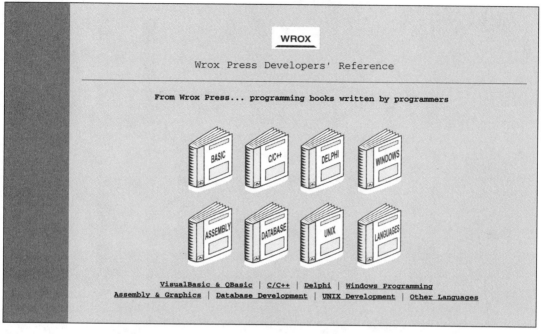

Professional Java Fundamentals

Shy Cohen
Tom Mitchell
Andres Gonzalez
Larry Rodrigues
Kerry Hammil

Wrox Press Ltd.®

Professional Java Fundamentals

Published by Wrox Press Ltd. 30 Lincoln Road, Olton, Birmingham, B27 6PA
Printed in Canada
Library of Congress Catalog no. 96-60892

ISBN 1-861000-38-3

Trademark Acknowledgements

Credits

Authors
Shy Cohen
Tom Mitchell
Andres Gonzalez
Larry Rodrigues
Kerry Hammil

Technical Reviewers
Rick Stones
Uwe Steinmueller
Ivor Horton
Jack Bakker
Ian Tomey
Julian Templeman
Ken Litwak
Betty Zinkann
Andrew Evans
Mark Webster
Markus Kohler
Srinivas Kankanahalli
Andres Gonzalez

Technical Editors
Gina Mance
Chris Ullman
Tim Briggs

Development Editors
David Maclean
Martin Tomlinson

Design/Layout
Neil Gallagher
Andrew Guillaume
Hetendra Parekh

Proof Reader
Pam Brand

Index
Simon Gilks

Cover Design
Third Wave

For more information on Third Wave, contact Ross Alderson on 44-121 236 6616
Cover photo supplied by The Image Bank

About the Authors

Shy Cohen

Shy Cohen is a Software Design Engineer working at Microsoft's R&D Center in Israel. He was an early adopter of Java, hooked on the new language ever since its early Alpha release days. He immediately recognized the potential of the new language both for Internet programming and as a general purpose one, and started spreading the word wherever he went, advising, lecturing and writing about it. In this book Shy aims to give the reader the hard won fruits of his study with Java.

To my wife Michal, who made it all possible.

Tom Mitchell

Tom Mitchell has been a programmer since 1985, working in languages ranging from IBM Basic, Assembly Language to, of course, Java. This is his first book and, now realizing how much work is involved, possibly his last. He can be reached at tjmitch@nac.net

Thanks to all the coauthors and the editorial team at Wrox for their patience, guidance and suggestions. Special thanks to Karen, Brian, Katie and Kevin for their love and encouragement.

Andres Gonzalez

Andres is a member of Technical Staff with Lucent Technologies Bell Labs (formerly AT&T Bell Laboratories), where he designs and develops protocol analyzer test systems for various telecommunication protocols like HDLC, X.25, ISDN, Frame Relay and Signaling System #7. His programming experience extends from assemblers, C, Visual Basic, MS Windows, X11 Windows, and Java on various Unix platforms, MS-DOS, and MS Windows. His personal interests include family, audio engineering, acoustics, guitars and rock, Mayan archaeology, Java and Internet technologies.

First and foremost, I would like to thank my wife, Rhonda, and our daughter, Brittany, for their support. Rhonda put some of her own personal goals on a back burner so I could be involved in this project. Finally, a thank-you goes to the boys in the band for being so patient about my recent Java obsession.

Larry Rodrigues

Lawrence H Rodrigues is a senior consultant with Compuware Corp. Milwaukee. His accomplishments include development of a number of 2D and 3D bio-medical image visualization features at GE Medical Systems, Milwaukee. His current areas of interest are, Image Visualization and Analysis, Data Compression, OOP and Java. He also the author of a number of publications.

I would like to express my gratitude to Compuware corp. for providing me the opportunity to work in Java. My thanks particularly goes to Pete Sampson, Tom Quinn and Ed Chaltry for their constant encouragement. I am grateful to my colleagues and friends, George Kowalski, Joel Wisneski, John Jurek, Nihar Shah, Jim Kohli and so many others for their valuable suggestions and comments. I am also grateful to my wife, Cloy, for reading and correcting the manuscript and my children, Joanne and Kenneth, for their patience and understanding.

Kerry Hammil

Kerry is a student by day and computer programmer by night. Her experience includes freelance programming and writing jobs. When not glued in front of her computer, she enjoys making and listening to music. Her ultimate goal in life is to make more money than Bill Gates.

CONTENTS

Table of Contents

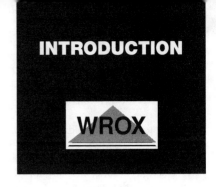

INTRODUCTION

Welcome to Professional Java Fundamentals, a book that aims to ride the second Java wave.

Once the initial euphoria at discovering Java has cooled, and you've got the basic language syntax off pat, you'll want to get down to coding some serious programs. The thirst for developer information just gets stronger, the more you do. This book provides you with in-depth coverage of a variety of subject areas, enabling you to use Java more effectively.

Who Should Read this Book?

The chapters in this book have been written by programmers for programmers. You should ideally be familiar with another language such as C++ or Visual Basic, and may be familiar with the basics of Java, though this is not assumed. You are looking for in-depth coverage of the advanced features of Java.

What's Covered in the Book

The book starts with a quick run-through the Java language. This acts both as a refresher and a reference to Java's syntax.

With these necessary introductions out of the way, we move on to a discussion of the implementation of object-oriented programming principals in Java. This takes two chapters–the first covering the basic concepts of OOP, the second looking at relations between classes. We then take a look at some of the fundamental Java classes and how they can be used.

The next two chapters look at how multithreading can improve the performance of a Java program and at the **Java.io** package, which encloses classes that provide a unified interface to the underlying system's input and output facilities.

Five chapters are then devoted to the Abstract Window Toolkit. The Abstract Window Toolkit or AWT is a collection of classes and interfaces encapsulating text fields, buttons, checkboxes and other user interface controls, along with the classes needed to handle layouts, graphics, text and event management. While being quite primitive and not overtly powerful the AWT does contain all the tools you'll need to build fully functional, window-based user interfaces which will run on any Java-enabled operating system or Internet browser. However, to get the best out of it, you'll need to delve into it quite deeply. Using the AWT requires an understanding of event-driven programming. The first chapter deals with event handling, the next outlines some fundamentals such as colors, clipping and fonts. The third chapter digs deeper into the graphics potential of the AWT and looks at the basic drawing primitives available, image handling and animation. The final two chapters encompass the GUI building blocks and the layout managers which place them at the correct points of the compass.

Once you're familiar with the file I/O, threads and the AWT, we take a look at Java's networking capabilities. The chapter includes two fairly extensive examples that tie together the knowledge you've gained from the previous chapters.

Two chapters on the building and designing of class libraries then show both the principles and practice of implementing a library of functions. Fundamental design considerations, API design and OOP design form the first of the chapters, while the second covers issues of coding, documentation, packaging and testing. Two example libraries are developed and an applet and application are introduced to show off the libraries to their best advantage.

The book ends with a chapter on native methods–interfacing Java to C++. This looks at the way Java can make use of C and C++ in application development to rectify current deficiencies in its own APIs, to make use of legacy code and to run CPU-intensive sections of code.

What Do You Need to Use this Book?

All you need is a computer and a recent version of Sun's JDK environment. This can be downloaded from:

> `http://java.sun.com/java.sun.com/products/JDK/index.html`

or by anonymous ftp from:

> `ftp://ftp.javasoft.com/pub`

> To run a program, type it in using a plain text editor and save it with a `.java` extension. It's usual to use the name of the class defined in the program as the filename e.g. `HelloWorld.java`. Then, from the command line, you can use `javac` to compile the program. Remember that Java is case-sensitive:
>
> `javac HelloWorld.java`
>
> Finally, to run the program, use `java` and the name of the class:
>
> `java HelloWorld`

Whether or not you have another development environment, such as Symantec's Café, Microsoft's Visual J++ or Sun's Java Workshop, is unimportant to the code working, but may improve the code's compilations and execution speed, provide an IDE with which you're more comfortable and have extensive online documentation and help.

Source Code

The complete source code from the book is available for download from:

```
http://www.wrox.com
```

We suggest you get hold of a copy, as it's useful to have the compilable code at your side when reading the book. We haven't included complete listings for all the code examples in this book because that would waste your time and good trees. Also some of the applications and applets are long and quite complex.

Conventions Used in this Book

To help you get the most from the text and keep track of what's happening, we've used a number of conventions throughout the book.

For instance:

> **These foreground boxes hold important information which is essential, or at least directly relevant, to the surrounding text.**

while,

> *Asides and interesting insights are presented like this.*

When we introduce them, we **highlight** important words. We show keyboard strokes like this: *Ctrl-A*.

We present code in two different ways:

```
In our code examples, this code style shows new, important,
    pertinent code;
while this shows code that's less important in the present context, or has been seen
before.
```

Finally, program output and screen text is represented like so:

Thank you for your patience!

Tell Us What You Think

We've worked hard to make this book as useful to you as possible, so we'd like to get a feel for what it is you want and need to know, and what you think about how we've presented (and represented) Java to you.

We appreciate feedback on our efforts and take both criticism and praise on board in our future editorial efforts. If you've anything to say, let us know on:

Feedback@wrox.com
or
http://www.wrox.com

Bookmark the site now!

Why Should I Return the Reply Card?

Why not? If you return the reply card in the back of the book, you'll register this copy of Professional Java Fundamentals with Wrox Press, and receive free information about our latest books. You'll also receive errata sheets when they become available or are updated (these will be updated on the Web page, too).

As well as having the satisfaction of having contributed to the future line of Wrox books via your much-valued comments and suggestions, you'll be given a free subscription to our hugely popular Developer's Journal. This bi-monthly magazine, read by all the software development industry, is invaluable to any programmer who wants to keep up with the latest techniques, as used by the best developers.

Wrox Press–The Reading Edge...

An Introduction to Java

Java's syntax and keywords are very similar to that of C and C++. Therefore, if you have programmed in either of these languages, you'll be pretty familiar with a lot of the concepts described in this chapter. If not, don't worry. This chapter is designed as a swift introduction to the basics of the Java language.

In the chapter we cover:

▲ The structure of a Java program

▲ Variables and data types

▲ Methods

▲ Expressions and operator precedence

▲ How to control program execution

Program Structure

Java is a structured language. Unlike BASIC and much like Pascal and C/C++, all programs in Java have the same form. This makes it easier for other people to read your code, and for the compiler to figure out what it is you want to do.

We'll start our examination of the Java language by using a simple example to illustrate many of the aspects of a Java program. The example is:

```
class HelloWorld {
        public static void main(String args[])
        {
                System.out.println("Hello World!");
        }
}
```

Let's examine this short program line by line.

The first line in this program declares a new class.

```
class HelloWorld {
```

Don't worry about the term class for the moment. We are going to look at classes in detail in Chapter 2. For now, all you need to know is that classes are the basic building block in Java and that, in order to run a Java program, you must create a class with the program's name.

The next line declares the **main** method:

```
public static void main(String args[])
```

Again, this will become clearer once we start discussing methods later in this chapter and object-oriented programming in the next. For now, you can just take my word for it that, if you want to run something in your program, you must write the line as it appears here.

> Although strictly not true, you can consider a method to be very much like a function in other languages.

The words before the word **main** describe the method:

▲ **public** means this method is accessible to other objects in the system, and so the system can start executing your program.

▲ **static** means that it belongs to the class (rather than to a specific instance of the class–all will be explained later).

▲ **void** means this method doesn't return any value.

The words **String args[]** describe the type of parameters this method accepts (in this case, an array of strings that were typed at the command line). We'll come back to **main** later on.

The next line has a single left curly bracket (**{**) that opens the body block. There's a matching right curly bracket (**}**) two lines below.

The next line calls for a system service to print out a text to the standard output device (usually the screen or console).

```
System.out.println("Hello World!");
```

As you will learn later, **System.out** points to an object that is an instance of the class **PrintStream**, and **println** is a method of that class (just like **main** is a method of the our **HelloWorld** class).

Blocks

Blocks are segments of your program that are enclosed in braces (the symbol '**{**' opens the block and the symbol '**}**' closes it). They define code units and divide your program both syntactically and logically by grouping related statements together. In the broadest sense, everything within matching braces can be thought of as one big statement. In fact, wherever a single statement can go, you can use a block. For example, if **a**, **b**, **c** and **d** are all integer variables then:

```
...
a=1;
b=2;
c=a+b;
d=c+a;
...
```

is the same as:

```
...
a=1;
b=2;
{
    c=a+b;
}
d=c+a;
...
```

or:

```
...
{
    a=1;
    b=2;
    c=a+b;
}
d=c+a;
...
```

In certain places, the compiler demands that you use braces or the code won't compile. Blocks are the only way to tell the compiler where one method or class ends and the next one begins.

> **Blocks also help you (or someone else reading your code) understand what is going on. It's good practice to follow a consistent notation when using blocks.**

Note that indenting and spacing is for the reader only. As far as Java is concerned this code fragment is the same as the previous ones:

```
...
a=1; b=2; c=a+b; d=c+a;
...
```

and so is this:

```
...
            a=1;
        b=2;
    c=a+b;
d=c+a;
...
```

Blocks can be (and usually are) hierarchical, i.e. one block can contain one or more subsidiary blocks. In the above **HelloWorld** program, we have one outer block that defines the **HelloWorld** class, and within it we have a method block called **main**. Many method blocks define further sub-blocks, as you will see in future examples.

Scope

In addition to grouping statements together, blocks define context and scope.

If we have a variable named **a** in a block **A**, and a sub-block of **A** defines a variable named **a**, then every reference to **a** within the sub-block would be to the **a** that was defined within that sub-block. If **A** had another variable **b**, and the sub-block did not declare any variable named **b**, then every reference to **b** in the sub-block would be to the **b** defined in the super-block **A**.

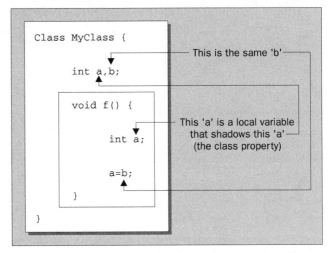

This may be a little confusing if you aren't familiar with structured languages. The next example should make things clearer though. Note that everything from the '**/***' to the '***/**' is a comment, and is ignored by the compiler (more about comments in a moment).

```
class TestScope
{
    static int a, b;        /* global definition of variables */

    public static void main(String args[])
    {
        a=1; b=2;           /* assign a value to the global variables */

        aIsAGlobal(); /* call the method aIsAGlobal()   */
                      /* to print the values of a and b */

        aIsALocal();  /* call the method aIsALocal()    */
                      /* to print the values of a and b */

    }

    static void aIsAGlobal()
    {
        System.out.println("b=" + b);   /* This would print 2 */
        System.out.println("a=" + a);   /* This would print 1 */
    }

    static void aIsALocal()
    {
        int a=4;    /* local definition of a overrides global definition */
```

```
        System.out.println("b=" + b);    /* This would print 2 */
        System.out.println("a=" + a);    /* This would print 4 */
                                /* as the local a overrides the global a */
    }
}
```

Header and Body

Java compilation units, (essentially files that end with a `.java` extension) are made of four parts (none of which is compulsory):

▲ Package declaration

▲ Import statements

▲ Definitions of interfaces

▲ Definitions of classes

We'll explain packages, importing interfaces and classes later on, but for now, note that:

▲ The package declaration states that all the classes and interfaces in the file belong to a Java package.

▲ The import statement asks for other classes and interfaces not defined in this compilation unit to be known to the compiler at compile time.

▲ The interface and class definitions supply the 'meat' of the compilation unit.

Comments

Comments can appear anywhere you can put a white space character (space, tab or carriage return) in a Java source file.

Comments are identical to those in C and C++. Everything between '`/*`' and '`*/`' is ignored by the compiler, and so is everything on a line to the right of two consecutive slashes. The following program is (as far as the compiler is concerned) identical to the first one:

```
// This is the Java version of the famous Hello World program
class HelloWorld
{
    public static void main (String args[])
    {
        /* Next line prints "Hello World" on the screen */
        System.out.println("Hello World");
    }
}
```

You can also write comments that begin with '`/**`' and end with '`*/`'. When you first look at this you might think to yourself "Hey, this is exactly the same as the previous one" and you wouldn't be wrong. As far as the compiler is concerned, everything between the '`/*`' and the '`*/`' is ignored, so the extra asterisk is the same as any other character. But the thing about this type of comment is that a special utility

11

called **javadoc** which comes with the JDK, can extract the text from these comments and create an HTML file that documents the public API of your classes or packages, using extra information supplied by the user if required.

The main() Thing

All Java applications (like our **HelloWorld**) must contain a **main()** method whose signature (definition) looks exactly like this:

```
public static void main(String args[])
```

The **main()** method in the Java language is similar to the **main()** function in C and C++. With C or C++, the run-time system starts your program by invoking the **main()** function. In your **main()** function you can then perform any task you require and call any other functions necessary to run your program. In Java, when you execute an application class using the Java interpreter, the run-time system starts your application by calling the class's **main()** method.

If you tried to run a class which didn't have a **main()** method with the Java interpreter, the interpreter wouldn't know which method to run first and would print an error message. The interpreter will also print an error message if the **main** method in your application class isn't declared in the correct way.

The main() Parameter

As we have seen above, the **main()** method accepts a single parameter: an array of strings. The values in this array are the words that were typed in at the command line when the application was invoked.

Note that you can use any name for the parameter as long as it's an array of strings. However, the name **args** is generally accepted as the one to use (like the **argv** and **argc** parameters to the C/C++ **main()** function).

> The C/C++ **main()** function accepts two parameters, while Java programs accept only one. The **args** parameter replaces **argv**. There's no need for **argc** because you can find the number of command line arguments using the array's **length** attribute (more about arrays in a moment).
>
> In C and C++, the system passes the entire command line to the **main()** function (including the name used to invoke it). In Java, the name of the application is the name of the class where the **main** method is defined, and you can always ask the system to tell you a class's name (using the **getName()** method). Therefore, the Java run-time system doesn't pass the class name used to invoke it to the **main** method; it only passes the items on the command line that appear after the class name.

A Short Example

The next little application prints out the arguments from the command line:

```
// This application prints out the command line arguments

class EchoCmdArgs
{
    public static void main (String args[])
    {
        int i=0;                        // i will iterate through the arguments

        while (i<args.length)
        {
            System.out.println(args[i]);  // Print out the argument
            i = i + 1;                    // Go to the next
        }
    }

}
```

This code example includes elements that are yet to be explained, such as variables, arrays, and loops. Don't worry if you don't understand it all right now. It'll soon be clear enough.

Variables and Data Types

Java is a **strongly typed language**. While in some languages variables can have any value assigned to them, Java's variables can accept only one kind of value, and that kind must be declared when the variable is declared.

Declaring Variables

Every variable in Java has a type that is either:

▲   One of the eight basic data types

▲   A class

▲   An array

A variable, whose type is one of the basic types, actually contains the data, but other variables are actually references to an object that lives elsewhere. We'll look at classes and arrays a bit later.

Variable declarations take this form:

```
variableType    variableName;
```

where **variableType** is the name of a known data type, and **variableName** is the name of a new variable. You can declare more than one variable of the same type in the same statement, using commas to separate the names and a semi-colon (;) to end the declaration like this:

```
variableType    VarName1, VarName2, ... , VarNameN;
```

For example:

```
int a;
int b;
```

is the same as:

```
int a, b;
```

Unlike BASIC and dBase, and like C and Pascal, in Java you must declare every variable you want to use *before you use it*. In Java (as in C++), you can declare a variable anywhere in your code, as long you do so before you use the variable for the first time.

Every local variable (a variable declared within a method) must be assigned a value before you first use it (for any other purpose other than assigning a value to it). If you try to use an uninitialized variable in your code, you'll get an error. You can assign a value to your local variables at declaration time using this syntax:

```
variableType   variableName = value;
```

where **variableType** and **variableName** mean the same as before, and **value** is the initial value assigned to your variable. If you declare more than one variable in the same statement, you can assign a value to each one like this:

```
variableType   VarName1 = value1, ... , VarNameN = valueN;
```

Of course, if you don't assign a value to a variable at declaration time, it will remain uninitialized.

The following code snippet demonstrates variable declaration and initialization:

```
int a;
int b=3, c;
int d, e,        // Declaration continues on next line (no semi-colon)
    f, g, h=5, i, j, k, l, m, n, o, p;
```

Here we created 16 variables named **a** to **p,** and assigned initial values to **b** (3) and **h** (5).

Because you can declare variables anywhere in the code, you'll often see code like this:

```
for (int a=0; a<10; a++) {...}
```

which has the same effect as:

```
int a;
for (a=0; a<10; a++) {...}
```

In the shorter version, **a** is defined in the scope where it's needed. It's recognized only within the **{...}** block that follows the **for** statement.

This kind of 'define where needed' programming uses scope to make your code clearer (readers don't have to ask themselves "Where did **a** come from and what is its value?"). It's considered good practice to declare and use locally needed variables (like counters and indexes) only where you need them.

Naming Variables

Java is case-sensitive, which means that you can have two different variables called **myvar** and **myVar**. However, you should avoid using misleading names like this.

There's no limit on the length of a variable's name, so use descriptive names to make your code clearer. Variable names in Java must begin with either a letter, an underscore (_) or a dollar sign ($). Subsequent characters can be any character, digit or Unicode character (character with a number above hex 00c0). Note however, that you can't use any of Java's reserved words (words that have special meaning in the language such as 'for' and 'if') as a variable name. Here's a list of all the reserved words in Java. (Note that some are reserved for future use and have no meaning in the language as it stands today.)

Abstract	boolean	break	byte	byvalue	case	cast
catch	char	class	const	continue	default	do
double	else	extends	false	final	finally	float
for	future	generic	goto	if	implements	import
inner	instanceof	int	interface	long	native	new
null	operator	outer	package	private	protected	public
rest	return	short	static	super	switch	synchronized
this	throw	throws	transient	true	try	var
void	volatile	while				

Primitive Data Types

Java has eight basic (or **primitive**) data types. There are four types which hold integers:

- ▲ **byte**
- ▲ **short**
- ▲ **int**
- ▲ **long**

Two types which hold floating point numbers:

- ▲ **float**
- ▲ **double**

One type which holds (Unicode) characters:

- ▲ **char**

And one logical type:

- ▲ **boolean**

These types are called primitive because they are built into the system and are the only things in Java that aren't objects. This makes it easier for programmers to use them and allows the system to implement them in a more efficient way. The primitive data types can also be accessed using classes, as we'll see later.

These data types are **machine independent**, which means that you can trust them to be the same on every system your code runs.

Type	Size	Type
byte	8-bit	Two's complement
short	16-bit	Two's complement
int	32-bit	Two's complement
long	64-bit	Two's complement
float	32-bit	IEEE 754 floating point
double	64-bit	IEEE 754 floating point
char	16-bit	Unicode character

Integers

Each integer data type can hold integer values according to its limits:

Type	Range
byte	-128 to 127
short	-32,768 to 32,767
int	-2,147,483,648 to 2,147,483,647
long	-9,223,372,036,854,775,808 to 9,223,372,036,854,775,807

You can't implicitly assign a value from a longer typed variable to a shorter typed variable, even if the actual value you want to assign is small enough to fit in the shorter typed variable. To do this you have to explicitly convert the value into a smaller type and then assign it. There are no restrictions on converting from a shorter typed variable to a longer typed variable.

> Converting from one type to another is called 'casting' (in Java, as well as other languages). To cast from one type to another, specify the type to convert to in parentheses before the value you wish to cast.

Floating Point

The floating point types are compliant with the international standard for floating point numbers IEEE 754. Float is a 32-bit single precision type and double is a 64-bit double precision type.

Type	Precision Range
long	$\pm1.40129846432481707e-45$ to $\pm3.40282346638528860e+38$
double	$\pm4.94065645841246544e-324d$ to $\pm1.79769313486231570e+308d$

Character

The char type can hold Unicode characters. Unlike C or C++ characters that can have only 256 distinct values, a Java character can have 16384 distinct values.

Boolean

Booleans can have only two values: true and false. Note that unlike C or C++, you can't cast an integer value into a boolean.

Literals

The term **literal** means that you mean what you write. When you write:

```
beastNum = sixSixSix;
```

you mean you want to assign to the variable **beastNum** the value of variable **sixSixSix**,. When you write:

```
sixSixSix = 666;
```

you literally mean that you want to assign to **beastNum** the *integer* value of 666.

Number Literals

There are several types of numeric literal.

The first type is the decimal integer literal. This type is written as a simple number. If you want a negative literal, you simply place a minus sign (–) before it. If the integer literal is small enough, you can assign it to a short or a byte. For example, –123 and 444444444 are decimal integer literals.

The second type is a decimal long literal. If a number is too big to be stored in an int, it's considered a long. You can explicitly specify that a literal number is long by appending either the letter 'l' or the letter 'L' to the end of the number. For example, 12345678901234 and –2L are decimal long literals.

Integer and long literals can also be written using octal or hexadecimal notation. Octal numbers are made up of the digits '0' to '7', and hexadecimal numbers are made up of the digits '0' to '9' and the letters 'a' to 'f' or 'A' to 'F'. A leading zero means the number is octal (007 has the decimal value 7, and 077 has the decimal value 63). A leading '0x' (a zero and a lowercase 'x') means the number is hexadecimal (0x007 has the decimal value 7, and 0x77 has the decimal value 119).

Floating point numbers are numbers written with a decimal point, or numbers written with or without a decimal point together with an exponent. If you want the number to be negative, place a minus sign before it. Floating point numbers are implicitly of the type double. You can explicitly make a float or double literal by respectively appending the letters 'f' or 'F' and 'd' or 'D'. Floating point numbers can also be written using the letter 'e' or 'E' followed by an exponent. For example, these are all floating point literals: 2.3, –45D, –12.5e, –2F.

Boolean Literals

A boolean literal represents a logical value and can be either true or false. For example:

```
boolean itIsRaining = true, itIsSunny = false;
```

You can use the keywords **true** and **false** wherever you need to assign or test a logical value.

Character Literals

Unlike C or C++, Java's characters are 16-bit Unicode characters.

You can write a character literal by surrounding a single character with single quotes (for example, 'a', 'b', '_', '@'). You use a backslash (\) to represent characters that are non-printable (e.g. tab, new line) or conflicting (e.g. a Unicode Greek 'A', as opposed to a Unicode Latin 'A'). These kinds of notation are known as **escape codes**.

The escape codes that are used to represent non-printable and other characters are:

Escape Code	Description
\t	Tab
\b	Back space
\r	Carriage return
\n	New line
\f	Form feed
\'	Single quote
\"	Double quote
\\	Backslash
\ddd	Octal representation of the character
\xdd	Hexadecimal representation of the character
\uddd	Unicode representation of the character

For example:

```
char newLine = '\n';
char sayItInOctal = '\101'; // This is the letter 'A'
```

You can also directly assign a Unicode value to a variable, for example:

```
char assignByUnicodeNumber = 66; // This is the letter 'B'
```

String Literals

We haven't yet discussed strings or the data type that holds them, but this is a good place to describe how to write string literals.

A string literal can be any number of characters enclosed in double quotes. You can use any Unicode character in a string, including escape codes. Sample strings are:

"This is a string. "
"This is a string,\nThat spans two lines. "   (Notice the new line escape code)
"This is the letter \\\101\'. "

To test how strings are displayed, you can modify our **HelloWorld** application to print your own strings. Simply replace the "**Hello World!** " string in this line:

```
System.out.println("Hello World!");
```

with your own string.

Arrays

Arrays are used to store a fixed length set of items of the same type. An array has 'slots' in which you can place the items, and which you can then use to refer to the different items. Java's arrays are true objects—more on this in the next chapter.

Since arrays are only used to hold things, they are not actually made of those things—a rolodex used to hold cards isn't a collection of cards, it's a rolodex. This isn't the case in C/C++ or Pascal, where arrays are really a collection of objects. When you declare an array in Java, you don't assign any memory to the items in the array. You don't even specify the length of the array—all that you specify is the type of object that may be stored in the array.

Declaration

The declaration of an array is as simple as that of any other variable. To specify that a variable refers to an array, you should place empty square brackets (**[]**) immediately after its name:

```
int  arrayOfIntegers[],  thisIsNotAnArray;
char arrayOfCharacters[];
```

or you can specify that all the variables in the statement are arrays by placing empty square brackets after the type, like this:

```
int[]  arrayOfIntegers, anotherArrayOfIntegers;
char[] arrayOfCharacters;
```

Assigning an Actual Array to an Array Variable

To assign an array to an array variable, you must create the array. The keyword that is used to create arrays is **new**. This is actually used to create all new objects, as you'll see in the next chapter.

The syntax for creating a new array and assigning it to an array variable is as follows:

```
arrayName = new arrayType [ sizeOfArray ];
```

For example, if you had an integer array variable **myArray**, then you could write:

```
myArray = new int[30];
```

This assigns a new array with 30 'slots' for integers to the array variable.

A good question would be "What value do the new array elements hold?" When you create a new array all the elements in it are initialized to default values:

- Numbers (of any type) to zero.
- Characters to '\0'.
- Booleans to **false**
- And everything else to **Null** ('null' is a keyword we are yet to encounter).

You can assign an array to an array variable when you create it, like this:

```
char myArrayOfCharacters = new char[26];
```

You can also assign an array filled with values to an array on creation:

```
int  arrayOfIntegers[]   = { 1, 2, 3, 4, 5 };
char arrayOfCharacters[] = { 65, 'B', '\103', 'D' };
```

You simply use the equals sign (=) like you do with plain variables, and then specify the array's elements surrounded by curly brackets, { and }. By doing this, you create an array in memory and assign the array variable to it.

Multi-dimensional Arrays

The arrays we've seen up to now have just one dimension. In some cases, however, we need arrays with more than one dimension (for example, to hold a matrix we would need a two-dimensional array).

Java doesn't have true multi-dimensional arrays, but achieves the equivalent functionality with an array of arrays.

The syntax used to declare multi-dimensional arrays is similar to that used to declare a one-dimensional array. Just add another pair or square brackets for every dimension you want to add. For example:

```
int  twoDimensions[][]       = new int [10][10];
char threeDimensions[][][]    = new char [2][2][2];
byte fiveDimensions[][][][][] = new byte [6][5][4][3][2];
```

Multi-dimensional arrays can be initialized in a manner similar to one-dimensional arrays. In a multi-dimensional array, every element in the highest level is an array rather than a value.

```
Int multiDimensions={ {1,2,3} , {11,12,13} , {21,22,23} }
```

The fact that Java uses arrays of arrays instead of true multi-dimensional arrays introduces the possibility of non-orthogonal arrays. These are arrays that have subdimensions of different sizes. For example, consider the following array:

```
int nonOrthogonal = { {0}, {0,1}, {0,1,2} }
```

Using Arrays

To access an array element you use a syntax very similar to that of C and C++. You specify the index of the element within the array in square brackets after the array variable's name. Like C/C++ and unlike Pascal, the index of the first array element in Java is zero. Here's an example using the arrays we declared before:

```
myArrayOfCharacters[0] = 'a';     // Put 'a' in the first slot of the array
twoDimensions[9][9] = 100;        // Put 100 at the LR corner of the matrix
myArrayOfCharacters[26] = 'z';    // OOPS !
```

The last line here is wrong as the array has 26 elements, but these begin at 0. The index of the last element in this array is therefore 25.

You can obtain the length of any array like this:

```
int arrayLength = someArray.length;
```

> Since Java doesn't use pointers to implement arrays, every array access operation is bound checked to ensure you are accessing an existing element. This eliminates the dangers of memory overrides and date destruction that you can find in C or C++.

Arraycopy

To duplicate arrays you must copy the content of one into another. The assignment operator (=) can't be used to copy the content of an array as it simply sets the two array variables to the same actual array. This means that the following code fragment:

```
int sourceArray[] = { 1, 2, 3, 4 },
    targetArray[] = new int[4];
targetArray = sourceArray;
targetArray[0]=5;
```

results in **sourceArray[0]** being equal to 5 as the two array variables are referencing the same actual array.

The Java system offers you an efficient way to copy arrays. Instead of using a loop like this:

```
for (int i=0; i< targetArray.length; i++) targetArray[i] = sourceArray[i];
```

you could call a Java system method to do the trick for you in a much more efficient way. The method's signature is:

```
public static void arraycopy(  Object src,
                               int src_position,
                               Object dst,
                               int dst_position,
                               int length)
```

and the method's parameters are:

- ▲ **src**–the source array
- ▲ **srcpos**–start position in the source array
- ▲ **dest**–the destination array
- ▲ **destpos**–start position in the destination array
- ▲ **length**–the number of array elements to be copied

The method copies elements from the source array, beginning at the specified position, to the specified position in the destination array. It doesn't allocate any memory for the destination array (the target array's memory must already be allocated when you call it). Here's an example:

```
int a1[] = {1, 2, 3, 4},
    a2[] = new int[4];
System.arraycopy(a1, 0, a2, 0, a1.length );
```

Note that this method can copy elements from *any* type of source array into *any* type of target array. Of course, this isn't always possible, so the method will throw an **ArrayStoreException** exception if an element in the source array couldn't be stored in the destination array due to a type mismatch (elements are not of the same type). The method throws an **ArrayIndexOutOfBoundsException** if the copy operation attempts to access data outside the bounds of either array.

> *Exceptions are an error reporting and recovery mechanism we are yet to discuss. For now it's sufficient to know that a thrown exception (if not handled in a special way) causes the program to stop and print an error message.*

Compound Data Types

Compound data types are actually classes. We'll thoroughly review compound data types in Chapter 4: Fundamental Classes–once we've learned a bit about classes. The only two compound data types I'm going to mention at this point are **String** and **StringBuffer**. As their names imply, these classes handle Java strings.

Strings

Unlike C or C++, Java strings are *not* an array of characters, but a special class of their own, with methods and all.

Java string literals are constants. Their values can't be changed after creation. The Java compiler makes sure that each string literal in your code actually results in a **String** object, so the code

```
String myString = "this is a string";
```

takes a string literal ("this is a string"), converts it into a **String** object in memory, and assigns **myString** as the handle to that object. The process of converting a literal into an object is called 'object construction', and will be covered in depth in the next chapter.

The same thing happens when you write:

```
System.out.println("Hello World!");
```

The string literal "Hello World! " is first converted into a **String** object, and then that object is passed to the **println** method which in turn prints its content to the console. If you don't follow it, don't worry—we'll explain this line in more detail in Chapter 2.

A less trivial example is:

```
String c = "Hello World!".substring(0, 5);
```

The **substring** method extracts a section of a string object and creates a new one with the value of that substring. This line instructs the compiler to:

▲ Create a temporary **String** object

▲ Invoke the temporary object's **substring** method

▲ Assign the newly created **String** object to c

An equivalent way of writing this is:

```
String tempString = "Hello World!";
String c = tempString.substring(0, 5);
System.out.println(c);
```

Comparing Strings

When you need to compare strings you should use the **equals(...)** method, rather than the comparison operator (**==**). Consider the expression:

```
(string1 == string2)
```

Here, **string1** and **string2** are **string handles** (not strings!). When you compare them Java compares the references, not the values of the objects. Therefore, the above expression will return true only if **string1** and **string2** reference the exact same object (i.e. somewhere in your code it said **string2=string1,** or vice versa).

Therefore, you should use the string method **equals** to check whether the two strings pointed to by **string1** and **string2** are the same. This method compares the string to a specified object. It returns true if the object is exactly equal to the string (i.e. it has the same length and the same characters are in the same order). You can write either:

```
( string1.equals( string2 ) )
```

or

```
( string2.equals( string1 ) )
```

StringBuffer

Java allows you to manipulate strings in an easy, BASIC-like fashion. A special class called **StringBuffer** makes string manipulation a breeze.

Have a look at this statement:

```
int a = 1;
String myString = "abc" + a;
```

At first, this looks wrong; how can you add a string and an integer? The answer is very simple: the plus sign simply means concatenation. When you write this statement, the compiler creates a temporary **StringBuffer** object, invokes the string buffer's **append** method for each object you wish to concatenate, and finally, creates a **String** object to which it can assign the **myString** string handle. If you used classes explicitly to perform the same string concatenation, it would look like this:

```
String myString = new StringBuffer().append("abc").append(a).toString();
```

(As you can see, the first way is much simpler. Don't worry about the exact meaning of this example right now. It will become clear once you have a little more experience with classes and methods).

StringBuffers allow you to concatenate many types of objects very simply. They also provide other means of changing strings, such as insertion and translation. For further details on **StringBuffer**, refer to the API documentation.

Methods

A method is basically a collection of statements that can be invoked and executed as a whole. They group together code statements that are needed to accomplish the task of the method. You can change and control a method's execution by passing parameters to it.

Methods are much like functions and procedures in other non-object-oriented programming languages, but unlike C++ (that has both methods and functions), in Java no code lives alone: every method *must* belong to a class. Unlike C++, you can't have any executable code (i.e. methods) outside the scope of a class. In fact, in Java you never 'declare' methods and implement them somewhere else in your code (a common practice in C++). The method's body is always written 'in place'.

Methods can be invoked either by the system (like the **main** method) or by another method that uses them to do some work.

> *The Java VM design imposes some limitations on a method's length. A compiled method's byte-code may not exceed 32K bytes. This, however, should never be considered limiting. In order to generate a byte-code of over 64K bytes, the method's definition would have to be over 2500 lines of code (approximately). Object-oriented programming is a modular approach, and so code tends to be broken into small functional modules.*

> *There's also a limit on the number of methods in a class. There can be **only** 65,536 methods in a single class. For the same reasons mentioned before, this should pose no problem whatsoever.*

Pascal distinguishes between functions and procedures. In Pascal, functions are used to calculate things; they take parameters and return an answer. Procedures, on the other hand, do things. They may take arguments, but they don't return any value.

C/C++ and Java don't follow that notion. In Java there's no such distinction, as the only things that can execute statements are methods. A method may or may not take parameters, and may or may not return a value.

Declaring Methods

Declaring a method in Java is very similar to C/C++. The syntax used is:

```
methodModifiers returnType methodName throws
```

where **returnType** is the type of value returned by the method and **methodName** is (surprisingly enough) the method's name. The **methodModifiers** and **throws** parts of the declaration are optional, and we won't use them at this time apart from using the keywords **public static** with the **main** method, and the keyword **static** with any other method. (These keywords have to be used so that we can call the methods without having to create an object.)

In Java, every method declaration implies that a method implementation follows immediately. One example we've already seen is the **main** method:

```
class someClass
{
    public static void main(String vars[])
    {
        // here comes the code that does the work
        ...
    }
}
```

This method doesn't return a value (it's declared as **void**) and takes an array of strings as an argument.

Another example would be:

```
class someOtherClass
{
    public static void main(String vars[])
    {
        // here comes the code that does the main work
        ...
    }

    static int aMethodThatReturnsAPrimitiveInteger()
    {
        // this method is called from another method.
        // it calculates a value and returns a primitive integer
        ...
    }

    static Integer aMethodThatReturnsAnIntegerObject()
    {
```

```
            // this method is called from another method.
            // it calculates a value and returns an integer object
            ...
      }
  }
```

Notice that all the methods are declared inside the scope of the class.

Method Return Values

In essence, a method's return value may be any type known to the class in which the method is declared. This could be a primitive type, a class defined within the same file or package, an imported class or an array of any of them.

To declare a method that returns an array, you should place the empty brackets used to denote an array ([]) either after the type's name or after the argument list's closing parenthesis. The next example illustrates both variations:

```
  class arrayDemo
  {
     ... // some other methods declared before

     static int[] aMethodThatReturnsAnArrayOfIntegers()
     {
        // this method returns an integer array
        ...
     }

     static int andAnotherOne() []
     {
        // and so does this
        ...
     }

     ... // some other methods declared after
  }
```

Method Arguments

The method's argument list appears in parentheses immediately following the method's name. In this list, each argument is described by a **type** and **name** pair, even if some or all of the arguments are of the same type. The arguments can be of any type and are separated by commas.

```
  public static void allIntegers (int a, int b, int c)
  {
     ...
  }

  public static void wrongDeclaration (int a, b, c) // OOPS !
  {
     ...
  }
```

Arguments Are Passed by Reference

Almost all types of method argument are passed by reference. The only exception to the rule is primitive data types, and this is because they are not objects and therefore can't be referenced. Passing by reference means that Java doesn't create a new object for the method call but simply passes a handle to the object you referred to when you invoked the method.

A Way to Change the Value

Passing by reference means that the handle to the object is passed, but can't be changed. If you reassign the handle inside a method, the original reference remains unaffected when the method returns.

Another problem arises from the fact that many objects can't change their values. If you modify a string, for example, a new object is created and pointed to inside your method, but when your method returns the handle, it will point to the previous string object. If you want to change the thing you pass, you need to pass something that *holds* a reference to an object, rather the actual reference itself. This is where arrays come in. An array holds references to an object, and thus, without changing the handle to the array, you can have an array entry reference the object you want to return. Here's a code snippet that shows you how to do this:

```
void someMethod()
{
   int i = 0;
   ...

   // Call returnANewValue() and have it compute a new value for i

int[] dummy = {i};      // create a dummy array to pass the reference in
   returnANewValue( dummy );    // dummy[0] is now updated
   i = dummy[0];               // get the new value
}

...

void returnANewValue(int[] a)
{
   ... // assign new value to a[0];
}
```

This cumbersome way of changing the value of a method's argument becomes pointless when dealing with objects and classes, as you'll later see.

Scoping Rules

Consider this code:

```
class scopeDemo1
{
   static int a;

   public static void main(String vars[])
   {
      a = 1;
      System.out.println("a=" + a );    // This line will print "a=1"
```

```
        printA();
    }
    static void printA()
    {
        int a = 2;
        System.out.println("a=" + a );     // This line will print "a=2"
    }
}
```

How does the compiler know what the **printA** method refers to? The answer is that it has to use the syntax of Java to resolve the issue. There can't be any ambiguity.

In Java, every variable and method name you use are first searched for in the current block–surrounded by **{** and **}**. If they aren't found there, the compiler goes up one scope level (to the block containing the current block) and searches there. If a name can't be resolved, the compiler will complain that the variable is undefined.

This code:

```
class scopeDemo2
{
    static int a = 1;

    public static void main(String vars[])
    {

        System.out.println( "a=" + a );             // prints "a=1"
        {
            int a=2;
            System.out.println( "a=" + a );         // prints "a=2"
        }

        {
            System.out.println( "a=" + a );         // prints "a=1"
        }
    }
}
```

would print

```
a=1
a=2
a=1
```

while this code:

```
class scopeDemo3
{
    static int a = 1;

    public static void main(String vars[])
    {

        System.out.println( "a=" + a );             // prints "a=1"
```

```
        {
          int a=2;
          System.out.println( "a=" + a );          // prints "a=2"
        }


        {
          int a=3;
          System.out.println( "a=" + a );          // prints "a=3"
        }
      }
    }
```

would print

```
    a=1
    a=2
    a=3
```

You can't always override an upper block's definition of a variable. If a method defined some local variable, no block within the method can override the definition. The next code snippet won't compile because **a** is already defined in the method.

```
    public static void main(String vars[])
    {
      System.out.println( "a=" + a );
      {
        int a=2;
        System.out.println( "a=" + a );
        {
          int a=3;                    // ERROR ! can't override 'a' here
          System.out.println( "a=" + a );
        }
      }
    }
```

Method Overloading

In Java (as in C++) methods are recognized by their full signature. A method's signature is the combination of its name, return type and the number, order, and types of parameters.This opens up some interesting possibilities.

Let's consider these statements:

```
    System.out.println( 10 );
    System.out.println( true );
    System.out.println("Hello" );
```

Here the **println** method is used to print various kinds of data types. You may wonder how it's possible for a method to accept different data types as an argument. Well, the reason is that there's actually more than one method named **println**. In fact, there are 10 methods with that name, and each of them accepts a different type of argument and knows how to print it. This is an example of **method overloading**–there are several versions of the same method with the same name and return type but different arguments.

> Overloaded methods must have different arguments and the same name and return type.

The **println** method versions are:

```
void println()
void println(Object o)
void println(String s)
void println(char[] cArray)
void println(char c)
void println(int i)
void println(long l)
void println(float f)
void println(double d)
void println(boolean b)
```

The compiler invokes the appropriate method by checking the number and type of the arguments you pass against the possible variations, and selecting the one that best fits the argument types. So, if you call it with an integer, then you invoke the 6th method, and if you call it with a string, you invoke the 3rd.

Method overloading is best used when you have methods that accept different types (or different numbers) of arguments, and perform the same thing. The **println** method, for example, prints its argument followed by a new line on the console. It would be tedious to have 10 different methods with 10 different names to do the same thing.

Another use for method overloading is when you have a method that, for the majority of the time, is used in one way rather than another. Take, for example, a method that synchronizes two sets of data—one is a database record, and the other is a class that represents the data stored in a database record in a more convenient way for your program. Most of the time you want to synchronize the two by taking the content of the database record and reflecting it in your class, but occasionally you want to update the database using the data in an object of the class (when you initialize it, for example).

If this is the method you use for synchronizing the data:

```
void synchronizeData( DBObject db, myClass c, boolean fromDBtoClass )
{
...
}
```

and most of the time you invoke it setting **fromDBtoClass** to true, you might consider overloading it with a shorter version that would only take 2 arguments:

```
void synchronizeData( DBObject db, myClass c)
{
    synchronizeData( db, c, true);
}
```

This method invokes the longer version, passing the supplied arguments and adding **true**. You can see that method overloading allows you to make your code a lot clearer and less tedious and error prone, and it does all that without the need to duplicate any code.

When overloading methods you have to take all parameter variations into account (this doesn't mean you have to implement every variation, just be aware of the possibilities). A parameter will always be promoted to a larger type that can hold it, so this code:

```
class TestOverLoading{
    static void Print(int w, int x)
    {
        System.out.println( "ints are " + w + " and " + x );
    }

    static void Print(float y, float z)
    {
        System.out.println( "floats are " + y + " and " + z );
    }

    public static void main(String vars[])
    {
        int a = 1, b = 2;
        float c = 3.1f;
        float d = 4.1f;

        Print(a,b);         // invokes Print(int , int)
        Print(c,d);         // invokes Print(float, float)
        Print(a,c);         // invokes Print(float, float) !!!
    }
}
```

may have undesired results, as **Print(a, c)** first promotes **a** to a **float**, and then invokes the **void Print(float, float)** method.

> *A standard convention for displaying the signature of a method is to write the method's name followed by the types of parameters in parentheses (for example, **void Print(float, float)**). A signature must be unique within the scope of the method.*

Expressions

In every procedural language, you tell the computer how to compute things you're interested in. A Java program is actually a sequence of expressions and flow control statements. In Java, every expression produces one of three things:

- ▲ A value (that can be used for further calculations or for assigning to a variable).

- ▲ A variable (in C, this is called an lvalue).

- ▲ Nothing (produced only by methods whose return type is **void**).

An expression that produces a variable may be used on either the left or the right side of the assignment operator (=). If it appears on the left, the value on the right is assigned to the variable. If it's on the right, the value of the variable is used in the context of the calculation.

An expression that produces a value can only be used on the right side of an assignment operator, unless it's a method that returns a value. In the latter case, the value is simply discarded. Note that this means you can't write statements like this:

```
int a=1, b=3;
a;         // Wrong ! - this produces a value
a+b;       // and this too
```

The type of value returned by every expression in a program must be known at compile time. This means that the compiler knows exactly what kind of operations can be performed on the resulting value. Java has no generic variable type (such as variant in Visual Basic).

Order of Evaluation

Every procedural language defines the order in which operations take place. Java has adopted the C/C++ notation and order of precedence.

The left side of a binary expression (i.e. one with two operands, one either side of the operator) is fully executed before the right side. This means that this expression

```
1 + (b=3) + b
```

would produce 7, no matter what **b** was prior to its execution (**(b=3)** assigns 3 to **b** and returns the value of **b**).

The expression to the left of an array's brackets (i.e. the array handle) is evaluated *before* the expression in the brackets. The following non-trivial example illustrates what I mean:

```
int[] a = {2, 1, 0}, b = {4, 5, 3}, c;
c = b;
b [ (b=a)[0] ] = 6;
System.out.println( c[2] );  // This prints out "6"
System.out.println( b[2] );  // This prints out "0"
```

Let's examine it, line by line.

The first line creates three array handles and initializes **a** and **b**. The second line makes **c** point to the same array as **b** does.

The third line is the tricky one. First, we take the array referenced by **b** and know that we're going to reference it. Then we go and calculate the inner expression. We first assign **b** to point to the same array as **a** does, and then we take the value in the 1st element in that array (2) to be used as the index to the array we're referring to in the outer expression. When we're done with that, we assign the value 6 to the 3rd element (whose index is 2) in the array we know we're referring to.

Because **c** pointed to the array we changed in the third line, when we print the value in the 3rd element in **c**, we get 6, while now **b** points to the same array as **a** does, and the 3rd element in it's zero.

As you can see, expressions like this are very hard to read and understand. The side effects of the expression are anything but clear, and coding like this is prone to error. For this reason, we strongly recommend that you don't use these types of 'shortcut'.

In a method call, all the arguments are calculated to produce a value before the method is invoked. Thus, when Java encounters a method call like this:

```
someMethod ( 1+1, 2+2)
```

it will first calculate 1+1 and 2+2 and only then invoke the method.

Every operand of an operator is fully calculated before the operator's action is performed.

Arithmetic Expressions

Java has 9 arithmetic operators:

Operator	Type	Meaning	Example
+	Unary	Promotion (see below)	+7
-	Unary	Promoting and arithmetic negation	-5
+	Binary	Adding	2 + 3
-	Binary	Subtracting	4 - 2
*	Binary	Multiplication	2 * 3
/	Binary	Division	4 / 2
%	Binary	Modulus	7 % 3
++	Unary	Increment	a++ or ++a
--	Unary	Decrement	a-- or --a

Promotion means that if the operand's type is either **byte** or **short**, the value used for the calculation is considered to be **int**.

The type of the outcome of an arithmetic expression depends on the type of the operands. An operator can only operate on operands of the same type, so if the two operands are not of the same type, the value stored in the operand of the smaller type (the one that hold numbers of lower values) is temporarily promoted to be of the same type as the other.

- If either is stored in a **double**, the other is temporarily stored in a **double**.
- If either is stored in a **float**, the other is temporarily stored in a **float**.
- If either is stored in a **long**, the other is temporarily stored in a **long**.
- Otherwise, both operands are temporarily stored in an **int**.

No operand works on a **byte** or a **short**, which may come as a bit of a surprise for C and C++ programmers. Since all operands are promoted to **int**s, the following statements would fail to compile:

```
byte a=2, b=3, c;
c = a + b;                 // this line fails
```

This is because the variables on the right get promoted to integers before being added, and then you can't assign the result to the smaller **byte** variable on the left.

> *In order to assign the result to **c**, you have to cast the result into a **byte** before assigning it. Here's how to do it:*

```
byte a=2, b=3, c;
c = (byte) (a+b);        // now it's ok to assign
```

Remember, an expression that takes only integer values as operands, will return only an **int** or a **long** (if the value is too big to be stored in an **int**). Thus **5/2** will return **2**, while **5f/2f** will return **2.5**.

The modulus operator returns the remainder of a division, thus **4%3** returns **1**.

The increment (**++**) and decrement (**--**) operators add or subtract 1 from the operand, whatever type it is. If the operands are on the left side of the variable (the prefix form of the operands), the variable's value is first incremented and then used in the expression. If the operands are on the right side (the postfix form), the value is first used for the expression and only then is the variable's value incremented.

Here's a short example to illustrate what I mean. The following code:

```
int a = 3;
System.out.println ( a++);
// Now 'a' equals 4
System.out.println ( ++a);
// Now 'a' equals 5
```

would print out:

```
3
5
```

Relational Operators

Java's relational operators are the same as C/C++'s. They are:

Operator	Meaning
= =	Equal to
!=	Not equal to
<	Smaller than
>	Larger than
<=	Smaller than or equal to
>=	Larger than or equal to

All the operators produce a boolean value: 'true' or 'false'.

As in C/C++ but not in BASIC, Java has different operators for comparison and assignment. To compare we use two adjacent equal signs (**==**) while for assignment we use only one (**=**).

> **Whenever you use booleans as arguments, be sure you're using == and not =, as these typos are very hard to trace. With all other types the compiler would complain that the result isn't a boolean and your code wouldn't compile.**

Bitwise and Logical Operators

Bitwise operators are used to manipulate the individual bits that make up an integral typed variable. These operations are:

Operator	Type	Meaning
~	Unary	Bitwise complement
>>	Unary	Signed right shift
>>>	Unary	Unsigned right shift
<<	Unary	Left shift
&	Binary	Bitwise AND
^	Binary	Bitwise OR
|	Binary	Bitwise exclusive OR (XOR)

Java also provides 'shortcuts' for bitwise operators:

Operator	Example	Meaning
>>=	x >>= y	x = x >> y
>>>=	x >>>= y	x = x >>> y
<<=	x <<= y	x = x << y
&=	x &= y	x = x & y
^=	x ^= y	x = x ^ y
|=	x |= y	x = x | y

Expressions that result in boolean values (like all the comparison expressions and methods returning boolean values) can be manipulated using logical operators. The logical operators are:

Operator	Type	Meaning
&&	Binary	Boolean AND (evaluates to true, if both operands are true).
&	Binary	Boolean AND (evaluates to true, if both operands are true).
||	Binary	Boolean OR (evaluates to true, if either operand is true).
|	Binary	Boolean OR (evaluates to true, if either operand is true).
^	Binary	Boolean exclusive OR (XOR) (evaluates to true, if exactly one operand is true).
!	Unary	Boolean NOT (negates the boolean value it operates on).

The difference between the && form and the & form of the AND operator is that in the && form, if the left operand evaluates to false, the right side isn't calculated, while in the & form both sides are calculated no matter what the result was. The && form can save time, while the & form can come in handy if calculating the right operand has 'side effects'.

The same applies for the || and | form of the OR operator.

String Manipulation

We've already seen the string concatenation operator (+). This operator takes strings and concatenates them to create a new string.

The operands for the concatenation operator should both be of the type **string**. If either of them isn't a string, it's converted to a string. Every object in Java has a default method called **toString** that returns a representation of the object in a string form. We recommended that you override this default method when you define your own type of objects.

Java also provides a 'shortcut' for concatenation in the form of a **+=** operator, so

```
string1 += string2
```

is the same as

```
string1 = string1 + string2
```

Assignment

The assignment operator assigns the value on the right side of the operator to the value on the left side. It also returns the value stored, so an expression like

```
a = b = c = d = 2;
```

will store **2** into **a**, **b**, **c**, and **d**. Since the right side is always evaluated before assignment, the order of events resulting from this expression is as follows:

```
d = 2;
c = d;
b = c;
a = b;
```

It would also make sense of this expression:

```
a = a + 5;
```

as first the right side (**a+5**) would be calculated, and only then the resulting value would be assigned to **a**. As this type of statement appears a lot in programs, Java adopted the C/C++ shorthand notation and added the following 'shortcuts':

Operator	Example	Meaning
+=	x += y	x = x + y
-=	x -= y	x = x - y
*=	x *= y	x = x * y
/=	x /= y	x = x / y
%=	x %= y	x = x % y

Precedence

The order in which an expression is evaluated is very important, and may affect the result of the expression. The expression **6+4/2** could have the value of **5** if you calculated from left to right, or **8** if you divided 4 by 2 and only then added the 6.

The following table shows the priorities of all of Java's operators. If an expression contains operators with different priorities, the higher priority operator takes action first. Operators of the same priority are executed from left to right.

The table lists all of the operators in Java. We've still to discuss some of them, but they are all listed in order to provide a source of reference.

Priority	Operator	Notes
15	[ ] ( ) .	Brackets ([]) are used for array access, and parentheses are used to group expressions together. The dot (.) is used for accessing object's methods and attributes.
14	++ -- ! ~ **instanceof**	**instanceof** returns true if an object is an instance of the class specified or any of the class's superclasses. It returns false otherwise.
13	**new** **(type)expression**	**new** creates new objects. The **type** casts the result of the **expression** to be of the type **type**
12	* / %	
11	+ -	
10	<< >> >>>	Bitwise shifts
9	< >	

Table Continued on Following Page

Priority	Operator	Notes
8	`==` `!=`	
7	`&`	Bitwise or Logical AND
6	`^`	Bitwise XOR
5	`|`	Bitwise or Logical OR
4	`&&`	Logical AND
3	`||`	Logical OR
2	`boolean expression ? expression : expression`	The 'conditional operator'. `boolean expression ? expression : expression` is short for `if (boolean expression) {expression} else {expression}`
1	`= += -= *= /= %= ^= &= |= <<= >>= >>>=`	Various

You can see that parentheses have the highest priority. This means you can use them to force an order of evaluation on any expression. You can also use them to show the order of evaluation in complex statements. There's no penalty for using parentheses–use them wherever you think they may help to make your code more readable.

Controlling Program Flow

Control is the ultimate goal. The programs we've seen up to now have been very straightforward. They did their thing in a linear way, starting at the top of the code block and working their way down, executing each instruction until they reached the last one.

Selecting the Execution Path

There are several ways in which you can condition the execution of a block of code.

The if Statement

To **condition the execution** of a block of code you can use the famous **if** statement. The syntax is the same as C/C++'s:

```
if ( Expression ) Statement;
```
or
```
if ( Expression ) Statement; else Statement;
```

The major difference between Java and C/C++ is the type of the **Expression**. Since Java has a true boolean primitive type, it uses a boolean value to condition the execution. This is different from C/C++, where the expression is an integer.

This eliminates one of the most common problems in C/C++ programming: possible wrong assignment.

When a C/C++ programmer writes

```
if (a=b) {...}
```

it's perfectly legal. A smart compiler may warn that there could be a mistake here, but would compile the code nevertheless. In Java, this wouldn't pass.

> **Attention C/C++ users!** In C/C++, an expression evaluates to `true` if it isn't zero. In Java, you have to use a `boolean` that evaluates to `true`. This code doesn't work in Java:
>
> ```
>         int val=0;        // init val to be zero
>         ...               // some code
>         val = 2;          // assign a value to val
>         ...               // some more code
>         if (val) {...}     // do something if val was assigned a value
> ```
>
> To check whether `val` isn't zero, you have to write it explicitly:
>
> ```
>         if ( val!=0 ) {...}
> ```
>
> because while `val` is an integer, the expression `val!=0` returns a boolean.

The **Statement** that follows the parentheses indicates either a single statement or a block of code. There's nothing special about this because, as you know, wherever you can put a single statement, you can also put a block.

When Java reaches an **if** statement, the expression inside the parentheses is evaluated first. The expression must return a boolean type value. In both forms, the **Statement** that follows the parentheses will be executed only if the expression returns **true**. In the second form, if the expression returns **false**, the statement that follows the keyword **else** is executed.

Remember, the **else** will refer to the last **if** in the same block that doesn't have an **else**. Consider the following (erroneous) code snippet:

```
boolean condition1, condition2;
... // Some code that assigns a value to condition1 and condition2
if ( condition1 )
     if ( condition2 )
       System.out.println("Both conditions are true");
else
   System.out.println("condition1 is false");
```

Here the **else** refers to the second **if** statement, despite the (deliberately) misleading layout, and so this code would print **condition1 is false** only if **condition1** was true and **condition2** was false.

The code can be fixed using a block. If we put the second **if** in an inner block, the **else** would refer to the first **if**.

```
if ( condition1 )
{
    if ( condition2 )
        System.out.println("Both conditions are true");
}
else
    System.out.println("condition1 is false");
```

The Conditional Operator

Java followed C/C++, and implemented a shorthand version of the **if...then...else** statement. It's most often used when you want to assign a value according to a condition. The conditional operator's syntax is:

conditionExpression ? expressionForTrue : expressionForFalse

As you can see it has two symbols (**?** and **:**) and three operands (an operator with three operands is called a **ternary operator**). The operands are all expressions.

As in the **if** statement, the first value must return a boolean. If the first expression (**conditionExpression**) evaluates to **true** then the second expression (**expressionForTrue**) is evaluated and its value returned. If the first expression evaluates to **false**, the third expression is evaluated and its value is returned.

Here's an example:

```
float x, y, max;
... // assign values to x and y
max = x>y ? x : y;
```

We use the conditional operator to check if **x** is greater than **y**, and if so, assign its value to **max**. If it's less than or equal to **y**, then **max** gets the value of **y**–short and elegant.

Since the value returned by the conditional operator may be assigned to a variable, both the second and third expressions must return a value of the same type. They must be one of the following:

▲   Both of a primitive arithmetic type

▲   Both booleans

▲   Both of a reference type

To read more on this, refer to the *Java Language Specification*.

The switch Statement

In programming, you often have to choose a path of action according to a single value. Here's a pseudo-code example from a rolodex system:

```
input a key from the user
if the key was 'n', go to name handling
if the key was 'a', go to address handling
```

```
if the key was 'p', go to phone handling
if the key was 'o', go to occupation handling
if the key was 'x', go to exit the system
otherwise, show a help screen
```

Here's a Java code that implements this action (key input excluded):

```
if        ( key == 'n' ) handleName();
else if ( key == 'a' ) handleAddress();
else if ( key == 'p' ) handlePhone();
else if ( key == 'o' ) handleOccupation();
else if ( key == 'x' ) exitProgram();
else                     showHelpScreen();
```

This form of using the **if** statement (called 'nested **if**') was so common, that long ago people decided there should be a mechanism to handle it. Today, many languages implement such a mechanism. It's called a **switch** statement.

The switch statement is used to select one of many possible actions using the different possible values of a single variable. Java's syntax for the switch statement is:

```
switch ( Expression )
{
    case Value1      :      Statement1;
    case Value2      :      Statement2;
    ...
    case ValueN      :      StatementN;
    default     :      defaultStatement;
}
```

You must have at least the **switch** and one **case**. The **default** clause is optional.

The **Expression**'s type and the type of different **Value**s must be either **byte**, **short**, **int** or **char**. The **Expression** can be a variable or method whose return value is also one of the four. You can't have two **Value**s with the same value, even if they aren't of the same type (this is because all the types are actually promoted to an **int** before they are compared).

When Java reaches a **switch** statement, the value of the expression is compared against all the cases, and execution jumps to the statement following the **case** that has a value equal to that of the expression. If no match is found and a **default** clause is present, the **defaultStatement** is executed.

Unless specifically instructed, Java will continue execution on through all of the other cases that follow the one selected. While sometimes this can be useful, more often than not you will want execution to stop before the next **case**, and continue at the instruction following the **switch** statement. You can stop execution by using the **break** keyword. This exits the current block. Note that you don't have to use a **break** after the **defaultStatement**, as it's the last option in the **switch**.

However, to reduce the possibility of bugs in your code, and to make it easier to read and maintain, we recommend the following:

▲ Always have a **default** (even if it does nothing).

▲ Always put the **default** last, because it's easier to read.

▲ Always use the **break** statement even if it's the last statement, to keep each of the cases in the same style and avoid 'fall through' errors when you add a new **case.**

▲ If you really do want to fall though to the next **case**, add a comment pointing this out.

Using the **switch** statement, our example would look like this:

```
switch ( key )
{
case 'n' : handleName();
          break;
case 'a' : handleAddress();
          break;
case 'p' : handlePhone();
          break;
case 'o' : handleOccupation();
          break;
case 'x' : exitProgram();
          break;
default  : showHelpScreen();
          break;
}
```

An example of using the **switch** statement without the **break** is:

```
switch (securityLevel)
{
    case 9 : // Levels 6-9 are for future use.
    case 8 : // For now they are the same as level 5, so the execution
    case 7 : // falls through these cases down to level 5.
    case 6 :
    case 5 : canKillProcess    = true;
    case 4 : canAddUsers       = true;
    case 3 : canMakeDirectories = true;
    case 2 : canCreateFiles    = true;
    case 1 : canReadFiles      = true;
             break;
    case 0 : kickUserOfTheSystem();
}
```

Note that although the **switch case** is useful and versatile, it's also very limited. You can only compare **int**s, and the only relation you can check for is equality.When you need to compare against integer values, use **switch**. When a more powerful comparison is needed, use nested **if**s.

Loops

In many programs you need to do something repeatedly, either the same way every time, or with some variations. There are several ways to do this in Java.

while Loops

The Java syntax of a **while** loop is very similar to that of C/C++.

```
while ( Condition ) Statement;
```

The **Condition** is a boolean expression, and the **Statement** could be either a single statement or a block. For each iteration of the loop, the **Condition** is first checked, and if it evaluates to **true** then the **Statement** is executed. After the **Statement** is executed, the **Condition** is checked again, and so on.

In the following example, we use a **while** loop to create the binary representation of a decimal number.

```java
class BinaryTrans
{
   public static void main(String args[])
   {
      int      integerValue  = 543;
      String   binaryValue   = "";

      System.out.print(integerValue + " = ");

      while (integerValue != 0)
      {
         // If the rightmost bit is 1, add "1" to the string
         if ( (integerValue & 0x1) == 1 )
            binaryValue = "1" + binaryValue;
         // Otherwise, add "0" to the string
         else
            binaryValue = "0" + binaryValue;

         // Shift 1 bit to the right.
         integerValue >>>= 1;
      }

      // Print the binary string
      System.out.println(binaryValue);
   }
}
```

The output of this example is:

```
543 = 1000011111
```

Can you guess the output that would have been produced if **integerValue** was 0? We'll get to that after we learn about **do** loops.

do Loops

A **do** loop is very much like a **while** loop, only it guarantees that the **Statement** is executed at least once (the condition expression is evaluated only after the statement has executed once). The Java syntax of a **do** loop is also very similar to that of C/C++:

```
do Statement; while ( Condition );
```

The **Condition** is again a boolean expression, and the **Statement** can be either a single statement or a block. For each iteration of the loop the **Statement** is executed and only after that is the **Condition** checked. If it evaluates to **true** then execution returns to the **Statement**; otherwise execution continues to the statement following the **do** loop.

Here's the same example in a **do** form:

```
class BinaryTrans
{
   public static void main(String args[])
   {
      int      integerValue = 543;
      String   binaryValue  = "";

      System.out.print(integerValue + " = ");

      do {
         // If the rightmost bit is 1, add "1" to the string
         if ( (integerValue & 0x1) == 1 )
            binaryValue = "1" + binaryValue;
         // Otherwise, add "0" to the string
         else
            binaryValue = "0" + binaryValue;

         // Shift 1 bit to the right.
         integerValue >>>= 1;
      } while (integerValue != 0);

      // Print the binary string
      System.out.println(binaryValue);
   }
}
```

The output from this example is the same as the output from the previous one. They act in almost the same way, with the only difference being that if **integerValue** is 0, the **while** loop produces an empty string (**binaryValue** remains "") while the **do** loop forces one iteration to be performed, meaning **binaryValue** contains "0".

for Loops

When you need to repeat a statement (or a block) a known number of times, or when you want to keep a count of the number of times you have been through the loop you should use a **for** loop.

The Java syntax of a **for** loop is:

```
for ( Initialization; Condition; Incrementation ) Statement;
```

Note that the semicolons are part of the statement. The **Initialization** and **Incrementation** could be any statement, and the **Condition** should return a boolean value of **true** in order for the **Statement** to be executed.

This example adds the numbers from 1 to 10:

```
int sum=0, n;
for (n=1; n<11; n++) sum+=n;
```

The elements of this syntax are optional. If you omit the **Initialization** part, you would have to initialize the counter before entering the loop.

```
int sum=0, n=1;
for (; n<11; n++) sum+=n;
```

If you leave the **Condition** part out, your loop would either go on forever (it's the same as having the condition be **true**), or you would have to break out of it on your own (more about that up ahead).

```
int i;
for (i=0;; i++) System.out.println( "counting " + i );
```

If you leave the **Incrementation** part out, you would have to increment your counter inside the **Statement**.

```
int sum=0, n;
for ( n=1; n<11; ) sum+=n++;
```

If you leave the **Statement** part out, your loop could only use the side effects of either the **Condition** or the **Incrementation** to do any actual work.

```
int sum=0, n;
for ( n=1; n<11; sum+=n++ );
```

> You can do even more using the comma operator. The comma operator allows more than 1 statement to be executed inside the sections of a for loop. Here's an example which computes the sum of partial sums of the numbers 1 to 4 (or put more simply: $(1)+(1+2)+(1+2+3)+(1+2+3+4) = 20$)
>
> ```
> int f=0;
> for (int i=0, sum=0; i<4; i++, sum+=i, f+=sum);
> ```
>
> We recommend you don't use the comma operator as it makes your code harder to read and maintain. Everything you can achieve by using the comma operator can be done in the body of the loop.

A typical use for **for** loops is to iterate through the elements of an array. Here's an example:

```
int myArray[], i, sum=0;

// create the array
myArray = new int[10];

// initialize the array
for ( i=0; i<10; i++ ) myArray[i] = i+10;

// sum the elements in the array
for ( i=0; i<10; i++ ) sum += myArray[i];
System.out.println( "the sum of 10 to 19 is " + sum );
```

You can declare a loop variable inside the loop (if you don't need it for anything else). For example:

```
for (int i=0; i<5; i++) System.out.println( "i= " + i );
```

Note though, that you can't redefine a variable that's already defined in the method. This wouldn't work:

```
int i=99;
for (int i=0 ;i<5; i++) System.out.println( "i= " + i );
System.out.println( "i= + i );
```

Which Loop Should You Use?

You can implement any type of loop using any other. Choosing what kind of loop to use is really a matter of programming style. There are some acceptable rules though:

▲ If you only want to execute the statement if a condition is true, use **while** loops.

▲ If you want to force a statement to execute at least once and therefore loop back only if a condition is true, use **do** loops.

▲ When you want to use an index, use **for** loops.

Endless Loops

To make a loop go on forever, you can use an empty **for** statement like this:

```
for (;;)  { ... }
```

a **while** statement like this:

```
while (true) { ... }
```

or a **do** statement like this:

```
do {...} while (true)
```

If Something Happens along the Way...

Sometimes, you don't want to go all the way through the loop's body.

Take, for example, the case where you're using many (not nested) **if**s inside the code of your loop, and you find a condition to be true. Once you have executed the action for this condition, you know that you don't need to go on checking all the other **if**s because they will evaluate to **false**. What can you do to finish this iteration through the loop and start the next one?

The solution is in the keyword **continue**. This keyword causes Java to stop executing the loop's body and continue iterating. Here's an example:

```
String inputString;
do
{
    ...// read the user's input into inputString
    if ( inputString.equals("send mail") )
    {
        sendMail(); // invoke mail sending method
        continue;
    }
    if ( inputString.equals("get mail") )
    {
        getMail(); // invoke mail retrieval method
        continue;
    }
    if ( inputString.equals("read mail") )
    {
        readMail(); // invoke mail reading method
        continue;
} while ( ! inputString.equals("bye") );
```

There are times when you need to break out of a loop in the middle. This could be because you've found an error, or some condition was met inside the loop, or indeed any of a number of things. The point is that you need to bail out, now!

The way to break out of loops is to use Java's **break** keyword. We've already seen that **break** can be used to exit the current block when used in a **switch** statement. The same applies here.

When you issue a **break** command, execution moves to the statement following the loop. The following example illustrates what I mean.

Assuming **myArray** holds a list of numbers, the following code checks if any two of them are the same. The focus is on breaking out of the loop as soon as we find out that two elements are equal.

```
int i=0, j=0, myArray[]={2, 5, 4, 6, 3, 4};

for ( i=0; i<myArray.length-1; i++)
    {
        for ( j=i+1; j< myArray.length; j++)
            if ( myArray[i] == myArray[j] )
                break;  // break out of the inner loop
            if ( ( j<myArray.length ) && ( myArray[i] == myArray[j] ) )
                break;       // break out of the outer loop
    }
    if ( myArray[i] == myArray[j] )
    System.out.println( "elements " + i + " and " + j + " are the same !");
```

Note that this example is intended to demonstrate how to break out of a loop (two nested **while**   loops would be easier to write, and clearer). In real life, you would hardly ever break from a **for** loop.

Labels

Labels are place markers. They are used to identify locations in your program, so you can refer to them. The syntax for labels is:

```
labelName  :  Statement;
```

Where the `labelName` is any legal name that isn't the name of a local variable, another (previously defined) label or the name of one of the method's arguments. The colons separate the label from the statement.

If you give a label to a loop statement, you can refer to it in your **break** and **continue** statements to specify what loop you wish to continue iterating or break out of. You can only break from or continue a loop which encloses the block that contains the **break** or **continue** keyword.

To refer to a label use:

```
break labelName;
```

or

```
continue labelName;
```

Labels may be useful when some condition is met inside an inner loop. Here's the previous example using labeled loops:

```
int i=0, j=0, myArray[]={2, 5, 4, 6, 3, 4};

outerLoop:

for ( i=0; i<myArray.length-1; i++)
{
    for ( j=i+1; j< myArray.length; j++)
        if ( myArray[i] == myArray[j] )
            break outerLoop;        // break out of the outer loop
}
if ( myArray[i] == myArray[j] )
System.out.println( "elements " + i + " and " + j + " are the same !");
```

However, we recommend you *don't* use labels. Instead of introducing unstructured flow control statements into your program (bugs, maintenance, readability–the usual issues), use the correct flow control mechanism.

Summary

This chapter has introduced you to the basics of the Java programming language. We started by looking at the structure of a Java program and then went on to look at some basic concepts in more detail. These included variables and data types, methods, expressions, and how to control program flow.

In Java, everything (apart from the primitive data types) is a class. This is a concept that we have somewhat brushed over in this chapter. We'll put this to rights in the next two chapters, which look in detail at object-oriented programming.

Object-Oriented Programming

This chapter provides an overview of object-oriented programming. We'll start by examining what classes and objects are, and then see how to use classes and objects in Java programs.

In this chapter, we'll look at:

▲ Classes and objects

▲ The buzzwords of OOP: encapsulation, inheritance, and polymorphism

▲ Class properties and methods

▲ How objects are declared, instantiated, and used

Concepts of Object-Oriented Programming

Object-oriented technology is basically made up of three elements: object-oriented analysis (OOA), object-oriented design (OOD), and object-oriented programming (OOP). OOA and OOD are well beyond the scope of this book (you want to learn Java, right?–pick up one of the many good books on OOA and OOD to learn more on these exciting topics). However, we'll try to cover the basics you need to lay the foundation for OOP.

Objects

A software object is really just like a real-world object, a self-contained entity with its own set of recognizable attributes. Clocks will serve as a good analogy.

Clocks are very common and there are different kinds of them. Some are plain and some are fancy, some have knobs and others have buttons. However, all clocks are functional devices, with a defined purpose and means of achieving it. Along with everything else, they need to function correctly.

A clock is basically a device to show time. It has an **internal representation** of the time (for example, a particular arrangement of wheels in an analog clock), an **external representation** (hands or digits), and various **methods** to set the time it holds.

The internal and external representation of the time aren't necessarily the same. For example, two digital clocks can store the time internally the same way (as a sequence of bits in a silicon chip), but one could display it using a large LED display on a billboard, while the other could use LCD digits on a wristwatch. Or you could have two clocks that use hands to show the time, one being an analog clock and the other being digital. Although the internal representation is different, they display data in the same way.

There can also be different ways to do the same thing with a clock. You can set the time by turning a knob or by pressing buttons.

Most objects are capable of being in different **states**. A trivial example is an alarm clock which can either be ringing or silent. Actually, if you think about it, every one of the 43200 different settings of the hands in an analog clock is a distinct state, as these states determine the time it shows.

Objects also have **methods** to get and set attributes and perform different operations. Some clocks **extend** the functionality of the basic clock. While an alarm clock extends the operation of a clock with functionality that's time-related, a calculator clock extends it with operations that may have nothing to do with time.

Software Objects

Software objects are modeled after real-world objects. They, too, have states and behaviors.

A **software object** is a self-contained entity that differs from plain data or plain code by the fact that it knows what it is and how to operate on itself. While a continuous sequence of bytes in memory could be an image, a string, or something else, a **String** object knows it is a string, and knows how to conduct string-related operations on itself.

There are many terms used to describe the things that hold the object's state. These include:

- ▲ Properties
- ▲ Attributes
- ▲ Variables
- ▲ Fields
- ▲ Data members

These terms are used by different people to describe the same thing: a state holder. Don't confuse the things that hold the state with the state itself: a 'property' isn't the same as a 'property value'.

The terms used to describe the mechanism by which we interface with software objects are:

- ▲ Functions
- ▲ Methods
- ▲ Messages

Software objects can be the digital representation of real-world objects. They can represent the relevant information needed by your program about the object's state, and expose the functionality your program needs.

For example, let's assume you want a gauge object to show the amount of free disk space on your hard-disk. Assuming you read the amount of free space yourself, you want the gauge to be able to present it. You would probably want to have properties representing the current value, minimum and maximum values which can be displayed, color of the gauge, and so on, and some methods to display the gauge (e.g. as a needle, a thermometer, etc.).

Software objects aren't just pale representations of physical objects. Software objects are also used to 'objectify' abstract concepts. For example, an 'Exception' is an object used by the Java system to represent erroneous situations. It holds the description of the error, and supplies methods to ask for the description of the error and the stack trace.

Classes and Instances

A class is a template (or blueprint) for software objects. In programming (as in the real world) you often need to have many objects of the same kind. Your wristwatch, for example, is one of many identical watches. It may be in a different state to the other ones (show a different time, have different alarm settings, and so on), but it has the same properties and methods. Using a single class, you can create many objects that have the same characteristics, but which can have different states. Each such object is an **instance** of the class.

Since each instance can have its own property values, a separate property memory space is needed for each object to hold its values. On the other hand, since the operations are the same for all the instances, they can (and do) share the same code to implement their methods.

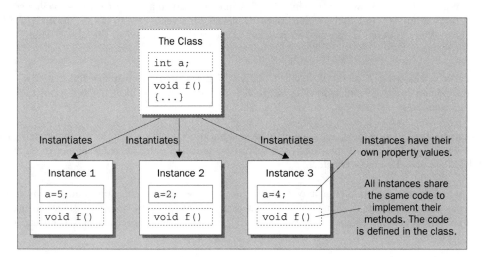

Encapsulation

Encapsulation is about separating the interface and the implementation. A good clock object would hide the internal implementation of time measurement and would supply us only with what we need to know. This would serve two causes:

- If users can't touch it, they can't break it.

- If you don't know what the inside looks like, it makes no difference if someone changes it (as long as it works the same way).

Let's examine these points:

If Users Can't Touch It, They Can't Break It

Sometimes, you have to protect your data. You don't want the user to be able to set all the properties directly because the damage might be irreversible. Therefore, you need to be able to hide the data and only allow it to be manipulated using your methods.

Say you have to build an interface to a computer-controlled surveillance camera. It's very simple: the user sets the value of a special parameter and the camera turns in that direction. The only problem is that the camera's axis motor is very delicate: if you set the value too high or too low, it will break.

"Okay", you say, "I'll have the users enter the input through a function that checks the value, and prevent the user from accessing it otherwise." Congratulations! You have just implemented data encapsulation.

If You Don't Know What the Inside Looks Like...

One of the major benefits of using a (good) interface is that it hides the implementation. This is true for all interfaces, but especially for object-oriented ones. An object-oriented interface doesn't need the user to tell it what data to work on, so if some internal data representation changes, it has no impact on your code.

Take, for example, a camera view object. This object is linked to an image source (the surveillance camera from the previous example), and updates the image displayed on screen whenever the **Update()** method is invoked. The picture's source is specified in a string property that is passed to the object when it's created.

For the first few versions, the camera view object obtained its images from an image file that was automatically updated every few seconds. The image file used to sit on the local file system of the surveillance computer.

Now you want to implement a new, Internet-enabled version and add the ability to set the image source to be a remote computer. This means the image source can be specified either as a file name, or as an Internet URL (Uniform Resource Locator).

While the internal source representation may change, the interface remains the same and no one using the object is affected by the change. Existing software that uses the camera view object continues to use it in the exact same way, and new software may continue using files or simply specify an URL instead of a file name.

To Sum Up

There are two main benefits of encapsulation:

- ▲ **Hiding implementation information**: the public interface is used by other objects, but the object's private information and helper methods (methods used internally within the object and not exposed for public use) are hidden from the other objects. You don't need to understand the way your watch works, you just need it to tell you the time.

- ▲ **Modularity of code**: if the system is well-designed, an object's source code can be maintained independently of the source code for any other object. This is very important when working on a large project.

Messages

The way to interact with objects is by sending them messages. Messages can be inquiring (tell me the time), commanding (set the time to 12:23AM), or both (turn the alarm off and tell me how long it's been ringing).

In programming languages, sending a message is often implemented as invoking a method. Method invocation can be seen as sending a message stating what we want to do, along with the information needed for that task.

A message can cause the object to change its state, report it (or some of the properties that comprise it), and possibly take some action. For example, when the graphics system sends a message to your object telling it to repaint, the object takes action in the form of displaying some graphics on screen. The interesting thing is that the object is actually doing so by sending messages back to the system, telling it to draw lines on the screen.

> *Another possible way (a less object-oriented one) to interact with objects is by directly manipulating exposed properties. This approach should be used only in those rare situations that necessitate it.*

Inheritance

By now, we know that an object is an instance of a class, and that a class defines the characteristics and behavior of all the objects created (instantiated) from it. We don't need to re-implement the behavior of the class for each object separately.

Now, say we want to create a new class of objects that's actually an extension of an existing class. For example, we may want to create an alarm clock class and already have a clock class.

Inheritance is the mechanism of deriving a new class from an existing one. The existing class is called a **base class** (or a **superclass**), and the new one is called the **derived class** (or **subclass**). The derived class has all the characteristics and behavior of the base class, plus any characteristics and functionality created by adding new properties and methods.

Inheritance relationships are often displayed using diagrams like this:

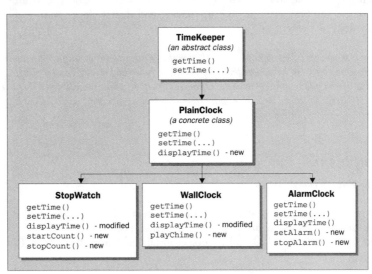

The derived class can also supply a behavior that overrides the behavior of the base class. For example, if the original clock class displayed the data using hands, the derived class could supply an overriding functionality and display the time using digits.

In some cases, a superclass can declare the behavior of an object, but not provide any concrete implementation (either for some of the methods, or all of them). For example, a generic clock may define a method to display the time, but not supply the actual implementation. A derived class could then come and, using the overriding mechanism, supply the actual implementation. A superclass like that is called an **abstract class** (referred to in C++ as a **virtual base class**), and the methods that are declared but not implemented are called **abstract methods** (or, in C++ terms, **virtual methods**).

> **Abstraction is the process of identifying an object from a few properties and methods. Abstract classes define a generic object; they form the top layer(s) of a class hierarchy and cannot be instantiated.**

Who Extends Who?

Inheritance is a great thing in terms of code reuse. If you need to implement two kinds of clocks–a regular clock and an alarm clock–you can fully implement the regular clock, and then just derive the alarm clock from it.

This is a very simple example. It's clear that an alarm clock extends the functionality of a regular clock, and so the order of inheritance is obvious. But what if you need to implement two different kinds of clocks–analog and digital. Which is the derived class in this case? It's not that simple: you can create either class and derive the other from it, overriding the functionality.

These kind of issues are the heart of object-oriented design (which, as mentioned earlier, we aren't going to cover in this book). OOD theory and programming experience are the tools you need to answer questions like this.

In this case, the right solution in terms of design would be to recognize that the common functionality comes from the fact that both the analog and digital clocks are clocks, and thus a third class–clock–should be introduced as the base class of both the analog and digital clock classes, which are therefore siblings (being both derived classes).

> *Some languages (C++ to name one) allow multiple inheritance. Multiple inheritance is a mechanism in which an object can have more than one base class, inheriting methods and properties from all of them. Java doesn't allow multiple inheritance; instead it offers (what is considered to be) a 'cleaner' mechanism, in which an object can implement a functionality that its superclass doesn't provide by implementing publicly declared interfaces.*

Polymorphism

(From Latin:'Poly' = many, 'Morph' = shape or form)

Polymorphism is a long word for a very simple concept. The basic idea is that invoking a method declared in the base class can produce different results from different objects. For example, an object instantiated from the Clock class and an object instantiated from the Alarm Clock class could both invoke the **displayTime** method and display the time in different ways (e.g. one could show 12:23 AM and the other 00:34). The method implementation is taken from the class the object was instantiated from.

This can be very useful. Take, for example, a 3D graphics software package. In this package all the 3D classes (e.g. Cube, Sphere, Pyramid, etc.) are derived from a common base class called '3D_object'. The 3D_object is an abstract class with some properties (the object's location in the 3D space, the object's color, etc.) and an abstract method called **drawImage**. Using this package you can store all the objects in the 3D world in an array (with elements of the type 3D_object), and then iterate through the elements of the array and invoke the **drawImage** method on all of them to draw our 3D world. For each object, the code that implements the method **drawImage** is taken from the object itself, and so cubes draw themselves as cubes, while spheres draw themselves as spheres. Now isn't that a natural way of doing things?

Classes in Java

Classes are the modular building blocks that are used to create Java programs and applets. Now that you know what makes up the inside of a class in terms of variables, expressions and methods, we can move on to talk about classes and how they are built in a more meaningful manner.

Class Members

Object-oriented methodology talks about **properties** and **methods**. These are commonly known as the members of a class and together they define the class.

In Java, properties and methods are declared and implemented in the same place: the class's body. This is unlike C++, where the classes are usually declared in a header file and implemented in a source file. Although you can declare properties and methods wherever you want in the class's body, it's common practice to declare them in this order:

- ▲ Constant properties (we'll talk about these in the next section)
- ▲ Variable properties
- ▲ Methods

In the following sections, we'll dive into the world of properties and methods, and see exactly how they're defined and used.

Properties

As you already know, properties hold an object's state. We use the term 'properties' to distinguish between the local variables of methods (variables declared inside a method's body) and the properties of a class (variables declared in a class but outside of the body of any of its methods). Properties are declared the same way as variables (as seen in Chapter 1). In this section, we'll see how to use an object's properties both from within and from outside the object.

The Dot Notation

When we want to refer to object properties and (as we shall see later) methods, we use the dot notation. This notation uses the object's name (the name you gave the *specific instance*) to identify it, and the property's (or method's) name, as defined in the class definition. Formally speaking, the notation is:

```
objectName.propertyName
```

Getting and Setting Values

Public properties (as opposed to 'private' properties) can be used in any expression, either as a value provider or as a place to store the result (just like any other variable). To get a value of a public property, you use the dot notation to identify the property.

Take, for example, a class called **My3DPoint**, used to define a point in a 3D space. This class has three public properties called **x**, **y**, and **z**. It also has a method called **distanceFrom**, that takes a point as an argument and returns the distance of the point the object represents from the point specified. Here's an example of how to change the **x** property of an instance of the **My3DPoint** class called **startPoint**:

```
startPoint.x = 0;
```

It's really quite straightforward. Here's the body of the **My3DPoint** class:

```
class My3DPoint
{
   public double x, y, z;

   public double distance (My3DPoint p)
   {
      // return the square root of the sum of squares
      return Math.sqrt( (p.x-x)*(p.x-x) +
                        (p.y-y)*(p.y-y) +
                        (p.z-z)*(p.z-z) );
   }
}
```

Note that we've used **p**'s properties as a source for the value we needed for the calculation. This is a very interesting example, because it shows that an object can accept another object of the same class as input, and shows how the object's properties are used in conjunction with the other object's properties.

Constant Properties

There are cases where you want to associate a specific constant value with a class and assign a name to it (like the boolean **TRUE** and **FALSE** constants, for example). This makes your code more readable and your life as a programmer a little less stressful, because names are usually easier to remember than numbers. For example, most C/C++ programmers would tell you that the maximum value for an integer is **MAXINT**–the name that's associated with that value.

In C/C++, you can use the **#define** preprocessor directive to associate the value with a reasonable name, and put it in the header file for the class. This is a very error prone option, as the name of the constants you define for your class might collide (name-wise) with names defined by other classes.

In Java, a constant is an integral part of the class. There are no header files, and all the information needed to use a class is encapsulated in it.

The way to declare a property as constant (i.e. read-only) is to precede it with the keyword **final**, and assign a value to it. **final** means that the value assigned to the property can't be changed.

The **Math** class defines **E** (the natural base) as a **final** property like this:

```
public final static double E = 2.7182818284590452354;
```

This line declares a publicly accessible (**public**), constant (**final**), class wide (**static**–more on this once we've looked at methods), **double** value called **E**, and assigns it the value 2.7182818...

Methods

Methods provide the class functionality. In Chapter 1, we saw how methods are declared and used. Here, we'll sharpen up our understanding of method invocation, and then examine two special kinds of method.

Calling Methods

Methods are invoked using the same dot notation as we saw above:

```
objectName.methodName
```

What we're actually doing is using the object's name as a way of creating a reference to an object. Following are some other ways of referencing objects.

If an expression evaluates to an object (for example, referring to an element in an array of objects), we can use the object to invoke the method. So this:

```
SomeObject myObjectsArray[];
... // add object references to the array
myObjectArray[2].myMethod();
```

is a legal thing to do.

Other expressions that evaluate to objects are references to properties that are objects (for example, the property **out** in the class **System**), so the invocation takes this form:

```
System.out.println(...)
```

If a method returns an object that itself has methods, it's also possible to do things like this:

```
void printClassName(Object obj) {
    System.out.println("The object\'s class name is " + obj.getClass().getName());
}
```

There's no limit to the level of concatenation. As long as an expression evaluates to an object reference, you can add a dot notation method call to the right of the expression.

this

The implementation of a method is common to all the instances of the class, but there are cases in which a method needs a handle to the actual instance it is being invoked from. In every method call (even if the method has no formal arguments), Java passes an implicit argument that's the handle to the actual instance used to invoke the method. This argument has the name **this**. (**this** is a reserved name in Java, and can't be used in any other way).

Using **this** is especially convenient for resolving ambiguity or providing access to otherwise hidden properties (remember, a variable name overrides the name of the class's property). Here's an example:

```
class ValueKeeper
{
   int val;

   public void setVal (int val)
   {
      this.val = val;   // Using this, we can assign the local variable val
                        // to the class's property val. Without the use of
                        // this the property val would be "shadowed"
                        // by the method's argument
   }

   public int getVal ()
   {
      return val;
   }
}
```

Class Properties and Methods

The properties and methods we've seen up to now were all attached to single instances of a class. Properties and methods of this kind are called **instance properties** and **instance methods**. To refer to an instance property or method, you must instantiate the class before you obtain the property or method from the instance.

On the other hand, there are methods and properties which belong to the class as a whole, rather than to any individual instance. These are called **static** methods and properties.

Static properties can be accessed from each instance as if they were an instance property, but if one instance changes a static property, all the other instances will see the new value. Static methods are like static properties in the sense that you don't need an instance in order to invoke them. They can, of course, only refer to static properties.

You could use static properties if you wanted all of a class's objects to know how many of them exist at any given time. A class-wide instance count property could provide just that with no programming overhead. Every time you create a new instance, the counter increases and every time an object is destroyed, the counter decreases.

The great thing is that if you want to check the value of the counter, you don't need a handle to an instance of the class to do so. Class-wide properties exist in the context of the class, and don't need an instance to carry them. We'll see an example of this in a minute.

To declare a property or method static, prepend the keyword **static** to the declaration (if you want to declare it **public**, use either **public static** or **static public**, they both mean the same). To access a static property or method from within an instance of the class, use it as if it was an instance variable. To access it from outside the class, you can either use the name of an instance of the class, or the class name.

Here's a (fairly extensive) example:

```
class StaticExample {
   static int       staticInt;    // a static property
   public static char staticChar;  // a static property
```

```
    int                    instanceInt;      // an instance property

    public static void setStaticInt(int v)
    {
        staticInt = v;                 // Here we use the static property as if
                                       // it was an instance property
    }

    public static int getStaticInt()
    {
        return staticInt;  // Same here
    }

    public void setInstanceInt(int v)
    {
        instanceInt = v;
    }

    public int getInstanceInt()
    {
        return instanceInt;
    }
}

class StaticTest {

    static StaticExample s;     // must declare s static - main is a static
                                // method and it uses s

    public static void main(String vars[])
    {
        // Working with the static members

        StaticExample.setStaticInt(13);
        System.out.println( StaticExample.getStaticInt() );

        StaticExample.staticChar = 'a';
        System.out.println( StaticExample.staticChar );

        // Working with an instance

        s = new StaticExample();           // here we create a new instance

        s.setStaticInt(13);
        System.out.println( StaticExample.getStaticInt() );
        System.out.println( s.getStaticInt() );

        s.staticChar = 'a';
        System.out.println( StaticExample.staticChar );
        System.out.println( s.staticChar );

        s.setInstanceInt(17);
        System.out.println( s.getInstanceInt() );
    }
}
```

The output of this program will be:

```
13
a
13
13
a
a
17
```

You can initialize a static property the same way you initialize an instance property. The initial value will be assigned before the first use of the object (assignment happens when the class is first loaded in your application), so you can safely use it whenever you want.

> Note that if all the methods and properties of a class are static, you can't instantiate or extend the class through inheritance.

System.out.println()

You're familiar enough with the following expression:

```
System.out.println(...)
```

However, you may not have understood exactly what it's doing until now. What you see here is an invocation of a method called **println**. This method belongs to an object called **out** which, in turn, is an instance of the **PrintStream** class that implements the standard output, and is itself a static member of the class **System**. The method **println** is invoked with the item whose value we wish to display.

When the **System** class is loaded into the application, it automatically creates **out** and all of its other static properties. We can then use them without having to create an instance of the **System** class.

Actually, you can't create an instance of System because all of its members (out, in, and the rest) are static. (It'd be nice though if you could get yourself a new computer by instantiating System, wouldn't it?)

Objects

The life cycle of every object in Java is made up of these 5 phases:

- Declaration of a handle to the object
- Instantiation
- Initialization
- Usage by referencing
- Destruction

Let's have a look at each of these.

Declaring an Object Handle

Objects that hang around in memory are of no use unless you have a way to reference them. To provide object access, Java uses object handles. Handles can be thought of as a leash on a wild animal. Once the first one is on, you can add as many as you like, but once the last leash is released, there's no way to put one back.

> *A word to the expert: handles are really indices into a table that holds the actual location of objects in memory. This method of indirect access enables Java to move objects around in memory (thus allowing better use of it in terms of fragmentation and—as we'll see later—garbage collection). While the object moves around, the entry in the table doesn't change so we always know where to find the object's actual address.*

Handle declarations take the same form as any other variable or property. Formally speaking, the syntax for declaring handles is:

```
ClassName handleName;
```

where **ClassName** is a name of a known class, and **handleName** is the name of the handle. A handle declaration is simply a way to notify the compiler that you'll be using **handleName** to refer to an object in memory that is an instance of the **ClassName** class.

> **Object handles can only be passed around in the application. You can't create a handle out of thin air (as you can do in C/C++ by assigning a value to a pointer, thus having it point to any location in memory); it must be given to you either by the run-time system (that created the object) or by someone else who has it.**

Unlike in C++, declarations do not instantiate objects. To instantiate an object in Java, you use the **new** operator.

Instantiating a New Object

The **new** operator instantiates a new object (as an instance of a specified class) by allocating memory for it and invoking a constructor method (a method used to initialize the state of the object). The syntax of **new** is:

```
new ClassName( Arguments )
```

Where **ClassName** is a name of a class, and **Arguments** are any arguments needed for one of the constructors (the parentheses are required, even if no argument is specified).

If you're thinking that this looks like we're calling a method without specifying an object or a class, then you're right. What you see here is the invocation of a constructor method for the specified object. This is the only case where we can use a class's name without specifying the method's name (or vice versa—use a method's name without specifying the class's name) because the constructor and the class have the exact same name.

Initializing an Object

When instantiating a new object, you often want to initialize it to a specific state. This can be done by assigning initial values to properties (resetting a counter, for example), or performing some initializing operation (like opening an output file).

The **constructor** is a method that has the same name as the class, and it's invoked when instantiating a new object. Every class has at least one constructor. If you don't want to perform any initialization code, Java provides you with a default constructor (that takes no arguments and does nothing). This is why every object instantiation looks like a method call. When invoking the default constructor, you don't pass any argument, but you still have to include the opening and closing parentheses of a method call.

Here's an example of using a default constructor:

```java
class Location {
    int    x = 0,
           y = 0;
    String description = "at home";

    public void SetPos (int x, int y, String d)
    {
        this.x = x;
        this.y = y;
        description = d;
    }

    public void PrintPos()
    {
        System.out.println( "I'm " + description + " ("+x+","+y+")" );
    }
}

class ConstructorTest {
    public static void main (String args[])
    {
        Location l = new Location();  // invokes the default constructor

        System.out.println();
        l.PrintPos();
        System.out.println();
        l.SetPos(1,1,"in the forest");
        l.PrintPos();
    }
}
```

This is the output you'll get when you run **ConstructorTest**:

    I'm at home (0,0)

    I'm in the forest (1,1)

Notice how the properties were initially set to the explicitly defined default values.

The constructor is called after the properties were initialized to their default values (as defined by Java—numbers to zero, characters to **\u0000**, and booleans to **false**), or any explicit value that you specify for them in your class definition.

The return type of a constructor is (implicitly) an instance of the class. You can't explicitly return any value from a constructor. The value returned is actually the implicit argument **this**.

A class can have many constructors by using method overloading. For example, the Integer class (a wrapper class for **int**s) has the two following constructors:

```
public  Integer(int  value)
public  Integer(String  s)
```

The first takes an **int** and sets it as the value of the instance. The second takes a **String** that holds an integer *in a textual form*, parses the string, and stores the value it represents. More on this class in Chapter 4.

Implicitly Calling the Constructor

When using methods that take strings as arguments, you often pass them a string literal. For example, one of the **println** methods is defined like this:

```
println(String s)
```

but we often use it like this:

```
System.out.println( "Hello world!");
```

How is it possible to use a string literal when the method expects a **String** object?

The answer lies in the fact that the method did get a **String**. Java came to our aid here (as in all other implicit casting cases), created the **String** object for us, and passed it on to the method. The only remaining question is "How did Java know to create the **String** object?"

When Java encounters a mismatch of types, it first tries to fix it itself. It does so by trying to create the object it needs from the one supplied. The way to create new objects is by calling a constructor, and since the **String** class has a constructor that takes a string literal, Java could automatically create a new **String** object by invoking that constructor. After creating it, Java passed it to the **println** method.

Although implicit construction of objects is helpful, bear in mind that invoking the constructor can have side effects. For example, if your constructor prints out a message, this message would also be printed when the constructor is implicitly invoked.

Summing Up Initialization

A constructor is a method of the class that is being invoked when you create a new instance. It can be used to initialize the state of the object before anyone handles it.

You can have multiple constructors using method overloading. The order of events when you create a new instance is shown as follows:

- ▲ Memory allocation for the new instance
- ▲ Initialization of properties to default values
- ▲ Calling the appropriate constructor

We'll meet constructors again in the next chapter.

> **Note that to assign a constant value to a property you don't need a constructor. When declaring a property, you can specify the initial value this property will have when an object in instantiated.**

Object Reference

The following class assigns constant values to the properties **x** and **y**:

```java
class Point {
    int x = 1, y = 1;      // <- initialize x and y to
                           // CONSTANT values

    void set( int x, int y )
    {
        this.x = x;
        this.y = y;
    }

    int  getX () { return x; }

    int  getY () { return y; }

    void printOut ()
    {
        System.out.println( x + " , " + y );
    }
}
```

You can't use a handle before you've assigned it to an actual object, so this wouldn't work:

```java
Point myPoint;          // handle declared
myPoint.set(1,2);       // <- ERROR: trying to use an unassigned handle !
```

However, once the object has been created in memory and you have a handle to it, you can start using it.

Look at the following example:

```java
class ShowMyPoint {

    public static void main (String args[])
    {
```

```
        Point p1, p2 = new Point();

        p1 = new Point();
        p1.set(1,10);

        p1.printOut();
        p2.printOut();

        p2 = p1;              // <- watch this one carefully

        p2.set(3,4);
        p1.printOut();
    }
}
```

Can you guess the output? Strangely enough, it is:

```
1 , 10
1 , 1
3 , 4
```

What went on here? We changed **p2**'s attributes and **p1** was affected. This was because (after the statement marked 'watch this one carefully'), **p1** and **p2** refer to the same object.

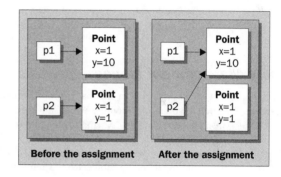

The statement

```
    p2 = p1;              // <- watch this one carefully
```

means we lose the object pointed to by **p2**, forever. We can't regain the handle to it, because no one has it any longer. What happened to that object? Does it remain in memory forever? Let's find out ...

Object Destruction

The last phase in an object's life is the destruction. This phase is, I believe, simultaneously the most easy and difficult to understand. It's easy because most of the time you don't even think about it, but when you start asking questions, there are a lot of mysteries to explore. Let's plunge in and learn about the power of Java's memory management mechanism, and how it affects Java programming.

When we don't need an object anymore, we want the memory space it occupies to be returned to the system's free memory pool. Java's memory management system uses an automatic mechanism to regain unused memory. This is unlike C/C++, which forces you to explicitly free memory you don't need (here, Java takes after languages like Lisp).

Java's memory management system remembers all the objects it had allocated memory to, and keeps track of all the references to them. When the reference count goes down to zero, the object can be deleted, and the memory it occupied reclaimed.

> *If you remember, you can only pass references. Here is one major benefit of the system. Since only object references can be passed, the system can figure out how many handles point to any object. If no handle points to an object, then no one can ever regain access to the object and the object can be freed from memory.*

> *This isn't true for classes which have only static methods and properties. For these classes there's one persistent instance that you can reference without a handle.*

The mechanism used for getting rid of never-to-be-used-again memory objects is called **garbage collection**. This technique was adopted by Java, from languages like Lisp, to ensure that all allocated memory is freed. It takes the memory management load off the programmer and makes sure everything goes on smoothly in terms of memory resource management. One of the major pitfalls when programming in languages like C or C++ is forgetting to free up memory—your application slowly consumes all the memory in the system, and when it suddenly crashes, you don't know why it did.

> *If you're coming to Java from C/C++, this may seem a little unnatural, but I'm sure you will grow to love it in no time (I did). Just don't get too used to it, and forget memory deallocation when you use C/C++!*

Memory Management Issues

The garbage collector runs silently in the background, making sure everything is okay in terms of memory management. Normally, you don't have to worry about it, but—if you wish to—you can give it 'hints' as to when an object won't be used again. Normally, the reference count goes down in two situations:

- ▲ When a *handle* (not necessarily the object) is deleted, as happens when a method returns and deletes all of the local variables from memory.

- ▲ When a handle is being assigned to another object.

The question is what to do if, in the middle of a method, you know that:

- ▲ You aren't going to use the handle anymore.

- ▲ The object occupies memory and you want it available for better use.

- ▲ You don't want to assign the handle to a new object.

The solution is to assign the handle to nothing (thus reducing the reference count to the referenced object). You do this by simply assigning it to **null**—a keyword that stands for '*a handle to nothing*'. The following code snippet illustrates the point:

```
int reallyBigObject bigOne;

bigOne = new reallyBigObject;
```

```
... // use bigOne
```

```
bigOne = null;                    // implicitly drop the handle
```

```
// forever process user requests...
for (;;)
{
   getRequest();
   processRequest();
}
```

The same goes for large arrays:

```
int i, a[];

a = new int[10000];

for (i=0; i<a.length; i++) a[i] = readData();
processArray( a );
a = null;
```

```
... // do other things
```

Remember that normally you shouldn't worry about this. The system is very capable of handling memory deallocation itself. Also, remember that assigning a handle to **null** doesn't invoke the garbage collector. It simply hints that the occupied memory may be freed.

Finalizers

When the reference count of an object goes down to zero, the object may be removed from memory by the garbage collector. In some cases, it's very important to detect the action of object deletion before it's executed, and do some pre-termination work. For example, if an object uses a system resource such as a file then it should release the resource when it's removed from memory, otherwise the system may run out of free file handles.

Java provides a simple solution to this problem in the form of the **finalize()** method (a finalizer is somewhat similar to a C++ destructor). A finalizer is used to doing all the housekeeping of object destruction (other than memory deallocation) such as:

- ▲ Closing open files
- ▲ Closing communication sockets
- ▲ Freeing up other system resources
- ▲ Any other task that must be performed upon termination

A finalizer is an instance method (not a class-wide one) that takes no arguments. The finalizer method *must* be named **finalize()** (this is unlike C++, where the finalizer of a class **myClass**   must be named **~myClass**). Here's an example:

```
class databaseConnection {
   databaseConnection( String DatabaseURL ) {
      // Open a database connection
      ...
```

```
    }

    boolean processRequest( String SQLQuery ) {
        // Do some work
        ...
    }

    ...   // Some other methods

    finalize() {
        // Close the database connection
        ...
    }
}
```

Finalizers are only executed *once* by Java. An object's **finalize()** method is called before the memory is freed, and the memory is only freed if–after the finalizer is done–the object remains unreferenced (a finalizer may assign the object's handle provided to it by **this** to another object, thus increasing the reference count).

If the Java interpreter terminates without deleting all the objects in memory, a finalizer may not be called at all. In this case, the operating system will take care of freeing all the resources held by your Java program.

Note that you can't be sure exactly when the **finalize()** method will be invoked. You can invoke the **finalize()** yourself, like any other instance method, but doing so does not cause the destruction of the object.

Finalizers are useful when you need to make sure the user of your class doesn't forget to release a resource before the object is destroyed. This mostly has to do with native methods (methods that are written in a language other than Java and compiled to native machine language). These methods don't enjoy the comfort of explicit deallocation of system resources provided by Java. Since such methods may use system resources that should be explicitly released (graphic display contexts, system file handles etc.), you must make sure they're released by providing a finalizer.

If your application runs long enough for the GC to be invoked, your objects release any unneeded resources when their finalizers are invoked. If the system exits without calling the finalizing methods, then it releases any resources your application holds by itself.

Putting It All Together

So far we've seen the core of Java's power: classes and objects. Before moving on to more advanced concepts and some examples of object-oriented programming in the next chapter, we'll sum things up in a simple (yet not trivial) example.

Example: The Vehicle Class

A vehicle (not a specific one, but a general vehicle) can be seen as an object. It has methods and attributes and we can model them in software.

Definition of a Vehicle

A vehicle is an object that travels from place to place, carrying people, pets and purchases. Let's list some of the properties of a vehicle:

`CurrentSpeed`	The speed the vehicle is traveling at.
`MaximumSpeed`	The maximum speed the vehicle can travel at.
`MinimumSpeed`	The minimum speed the vehicle can travel at (i.e. reverse).
`CurrentPassengerCount`	Self explanatory.
`MaximumPassengerCount`	Same here ...
`CurrentCargoLoad`	And here ...
`MaximumCargoLoad`	And here.
`Name`	Every vehicle has one (either a brand name, a number plate or a name given to it by the owners...).

(There are more, but these will do for our example.)

A vehicle also has the following methods:

`SpeedUp()`	Accelerate, if not at the maximum speed.
`SlowDown()`	Decelerate, if not at the minimum speed.
`MakeSound()`	Ring a bell, sound a horn, etc.

(Again, we'll keep the list short and simple.)

Creating the Vehicle Class

Now that we know what a vehicle is, and what its attributes are, let's see how these attributes are implemented in our Java class.

To make the code readable, I've listed it all in one chunk. The various parts are pointed out by the comments.

```
class Vehicle {              // Class declaration

    / ************          // The properties
     * Properties  *
     ************/
    int    currSpeed,
           maxSpeed,
           minSpeed,
           currPsgrCount,
           maxPsgrCount;

    float currCargo,
          maxCargo;

    String name;

    /*********               // The methods
     * Methods *
     *********/
    Vehicle(String name)     // The constructor
      {
```

```
            this.name = name;
    }

void speedUp(){                    // Other methods...
        if (currSpeed<maxSpeed)
            currSpeed++;
    }

    void slowDown() {
        if (currSpeed>=minSpeed)
            currSpeed--;
    }

    void makeSound() {
        System.out.println("Beep");
    }
}
```

As you can see, the mapping of our theoretical design to a Java class was really straightforward. It's often harder to think of the right model than it is to code it (our example was *so* simple that it really took no effort to design it).

Using the Vehicle Class

OK, now let's create a test class:

```
class TestDrive {

    public static void main (String args[])
    {
    Vehicle myCar;                              // Declaration of a handle to the object

                                                // Create a car and let it roll...
        myCar = new Vehicle("K.I.T.T");         // Instantiation and Initialization
    myCar.maxSpeed  = 100;                      // Usage by referencing
    myCar.currSpeed =  10;                      // here too

                                                // "Press the gas" 100 times
        for (int i=1; i<100; i++) myCar.speedUp();          // and here
        System.out.println(myCar.name +                     // and here
                         "'s speed is " + myCar.currSpeed);  // and here
        myCar.makeSound();                                   // and here
    }
}
```

The **main()** method of the **TestDrive** application creates a **Vehicle** object named **myCar**. The next statement instantiates and initializes the object. We could have also done it like this:

```
Vehicle myCar = new Vehicle("K.I.T.T");     // Declaration, Instantiation and Initialization
```

This single statement performs all three actions at once: declaration, instantiation, and initialization.

As you may have noticed, there's no explicit object destruction phase (can you tell when the **myCar** object is made a candidate for garbage collection?).

Summary

This chapter has introduced you to the basic concepts of object-oriented programming. We've discussed inheritance, polymorphism and encapsulation and seen how to create and use classes and objects. We've also looked at how to get and set property values and how to call methods, including using the reserved word **this**. You should be familiar with the differences between static and instance properties and methods.

We've looked at the life-cycle of an object, and examined each of the phases: declaration, instantiation, initialization, object reference and destruction.

The discussions of this chapter form the basis of Chapter 3 which continues our look at object-oriented programming.

Class Relations

In the last chapter, we reviewed OOP principles and the way you set up, use and destroy an object in Java. In this chapter, we'll look at the ways in which classes are related, using those OOP buzzwords:

- Inheritance
- Abstraction
- Polymorphism

We'll also look at package creation and use, and Java's comprehensive exception handling.

Inheritance

Inheritance is a key concept in object-oriented programming. It allows us to create new classes based on an existing class, without re-implementing the functionality of that existing class.

Java's syntax for declaring a derived class is:

```
class DerivedClass extends BaseClass
```

where **BaseClass** is the name of the base class we want to extend, and **DerivedClass** is the name of the new class.

Every class that does not explicitly extend any other class, implicitly extends Java's most basic class, called **Object**. **Object** is the only class that does not inherit from any other class.

Let's look at a simple example:

```
class Value {
    int val=0;
    int getVal() {
        return val;
    }
    void setVal( int val ) {
        this.val = val;
    }
}

class PrintableValue extends Value {
    PrintVal() {
        System.out.println( val );
```

```
        }
    }

    class InheritanceTester {
        public static void main (String args[] ) {
            Value a = new Value();
            PrintableValue b = new PrintableValue();

            a.setVal(5);
            b.setVal( a.getVal() );
            b.PrintVal();
            System.out.println( a.getVal() + " = " + b.getVal() );
        }
    }
```

The output of **InheritanceTester** is:

    5
    5 = 5

Notice how we got the **PrintableValue** methods **setVal** and **getVal** for free by deriving it from **Value**.

Casting

We have already seen casting with primitive types (an **int** being converted to a **float**, etc.). Casting means that we wish to refer to an object of type X as if it were of type Y.

Casting objects in Java is a little different from casting in C/C++. While in C/C++, one can cast from any type to any other type; in Java, you can only cast something of type X into some type Y if:

▲ X is the same as Y, or

▲ The base class of X could be cast to Y.

Here's an example:

```
class A {
    int a;
}

class B extends A {
    int b;
}

class C extends B {
    int c;
}

class TestCasting {
    public static void main (String args[] ) {
        B myB = new B;
        C myC = new C;
```

```
        myC.a = 1;
        ((B)myC).a = 2;        // the base class of C is the same as B,
                               // so C can be cast to B.
        ((A)myC).a = 3;        // the base class of C can be cast to A,
                               // so C can be cast to A.

        System.out.println( myC.a );    // output is: "3"

        ((A)myC).b = 1;        // Breaks on compilation - A has no property
                               // called b, so we can't refer to it

        myB.b = 1;
        ((C)myB).c = 2;        // Runtime exception - an object from
                               // class B can't be cast to class C.
    }
}
```

Here we show how **myC.a** can be successfully cast to classes **A** or **B**. Then we show two illegal casts, the first which the Java compiler notices, the second which causes an exception when the program is run.

Overriding Parent Methods

A derived class can implicitly inherit the implementation of the methods in the base class, but it can also provide its own implementation. This allows the derived class to change the behavior of methods when they are invoked.

Here is an example of two classes being derived from our hypothetical **Vehicle** class and overriding the **makeSound** method:

```
class Scooter extends Vehicle {
    ...
    makeSound() { System.out.println("Beeeeeeep"); }
}

class Boat extends Vehicle {
    ...
    makeSound() { System.out.println("Tooooooo"); }
}
```

When we instantiate a **Scooter** object or a **Boat** object, the object created is identical to a **Vehicle** object, except for the implementation of **makeSound** method. The fact that only the implementation is different makes polymorphism possible.

Shadowed Properties and Methods

In the same way that method argument names can shadow class property names, derived class properties may shadow base class properties or methods.

Shadowed properties are properties that have the same name as properties in the base class. Shadowed methods are methods that have the same **signature** (not just the same name, but also the same return type and the same number, order and type of arguments).

Here is an example of a shadowed property:

```
class X {
    int p;
}

class Y extends X {
    int p;
    ...
}
```

Referring to Shadowed Properties

If, in class **Y**, we wish to refer to the property **p** of a base class (i.e. **X.p**), we need a way to distinguish it from **Y**'s property **p**. To specify **p** as the property of the base class, we precede it with the keyword **super**:

```
class Y extends X {
    int p;
    Y( int val ) {
        p = 1;
        super.p = 2;
    }

    printMe () {
        System.out.println (super.p + " " + p);
            // output is: "2 1"
    }
}
```

Another option is to cast the object to the base class, but this way is both cumbersome and error prone. Although it isn't recommended, you can cast to the base class like this:

```
    Y( int val ) {
        p = 1;
        ((X)this).p = 2;
    }
```

Referring to Shadowed Methods

The same applies to shadowed methods. Here's an example:

```
class AuditedValue extends Value {
    void setVal( int val ) {
        System.out.println( "Old value" + val );
        super.setVal( val );
        System.out.println( "New value" + val );
    }
}
```

However, unlike property shadowing, you can't cast an object to another class to get it to behave as that other class. The only way you can access a base class behavior is by using the **super** keyword. This means that you can only invoke the implementation of the direct base class of the referred object (in other words, you can only go up one level in the inheritance tree). Although this seems like a restriction, the benefits are enormous as we will soon see.

The following example illustrates the effect (actually the lack of it) of casting on the behavior of an object:

```
class TryToFoolTheSystem {
    public static void main (String args[] ) {
        AuditedValue privilege = new AuditedValue();

        System.out.println("Nothing is going on...");
        ((Value) privilege).setVal(4);   // Try avoiding the printing
                                          // of audit information
    }
}
```

This example would print out:

```
Nothing is going on...
Old value 0
New value 4
```

Benefits of Using the Base Class's Implementation

By using the base class's implementation:

▲ We don't need to know the implementation details of the base class, which is important if we weren't the ones who wrote the base class.

▲ We don't need to duplicate the effort of writing and testing the code that does the basic work.

▲ If the base class changes, our code changes with it.

It's good practice to use the implementation the base class provides, rather then re-writing it—even if it's only a single line of code. Doing so contributes to a code which is more maintainable, robust, adaptive and encapsulated (other buzzwords omitted to save trees).

Base Class Constructors

Almost every class is derived from another class, the only exception being **Object**—the ancestor of *all* classes. If the base class for some class isn't specified, it means that the class is implicitly derived from the class **Object**.

Every object in Java has a constructor. If you don't implement a constructor for your class, Java provides a default constructor for you. The default constructor of the derived class does nothing but invoke the constructor of the base class:

▲ If your class is implicitly derived from **Object**, the constructor provided takes no arguments and calls **Object**'s constructor (which does nothing as far as a Java programmer is concerned).

▲ If you derive your class from a base class that has a constructor that takes no arguments (either explicitly implemented or the default), that constructor will be invoked (even if the base class has other constructors that take arguments).

▲ If you derive your class from a class that has a constructor which takes arguments, then you must pass the arguments to that constructor. If the base class has more then one constructor then you need to specify which constructor to call.

Again, we can use **super** to invoke the constructor of the base class like this:

```
class Car extends Vehicle {
    String model;
    Car (String model, String name){
        super(name);    // Invokes the Vehicle's constructor
                        // with the required parameter.
        this.model = model;
    }
}
```

The constructor invoked is the one with a signature that matches the parameters passed. If a class has more than one constructor, the ambiguity is resolved using the same rules used in method overloading.

The mystery of the default constructor can be summarized with this rule:

▲ If the first statement in a constructor is neither a call to **super** nor a call to another constructor in the same class, then Java implicitly inserts the statement **super()** as the first statement of the constructor.

The outcome is that while constructors can invoke other constructors in the class, eventually one constructor must invoke (either implicitly or explicitly) a constructor of the base class. The first constructor to run would be the constructor of **Object** (that's always true), followed by constructors for each of the base classes of the instantiated class, and finally the constructor originally invoked.

Here's an example to illustrate this:

```
class A {    // implicitly extends Object
    int a;

    A() {
        // implicit call to super()
        a = 0;
    }

    A(int a) {
        this.a = a;
    }
}

class B extends A{
    int b;

    B(int a, int b) {
        // implicit call to super()
        this.a = a;
        this.b = b;
    }
```

```
        B(int b) {
           this.B( 1, b );
        }
   }

   class C extends B{
      int c;
      C(int c) {
         super(3);
         this.c = c;
      }

      void Display() {
         System.out.println( "a=" + a + " b=" + b + " c=" + c);
      }
   }
```

When instantiating an object from the class **C**, the constructor explicitly invokes the second constructor of class **B**, which explicitly invokes the first constructor of class **B**, which implicitly invoked the first constructor of class **A** which implicitly invokes the constructor of **Object**. So the statement,

```
   C triplet = new C(5);
```

results in the following chain of calls:

The constructors are executed down the inheritance tree; from **Object**'s constructor, to **C**'s. If we invoke **Display** on **triplet**, we would get the following output:

    a=1 b=3 c=5

Using init()

Java allows you to use a special method, **init()**, which allows several constructors to share common initialization code. What is so special about **init()**? We can use any method to share common code, but there are some special things that only **init()** can do.

Java treats **init()** in a special way. While method overloading is available throughout the language, **init()** is the only method that completely obscures any of its other implementations in any context other than the one from which it is called. The following example illustrates what I mean:

```
   class BaseClass {
      BaseClass() {
         init();
      }

      void init() {
         System.out.println("init of BaseClass");
      }
```

```
    }

    class DerivedClass extends BaseClass {
        DerivedClass() {
            // This will invoke the BaseClass constructor which
            // will invoke DerivedClass.init();
        }
        void init()
        {
            System.out.println("init of DerivedClass");
        }
    }

    class TestInit{
        public static void main(String args[])
        {
            BaseClass b = new BaseClass();
            DerivedClass d = new DerivedClass();
        }
    }
```

The method **init()** defined in the derived class obscures **init()** in the base class when a method from the derived class is invoked. The result is that **BaseClass.init()** is never called when a **DerivedClass** object is created. Calling **new DerivedClass()** invokes the **DerivedClass** constructor, which invokes the **BaseClass** constructor, which invokes the **init()** implementation from **DerivedClass**. This would happen even if you try forcing the type of **init()** to that of the base class using explicit casting like **((BaseClass)this).init()**.

The output of **TestInit** would be:

```
init of BaseClass
init of DerivedClass
```

Abstraction

When we introduced the **Vehicle** class it had a method called **makeSound()**:

```
class Vehicle {

    ... // all the other properties and methods

    void makeSound() {
        System.out.println("Beep");
    }
}
```

Since a generic vehicle may or may not make a sound, and since any sound it makes can be whatever the designer wants, we implemented the **makeSound()** method without much thought, counting on the derived classes to override it.

When designing software, it's common to have a generic base class whose implementation is sure to be overridden by any derived class, or (unlike the very simple case we presented) whose implementation is so free that no default implementation can be provided.

In the past, programmers have solved this problem by leaving the body of such methods empty, that is, providing no implementation to the method, or putting in a stub, as we did above. This is poor practice, as a programmer can't know what methods need to be overridden and what methods are provided with a default implementation from the base class's method declarations. A language construct was needed to differentiate these two cases, abstract classes and methods.

Abstract Classes and Methods

The **abstract** keyword enables us to declare classes with methods that have no default implementation. To declare an abstract class, you should add the **abstract** modifier to the class's declaration. For example:

```
public abstract class anAbstractClass {...}
```

To declare an abstract method, you should add the **abstract** modifier to the declaration, and instead of a body put a semicolon. For example:

```
public abstract void anAbstractMethod(...);
```

> Note that only abstract classes may have abstract methods. It's a compilation error to declare an abstract method in a non-abstract (sometimes referred to as 'concrete') class. Obviously, not all the methods of an abstract class have to be abstract, only those for whom there's no obvious default implementation.

The Abstract Base Class

Since an abstract class may have methods with no implementation, it's impossible to instantiate an object from an abstract class. Abstract classes are used as a common base class for a set of derived classes.

Below is our Vehicle example, revised to use abstract classes. I've removed all reference to the unused common attributes (i.e. class properties), as they obscure the purpose of the example. The only property left is **name**, because it illustrates the nature and purpose of the abstract class.

```
class Vehicle {
    /* Properties */
    String name;

    /* Methods */
     public Vehicle(String name)
    {
        this.name = name;
    }

    public abstract void speedUp();
    public abstract void slowDown();
    public abstract void makeSound();
}
```

We will further investigate the use of abstract classes when we look at polymorphism in a later section.

Interfaces

Having covered classes, inheritance and abstract methods, we need to make a distinction between the **class** and the **type** of the object:

▲ The class of an object defines the way an object represents its state and the way it implements its various operations.

▲ The type of an object defines the messages the object is capable of receiving.

Inheritance gives us a way to change the implementation of a method without changing the set of methods the class provides, thus allowing the base class and the derived class to be of the same type. We're now going to look at a new concept that separates a class's functionality, as represented in a class's method interface, from any specific class.

Generally speaking, an object has many types—each type is defined by a subset of messages the object is capable of receiving.

Take, for example, an object that has methods for storing, retrieving and printing strings. If you look at one subset of the object's methods, you would say it is a 'Storage Provider'. If you look at another, you would say it is 'Printable'. Which one is it?

The answer is both. In the object model, as seen by Java, an object can be both a 'Storage Provider' and 'Printable' at the same time. When we examine the object we give no greater importance to either subset, so we can say it is a 'Printable Storage Provider Object' or a 'Storage Providing Printable Object' and be right in both cases.

In Java, sharing a common functionality does not necessarily imply being derived from a common base class. While a Truck class could be derived from the class Car, it can implement any other functionality not found in the Car class but common to a set of other classes, for example, 'Storage Provider', using the **interface** mechanism.

An interface describes the type of functionality an object is able to provide. It declares a set of messages, providing only the messages' signatures, that a class must fully implement in order to be of that type.

> *An interface is like a pure virtual base class in C++ in the sense that it supplies no functionality. We'll come back to the differences between abstract classes and interfaces later.*

Identifying the Interface

Recognizing that some functionality may be common to many objects requires a broad view of your system, and an understanding of affiliations amongst the objects. You can either over-interface a class, taking things that truly belong to the class and making them an interface, or under-interface, by overlooking a common functionality some classes in your system share.

Not every common functionality must form an interface. An interface is used to provide a way to refer to different classes as being of the same type. If two classes share a common functionality which doesn't need to be referred to polymorphically using that common interface (i.e. by invoking the methods of the interface on objects of the classes and treating them as instances of the interface), there is no point in making the common functionality a declared interface.

Here is an example to make things clearer. Say you are developing a basketball arcade game. Among the classes of the game there are two classes with a common functionality who's signature is **void play()**. These classes are **BasketballPlayer**, for which **play** means running around the court trying to help your team win, and **TimeKeeper**, for which **play** means playing a tune when there are only a few seconds left. Although the two classes share a common interface, there is no point in creating a **Player** interface with a method **void play()** as the two classes would never be handled polymorphically.

Declaring an Interface

After recognizing the interface, we come to the declaration phase. When declaring an interface, we state all the methods and properties that are associated with the interface. The actual implementation is left for the class's body.

Let's take, for example, a composite object: a clock with a lamp. In our world of objects, this clock would be a class derived from a **Clock** class, and implement an **Illuminating** interface.

Interfaces are declared very much like classes. The syntax for interface declaration is:

```
interface InterfaceName { InterfaceBody }
```

where **InterfaceName** is any name that is also valid as a class name. The **InterfaceBody** can contain method declarations and constants (i.e. **static final** properties). Method declarations look very much like methods, except for the fact that they have no body. Instead of the body they have a semicolon.

Here is an example:

```
public interface Illuminating {
    // state constants
    static final bool LIGHT_ON  = true;
    static final bool LIGHT_OFF = false;

    // Methods
    void turnOn();
    void turnOff();
    bool toggle();
    bool getState();
}
```

All the methods of an interface are (implicitly) abstract. If you wish to emphasize the abstraction of your methods, you may precede any method declarations with the **abstract** keyword, but it's redundant and the compiler ignores it.

Implementing Interfaces

A class that wants to be recognized as implementing an interface must be declared something like:

```
class Foo implements Bar { ... }
```

The declaration assures the class user that every object instantiated from that class implements every method defined in the interface.

The keyword **implements** is a part of the class declaration. If you want to use it, it should come after the **extends** clause if it exists or directly after the method's declaration if it doesn't. Following **implements** is a list of interfaces the class implements. Unlike class extensions (where there is only single inheritance), in Java you can implement as many interfaces as you like.

When implementing an interface, you should provide an implementation to every method defined in the interface. The class that extends the interface, also 'inherits' any constants defined in the interface, and may use them as if it defined the constants itself.

What if a class implements two interfaces that have the same method defined in them? That is, class A implements the C and D interfaces, and C and D both have a method F in them.

- If the method's signatures are different, the methods are overloaded just like any other two methods that share a name.

- If the signature is the same, the method implementation simultaneously belongs to both interfaces (i.e. you only need to implement the method once to satisfy all the interfaces).

The answer is really very simple, but it teaches us something. When we are looking at a class, we look at the types of interfaces it has, one interface at a time. If all the methods in the interface are supported, the class is considered to be implementing that interface. This makes it possible for two interfaces to share a single method implementation.

The following example shows two classes implementing the same interface (irrelevant method bodies have been omitted):

```
interface Annoying {
    void doAnAnnoyingThing();
}

class ComputerVirus extends ComputerProgram implements Annoying {

    ComputerVirus() {...}

    void multiply() {...}

    void doAnAnnoyingThing() {
        System.out.println("Booooooo");
    }
}

class BrokenCar extends Car implements Annoying {

    BrokenCar()  {...}
```

```
    void doAnAnnoyingThing() {
       // The two following properties are inherited from CAR
       Oil = 0;                       // implement an oil spill
       fuse[4] = BURNED;              // burn the ignition fuse

       // Print annoying message
       System.out.println("I won't start !...");
    }
}
```

Here's a long example showing a class implementing two interfaces (again, irrelevant method bodies are omitted). Notice the use of constants 'inherited' from the interfaces.

```
class Clock {
    // Properties
    int time;
    ...

    // Methods
    ...
    void ClockTick () {
       time ++;
       updateDisplay();
    }
    ...
}

public interface Illuminating {
    // state constants
    static final bool LIGHT_ON  = true;
    static final bool LIGHT_OFF = false;

    // Methods
    void turnLightOn();
    void turnLightOff ();
    bool toggleLight ();
    bool getLightState();
}

public interface AlarmGeneratingDevice {
    // state constants
    static final bool ALARM_ON  = true;
    static final bool ALARM_OFF = false;

    // Methods
    void setAlarm(int time);
    void enableAlarm(bool newState);
    bool isEnabled();
    void turnAlarmOff ();
    bool getAlarmState ();
}

class BedSideClock extends Clock implements AlarmGeneratingDevice, Illuminating {
    // Added properties
    int  alarmTime;
    bool alarmEnabled, alarmState, light;
```

```
// Constructor
BedSideClock() {...}

// Overriding the ClockTick method to support alarms
void ClockTick () {
    super.ClockTick();
    if ( (time == alarmTime) && (alarmEnabled) ) {
        alarmState = ALARM_ON;
        System.out.println("Beep Beep");
    }
}

// Implementation of the Illuminating interface
void turnLightOn()          { light = LIGHT_ON;   }
void turnLightOff()         { light = LIGHT_OFF;  }
bool toggleLight ()         { light = !light;     }
bool getLightState()        { return light;       }

// Implementation of the AlarmGeneratingDevice interface
void setAlarm(int timeToSet)     { alarmTime = timeToSet;   }
void enableAlarm(bool newState)  { alarmEnabled = newState; }
bool isEnabled()                 { return alarmEnabled;     }
void turnAlarmOff()              { alarmState = ALARM_OFF;  )
bool getAlarmState()             { return alarmState;       }
}
```

A class may only partially implement an interface. This class *must* be an abstract class and leave the implementation of the rest of the interface to its derived classes. Here's an example:

```
interface YesNo {
    public void JustSayNo();
    public abstract void SayYes();
}

abstract class CantSayYes implements YesNo
{
    public void JustSayNo()
    {
        System.out.println("NO!");
    }
}
```

Extending Interfaces

New interfaces may extend an existing interface, much like a new class can extend an existing class. A very important difference though, is that, unlike classes, interfaces can extend more then one base interface.

Here's an example. Assuming we have two interfaces, **A** and **B**, and we want a single interface, **C**, to combine them both. The code would look like this:

```
public interface A {
    int propOfA = 1;
    void a();
```

```
    }

    public interface B {
        int propOfB = 2;
        void b();
    }

    public interface C extends A, B {}
```

We can also add new methods and interfaces to the new interface, just as we can with new classes. Here's an example:

```
    public interface D extends A, B {
        String propOfD = "I implement the interface D";
        bool newMethod();
    }
```

A class that implements an interface X that extends other interfaces must implement all the methods defined in X, as well as all the methods in the interfaces that X extends. Such a class also 'inherits' all the constants defined in X and all the interfaces it extends.

The Difference between Interfaces and Abstract Classes

Some may say interfaces are like classes where all the methods are abstract, but that isn't true. There are fundamental differences between the two:

- ▲ A class may provide an implementation for any method, an interface cannot provide any implementation.

- ▲ A class may have any properties, an interface can have only constant properties.

- ▲ Derived classes can inherit methods and properties from a single base class, while any class may implement as many interfaces as it needs to.

Polymorphism

Although this isn't a book on object-oriented programming or software design, it's important to devote a section to polymorphism, as it's a key concept in object-oriented programming in Java. We'll concentrate on the implementation of polymorphism in Java programs, showing practical examples of how you can use it in your applications.

In a 'live' Java program, objects request other objects to perform actions by invoking their methods. The **client** (the requesting object that uses a service) and the **server** (the complying object that supplies the service) have a per-request role. An object can change roles many times during the program, performing as a client in some interactions and as a server in others.

Polymorphism minimizes the assumptions a client object needs to make about the nature of the server object. The client only needs to know that the server supports a specific interface. Here I mean 'interface' in the broad sense, i.e. in addition to the interface declarations the client needs to know both classes' signatures (the collection of all the class properties and method signatures).

Treating Objects Polymorphically

So, how do we make use of polymorphism?

Passing Handles to Methods

Methods can require object handles as arguments. The handles can be used by these methods to invoke the methods of the objects which they reference.

Let's assume that:

▲ The method to which a handle is passed expects the handle to reference an object of the class **A**,

▲ Class **B** extends class **A**. Since every instance of the class **B** can also be seen as an instance of the class **A**, that method will also accept objects of class **B**.

We have already seen that sending the same message to different classes derived from the same base class can result in various actions. The method's implementation is always taken from the class the object was instantiated from.⌡

An example would be the simple extension of existing code. Let's assume we have a warehouse application. This application can print the description of every object in the warehouse by invoking the **describe()** method of the object. All the classes of warehouse object in the application extend a base class called **WarehouseObject** that defines **describe()** and other methods and properties (that base class would probably be abstract). If we want to add a new kind of item to the warehouse, we would simply create a new class by extending **WarehouseObject**. The description printing method need not be altered to support the new class, as it accepts a **WarehouseObject** handle, and our new class supports the **WarehouseObject** interface.

Another simple example for the use of this feature is for debugging. In this example, we want to see the changes in an object of the class **Value** throughout the life of the program. In the program there is only one instance of the class, and a handle to it is passed as an argument to various methods that change its value by invoking appropriate value-changing methods in the object.

To debug the application we would create a new class called **AuditedValue** which would extend **Value** by adding debug printouts in the relevant value-changing methods. Then, instead of instantiating a single **Value** object, we would instantiate a single **AuditedValue** object. This change results on values being recorded whenever they change. This modification would have no other effect on the application, and no other changes are needed in any of the other methods.

Here's how it's done:

```
class AuditedValue extends Value {
    void setVal( int val ) {
        System.out.println( "Old value" + val );
        super.setVal( val );
        System.out.println( "New value" + val );
    }
}
```

```
class UnderTest {
   Value a;

   a= new AuditedValue();  // used to be: new Value(),
                           // chanced for testing...

   ... // other properties and methods

   public void DoSomething () {
      ...
      System.out.println("Expecting old value to be 3");
      a.setVal(6);
      ...
   }
}
```

If you get something like this (start of output listing omitted):

```
...
Expecting old value to be 3
Old value 0
New value 4
```

then you know there is something wrong in the way you handle that value. The change list can lead you in the right direction towards finding the problem.

A Collection of Related Objects

Arrays of objects are common things in applications. Traditional arrays hold objects of one kind that are related in some way. Java's arrays consider the interface their objects support. They are declared as collections of objects with a common interface, and would store any object that supports that interface.

Widening the definition of arrays, along with the strength of Java's arrays, allows us to do things like:

- Storing various **Vehicle**s in an array and then makings them all beep.
- Printing a store's catalog by iterating through the inventory list, invoking the **describe()** method for each item and printing it.

The same method described here could be used in an object-oriented graphic application where you place various graphic elements in an array, and then invoke the **drawOnScreen()** method for each one. This isn't just a nice idea; many commercial applications do just that when displaying graphics or text. This way every object will draw itself the way it should be drawn. The responsibility is moved to the object instead of the calling code, and that's part of what being object-oriented is all about.

Dynamic Method Lookup

How does the compiler know what method body (i.e. implementation) to invoke at run time when you specify a method call? The answer is that the compiler can't know that at compile time, and so it uses a mechanism called **dynamic method lookup** to find which implementation to execute. This mechanism uses the object's handle to find the actual type of the object, and thus the right implementation.

91

The process of method lookup takes time. While in many cases this may not be important, there are times where it is. Luckily enough, Java provides a way to control the way methods are looked up. It only uses dynamic lookup in cases where there may be ambiguity.

The compiler uses direct method calls in the following cases:

▲ `static` methods–They may not be overridden.

▲ `private` methods–They are not inherited.

▲ `final` methods–They too may not be overridden.

These types of methods may only be used in the class where they were defined, so there is no chance of ambiguity.

> *The process of dynamic method lookup is very similar to the one in C++'s. The difference is that in C++ you have to specify you want run-time lookup by making the method virtual, while in Java this is the default.*

Determining Object Type

Sometimes it's important for the programmer to know the type of an object that is attached to a handle.

For example, let's assume we have a word processor which the user can use to combine plain text with other non-plain-text objects (like pictures and graphs). I will refer to the characters that make up the plain text and the other elements by the collective name glyphs.

To store the glyphs in a sequence we use some kind of data structure that allows use to iterate through the elements. To display a section of the document on screen, we iterate through the glyphs that reside in that section and invoke the **drawOnScreen()** method for each one of them.

The word processor has a mode where, for better performance, only plain text elements are displayed. In that mode we would like to be able to tell plain text elements from others. How can we do it?

Using objects polymorphically raises some very interesting questions:

▲ How can we determine the type of a generic object?

▲ How can we detect if the object's class is a subclass of a given class?

▲ How can we find if an object implements interface X?

This section will try to answer these questions and others.

The instanceof Operator

The **instanceof** operator is a language mechanism that enables us to compare the type of an object with a specific type. The syntax for **instanceof** is:

```
objectHandle instanceof Type
```

where **objectHandle** is a handle to the object we wish to check, and **Type** is some well-known type (a class or an interface) that was either defined in your program or **import**ed from a package. The expression returns true if the type of **objectHandle** and **Type** are the same.

The following example shows a section of a word processor code. In this word processor, each document is made of textual objects (characters, words and paragraphs) and non-textual objects (drawings and charts). All the textual elements are derived from the **TextualObject** class, and all the graphical objects are derived from the **GraphicalObject** class. Both **TextualObject** and **GraphicalObject** are derived from the **DocumentObject** class. The entire document is stored in an array that holds **DocumentObject** objects.

This word processor has two modes, a graphical mode and a textual mode. In the textual mode, only **TextualObject** elements are displayed, and in the graphical mode all the objects are drawn on screen. The method used to draw the elements is **drawIt()** defined in **GraphicalObject**.

```
...
for (j=0; j++; j<document.length)
{
    // if we are in textual mode and the next object is graphical
    if( textMode && (document[j] instanceof GraphicalObject) )
        // skip it
        continue;
    else
        // otherwise, draw the element in the current graphic context
        // (either screen or printer)
        document[j].drawIt( currGraphicContext );
}
...
```

Using Class Methods

Java's class library includes a class called **Class**. It's derived from the class **Object**, and contains the run-time representations of each class in the system. A **Class** isn't modifiable at run time.

The **Object** class has a method called **getClass()** that returns the **Class** object associated with the class of the instance this method is invoked on. Since **Object** is the base class of all the classes in the system, this method exists in every class.

The **Class** class has methods that allow more sophisticated queries on classes than those possible using **instanceof**. Some of the methods defined in **Class** are:

Name	Description
forName(String)	Returns the runtime **Class** descriptor for the specified class name.
GetInterfaces()	Returns an array of the interfaces this **Class** supports.
GetName()	Returns the name of the **Class**.
GetSuperclass()	Returns the superclass of the **Class**.
IsInterface()	Returns a boolean indicating whether or not this **Class** is an interface.

Table Continued on Following Page

Name	Description
NewInstance()	Creates a new instance of this **Class**.
ToString()	Returns the name of this class or interface. The words 'class' or 'interface' are prepended to the name according to the nature of the **Class** object.

The **Class** class is reviewed in more details on the next chapter. Meanwhile, here is an example of how **Class** is used:

```
void printObjectClassName(Object myObj) {
    System.out.println("The class of " + myObj +
                       " is " + myObj.getClass().getName());
}
```

Some C++ class-libraries also add such methods to their basic class (and of course to all the classes derived from it), but, as in the case of **Class***, such methods create a large overhead and require further analysis of their output to determine if the object is of a particular type. When* **instanceof** *is enough, it should be used in preference.*

> Remember you have to use casting if you wish to manipulate an object in a way that isn't possible given the type of the handle that points to it. For example, if class B extends class A, and you have a handle of the type A that actually points to an object instantiated from B, and you wish to invoke a method that only exists in B, you would have to use explicit casting.

Access Modifiers

One of the concepts we mentioned when we initially talked about object-oriented programming was **encapsulation**, how you don't want to expose all of your class's properties or methods for everyone to see, change or use.

Access modifiers are a construct that control the 'visibility' of class elements (properties or methods).

P for Protection

The keywords to control access are:

- **public**
- Friendly (**package**)
- **protected**
- **private**

Let's examine them one by one:

public

When applied to a class, the keyword **public** makes the class visible everywhere (we haven't yet seen any case in which a class was not visible, but we will when we talk about packages). When applied to a class element (property or a method), that element is made visible to code outside the class.

Friendly

Although we will talk about packages later on in the book, it's important to mention them in this context because of the effect they have as access controllers.

A package is a collection of related classes that has a common name. We 'import' the contents of these packages into many of our applications. To do this, we declare that all the classes in a source file belong to a certain package using the **package** keyword (we'll see the exact details later). We declare the use of classes from a package with the **import** statement.

Every class that isn't implicitly declared as belonging to some package is explicitly assigned to the default package, along with all the other unassigned classes.

The default access (i.e. when you use no construct to change the protection level) is a package level visibility. This level of protection is called **friendly** access. Every class, interface, method and property are visible to any class in the package.

protected

Using this access modifier, a class **X** can grant access to its methods and properties to classes from other packages. This access is granted only to classes that extend the class, allowing them to 'touch' the details of the implementation of the base class. For the rest of the discussion on protected methods and properties we will refer to them by the collective name 'elements' as they are the elements of which classes are made.

The extending class Y may only reference a protected element of the class X using the **super** keyword (for access to elements in objects of the class X) or a protected element inherited from the class X using handles to objects of the class Y or classes derived from Y. Y may not access a protected element of an object instantiated from the class X

If the protected element is a constructor then it can only be invoked by using **super()** or the method **newInstance** of the class **Class** (see Chapter 4 for a discussion of the class **Class**).

private

A class may have methods that are only meant for internal use. They could be used in your code to create greater modularity, to express the internal or logical structure of the object, to help keep the other methods small or for any other purpose. The main thing is that you don't want to expose them to the outside world.

For such methods you should use the **private** modifier. **private** methods are visible only inside the class they were defined in.

Some Final Words on Protection

The **final** keyword is used to declare methods whose implementation should not change once it's declared. We've seen the **final** keyword used to declare constant properties. A constant property's value can't change, and so the analogy is simple: the same way we define a value for a constant property, we define an implementation for a **final** method, and neither can change once defined.

Preventing Method Override in Derived Classes

final methods can't be overridden by derived classes. You should use them wisely, as they give you control over what you (or anybody else extending your code) can do, and, at the same time, can cause unforeseen difficulties.

Given the above definition, it's clear that a method can't be both **final** and **abstract**. If it could, then there could never be an instance of the class, or any other class derived from it, because you can't instantiate abstract classes.

Packing Things

Once upon a time, so legend has it, file systems were 'flat'. They only had files, and there was no notion of directories and subdirectories. As people started to use more and more files, they had to separate the files by category to make their file system manageable, and allow for two files to have the same name. This led to the creation of directories.

Being sensitive to the requirements of modern software development, Java allows the programmer to use software components developed by others. These components come in the form of classes you can incorporate into your application, and the most basic classes are the ones that come with the Java run-time system. With an ever-growing base of software components, programmers need a way to organize classes in a manageable way.

What are Packages?

The Java Language Specification defines a package as a collection of Java classes and interfaces. Packages are a tool for creating a hierarchy in Java's name space, providing both manageability and resolution of naming conflicts.

The classes in a package are almost always related in some way, and the package that binds them is usually named according to that relation using a methodology that creates names which are both descriptive and unique. A package we have used many times (though at the time we didn't recognize it as such) is the **java.lang** package (the dot is a part of the name). The classes in that package are the Java language classes such as **System** and **String**.

Every Java class and interface name is contained in some package. Every class that isn't implicitly declared as belonging to some package is explicitly assigned to the default package–a package that bundles all the classes not assigned to a specific package.

The Package Naming Convention

Since no one is responsible for allocating package names, package names might collide (i.e. two packages might have the same name) and thus packages could lose their whole purpose-creating a unique name spaces. You wouldn't be able to use those two packages in your applications at the same time, because packages are referred to by name, and Java wouldn't know to which you are referring. To avoid such name clashes, a naming convention was introduced.

The name you give your package is made of two parts. The first is the name of your organization and the second is a descriptive name of your collection of classes. The two parts are made of words connected by periods. The parts themselves are connected by periods. By convention, the names of the packages start with a lower case letter, to distinguish them from class names.

Keeping the names of your class collections unique isn't a big problem. The real problem could be in keeping your organization name unique. No one can prevent two companies using the same abbreviation or two companies from different countries from having the same name. Luckily enough there is a unique identifier for each organization on the Internet: its Internet domain name. The convention is to use the reversed domain name of your organization, so if, for example, you develop a package in **cs.technion.ac.il** then you should use **il.ac.technion.cs** to identify your organization.

Here is another example, your company is called Hyper Gnome and your package is a collection of classes that control the hyper-space engines of an intergalactic destroyer. In this case, you would probably call your package,

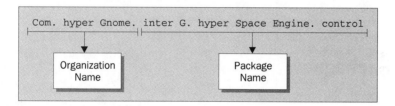

or something like that.

Two exceptions to the rule are the **java** and **sun** packages. These packages were created and put to public use before the convention was introduced, and so they enjoy earlycomer's rights.

The Directory Structure

Java expects your file system directory structure to be the same as your program's package structure. The **CLASSPATH** environment variable identifies the location where Java starts looking for your classes, so if in your system **CLASSPATH** points to a subdirectory called **classes**, a partial view of your directory and file system should look something like this:

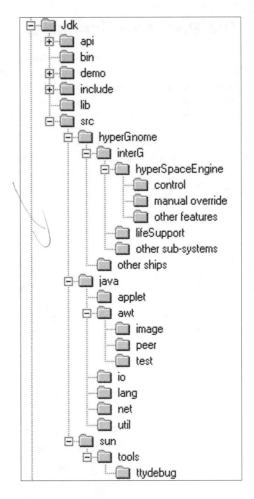

Creating Packages

To create a new package, you simply have to follow four simple steps. But first, some very important notes.

> The steps described here are for people using the command line JDK program files to compile and create packages. If you are using a development environment (like Microsoft's VJ++, Sun's Java Workshop or Symantec's Cafe), you should consult your manual.
>
> These instructions also assume you are using a DOS shell. If you are using UNIX or Macintosh, you should use the corresponding operations to achieve the same result. If you are not sure what you should do, consult your operating system manual.
>
> These steps can result in loss of data and other harmful things, and should be performed only if you know exactly what you are doing.

Create New Directories

The first step is to create the source and class directories. Here **YRODN** stands for Your Reserved Organization Domain Name.

```
MD   SomePath\src\YRODN\NameOfNewPackage
MD   SomePath\classes\YRODN\NameOfNewPackage
```

Copy the Source Files

The next step is to copy the source (`*.java`) files to the package source directory (if they are not already there).

```
copy  SourcePath\*.java  SomePath\src\YRODN\NameOfNewPackage
```

Add the Package Statement

As I've said when we talked about access modifiers, we declare that all the classes in a source file belong to a certain package using the **package** keyword. **package** must be the first non-commented line in the source file. You must add this line to every source file in your package.

```
package  YRODN.NameOfNewPackage;
```

Compile the Package

To compile the package we use a special switch in the compiler, telling it to combine all the classes from the source directory into a single package. We need to specify both the source directory (directory of the `*.java` file) and the target directory (the directory in which the package will be created).

```
javac -d SomePath \classes SomePath\src\YRODN\NONP\*.java

NONP = NameOfNewPackage
```

Adding a Class to an Existing Java Package

To add a class to an existing package simply add the source file to the source directory and recompile.

Using Packages

Having created your package, how do you import it into your Java code and how do you ensure the Java compiler knows where to look for the package?

Importing a Class

To use the classes in a package you need to import them into your source file. Once imported, all the public classes are visible.

To import a class from a package you should add an **import** statement to the top of your source file. For example, if you want to include the magma flow control class from the intergalactic destroyer hyper-space engines package you would include this line:

```
import  com.hyperGnome.interG.hyperSpaceEngine.control.MagmaFlow
```

This is a rather long statement. Imagine you wanted to include 40 such classes. This could be cumbersome. To solve that problem you can use an asterisk to say '*All* the classes defined in this package'. The asterisk includes only the classes defined in the package whose name you specified, it doesn't include any other packages, not even if their name begins with the same name. For example, if the intergalactic destroyer control package hierarchy has some general classes in **com.hyperGnome.interG.hyperSpaceEngine** and you specified their inclusion by,

```
import  com.hyperGnome.interG.hyperSpaceEngine.*
```

then **com.hyperGnome.interG.hyperSpaceEngine.control.*** would not be included.

Importing an entire package does not change the size of the compiled class file, as only referenced classes are actually included in your application. It does lengthen the compile time and increases the chances of name conflicts. We, therefore, recommend that you import only the classes you need.

Some Setup Issues

In order for Java to know where your directory tree starts to reflect the class structure, you must specify the path to the classes. This is done by setting an environment variable called **CLASSPATH** to that point in the directory tree. **CLASSPATH** must point to the directory above the classes.

For example, if your classes are stored in a subdirectory named `c:\java\lib\classes\*` as in:

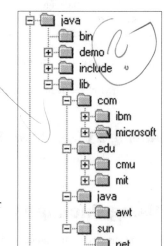

You should set your **CLASSPATH** to point to `c:\java\lib\classes` and so when you refer to **edu.cmu.cs.util.UtilityClass** Java knows exactly where to find it.

You can add as many directories as you like to the path (separated by the system's path separator character: '**:**' for UNIX, '**;**' for Windows). The order in which you specify the directories is the order in which the classes will be searched (in a left-to-right order). If you have two classes with the same name, the first one that Java finds will be used.

Making Exceptions - The Fine Art of Error Handling and Reporting

Exceptions are a mechanism used in various object-oriented programming languages to report and handle errors. In this chapter we will explore the exception mechanism and learn about the various error objects that may be 'thrown' at us by Java.

Every program you will write (except for really trivial ones) will have to deal with errors. It could be that a file operation fails, the user enters an invalid value in a dialog box, the network connection hangs up, the program tries to access an out-of-bounds array element, and so on.

There are two main operations associated with exceptions. The first is to **raise** or **throw** an exception, and the other is to **handle** or **catch** an exception. The first is used to describe the event of reporting an error, and the other the event of dealing with it. The terminology used by Java is the throw-catch terminology that is also used in C++.

Traditional Error Management vs. Exceptions

Traditional error reporting involves methods returning error codes. A method indicates that something bad happened while it was running, and leaves the cleaning up to the method that called it.

Let's look at an example. To keep things simple and concentrate on the real issues, the next few methods are written in pseudo-code (using plain English to show the algorithm).

This method is a part of a web browser, it loads the entire content of a remote HTML page (a page on an Internet server) into memory:

```
pageHandle ReadPageToMemory ( URL )
{
    open connection to the URL
    obtain the size of the page
    allocate memory for the page
    load the page into memory
    close the connection
    return a reference to the allocated memory in pageHandle
}
```

This method is really straightforward, but it's missing a lot of error-handling code. What happens if:

▲ The connection can't be opened?

▲ The size of the page can't be obtained?

▲ Memory allocation fails?

▲ The load operation is unsuccessful?

▲ The connection is broken during one of the transmissions?

▲ And so on...

The solution is for these methods to return an error code indicating whether their operation was successful or not. With each method returning an error code, the code that was once simple now looks like this:

```
errorCode ReadPageToMemory ( URL, PageObject )
{
    errorCode err = 0

    open connection to the URL
    if the URL was opened okay
    {
        obtain the size of the page
        if the size was obtained
        {
            allocate memory for the page
            if allocation was successful
            {
                load the page into memory
                if loading failed
                {
                    err = 4
                }
            }
            else // memory allocation failed
            {
                err = 3
            }
        }
        else   // could not get the page's size
        {
            err = 2
        }
        close the connection
        if the the connection could not be closed and err = 0
        {
            err = -1   // data was loaded okay, but
                       // there still may be a problem
        }
    }
    else    // could not open the connection to the URL
    {
        err = 1
    }

    if err is equal or less than 0
    {
        store a reference to the allocated memory
            in a property of pageObject
    }

    return err
}
```

Wow! The original six statement method has inflated into an eighteen statement monster. The size of the code tripled, and now our original algorithm is so hidden in all the error handling that the once simple method is now a disaster. Imagine what it's like to maintain such code...

Exceptions separate the error handling from the error reporting. When an exception is thrown, the original flow of the program is interrupted, and control is transferred to the error handling code. The error handling code is separated from the main code, and adds no overhead at run time. It's only when an exception occurs that the error handling code springs to action. This is contrary to traditional interleaved handling that adds both execution overhead and lessens the readability of the code.

This is what exception handling code for the above method would look like:

```
pageHandle ReadPageToMemory ( URL ) might throw exceptions
{
    try to execute these commands
    {
        open connection to the URL
        obtain the size of the page
        allocate memory for the page
        load the page into memory
        close the connection
        return a reference to the allocated memory in pageHandle
    }
    if something bad happens do this
    {
        // notify the caller and let it handle the error
        throw a full description of the error to the caller
    }
}
```

See how instead of checking each operation this code simply checks for any error, and lets the caller handle it just like the traditional code did. Two things gained by this are:

- The main code stays intact, and error checking statements don't clutter the method.

- The error handling code is all in one place, making it easier to verify and maintain.

The error handling code back at the calling method is much the same in both cases. Using the traditional way, the error code has to be checked against every value, while using the exception model the thrown object's type has to be identified.

One of the strongest reasons for using exceptions to report critical errors is that the caller cannot ignore an exception like a simple error code. This takes the sting off one of the worst nightmares of software testers: silent errors. A silent error is an error that is reported but ignored, and these errors seem to be hard to catch. Using exceptions forces the user of the method to either handle them in some way or to declare that someone else must.

The Way Exceptions Work

If you look at your application at any given time, the statement currently being executed belongs to some method–let's call that method X. X was called from another method, Y, and when X returns, the next statement executed in Y will be the one following the call to X. This is true for all the methods, except for **main** of course. **main** was not invoked by any statement in your application. It was invoked by the system.

The sequence where a method calls another method which calls another one is commonly referred to as a **call stack**. Imagine a stack where every time a method is invoked, the location of the statement that called it is pushed on the top of the stack, and whenever a method returns, the location of the next statement to run is popped off the top of the stack so that the calling method may be resumed.

This description isn't far fetched. This is actually the way method calls are implemented in Java and most other languages. Most of the time the stack hold many other things (like the local variables of the methods that were called), but the main idea is exactly as I've displayed it.

Call stacks have a top and a bottom. The stack's top is the place where the stack begins, the bottom is the place where the stack ends and where you push new things onto the stack. This terminology may seem reversed, but it has deep roots. It originates from the way call stacks are commonly implemented in the computer's memory, where the stack begins at the highest location in memory and works its way down. 'Going up the call stack' means going to the methods that invoked the current one.

Once an exception is thrown, the system tries to find a method that is waiting to catch it. It goes up the call stack, popping off the elements, looking for an error handler that can accept the error object, until it finds such a handler or completely empties the call stack by popping **main** out. In the first case, execution transfers to the error handler, and in the second, the system halts the execution of the application and prints out a description of the exception. The fact that the system searches for an error handler up the call stack makes propagating errors trivial.

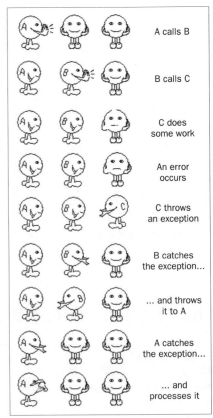

A calls B

B calls C

C does some work

An error occurs

C throws an exception

B catches the exception...

... and throws it to A

A catches the exception...

... and processes it

In some cases, though, the direct caller (the method that contains the statement that called the method in which the exception was generated) does not want to handle the error, or simply can't handle it.

Take, for example, a class library where a public class uses a private class. A public class's method, B, is invoked by a method in your application, A. B then goes on and invokes a private class's method, C, and that method throws an exception. We now have a case where A invoked B which invoked C, and C threw an exception. B needs to propagate that error back to A, so that A will decide what to do with it.

Using traditional error handling, B would have to add special code to recognize the error, catch it and re-throw it. This code has nothing to do with the operation of B, it adds to the complexity of the method and has to be checked and verified.

Using exceptions, B wouldn't have to do a thing. Idleness accomplishes just what we want, because exceptions are seamlessly propagated as a default. However, as we'll soon see, propagating exceptions does require some effort by the 'middleman' methods, not in the sense of actual handling but in the sense of declaring the fact that they may throw exceptions.

In Java, exceptions are actually objects that are instances of classes that are derived from the **Throwable** (**Throwable** is defined in the **java.lang** package). The exception objects con rules of objects, except for the fact that none of your classes has to hold a reference to them. Regular objects are gone as soon as there is no reference to them. Once an exception is gen method that created it exits and thus it seems like no one knows of its existence. This isn't true, the exception object is held by the system until it can find an appropriate handler, and so it's the system which holds the reference and the exception object isn't lost.

As exceptions are instances of classes, you can create related 'groups' of exceptions by deriving them from the same base class.

For example, Java's built-in exception classes declare the exception class **IndexOutOfBoundsException** and then derive two classes from it:

▲ **ArrayIndexOutOfBoundsException**

▲ **StringIndexOutOfBoundsException**

If you want to catch any 'index out of bound' exception then you can catch **IndexOutOfBoundsException** (remember, both **ArrayIndexOutOfBoundsException** and **StringIndexOutOfBoundsException** classes are also of the type **IndexOutOfBoundsException**), but if you are interested only in 'array index out of bound' exceptions, you need catch only **IndexOutOfBoundsException** objects.

Catching

If catching fish was as easy as catching exceptions, I think fishing wouldn't be much of a hobby. To catch an exception you need only surround the place from which it may pop with a **try-catch** block, and if an exception is thrown out of any method in the block you will get a chance to catch it. It's like sitting at the river bank, putting a net in the water, and any time a fish swims by, someone asking you, "Would you like to catch this fish?".

Catch Me If You Can

The **try-catch** block is a language construct used to declare and implement exception handling. The syntax for a try-catch block is:

```
try
{
    Statements that may throw exceptions
}
catch (ExceptionType1 variable1)
{
    Code to handle exceptions of type ExceptionType1
}
catch (ExceptionType2 variable2)
{
    Code to handle exceptions of type ExceptionType2
}
```

```
...  (more catch statements may come here)

catch (ExceptionTypeN variableN)
{
    Code to handle exceptions of type ExceptionTypeN
}
finally
{
    Statements that must be executed, no matter what !
}
```

As you can see, a more descriptive name might be 'Try, catch-one-or-more and optionally-one-finally' block, but that would be somewhat long, don't you think?

If an exception is thrown by any of the statements in the **try** block, be they exceptions thrown by methods that are invoked in the block or exceptions generated by a statement in the **try** block (like index errors), the thrown object's type is compared against the types found in the **catch** blocks' headers.

The **catch** blocks' headers look much like method declarations, having a typed argument in parentheses. The argument type declares the type of exception that the handler is willing to handle, and must be the name of a class derived from the **Throwable** class.

Like method overloading, the exception type is compared with the type of exception the **catch** block is willing to accept, and if a match is found, then the statements in the **catch** block are executed. The catch blocks are checked one by one in the order in which they appear.

The handler found in the **catch** block can refer to the exception using the argument that the **catch** statement declared. Being an object, you access the properties and methods of an exception in the exact same way that you access the properties and methods of any other object.

The **Throwable** class (the base class for all exceptions and other errors) provides a method named **getMessage()** that prints a string with some information about the error that occurred. The **Throwable** class also implements three methods for filling in and printing out the contents of the call stack at the time when the exception occurred. The filling method is mainly used when re-throwing an exception (which we'll get to later on), while the two printing methods are mainly used for debugging. Subclasses of **Throwable** can add methods and properties, providing more information and functionality.

The following code snippet illustrates how to wrap a single statement in a **try** block, and then catch exceptions generated by it:

```
...
try {
    characterArray[i++] = URLPageBuffer.getNextChar();
}
catch (ArrayIndexOutOfBoundsException e)
{
    System.err.println("Caught ArrayIndexOutOfBoundsException: " +
                       e.getMessage());
    System.err.println("Reason: URL page buffer size is differrent" +
                       " then the reported page size!");
}
catch (Exception e)
```

```
    {
        System.err.println("Caught a general exception: " +
                            e.getMessage());
    }
    ...
```

The **IndexOutOfBoundsException** that is caught by the first handler is generated by the actual array assignment. This is an example of an exception that is generated directly by the code in the **try** block, as opposed to the **Exception** that is caught by the second **catch** block, which may be generated by the method call.

Because the exception's type is tested against the arguments of each of the **catch** blocks in order, the **IndexOutOfBoundsException** exception is caught by the first handler. Other exceptions don't match the first type, so the 'catch all exceptions' second **catch** block handles them (being the base class for all exceptions, **Exception** is the type of every exception).

finally

The **finally** block is an optional block that contains statements that must be executed, regardless of anything that happens at run time. It's usually used for freeing up resources taken by the **try** block.

Take for example a case where the **try** block opened a file. This file must be closed, even if an exception is thrown somewhere within the **try** block. Since the execution of the program may be transferred to an error handler, which in turn may decide to return from the method, there is no other way to make sure the file is closed other then using a **finally** block. The statements in the **finally** block are executed whether an exception was thrown or not, even if the error handler code returns from the method, throws another exception, or anything else. Simply put, a **finally** block is always executed!

Some people may argue that **finally** is redundant because everything can be accomplished by other means. You can add the finalization code at the end of the **try** block, and then again at the end of each error handler. You would have, of course, to add a general catch-it-all handler to catch all the exceptions you are not interested in and add the finalization code there too, so that no exception gets by without you closing the file first.

So if you don't use a **finally** block, you have to change the code completely, making sure you don't **return**, **break** or **continue** without closing the file. You then have to wrap it again to make sure that even if one of your handlers threw an exception the file would still close.

Finally, you end up with,

▲   The same code duplicated many times in the same method

▲   The main algorithm obscured by the finalization chunks

▲   Error prone, fragile code

and the whole purpose of handling errors using exceptions is completely missed.

Throwing

In general, every method must state the types of exception it may throw.

> Apart from declaring the types of exceptions it throws, a method must catch every exception that may be thrown by a subsequent method it invokes, or declare that the exception may propagate through it.

Any exception that may be thrown by a method is really a part of the method's interface, just like the type and number of arguments, or its return value. Anyone who wishes to invoke a method must know about the exceptions that a method may throw in order to be able to decide what to do when they are thrown.

Being a part of the method's interface, the exceptions that may be thrown are listed as a part of the method declaration. The syntax for declaring the types of methods that may be thrown is,

```
MethodDeclaration   throws ExceptionType1, ... ExceptionTypeN
```

where the **MethodDeclaration** is the same as we've seen before (modifiers, return type, method name and list of arguments) and after the **throws** keyword comes the list of the types of exceptions that the method may throw.

Java has many exception classes, and you can derive classes of your own from these. A special subset of exceptions are the run-time exceptions, derived from the **RuntimeException** class, which may be thrown during the execution of a Java application. They include:

- Negative array size exception–Thrown upon an attempt to create an array with a negative size.

- Indexing exceptions–Thrown upon an attempt to access an array element through an index that is too large.

- Pointer exceptions–Thrown upon using a null reference to access an object, and arithmetic exceptions, such as division by zero.

Since run-time exceptions are so common, and may be thrown by almost any method, the compiler doesn't require that you catch or declare them (although you may). This is the only exception to the rule.

You will soon learn how to create exception classes of your own. Do not be tempted to declare your exceptions as run-time exceptions (by deriving them from **RuntimeException**) because that defies the whole purpose of throwing exceptions. It may seem tedious to declare your methods as throwing an exception, making it compulsory to wrap calls to them in **try-catch** blocks, but this is the only way to make sure that anyone who uses your classes will consciously have to decide what they want to do when your method throws the exception.

As you see, propagating any exception other than run-time exceptions does require some effort on the part of the 'middleman' methods. Any non-run-time exceptions that can be thrown within a method (by calls to subsequent methods) must be declared in the **throws** part of the method's declaration.

How to Throw Exceptions

In order to throw an exception you must first list the type of the exception to be thrown in the **throws** part of the method's declaration.

After declaring the type of the object to be thrown, you can simply throw the object using the **throw** statement. The syntax for the **throw** statement is:

```
throw objectToBeThrown
```

where **objectToBeThrown** is a **Throwable** object (an instance of the **Throwable** class or any class derived from it). It's a compile time error to try to throw an object that is not **Throwable**. You can throw any **Throwable** object, either defined in Java's class hierarchy or of your own device.

Creating Your own Exception Classes

When it comes to throwing exceptions you have two choices:

▲ Use an exception class written by someone else, for example, one of the exception classes in Java's class hierarchy.

▲ Write your own class.

Object-oriented design is pro-reuse. You should try to use one of the many exception classes Java provides you with, be it a specialized exception like a **ProtocolException** that you can throw in your special protocol class, or a general purpose exception, like **Exception**. Though the exception classes provide an extensive resource to draw upon, there are three reasons to create your own exception classes:

▲ The nature of your exception isn't represented by any of the exceptions in the class hierarchy.

▲ Your code throws several related exceptions, and you want to be able to refer to them in a common manner (i.e. use your own common base class for all of your exceptions).

▲ You want to make your class package self-contained because you don't want to rely on other packages for supplying any classes.

Since Java exceptions must be **Throwable** you may think that it is obvious to derive your classes from **Throwable**. Looking deeper in the class tree you will see that **Throwable** has two subclasses that divide the world of problems in two:

▲ The first is the familiar **Exception**.

▲ The second, **Error**, is reserved for abnormal events that should never occur. We recommend that you do *not* to try and catch such events.

You wouldn't want to derive your exception class from **Error**, unless you don't wish them to be caught, so most, if not all, of your exception classes will be derived from **Exception**.

You may decide to derive your exception class from a class further down the hierarchy tree. It's wise to do so if you need to throw an exception that fits into a set of exception classes, but doesn't exactly match any of the subclasses of that group. For example, you may want top throw an I/O error exception that doesn't match any of the subclasses of **IOException**, so you should derive your exception class from **IOException**. Remember, resist the temptation to derive your classes from **RuntimeException**.

Here is an example of creating an exception class to be used in a package. It defines two classes, a **Queue** class and an exception class that may be thrown by the **Queue** object.

```java
package queue;

import java.util.Vector;

public class EmptyQueueException extends Exception
{
    public int capacity;

    public EmptyQueueException()
    {
        super("The queue is empty");
    }
}

public class Queue
{
    private Vector v;

    public Queue()
    {
        v = new Vector();
    }

    public void addToBack( Object o )
    {
        v.addElement( o );
    }

    public Object removeFront()
    throws EmptyQueueException, CloneNotSupportedException
    {
        Object o;
        EmptyQueueException x;

        if (v.isEmpty())
        {
            x = new EmptyQueueException();
            x.capacity = v.capacity();
            throw x;
        }

        o = v.elementAt(0);
        v.removeElementAt(0);

        return o.clone();  // may throw CloneNotSupportedException
    }
}
```

Benefits of Exceptions

Using exceptions to handle errors gains the following advantages over traditional error handling:

- ▲ Separation of the error handling code from the main algorithm.
- ▲ Seamless propagation of errors up the call stack.
- ▲ The ability to group and differentiate errors by type.
- ▲ The must-be-executed-no-matter-what code is simple to introduce and recognize.
- ▲ The ability to generate error reports which can't be ignored.
- ▲ The ability to attach any related information in the exception class's properties along with methods to perform exception-specific actions.

When not to Use Exceptions

Although exceptions are a great mechanism for error handling, they carry with them the overhead of instantiating a new object, rolling back the call stack and propagating the errors to the calling methods. This takes time.

Also, not all the situations that are not strictly 'normal' demand the full attention of the user. Some may be ignored and others can be reported in other ways.

An example of a situation that is 'not 100% OK' but can be ignored is a case where a method requests you pass it an array to fill. That method expects the array to be ten elements long, but the array you pass is of a different length. If it's shorter then this is clearly an error worth throwing an exception for, but if it's longer you may decide you not need any indication of that. After all, there's nothing wrong with what you've done, and the application works fine. It might indicate something deeper in the application is wrong, but it could also be intended.

A very good example for reporting an error in another way is provided by the I/O classes. These classes use exceptions to report most exceptional situations, but not all of them. Reaching the end of a file is definitely not a normal situation, but is also not worth throwing an exception for. It happens almost every time you read a file, and may even be considered as a good sign (indicating your work is done). Since the reading methods all return a positive number for successful reading, the negative number –1 was selected as the end-of-file indicator. Since you're probably storing the return value in a variable anyway, there is no reason to make you use special error handling code to detect it's value as –1. You can simply compare the returned value to –1 and decide what to do if they are equal.

Here are a few rules to help you know when to use exceptions and when not:

- ▲ Use exceptions only in cases where the error disrupt the normal flow of the program.
- ▲ Use exceptions then they make your application simpler. Don't force the user of your methods to wrap every line in a **try-catch** block, or they will most likely wrap the entire method in a general catch-all **try-catch** block and ignore the type of the exception object.
- ▲ Don't use exceptions when there is a natural alternative (usually for simple tests).

Exception Thrown within a Finalizer

If an object has a finalizer method, this method is invoked by the system before the object is garbage collected. Since a finalizer is a method, like any other method it may throw exceptions at will.

A finalizer is invoked from the context of the run-time system. It has no caller in the usual sense and thus no one gets a chance to handle the exceptions it throws. For that reason, exceptions thrown within a finalizer are ignored.

Rethrowing

How can you handle an exception within a method, but still allow any calling methods to subsequently handle the exception as well? To handle the exception you must catch it. In order for a calling method to handle it, the exception must propagate through your handler. The solution is simply to rethrow the exception.

Rethrowing means catching the exception, doing whatever it is you want to do, and then throwing the object you caught again.

```
import com.WROX.java.examples.queue.*

public class Rethrower
{
    public void Rethrow() throws EmptyQueueException
    {
        Queue  q=new Queue();
        Object o;

        try
        {
            o = q.removeFront(); // Cause an EmptyQueueException to be thrown
        }
        catch (EmptyQueueException eqx)
        {
            System.err.println("Well, what do you know?" +
                              " The queue was empty !");
            throw eqx;
        }

        // Execution won't get here because if the exception that is
        // allways thrown...

        System.out.println("You will never see this printed...");
    }
}
```

Cloning Objects

Having discussed interfaces, access modifiers and exception handling, we can now look at how you might clone objects, i.e. create an exact and distinct duplicate of an object.

The **Object** class has a **clone()** method that does the job for you. Since *every* Java object is a descendant of **Object**, every object has the **private** method, **clone()**. **clone()** creates an exact memory replicate of the object that invoked it and returns a handle to the copy.

To enable cloning, an object must implement the **Cloneable** interface. If you invoke the **clone()** method on an object that does not support the **Cloneable** interface you will get a **CloneNotSupportedException** exception.

Since **clone()** doesn't know the type of object that invokes it, it always returns a reference to an **Object**. You must explicitly cast the returned handle to the calling object's class.

Here is an example of cloning. The **try** and **catch** statements deal with exceptions, making sure that, if cloning fails you get a **null**, and otherwise you get the desired handle.

```
class Point implements Cloneable {
   public int x,y;

   public Point( int x, int y )
   {
      this.x = x;
      this.y = y;
   }

   public void printIt()
   {
      System.out.println( "x= " + x + " y= " + y );
   }

   public Point cloneIt()
   {
      Point me;

      try {
         me = (Point) this.clone();
      }
      catch (CloneNotSupportedException e)
      {
         return null;
      }
      return me;
   }
}

class CloneTest {
   public static void main (String args[])
   {
      Point p1 = new Point(2,1);
      Point p2;
```

```
        p2 = p1.cloneIt();
        if ( p2!=null )
        {
            p1.printIt();
            p2.printIt();
            p2.x = 9;
            System.out.println();   // Print a separating line
            p1.printIt();
            p2.printIt();
        }
        else
            System.err.println("p1 could not be cloned");
    }
}
```

The output you get when you run **CloneTest** will be:

```
x= 2 y= 1
x= 2 y= 1

x= 2 y= 1
x= 9 y= 1
```

Notice the face that since the **clone()** method is private we had to introduce the public method **cloneIt()** to expose the desired functionality.

Summary

In this, the second of the chapters discussing OOP in Java, we've reviewed:

- ▲ Inheritance
- ▲ Abstraction
- ▲ Interfaces
- ▲ Polymorphism
- ▲ Access modifiers
- ▲ Packages
- ▲ Exception Handling

Fundamental Classes

Java is object oriented from the ground up. In C++, for example, the programmer uses object-oriented technology built on top of the good-old-procedural-C system interface. In Java, the whole run-time system is object oriented. All the run-time classes (except **Object**) are extensions of other classes and they're all arranged in functional packages.

In this chapter, we'll look at some of the fundamental classes in Java. In particular, we'll cover:

- ▲ Wrapper classes:
  - **Object**
  - **Boolean**
  - **Character**
  - **Number** and its derived classes **Double**, **Float**, **Integer**, and **Long**
  - **String** and **StringBuffer**
- ▲ Data structures:
  - **BitSet**
  - **Enumeration**
  - **Vector** and the **Stack** class which extends it
  - **Hashtable**
- ▲ Other interesting classes:
  - **Math**
  - **Class** and **ClassLoader**
  - **Applet**

The Java Packages

Some of the classes in Java encapsulate the functionality of the underlying system, providing a system-independent interface to facilities common to all the systems (the console, the file system, etc.). Other classes encapsulate more virtual concepts, like data types and data structures.

The different packages are as follows:

- ▲ **java.lang**–This contains the basic Java classes, such as numeric classes, strings and objects, along with several other classes to control the compiler, run time, security, and threads. It contains the classes of most of the basic exceptions and errors that might be thrown during the execution of a program such as index errors, run-time exceptions, and security exceptions. *This package is implicitly imported in every Java program.*
- ▲ **java.io**–Contains classes to manage input and output streams, files, and related resources. The exceptions in this package are all I/O related.

▲   **java.util**–Contains miscellaneous utility classes, including generic data structures (hash table, stack, etc.), date and time, random number generation, system properties and others.

The exceptions defined in this package are specific to data structures.

▲   **java.net**–Contains classes that support network communication, including URLs, sockets, IP addresses, and others. The exceptions defined in this package are specific to networking.

▲   **java.awt**–This large package contains classes to manage the graphic user interface (GUI) components such as windows, menus, fonts, buttons, lists, and others. Other classes handle generic objects like points, rectangles, frames, and so on. Yet other classes handle object layout, insets, and other things you need in a GUI environment. This package contains a single exception that's thrown when an AWT error occurs, and a single error that's thrown when a really serious AWT error occurs.

▲   **java.awt.image**–Contains classes for managing images. These include color models, color filtering, grabbing snapshots, and more.

▲   **java.awt.peer**–This package contains interfaces to connect AWT components to the platform-specific GUI implementation (such as Motif widgets or Microsoft Windows controls).

▲   **java.applet**–This package contains the Applet class along with interfaces that enable an applet to communicate with its environment and play music.

The Object Class

The **Object** class is the ancestor of all other classes in Java, including your own classes. This means that its methods are common to all Java objects. The **Object** class is in the **java.lang** package which is implicitly imported into every source file.

Every class you create that doesn't specifically extend any other class extends **Object**. Thus,

```
class myClass {...}
```

is equivalent to

```
class myClass extends Object {...}
```

Here's the definition of the methods in the **Object** class.

```
public   class   java.lang.Object
{
    //*************
    // Constructor
    //*************
    public Object();


    //***********
    //  Methods
    //***********

    // Content related methods
    public boolean equals(Object object);
    public String toString();
    protected Object clone();
```

```
    public int hashCode();

    // Thread synchronization related methods
    public final void notify();
    public final void notifyAll();
    public final void wait();
    public final void wait(long  timeout);
    public final void wait(long  timeout, int  nanos);

    // Miscellaneous methods
    protected void finalize();
    public final Class getClass();
}
```

As you can see, there are two **protected** methods in the class. These methods (**clone()** and **finalize()**) don't do any real work when invoked on an **Object**. The first just throws a **CloneNotSupportedException** to indicate that the class **Object** doesn't support cloning, and the second does nothing because no finalization is needed for generic **Object**s.

If you declare that a derived class implements the **Cloneable** interface, invoking **clone()** on an object of that class creates a clone of that object (there's no need to give any implementation of **clone()**, the implementation in **Object** does the work). The other methods are as follows:

equals
Compares two objects. This is overridden by many classes to properly implement their specific content comparison.

toString
Returns a string representation of an object. Overridden by many classes to properly represent their content.

clone
Returns an exact duplicate of an object. Cloning doesn't involve invoking any constructor, it copies only memory content.

hashCode
Calculates a hash code value for the object. We'll get back to hash codes later in this chapter when we talk about hash tables.

notify
notifyAll
wait
These methods are used to synchronize threads. They're discussed in Chapter 5: Threads.

Finalize
Overridden by some classes to perform a finalization sequence when an object of the class is garbage collected.

getClass
Returns a **Class** object that holds information about the class of the current object. We discuss the **Class** class later on in this chapter.

Wrapping the Basic Data Types

There's a triple advantage to using classes to encapsulate the basic data types:

- ▲ The methods of the classes provide a way to construct, query, and manipulate the various data types.

- ▲ The constant properties provide commonly used (and sometimes hard to produce) values such as **Integer.MAX_VALUE**, **Float.NEGATIVE_INFINITY**, **Double.NaN** and others.

- ▲ Most of Java's utility classes require the use of objects. Since primitive data types are not objects in Java, they need to be wrapped.

Following are short descriptions of the wrapper classes. Notice that some methods are class-wide (static) while others need an object.

Although what follows is rather a reference manual style coverage of the methods, we recommend that you go through it so you know what's in your toolkit. As you read through the class descriptions, you'll get acquainted with the style of the class library. Once you get to know the look and feel of the class library, you'll feel a lot more at home with Java. Last but not least, you'll also learn about caveats and pitfalls you should be aware of.

The chapter contains examples to demonstrate the use of just a small fraction of the methods and properties of the classes we'll describe. They show some of the more interesting features and oddities of the classes, but not all of them. You're encouraged to try out the things that interest you and which aren't covered here, yourself.

Some statements in these examples might be a little confusing. If so, look carefully at the order of execution (precedence of operations, dot notation, etc.) and compare your view of what the statements do with the actual results.

The java.lang Package

Boolean

The **Boolean** class provides a wrapper for boolean data values, and serves as a place for boolean-oriented operations.

It has two static properties used to assign values to **Boolean** objects:

```
public final static Boolean TRUE;
```
Assigns a **Boolean** to be true.

```
public final static Boolean FALSE;
```
Assigns a **Boolean** to be false.

The constructors of the **Boolean** class allow you to specify the initial value either as a boolean or as a string. Whenever a string is used to assign a value to a **Boolean**, its value is considered true if the string is equal to 'true' (case is ignored).

```
public Boolean(boolean value);
```
Constructs a **Boolean** object and initializes it to the value specified in **value**.

```
public Boolean(String s);
```
Constructs a **Boolean** object and initializes it to the value specified in **s**.

The following methods are value-related:

```
public boolean booleanValue();
```
Returns the value of the **Boolean** object as a boolean.

```
public static Boolean valueOf(String s);
```
Returns the boolean value that's stored in **s** in string format.

```
public static boolean getBoolean(String propertyName);
```
Returns a boolean value that's represented in string format in a system property. System properties, like **CLASSPATH** for example, are set on the host system and can't be accessed by applets.

```
public String toString();
```
Returns a new **String** object representing the **Boolean**'s value. This method overrides **toString()** in the **Object** class.

Other methods of the class have to do with comparing **Booleans** and creating hash codes. We discuss hash codes later when we talk about data structures.

```
public boolean equals(Object object);
```
Compares the **Boolean** object with the specified **object**. This method returns true if the objects are the same, false otherwise. This method overrides **equals()** in the **Object** class.

```
public int hashCode();
```
Returns a hash code for the **Boolean**. This method overrides **hashCode()** in the **Object** class.

The following code snippet illustrates the usage of the **Boolean** class:

```
// assigning a value by creating a new object
Boolean b1 = new Boolean(true);

// assigning a value by using a static property
Boolean b2 = Boolean.FALSE;

// Printing the value by implicitly invoking toString()
System.out.println(b1 + " " + b2);

// Obtaining the underlying data type & performing operations
System.out.println(b1.booleanValue() && b2.booleanValue());
```

The printout from this code is:

```
true false
false
```

Character

The **Character** class provides a wrapper for character data values and serves as a place for character-oriented operations. It has static properties used to assign values to **Character** objects and convert characters to numbers.

> **public final static int MAX_RADIX;**
> The largest allowed value for the radix argument in radix-conversion methods. These methods include **digit** and **forDigit** in this class, and the **parseInt** method in the class **Integer**.
>
> **public final static int MIN_RADIX;**
> The smallest allowed value for the radix argument in radix-conversion methods.
>
> **public final static char MAX_VALUE;**
> The largest value assignable to the type **char** ('**\uffff**').
>
> **public final static char MIN_VALUE;**
> The smallest value assignable to the type **char** ('**\u0000**').

The class has a single constructor that initializes the object to a specified Unicode value.

> **public Character(char value);**
> Constructs a **Character** object initialized to the specified value.

ISO-LATIN-1 (also known as ISO8859-1) is a Unicode character set that Java defines as the 'standard' character set. This character set contains characters from the Latin alphabet that are suitable for English and most West-European languages.

Although Java is very portable and supports internationalization in a manner only few other languages do, its Anglo-centric approach may lead to some difficulties when porting an application from English to other languages. For example, if you try to port an English version of a program to some European language (translating the user interface), and your program tries to uppercase an input string, it will fail to manipulate the non-ISO-LATIN-1 characters such as the German ess-zed, even though they may have corresponding uppercase characters.

If you plan on internationalizing your application, take care not to use ISO-LATIN-1 dependent methods.

The **Character** class's methods have to do with the value of the object and transformation from characters to numbers:

> **public char charValue();**
> Returns the underlying character value of a **Character** object.
>
> **public String toString();**
> Returns a new **String** object representing the **Character**'s value. This method overrides **toString()** in the **Object** class.
>
> **public static int digit(char ch, int radix);**
> Returns the numeric value of the character digit using the specified radix. If the character isn't a valid digit in the specified radix, it returns –1. For example, **Character.digit('f', 16)** returns 15 which is the value of the digit 'f' in the hexadecimal base (radix 16).

```
public static char forDigit(int digit, int radix);
```
The reverse of **digit()**. Returns the character value for the specified digit in the specified radix. If the digit isn't valid in the radix, the character 0 is returned.

The following methods query and modify the content of the **Character** object.

```
public static boolean isLowerCase(char c);
```
Returns true if the character is an ISO-LATIN-1 lowercase, false otherwise.

```
public static boolean isUpperCase(char c);
```
Returns true if the specified character is an ISO-LATIN-1 uppercase, false otherwise.

```
public static boolean isDigit(char c);
```
Returns true if the specified character is an ISO-LATIN-1 digit, false otherwise.

```
public static boolean isSpace(char c);
```
Returns true if the specified character is an ISO-LATIN-1 white space according to Java, false otherwise. Java defines the following characters as white space characters: space (' '), tab('\t'), form feed ('\f'), line feed ('\r') and new line ('\n').

```
public static char toLowerCase(char c);
```
Returns the matching lowercase character value of the specified uppercase ISO-LATIN-1 character. If **c** isn't an uppercase letter the method returns it unmodified.

```
public static char toUpperCase(char c);
```
Returns the matching uppercase character value of the specified lowercase ISO-LATIN-1 character. If **c** isn't a lowercase letter the method returns it unmodified. Note that only ISO-LATIN-1 lowercase characters are acceptable. Other lowercase characters (like German ess-zed and Latin small-letter y dieresis) are not included, even if they have corresponding uppercase characters.

Other methods of the class have to do with comparing **Character**s and creating hash codes:

```
public boolean equals(Object object);
```
Compares the **Character** object with the specified **object**. This method returns true if the objects are the same, false otherwise. This method overrides **equals()** in the **Object** class.

```
public int hashCode();
```
Returns a hash code for the **Character** object. This method overrides **hashCode()** in the **Object** class.

The **Character** class is most useful for converting and querying characters. Most of its properties are static and accept **char**s, allowing the manipulation of unwrapped characters. The following code snippet stresses the point.

```
// Manipulating characters

System.out.println( Character.isLowerCase('A') );
System.out.println( Character.toLowerCase('A') );

// Converting characters to digits

System.out.println( "\'a\' is " +
   ( Character.isDigit('a') ? "" : "not ") +
```

```
            "a digit. " +
            "its value in base " + Character.MAX_RADIX +
            " is " + Character.digit('a',Character.MAX_RADIX) );

    System.out.println( "\'9\' is " +
        ( Character.isDigit('9') ? "" : "not ") +
            "a digit. " +
            "its value in base " + Character.MAX_RADIX +
            " is " + Character.digit('9',Character.MAX_RADIX) );
```

As you can see, there's no need to wrap **char**s in order to query and manipulate them. The output of this code snippet is:

```
false
a
'a' is not a digit. its value in base 36 is 10
'9' is a digit. its value in base 36 is 9
```

Number

Number serves as an abstract superclass for all the numeric types. Its abstract methods provide common cast-like functionality to all of its subclasses.

> **public abstract int intValue();**
> Returns the value of the number converted to an **int**.

> **public abstract long longValue();**
> Returns the value of the number converted to a **long**.

> **public abstract float floatValue();**
> Returns the value of the number converted to a **float**.

> **public abstract double doubleValue();**
> Returns the value of the number converted to a **double**.

We'll see these methods being overridden by the **Double**, **Float**, **Integer**, and **Long** classes.

Double

The **Double** class descends from **Number**. It provides a wrapper for double precision data values and serves as a place for double-oriented operations. Java uses the IEEE 754 standard of representing floating point numbers.

The static properties of the class define a set of values that can be assigned to a **Double** object.

> **public final static double MAX_VALUE;**
> The maximum value that a double precision floating point number can have (1.79769313486231570e+308d). Only the most significant digits are stored.

> **public final static double MIN_VALUE;**
> The minimum value that a double precision floating point number can have (4.94065645841246544e–324d). Again, the actual number of significant digits is limited.

```
public final static double POSITIVE_INFINITY;
```
The IEEE 754 value for double precision positive infinity.

```
public final static double NEGATIVE_INFINITY;
```
The IEEE 754 value for double precision negative infinity.

```
public final static double NaN;
```
The IEEE 754 value for double precision Not-a-Number.(**NaN** is the answer you get when dividing zero by zero, for example). **Nan** isn't equal to anything, including itself.

The constructors allow the initial value to be given either as a double or a string.

```
public Double (double value);
```
Constructs a **Double** object initialized to the specified double **value**.

```
public Double(String s) throws NumberFormatException;
```
Constructs a **Double** object initialized to the value stored in **s** in string format. This method throws a **NumberFormatException** if **s** doesn't contain a parsable number.

The following methods transform doubles to other types, and vice versa:

```
public long longValue();
```
Returns the long value of the **Double** object by casting to a **long** (truncating rather than rounding). This method overrides **longValue()** in the **Number** class.

```
public float floatValue();
```
Returns the **float** value of the **Double** object. This operation may result in loss of precision. Overrides **floatValue()** in the **Number** class.

```
public double doubleValue();
```
Returns the **double** value of this **Double**. Overrides **doubleValue()** in the **Number** class.

```
public int intValue();
```
Returns the integer value of the **Double** object by casting it to an **int** (truncating rather than rounding). Overrides **intValue()** in the **Number** class.

```
public static Double valueOf(String s) throws NumberFormatException;
```
Creates and returns a new **Double** object initialized to the value stored in **s** in string format. This method throws a **NumberFormatException** if **s** doesn't contain a parsable number

```
public String toString();
```
Returns a **Sting** representing the value of the **Double** object. This method overrides **toString()** in the **Object** class.

```
public static String toString(double d);
```
Returns a **Sting** representing the value of **d**.

The following methods query the **Double** object or double values:

```
public static boolean isNaN(double v);
```
Returns true if **v** has a **NaN** value, false otherwise.

```
public boolean isNaN();
```
Returns true if the **Double** object has a **NaN** value, false otherwise.

```
public static boolean isInfinite(double v);
```
Returns true if **v** has a **POSITIVE_INFINITY** or **NEGATIVE_INFINITY** value, false otherwise.

```
public boolean isInfinite();
```
Returns true if the **Double** object has a **POSITIVE_INFINITY** or **NEGATIVE_INFINITY** value, false otherwise.

Two methods of the class deal with comparing **Double**s and creating hash codes:

```
public boolean equals(Object object);
```
Compares the **Double** object with the specified **object** and returns true if they are equal, false otherwise. This method overrides **equals()** in the **Object** class.

```
public int hashCode();
```
Returns a hash code for this **Double**. Overrides **hashCode()** in the **Object** class.

To be pragmatic, when used in conjunction with hash tables, this method considers two **NaN** double values to be equal, making it possible to find **NaN** values in the table (we review hash tables later in this chapter). This is in contrast to the IEEE 754 standard. To correctly compare two **Double**s, use the **==** (equality) operator.

The following methods expose Java's internal representation of double precision floating point numbers:

```
public static long doubleToLongBits(double value);
```
The result is the 64-bit representation of the floating-point **value** according to the IEEE 754 floating-point 'double format' bit layout.

```
public static double longBitsToDouble(long bits);
```
Returns the **double** corresponding to the provided bit representation.

The internal representation of double precision floating point numbers is in accordance with the IEEE 754 standard. This standard defines a 64-bit representation where bit 63 represents the sign of the floating-point number; bits 62–52 represent the exponent; and bits 51–0 represent the mantissa of the floating-point number. It's the mantissa's length that limits the precision.

The following table lists the bit representation of the special numeric values:

Value	Representation
Positive infinity	**0x7ff0000000000000L.**
Negative infinity	**0xfff0000000000000L.**
Not-a-Number	**0x7ff8000000000000L.**

Float

The **Float** class descends from **Number**. It provides a wrapper for float data values, and serves as a place for float-oriented operations.

The static properties of this class have the same meaning as those of the **Double** class, only with different values. The maximum value a single precision floating point number can have is 3.40282346638528860e+38, and the minimum value is 1.40129846432481707e-45. Again, the actual number of digits is limited, so only the most significant digits are stored.

The methods of the **Float** class are the single precision floating point equivalent of the methods in the **Double** class, so I will describe only the differences. For the full listing of methods, refer to the API.

The internal representation of double precision floating point numbers is in accordance with the IEEE 754 standard. This standard defines a 32-bit representation where bit 31 represents the sign of the floating-point number, bits 30–23 represent the exponent, and bits 22–0 represent the mantissa of the floating-point number.

The following table lists the bit representation of the special numeric values:

Value	Representation
Positive infinity	`0x7f800000.`
Negative infinity	`0xff800000.`
Not-a-Number	`0x7fc00000.`

Here's code snippet that illustrates some interesting things about Java's numeric value representation. This example uses both **Float**s and **Double**s. Since in this example we don't cross the boundary of precision that differentiates single precision floating point numbers from double precision floating point numbers it will produce the exact same output whether we use **Float**s or **Double**s. (Try using **2e-100** instead of one of the floating point literals and see what happens if you replace **Double**s with **Float**s).

```
// Parsing and manipulating the underlying value
System.out.println( (Double.valueOf("128.5532").intValue() ));
Float f1 = new Float(3.8),
      f2 = new Float(3.4999999999999999);
System.out.println(f1.intValue() +" "+ f2.intValue() );
// Yes - division by zero is allowed for non-integer numbers
if (Float.isNaN(0f/0f) )
   System.out.println("It's not a number");
System.out.println( f1.floatValue() + 5 );

// Playing around with infinity
System.out.println(Double.POSITIVE_INFINITY);
System.out.println(Double.NEGATIVE_INFINITY);
System.out.println(Double.NEGATIVE_INFINITY+10000000);
System.out.println(Double.POSITIVE_INFINITY+Double.NEGATIVE_INFINITY);
System.out.println(Double.isInfinite(Double.NEGATIVE_INFINITY));

// Not numbers
f1 = new Float(Float.NaN);
```

```
f2 = new Float(Float.NaN);
System.out.println( (f1==f2) + " " + f1.equals(f2) );
```

The output of this code snippet is very interesting. See how **NaN**s and infinite values affect and are affected by other values.

```
128
3 3
It's not a number
8.8
1.#INF
-1.#INF
-1.#INF
true
false true
```

Integer

The **Integer** class descends from **Number** and provides a wrapper for integer values. It has static properties that you can use to assign or compare values of integers.

> **public final static int MIN_VALUE;**
> The minimum value an **Integer** can have (0x80000000 in hexadecimal base or –2147483648 in decimal base).

> **public final static int MAX_VALUE;**
> The maximum value an **Integer** can have (0x7fffffff in hexadecimal base or 2147483647 in decimal base).

The constructors allow the initial value to be given either as an integer or a string.

> **public Integer(int value);**
> Constructs an **Integer** object initialized to the specified int **value**.

> **public Integer(String s) throws NumberFormatException;**
> Constructs an **Integer** object initialized to the value stored in **s** in string format (the radix used for the conversion is 10). This method throws a **NumberFormatException** if **s** doesn't contain a parsable number.

The following methods transform integers to other types and vice versa.

> **public static int parseInt(String s, int radix) throws**
> **NumberFormatException;**
> Returns the integer value represented in the string **s** in the specified **radix**. This method throws a **NumberFormatException** if **s** doesn't contain a parsable integer.

> **public static int parseInt(String s) throws NumberFormatException;**
> This method's operation is equivalent to **parseInt(s, 10)**.

> **public static Integer valueOf(String s, int radix) throws**
> **NumberFormatException;**

Creates and returns a new **Integer** object initialized to the value stored in **s** in the specified radix. This method throws a **NumberFormatException** if **s** doesn't contain a parsable number

```
public static Integer valueOf(String s) throws NumberFormatException;
```
This method's operation is equivalent to **valueOf(s, 10)**.

```
public double doubleValue();
public int intValue();
public long longValue();
public float floatValue();
```
Returns the value of the **Integer** object in the specified format.

```
public String toString();
```
Creates and returns a new **String** object representing the value of the **Integer** object. This method overrides **toString()** in the class **Object**.

```
public static String toString(int i, int radix);
```
Creates and returns a new **String** object representing the value of **i** in the specified **radix**.

```
public static String toString(int i);
```
Creates and returns a new **String** object representing the value of **i** in the radix 10.

Two methods of the class deal with comparing **Double**s and creating hash codes:

```
public int hashCode();
```
Returns a hash code for this **Integer**. This method overrides **hashCode()** in the class **Object**.

```
public boolean equals(Object object);
```
Compares the **Integer** object with the specified **object** and returns true if they are equal; returns false otherwise. This method overrides **equals()** in the class **Object**.

System properties (or 'environment variables') are configured outside of Java in a system-dependent way. The following methods interact with the host system to retrieve the value of numeric system properties and store them in **Integer** objects.

```
public static Integer getInteger(String propertyName);
```
Returns a new **Integer** object from the value represented in string format in a system property. If the specified property doesn't exist, this method returns **0**.

```
public static Integer getInteger(String propertyName, int defaultVal);
```
Returns a new **Integer** object from the value represented in string format in a system property. If the specified property doesn't exist, this method returns **defaultVal**.

```
public static Integer getInteger(String propertyName, Integer defaultVal);
```
Returns a new **Integer** object from the value represented in string format in a system property. If the specified property doesn't exist, this method returns **defaultVal**.

The system property querying methods deal with numbers specified in decimal, octal or hexadecimal format.

Using different radixes to create and display integer values is very easy. (This could come in handy when doing business with 6-fingered aliens). Here's a code snippet that illustrates the point.

```
// Parsing a string representation of a value
System.out.println(Integer.parseInt("128"));
System.out.println(Integer.parseInt("10000000", 2));

// Displaying a number in radix 12
System.out.println(Integer.toString(128, 12) );
```

The output from this is:

```
128
128
a8
```

Long

The **Long** class descends from **Number**. It provides a wrapper for long numeric values, and serves as a place for float-oriented operations.

As with the two floating point classes, the methods and properties of the **Long** class are the long versions of those of the **Integer** class, so I'll only describe the differences.

The minimum value a **Long** can have is –9223372036854775808 (or 0x8000000000000000 in hexadecimal base) and the maximum value is 9223372036854775807 (or 0x7fffffffffffffff in hexadecimal base).

When converting a **Long** to an **int** using

```
public int intValue();
```

significant digits may be lost in the conversion.

The methods for retrieving system properties are:

```
public static Long getLong(String propertyName);
public static Long getLong(String propertyName, long defaultVal);
public static Long getLong(String propertyName, Long defaultVal);
```

String

String is a class that represents character strings.

As mentioned before, strings are immutable and their values can't be changed after creation. Every string in Java is contained in a **String** object. Even string constants are wrapped in a **String** object (the compiler takes care of this automatically). This opens the door for some really weird statements like this:

```
System.out.printf( "sub-string".substring(0,3) );
```

This is a funny way to print out the word 'sub'. The **substring()** method is invoked on the implicitly created **String** object.

The **String** class has many constructors.

> ```
> public String();
> ```
> Constructs a new empty **String** object.

> ```
> public String(String value);
> public String(StringBuffer buffer);
> public String(char value[]);
> ```
> Constructs a new **String** object that's a copy of the specified **String**, **StringBuffer** or array of characters.

> ```
> public String(byte charArray[],int hibyte, int offset, int count);
> ```
> Constructs a new **String** object initialized to the specified subarray of **count** characters, starting at the specified **offset**. Java strings are made of Unicode characters that are 16 bits wide, while a byte is only 8 bits wide. The value taken from each byte in the array is placed in the lower 8 bits of the corresponding character. The upper 8 bits are set to the value specified in **hibyte**. This method throws a **StringIndexOutOfBoundsException** if the **offset** or **count** arguments are invalid.

> ```
> public String(char charArray[],int offset, int count);
> ```
> Same as invoking the previous method with **hibyte** equals to 0.

> ```
> public String(byte charArray[],int hibyte);
> ```
> Another variation. This one uses all the characters in the array (**offset** equals 0 and **count** equals **charArray**.length).

The following methods query the content of the **String** object.

> ```
> public int length();
> ```
> Returns the length of the **String** (the number of 16-bit Unicode characters in the string).

> ```
> public char charAt(int index);
> ```
> Returns the character at the specified **index**. This method throws a **StringIndexOutOfBoundsException** if the **index** is less than 0 or not less than **length()** (remember, the first character's index is 0).

> ```
> public int indexOf(int ch);
> public int indexOf(int ch, int fromIndex);
> public int lastIndexOf(int ch);
> public int lastIndexOf(int ch, int fromIndex);
> ```
> Return the index within the **String** object of the first occurrence of the specified character, starting the search **fromIndex** characters from the start or end, searching forward or backward respectively. The methods return −1 if the specified character isn't found.

> ```
> public int indexOf(String str);
> public int indexOf(String str, int fromIndex);
> public int lastIndexOf(String str);
> public int lastIndexOf(String str, int fromIndex);
> ```
> Same as the previous methods, only these methods search for a string instead of a single character.

```
public boolean startsWith(String prefix);
public boolean startsWith(String prefix, int toffset);
```
Return true if the **String** object contains the **prefix** starting at the specified **offset** or first character, false otherwise.

```
public boolean endsWith(String suffix);
```
Returns true if the **String** object ends with the specified **suffix**, false otherwise.

The **String** class has several methods to compare the content of a **String** object.

```
public boolean equals(Object anObject);
```
Compares the **String** object with the specified **object** and returns true if they are equal, returns false otherwise. This method overrides **equals()** in the **Object** class.

```
public boolean equalsIgnoreCase(String anotherString);
```
Returns true if the **String** object is equal (in length and content) to the specified **String** object, ignoring case, false otherwise.

```
public int compareTo(String anotherString);
```
Lexicographically compares the **String** object with another **String** object. (The return value is explained below.)

```
public boolean regionMatches(boolean ignoreCase, int toffset, String
other, int ooffset, int length);
public boolean regionMatches(int toffset, String other, int ooffset, int
length);
```
Determines whether two regions in the **String** object and the other **String** are equal. The methods compare **length** characters, starting with the **toffset** and **ooffset** characters respectively. (The return value is explained below.) With the first version you can specify if you want case match or not. The second version requires case match.

A lexicographic comparison returns 0, a positive or a negative value according to the following algorithm:

1 Initialization: Let j equal 0 (indexing starts at 0).

2 Check for equal length strings: If both strings are j characters long return 0.

3 Check for one string longer than the other: If the first string is j characters long (implying that the second is longer), return a negative value. If the second string is j characters long (implying that the first is longer), return a positive value.

4 Check for different characters: If the Unicode value for the character with index j in the first string is higher than in the second string, return a positive value. If the Unicode value for the character with index j in the second string is higher than in the first string, return a positive value.

5 Go to next character: Increase j by 1 and go to step 2.

This algorithm returns 0 only for strings with identical length and content (you can also say that this method returns 0 if and only if **equals()** returns **true**).

The region matching method returns true if:

- The starting positions are greater than 0 and less than the length of the corresponding strings.
- The offsets plus the length are less or equal to the length of the corresponding strings.
- The regions contains the same characters in the same order.

It returns false otherwise.

The following method has to do with hash tables:

```
public int hashCode();
```
Returns a hash code for the **String** object. This method overrides **hashCode()** in the class **Object**.

The following methods manipulate the content of the **String** object.

```
public String concat(String str);
```
Concatenates the content of the specified string to the end of the **String** object and returns the outcome in a new **String** object (remember, .**String** objects are immutable–they can't be changed after creation).

```
public String replace(char oldChar, char newChar);
```
Replaces all the occurrences of **oldChar** in the **String** object with **newChar** and returns the outcome in a new **String** object.

```
public String toLowerCase();
public String toUpperCase();
```
Converts all the characters in the **String** object to lower or uppercase and returns the outcome in a new **String** object.

```
public String trim();
```
Trims the leading and trailing white space characters from the **String** object and returns the outcome in a new **String** object.

The following methods transform the value of their arguments to their **String** representation.

```
public static String valueOf(Object object);
```
Returns a **String** that represents the **String** value of the specified **object**. The object defines how to represent itself by overriding the **toString()** method in the class **Object**, providing its own implementation.

```
public static String valueOf(char data[]);
public static String valueOf(char data[], int offset, int count);
```
Returns a **String** that's made of the same characters in the same order as the ones in the specified character array. You can specify the **offset** to start from and the number (**count**) of characters to take.

```
public static String copyValueOf(char data[]);
public static String copyValueOf(char data[], int offset, int count);
```
Same as the previous classes only these methods first create a copy of the specified character array and then construct the **String** object 'around' it.

```
public static String valueOf(boolean b);
public static String valueOf(char c);
public static String valueOf(int i);
public static String valueOf(long l);
public static String valueOf(float f);
public static String valueOf(double d);
```
Returns a **String** object that represents the content of the specified argument.

These methods return a substring of the **String** object.

```
public String substring(int beginIndex);
public String substring(int beginIndex, int endIndex);
```
Return a substring of the **String** object starting with the **beginIndex** character (inclusive) and ending with the last character or **endIndex** (exclusive).
A **StringIndexOutOfBoundsException** is thrown if the **beginIndex** or the **endIndex** is less than 0 or greater than **length()**.

These methods expose the content of the **String** object as bytes, chars and another **String** object.

```
public void getBytes(int sourceStartPos, int sourceEndPos, byte
destination[],int dstStartPos);
public void getChars(int sourceStartPos, int sourceEndPos, char
destination[],int dstStartPos);
```
Copies bytes or characters from the **String** object starting with character number **sourceStartPos** and ending with character number **sourceEndPos** into the specified byte or character array starting at the **dstStartPos** element in the array.

```
public String intern();
```
Returns a **String** that's equal in content to the **String** object but which is taken from a pool of unique strings.

```
public String toString();
```
Returns the **String** itself. This method overrides **toString()** in the **Object** class.

```
public char[] toCharArray();
```
Creates and returns a new character array containing the characters of the string in the **String** object.

The **intern()** method return value is taken from a unique pool of strings. This guarantees that if **s1** and **s2** are **String** objects and **s1.equals(s2)** then **s1.intern()** == **s2.intern()** because they refer to the same object.

The **toString()** method really does nothing except return **this**, but it's important for the completeness of the class model. It enables you to invoke the **toString()** method on any object, making sure you get the right result.

Here's a code snippet that demonstrates some of the functionality of the **String** class.

```
// String manipulation - The String object is implicitly created

System.out.println( "sub-string".substring(0,3) );
```

```
System.out.println( "lava".replace('l', 'j') );

// Breaking up a sentence to words by looking for spaces

String sentence = "This is a sentence";
int wordStart = 0,
    wordEnd   = sentence.indexOf(' ');

while (wordEnd!=-1)
{
  // Print out next word
  System.out.println(sentence.substring(wordStart,wordEnd));

  // Update word start and end
  wordStart = wordEnd+1;
  wordEnd = sentence.indexOf(' ', wordEnd+1);
}

// Print the last word (there are no more spaces so wordEnd is -1
System.out.println( sentence.substring(wordStart) );
```

The output of this code snippet is:

```
sub
java
This
is
a
sentence
```

StringBuffer

StringBuffer is a class that represents character strings. Unlike **String**, a **StringBuffer**'s content can be modified.

String buffers can be used instead of the string concatenation operator (in fact, a Java compiler can translate every string concatenation to **StringBuffer** operations to achieve the desired result).

For example, if **sum** is an **int**eger and **item** is a **String**, then this statement:

```
"There are " + sum + " " + item + "s in the store."
```

is equivalent to:

```
new StringBuffer().append("There are ").append(sum)
                .append(" ").append(item).append("s in the store")
            .toString()
```

This statement first creates a new (empty) string buffer. It then appends the string representation (as determined by its **toString()** method) of the operands in turn, and finally returns the contents of the string buffer as a **String** object. (The **append()** and **toString()** methods are described below.)

A **StringBuffer** object has an internal buffer with a certain capacity. As long as the length of the character sequence contained in the string buffer is less than the capacity of the buffer, that buffer is used. If the string buffer is manipulated in such a way that the internal buffer isn't enough, a new and larger internal buffer is automatically allocated to contain the longer string.

The **StringBuffer** class has 3 constructors:

```
public StringBuffer();
public StringBuffer(int length) throws NegativeArraySizeException;
```
Constructs an empty **StringBuffer** object with an internal capacity of the specified **length** or (if the **length** isn't specified) 16 characters. If **length** is negative a **NegativeArraySizeException** is thrown.

```
public StringBuffer(String str);
```
Constructs a new **StringBuffer** object initialized to the contents of the specified string. The initial capacity of the string buffer is 16 characters more than the length of the specified string (**str.length()+16**).

The following methods handle the length and capacity of the **StringBuffer** object.

```
public int length();
```
This method returns the actual length of the string (not the size of the internal buffer) in the **StringBuffer** object.

```
public void setLength(int newLength) throws IndexOutOfBoundsException;
```
If the current length of the string in the string buffer is more than the **newLength**, the string is truncated at the new length. If the string is shorter, the string is appended null characters (**'\u0000'**) so that it becomes **newLength** characters long. This method throws an **IndexOutOfBoundsException**. if **newLength** is negative.

```
public int capacity();
```
This method returns the size of the internal buffer of the **StringBuffer** object.

```
public void ensureCapacity( int minimumCapacity);
```
If the current capacity of this **StringBuffer** object is less than the **minimumCapacity**, then a new internal buffer whose size is at least **minimumCapacity** is allocated and the current string is moved to it. If the **minimumCapacity** argument is less than or equal to 0, this method does nothing.

The following methods handle individual characters within the **StringBuffer** object.

```
public char charAt(int index) throws IndexOutOfBoundsException;
```
Returns the specified character from of the string, as indicated by the **index** argument.

```
public void setCharAt(int index, char newCharacter) throws
IndexOutOfBoundsException;
```
Replaces the **index**-th character in the string contained in the string buffer with the **newCharacter**.

```
public void getChars(int srcBegin, int srcEnd, char destination[],int
dstBegin) throws NullPointerException, IndexOutOfBoundsException;
```
Copies characters from the internal string buffer to the specified destination, starting with the character whose index is **srcBegin** (inclusive) and ending with the character whose index is **srcEnd** (exclusive). The total number of characters to be copied is **srcEnd-srcBegin**. The characters are copied into the **destination** starting at the **sdtBegin** character.

If **index** is less than 0 or not less than the length of the string contained in the string buffer, the method throws an **IndexOutOfBoundsException**.

If **destination** is **null**, then a **NullPointerException** is thrown. If either of the indexes is negative, or not less than the length of its corresponding string, or the number of characters to copy plus the starting destination is not less than the length of the target, this method throws an **IndexOutOfBoundsException** and the destination is not modified.

The following methods append the string representation of the argument to the **StringBuffer** object (the character representation of a **null** string is the string 'null').

```
public StringBuffer append(Object object);
public StringBuffer append(boolean b);
public StringBuffer append(char c);
public StringBuffer append(int i);
public StringBuffer append(long l);
public StringBuffer append(float f);
public StringBuffer append(double d);
public StringBuffer append(String str);
public StringBuffer append(char[] str) throws NullPointerException;
public StringBuffer append(char[] source, int offset, int length) throws
NullPointerException, IndexOutOfBoundsException;
```

These methods return a reference to the **StringBuffer** object.

The last method appends **length** characters from the **source**, starting at the specified **offset**, to the current content of the string buffer. If the **source** is **null**, it throws a **NullPointerException**. If the **offset** is less than 0 or the **offset** plus the **length** are not less than the length of the string, it throws an **IndexOutOfBoundsException**.

The following methods insert the character representation of the specified argument to the string buffer at the specified **offset**. If the **offset** is negative or not less than the length of the string, these methods throw as **IndexOutOfBoundsException**.

```
public StringBuffer insert(int offset, Object object)throws
IndexOutOfBoundsException;
public StringBuffer insert(int offset, boolean b) throws
IndexOutOfBoundsException;
public StringBuffer insert(int offset, char c) throws
IndexOutOfBoundsException;
public StringBuffer insert(int offset, int i) throws
IndexOutOfBoundsException;
public StringBuffer insert(int offset, long l) throws
IndexOutOfBoundsException;
```

```
public StringBuffer insert(int offset, float f) throws
IndexOutOfBoundsException;
public StringBuffer insert(int offset, double d) throws
IndexOutOfBoundsException;
public StringBuffer insert(int offset, char[] str) throws
NullPointerException, IndexOutOfBoundsException;
public StringBuffer insert(int offset, String str) throws
IndexOutOfBoundsException;
```

These methods return a reference to the **StringBuffer** object.

One more method is:

> ```
> public StringBuffer reverse();
> ```
> Reverses the string contained in the string buffer. This method returns a reference to the **StringBuffer** object. Note that this method is new in Java!!

The last method in this class returns the content of the **StringBuffer** object in a way that can be manipulated by other classes.

> ```
> public String toString();
> ```
> Returns a new **String** object containing a copy of the string the string buffer contains. This method overrides **toString()** in the **Object** class.

When used like this:

```
// Reversing the content of a string buffer
// and then (implicitly) transforming it to a String
//(as there's no method to directly print a StringBuffer object)
System.out.println( new StringBuffer("esrever").reverse() );
```

The last statement produces this output:

```
reverse
```

The string buffer's content is transformed to a **String** when the **println()** method invokes its **toString()** method.

java.util

Java's utility package **java.util** contains a collection of classes that provide an implementation for common data structures. This goes hand-in-hand with the object-oriented notions of abstraction (you don't need to know how a hash table is implemented in order to store things in it) and code reuse (write it once, use it again and again).

It's out of the scope of this book to explain what data structures are or what they're used for. We'll just examine the interface to the classes.

BitSet

BitSet is a class that encapsulates bit set related operations. Each bit has a value of either 'true' or 'false' (sometimes called 'set' and 'clear', or 1 and 0). The individual bits can each be examined and modified. Entire **BitSet** objects may be used to modify the contents of other **BitSet** objects using logical operations. The **BitSet** grows as needed to allow access to arbitrary bits, there's no need for a programmer to explicitly set its size.

The **BitSet** class has two constructors.

> **public BitSet();**
> **public BitSet(int initialSize);**
> Constructs a new **BitSet** object with all the bits set to false. If an initial size is specified, the created object is created with a size of at least **initialSize** bits, otherwise, the **BitSet** is initialized to an arbitrary length. Initially, all the bits in the set are assigned the value false.

The class has methods for changing and querying individual bits within the bit set.

> **public boolean get(int bit) throws IndexOutOfBoundsException;**
> Returns true if the bit with index **bit** has the value true; otherwise, it returns false.

> **public void set(int bit) throws IndexOutOfBoundsException;**
> Sets the bit with index **bit** in the **BitSet** object to the value true ('set'). If **bit** isn't smaller than the current number of bits in the **BitSet** (as returned by **size()**), the **BitSet** is dynamically increased to include the referenced bit.

> **public void clear(int bit) throws IndexOutOfBoundsException;**
> Being the reverse of **set()**, this method sets the value of the specified bit in the **BitSet** to false ('clear'). Dynamic sizing and indexing bounds are the same as for **set()**.

If **bit** is negative, these methods throw an **IndexOutOfBoundsException**.

Other methods manipulate the whole bit set.

> **public void and(BitSet set);**
> **public void or(BitSet set);**
> **public void xor(BitSet set);**
> These methods perform the specified bit-wise operation on every bit in the **BitSet** object and the corresponding bit in the specified **set**.

Other methods of the class are:

> **public int size();**
> Returns the number of bits actually allocated in the **BitSet** object.

> **public boolean equals(Object object);**
> Compares the **BitSet** object with the specified **object**. Returns true if the other object is a **BitSet** and for every bit index **i**, the **get(i)** returns the same value for both objects. This method overrides **equals()** in the **Object** class.

public int hashCode();

Returns a hash code for the **BitSet** object. The hash code depends on the values of the different bits, and may change if they do. This method overrides **hashCode()** in the **Object** class.

public Object clone();

Returns a new **BitSet** that is equal to the **BitSet** object. This method overrides the **clone()** method in the **Object** class.

public String toString();

Returns a new **String** object that contains a string that lists the indexes of all the bits that are set to 'true' (see the example below). This method overrides **toString()** in the **Object** class.

Here's an example that uses a **BitSet**.

```
import java.util.*;

class BitSetTest
{
    public static void main(String args[])
    {
        BitSet bs1 = new BitSet(5),
               bs2 = new BitSet(70);

        // Display number of allocated bits
        System.out.println(bs1.size() + " " + bs2.size() );

        // Compare bit sets
        System.out.println(bs1.equals(bs2) );

        // Modify both bit sets and compare again
        bs1.set(0);
        bs2.set(0);
        System.out.println(bs1.equals(bs2) );

        // Modify only one bit set, print the size and compare
        bs1.set(200);
        System.out.println(bs1.size() + " " + bs2.size() );
        System.out.println(bs1.equals(bs2) );

        // Implicitly invoke toString()
        bs2.clear(0);
        System.out.println( bs1 +" "+ bs2 );
    }
}
```

When I run it on my PC, the application prints this on the console:

```
64 128
true
true
256 128
false
(0, 200} {}
```

The actual size used to store the bits (as reported by `size()`) may vary across different implementations of Java. This isn't an issue as far as portability and system independence are concerned, as it doesn't change the behavior of the `BitSet` class.

Enumeration

The `Enumeration` interface isn't a data structure but rather an interface used by data structures to expose the elements they contain in a sequential fashion. This interface provides a way for its implementor to enable sequential access to objects. While you may not assume any specific order, the implementor guarantees you iterate through all the elements. As long as there are more objects to access, as indicated by the `hasMoreElements()` method returning true, the `nextElement()` method returns the next object in the series.

```
public abstract boolean hasMoreElements();
public abstract Object nextElement();
```

An example usage of an `Enumeration` of the elements of a `Vector` can be seen near the end of the next section.

Vector

`Vector` is a class that, like an array, contains items that can be accessed using an index.

A `Vector` has two major characteristics that make it unlike an array:

▲ It can dynamically change its size as elements are added to and removed from it.

▲ It's a heterogeneous container, meaning it can store a mixture of objects of different types.

While more versatile than an array, a vector has a lower performance, so when an array is suitable for the job (i.e. the objects are all from the same type and you know how many there are up front), you should use an array.

Like a `StringBuffer`, a `Vector` has an internal array of references with a certain capacity. As long as the number of elements in the vector is less than the length of the array, that array is used. If the vector is manipulated in such a way that the internal array is too small to contain all the references, a larger internal array is allocated. This process is opaque to the user of the `Vector` class.

The `Vector` class has 3 constructors.

```
public Vector();
public Vector(int initialCapacity);
public Vector(int initialCapacity, int capacityIncrement);
```
Creates a new, empty, `Vector` object. If an initial capacity is specified, the new object is created with a capacity of at least `initialCapacity` elements, otherwise, the `Vector` is initialized to an arbitrary capacity. Initially, all the elements handles are set to `null`.

Whenever there's a need to increase the capacity of the `Vector`, the new internal array size is incremented by a fixed amount. If you have some knowledge of the amount of elements you add each time, you may set the increment size in the constructor.

You can manage a vector's content by adding and removing elements.

```
public final void addElement(Object object);
```
Adds a new reference to the object as the last element in the vector, increasing its size by 1.

```
public final void insertElementAt(Object obj, int index) throws
IndexOutOfBoundsException;
```
Inserts a new element reference in the specified **index**, 'pushing' all the references from **index** onwards 1 index up.

```
public final boolean removeElement(Object object);
```
Removes the first occurrence of a handle to the specified object from the vector. If such a reference is found and removed, the method returns true, otherwise the vector remains unchanged and the method returns false.

```
public final void removeElementAt(int index) throws
IndexOutOfBoundsException;
```
This method removes the element in the specified **index** from the **Vector**, decreasing the size of the **Vector** by 1 and 'pulling' all the references from **index** onwards 1 index down.

```
public final void removeAllElements();
```
Removes *all* the element references from the **Vector**, leaving it empty.

The following methods query and set the size, capacity and content with no regard to the actual element references.

```
public final int size();
```
Returns the number of object references in the **Vector**.

```
public final boolean isEmpty();
```
Returns **true** if and only if the **Vector**'s size is zero.

```
public final void setSize(int newSize);
```
Changes the size of the **Vector** object to **newSize**. If the new size is smaller than the old size, then the method removes all references with an index that isn't smaller than the new size. If the new size is larger than the old size, new **null** items are added at the end of the **Vector**.

```
public final int capacity();
```
Returns the current capacity of the **Vector**.

```
public final void ensureCapacity(int minCapacity);
```
Makes sure there's room for at least **minCapacity** object references in the **Vector** by resizing the internal array, if needed.

```
public final void trimToSize();
```
The capacity is trimmed down to the actual number of element references in the **Vector**.

Four methods facilitate accessing single elements.

```
public final Object elementAt(int index) throws
IndexOutOfBoundsException;
```
Returns the item with the specified **index**.

```
public final void setElementAt(Object object, int index) throws
IndexOutOfBoundsException;
```
Replaces the current element at the specified **index** with the new **object**.

```
public final Object firstElement()throws NoSuchElementException;
public final Object lastElement()throws NoSuchElementException;
```
These methods return the first or last element in the vector. If the vector is empty these methods throw a **NoSuchElementException**.

The following method returns the entire content of the vector.

```
public final void copyInto(Object objectArray[]) throws
IndexOutOfBoundsException;
```
Copies all the object references in the **Vector** object into **objectArray**. This method throws an **IndexOutOfBoundsException** if **objectArray** is smaller than the size of the **Vector**.

These methods query and search a **Vector** for a specific element.

```
public final boolean contains(Object element);
```
Returns true if the **element** is referenced by some entry in the **Vector**.

```
public final int indexOf(Object element);
```
Returns the index of the first entry in the **Vector** that references the specified **element**. If no such entry exists, the method returns –1.

```
public final int indexOf(Object element, int minIndex) throws
IndexOutOfBoundsException;
```
Returns the first index of the entry greater than **minIndex** in the **Vector** that references the specified **element**. If no such entry exists, the method returns –1.

```
public final int lastIndexOf(Object elem);
```
Returns the index of the last entry in the **Vector** that references the specified **element**. If no such entry exists, the method returns –1.

```
public final int lastIndexOf(Object elem, int maxIndex) throws
IndexOutOfBoundsException;
```
Returns the first index smaller than **maxIndex** of the entry in the **Vector** that references the specified **element**. If no such entry exists, the method returns –1.

These methods throw an **IndexOutOfBoundsException** if the specified index is negative or not less than the **Vector**'s size (the first index is 0, and so the last is **size()-1**).

The **Vector** class provides an **Enumeration** object that enables you to easily iterate through the elements of the object:

```
public final Enumeration elements();
```
Returns an enumeration of the elements in the **Vector**.

You might use the **Enumeration** object to list the type of objects in a vector. Assuming **v** is a vector with elements, the following code would print the type of each element:

```
for (Enumeration e = v.elements(); e.hasMoreElements();)
{
    System.out.println(e.nextElement().getClass().getName());
}
```

(This example uses a **Class** object; the **Class** class is described later in the chapter.)

The other methods of the **Vector** class are:

> **public final String toString();**
> Lists all the elements in the vector by invoking the **toString()** method on each one. A **null** reference is displayed as the string **"null"**. This method overrides **toString()** in the class **Object**.

> **public Object clone();**
> Returns a copy of the **Vector**. This method overrides **clone()** in the class **Object**.

The following example illustrate some of the features of the **Vector** class.

```
import java.util.*;

class VectorTest
{
    public static void main(String args[])
    {
        Vector v1 = new Vector(3),
                v2;

        v1.addElement( new StringBuffer("a") );
        v1.addElement( new StringBuffer("b") );
        v1.addElement( new StringBuffer("c") );

        v2 = (Vector) v1.clone();

        System.out.println( v1 );
        System.out.println( v2 );
        System.out.println();

        ((StringBuffer) v1.elementAt(0)).append("A");

        System.out.println( v1 );
        System.out.println( v2 );
        System.out.println();

        v1.removeElementAt(0);

        System.out.println( v1 );
        System.out.println( v2 );
        System.out.println();

        for(Enumeration e=v2.elements(); e.hasMoreElements(); )
            System.out.println( e.nextElement() );
    }
}
```

The output of this example code is:

```
[a, b, c]
[a, b, c]

[aA, b, c]
[aA, b, c]

[b, c]
[aA, b, c]

aA
b
c
```

Stack

The **Stack** class extends **Vector** and adds five operations that allow you to treat a vector as a stack. It has one constructor:

```
public Stack();
```
Creates an empty stack.

The other methods of the class allow the underlying **Vector** object to be treated as a stack.

```
public Object push(Object item);
```
Pushes the **item** onto the top of the **Stack** object.

```
public Object pop() throws EmptyStackException;
```
Removes the object at the top of the **Stack** and returns it.

```
public Object peek() throws EmptyStackException;
```
Returns a handle to the object at the top of the stack without removing it.

```
public boolean empty();
```
Returns **true** if there are no object references in the stack.

```
public int search(Object object);
```
Returns the distance from the top of the stack at which the specified **object** handle is located. If the object handle isn't found on the stack, this method returns –1.

If the stack is empty **pop()** and **peek()** throw an **EmptyStackException**.

Hashtable

The **Hashtable** class extends the abstract class **Dictionary**, adding functionality to implement a hash table. **Dictionary** isn't discussed in this book, and isn't needed in order to understand how a hash table works.

> The following paragraphs cover fairly advanced material. If you don't know how a
> hash table stores elements, you can skip them, as they are intended to refresh your
> memory rather than teach. In general, you don't need to know how a hash table
> works in order to use it—you just have to understand the interface.

A hash table's efficiency is determined by two factors: its capacity and its load factor. The capacity is the number of different 'buckets' the data items are mapped to. The load factor is a number in the range 0 to 1. When the current load (defined as the current number of data items divided by the current capacity) exceeds the load factor, the capacity is increased to reduce it and the data is rehashed.

Data items are inserted into the hash table according to their hash code. A good hash code function distributes the data items evenly across the hash table. In hash tables, there is always a trade off between memory consumption and seek time. If every element maps to a different 'bucket', the average search time will be fixed. (In computer science talk it's called O(1).) If all elements map to a single 'bucket', the average seek time will have a linear ratio to the number of elements in the table. (That's O(n/2) which is the same as O(n) where n is the number of data items.)

Higher load factors utilize memory more efficiently at the expense of a longer average lookup time. Lower load factors speed up the search time at the expense of greater memory consumption.

If you know in advance that many data items are about to be inserted into the hash table, make it large enough to remove the overhead of rehashing and gain performance.

The **Object.hashCode()** method is provided to simplify the use of hash tables. When invoked on the same object, this method should return the same value. (The value may change from one execution to another, but during a single execution the value will be the same.) Furthermore, the hash code of two equal objects, as determined by the **equals()** method of their class, will be the same.

Most classes override this method to better implement their hash value function.

The **Hashtable** class has three constructors.

```
public Hashtable();
public Hashtable(int initialCapacity);
public Hashtable(int initialCapacity, float loadFactor);
```
Construct and initializes a new **Hashtable** object. The initial capacity and load factor are either specifically stated or set to default values. The hash table is empty on creation.

These methods query and modify the content of hash table elements.

```
public Object get(Object key);
```
Returns the object associated with the specified **key**, or **null** if no such element exists. This method implements the **get()** method of the **Dictionary** class.

```
public Object put(Object key, Object value);
```
Inserts the data item with the specified **value** to the hash table, associating it with the specified **key**. Neither the **value** nor the **key** may be **null**. This method implements the **put()** method of the **Dictionary** class.

```
public Object remove(Object key);
```
Removes the element associated with the specified **key** from the hash table. This method returns a handle to that object, or **null** if the object isn't found. This method implements the **remove()** method of the **Dictionary** class.

The following methods query the content of the entire hash table

> `public void clear();`
> Removes all the data elements and their associated keys from the **Hashtable** object.

> `public boolean containsKey(Object key);`
> `public boolean contains (Object value);`
> Returns true if there's at least one entry in the hash table for which the **key** or **value** is equal to the specified argument, as determined by the **equals()** method; otherwise this method returns false.

> `public boolean isEmpty();`
> Returns true if the hash table's size is 0. This method implements the **isEmpty()** method of the **Dictionary** class.

> `public int size();`
> Returns the number of data items in the hash table. This method implements the **size()** method of the **Dictionary** class.

The following methods allow the keys and data items to be walked through in a sequential manner.

> `public Enumeration keys();`
> `public Enumeration elements();`
> Return an enumeration of the keys or elements in the hash table.

Other methods of the class are:

> `public Object clone();`
> Returns a copy of the hash table. The hash table is cloned but not the keys or data items (they're shared among all copies). This method overrides the **clone()** method of the **Object** class.

> `public String toString();`
> Returns the list of the data items and their associated keys in the **Hashtable** in string format. This method overrides the **toString()** method of the class **Object**.

The following example illustrates some of the features of the **Hashtable** class.

```
import java.util.*;

class HashtableTest
{
    public static void main(String args[])
    {
        Hashtable h = new Hashtable();

        // Insert String elements to the hash table
        h.put(new Integer(1), "one");
        h.put(new Integer(2), "two");
        h.put(new Integer(3), "three");

        // Query the hash table
        System.out.println( h.contains("three") );
```

147

```
         System.out.println( h.contains("four") );

         // Using enumerations to walk through the content of the table
         Enumeration keys = h.keys();
         Enumeration elements = h.elements();
         while (keys.hasMoreElements())
         {
             System.out.println("key = " + keys.nextElement() +
                 " \t element = " + elements.nextElement() );
         }

         // Implicitly invoking toString()
         System.out.println( h );

         // Getting and removing elements
         Integer i = new Integer(2);
         System.out.println( h.get(i) );
         h.remove(i);
         System.out.println( h.get(i) );
     }
 }
```

The output of this example is:

```
true
false
key = 3          element = three
key = 2          element = two
key = 1          element = one
{3=three, 2=two, 1=one}
two
null
```

Other Classes and Interfaces

Math

Math is a final static class that extends **Object**. It contains methods to perform all the basic mathematical functions along with the double precision floating point representation of e and π. The **Math** class is found in the **java.lang** package.

Since the methods and properties of this class are very straight forward, only a short description of each of them will be supplied.

▲   **E**–The double precision floating point representation of the value e, the base of the natural logarithms.

▲   **PI**–The double precision floating point representation of the value p, the ratio of the circumference of a circle to its diameter.

Of course these values are not the real values of e and π but rather the closest numbers possible in Java. This is because both e and π are irrational numbers with an infinitely long decimal fraction part while double precision floating point values have a limited precision.

These are the rounding methods:

```
public static int abs(int a);
public static long abs(long a);
public static float abs(float a);
public static double abs(double a);
```
Returns the absolute value of the argument.

```
public static double ceil(double a);
```
Returns the smallest whole number greater than or equal to **a**.

```
public static double floor(double);
```
Returns the largest whole number less than or equal to **a**.

```
public static double rint(double);
```
Converts a double value into an integral value in double format.

```
public static int round(float);
public static long round(double)
```
Rounds the value of the argument. The methods add 0.5 to the argument and then return the largest integral value less than or equal to the result.

Trigonometric methods:

```
public static double acos(double a);
```
Returns the arc cosine of **a**, in the range of 0 through π.

```
public static double asin(double a);
```
Returns the arc sine of **a**, in the range of $-\pi/2$ through $\pi/2$.

```
public static double atan(double a);
```
Returns the arc tangent of **a**, in the range of $-\pi/2$ through $\pi/2$.

```
public static double atan2 (double a, double b);
```
Returns the angle θ of the (r, θ) polar coordinates pair corresponding to the (**a**, **b**) Cartesian coordinates pair.

```
public static double cos(double a);
```
Returns the trigonometric cosine of **a**.

```
public static double sin(double a);
```
Returns the trigonometric sine of **a**.

```
public static double tan(double a);
```
Returns the trigonometric tangent of **a**.

Power, exponent and their reverse:

```
public static double exp(double a);
```
Returns e raised to the power of **a**.

```
public static double log(double a);
```
Returns the natural logarithm of **a**.

```
public static double pow(double a, double b);
```
Returns **a** raised to the power of **b**.

```
public static double sqrt(double);
```
Returns the square root of **a**.

Minimum and maximum:

```
public static int max(int a, int b);
public static long max(long a, long b);
public static float max(float a, float b);
public static double max(double a, double b);
```
Returns the value of the greater of the arguments.

```
public static int min(int a, int b);
public static long min(long a, long b);
public static float min(float a, float b);
public static double min(double a, double b);
```
Returns the value of the smaller of the arguments.

The other methods of the **Math** class are:

```
public static double IEEEremainder(double, double);
```
Returns the remainder of f1 divided by f2 as defined by IEEE 754.

```
public static double random();
```
Returns a pseudo-random number in the range 0 through 1.

Classes and Class Loaders

Class - Accessing Class Information

Derived from **Object**, **Class** is a class that encapsulates the properties of Java classes and interfaces. Every class and interface in a Java application (both Java's and your own) has a **Class** object associated with it. The **Class** objects are constructed automatically by Java as it loads the classes of the application. There's no public constructor for **Class** objects.

The **Class** class is found in the **java.lang** package.

The **Class** object of any object can be obtained using the **getClass()** method inherited from **Object**.

You can generate your own **Class** objects by using a class loader. We'll discuss the **ClassLoader** class in a moment.

Following is a list all the public methods of the **Class** class with short description. For the complete description refer to the API.

> **public static Class forName(String name);**
> Returns the **Class** object for the specified class **name**.
>
> **public ClassLoader getClassLoader();**
> Returns the **ClassLoader** class associated with the **Class** object.
>
> **public Class[] getInterfaces();**
> Returns an array of the interfaces the class supports.
>
> **public String getName();**
> Returns the name of the class.
>
> **public Class getSuperclass();**
> Returns a handle to the superclass of the class.
>
> **public boolean isInterface();**
> Returns a boolean indicating whether the **Class** object is associated with an interface rather than a class.
>
> **public Object newInstance();**
> Creates a new instance of this class (this has the same effect as if you invoked the class's constructor with no arguments).
>
> **public String toString();**
> Returns the name of this class or interface, prepending the word 'class' or 'interface' to the name according to the nature of the **Class** object.

Here's an example of using the **Class** class:

```
class ClassTest
{
    public static void main(String args[])
    {
        // Create a new object
        ClassTest t = new ClassTest(),
                other = null;

        t.sayHi();

        // Use the Object.getClass() method
        Class c = t.getClass();

        // Implicitly invoke toString()
        System.out.println( c );

        // Create a new object using newInstance()
        try {
```

```
        other = (ClassTest) c.newInstance();
    } catch (Exception e) {
        System.out.println(e);
        System.exit(1);
    }

    // Invoke a method of the new object
    other.sayHi();
}

void sayHi()
{
    System.out.println("Hi");
}
}
```

The output of this example is:

```
Hi
class ClassTest
Hi
```

ClassLoader - Loading Classes at Run Time

Loading classes in run time is an amazing feature of Java. Just think of all the things you can do with this:

▲ Shorten the load time of applets by first loading only a tiny kernel and then adding only the capabilities you need.

▲ Save memory that's taken up by rarely used features.

▲ Extend your application dynamically, adding new features to an existing code *without* changing it.

▲ Patch an application without taking it all off line, just unload the piece that needs to be patched, patch it, and load it back.

▲ And much more...

When running a Java program, you never have to explicitly load *all* the classes that make your applications, you only need to specify the main class. The Java run-time system—either the one embedded in a web browser or the stand-alone interpreter—uses a dynamic class loading mechanism to load them for you. It examines the references to other classes, loads all the classes needed by your application automatically and starts the run of the application.

When you wish to add your own on-the-fly class loading, you can use the same mechanism Java uses, programmatically. This feature is available through subclasses of the abstract class **ClassLoader** that's found in the **java.lang** package. These classes load other classes from any source (local file system, the network, etc.) and provide a **Class** object you can instantiate using **Class.NewInstance()**.

```
public abstract class java.lang.ClassLoader extends java.lang.Object
{
    // Constructors
    protected ClassLoader();
```

```
    // Methods
    protected final Class defineClass(byte  data[], int  offset,
                                      int  length);
    protected final Class findSystemClass(String  name);
    protected abstract Class loadClass(String  name, boolean  resolve);
    protected final void resolveClass(Class  c);
}
```

As you can see, **ClassLoader** is an abstract class. You should extend it to create your own special loader.

An instance of a class often references other classes. To determine these classes, Java obtains the **ClassLoader** of that instance and tells it to load the referenced classes–assuming the object handle is **theObject**, it does the equivalent of:

```
theObject.getClass().getClassLoader().loadClass("referred class",  resolve);
```

If Java only needs to determine if the class exists (and if it does exist to know its superclass), it invokes the method with the **resolve** flag set to false.

If the referred class is being instantiated or any of its methods are being called, the class must also be resolved. Java invokes **loadClass()** with the **resolve** flag set to true. In this case, your implementation should invoke the **resolveClass()** method.

Following is a skeleton implementation of a class loader. In order to be able to instantiate your class, you must define the method **loadClass()**.

Your class loader should obtain the bytecode (the bytes that make up the class's code) of the class to instantiate. This can be obtained from **.class** files on your local file system or the network, a compressed class file or any source you fancy. Once loaded, your implementation should invoke the **defineClass()** method to create a class instance.

To avoid unnecessary lengthy load operations, most class loaders implement a cache of previously loaded classes using a hash table. Once a class is loaded once, successive loads are much faster.

Here's a skeleton of a class loader. In order to create your own loader, fill in the missing parts (the initialization of the class and the actual loading mechanism).

```
import java.util.*;

class MyClassLoader extends ClassLoader
{
    Hashtable classCache;

    public MyClassLoader(String sourceIdentifier)
    {
        // Initialize
        ...
    }

    public  synchronized Class loadClass(String name, boolean resolve)
    {
        // Check to see if we have the class cached
        Class c = (Class) classCache.get(name);
```

```
    if (c == null)
    {
        // Class was not loaded previously, need to load it

        byte  data[] = null;  // this byte array will hold the bytecode.

        // load the class - here you implement your own loading
        ...

        // The class is defined and stored in the cache for future use
        c = defineClass(data, 0, data.length);
        classCache.put(name,  c);
    }

    if (resolve)
        resolveClass(c);

    return  c;
    }
}
```

Example usage of the class is:

```
ClassLoader myLoader = new myClassLoader("packedClass.zip");
Class       main     = myLoader.loadClass("SomeClass", true).newInstance();
```

The Applet Class

Applets are probably the spark that started the Java rush. They were the first interactive content of the web and took the WWW into a new era.

Applets are actually classes derived from the **Applet** class (found in the **java.applet** package). This class defines the basic functionality for applets, and all other applets override the (do-nothing) default implementation to create swirling applications rich with graphics, animation, and sound.

Unlike applications that run on their own, applets run inside Java-aware applications like a web browser. They don't have a single entry point (like **main()** for applications) but rather provide a set of methods that are called 'from the outside' by the Java enabled applications they run in. These methods define the applet's behavior in regards to external events.

The Major Events in an Applet's Life

Applets have a very simple life cycle. They're first loaded and get a chance to initialize, they then start running and may be stopped and restarted many times before finally being unloaded.

The following diagram depicts the life cycle of applets along with the different methods that are being called on state transition.

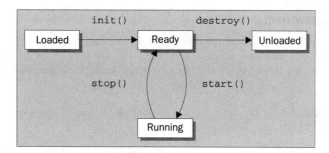

The default implementations of these methods do nothing. Classes that wish to:

- Initialize themselves
- Do something special when they enter the 'running' state
- Do something special when they stop running, or
- Cleanup before being unloaded

should override the relevant method(s). It isn't necessary to override any of the methods for your applet to do something useful.

init()

The **init()** method is the place to perform any initialization your class needs in order to start running. This may include loading images and sound, setting up parameters, and so on.

start()

This method is invoked before your applet enters the 'running' state. If your applet kicks off threads, this is a good place to start them running (threads are discussed in the next chapter). Note that **start()** may be invoked more than once during the lifetime of your applet.

stop()

This method is invoked whenever your applet exists in the 'running' state. By default, when the browser leaves the page that displays your applet, the applet continues to run, consuming CPU time and other resources. If your applet does nothing meaningful, you should override the **stop()** method. Animating an image that isn't displayed is considered not meaningful, but performing a calculation or fetching a file from a remote server may be considered meaningful.

destroy()

This method is invoked before the applet is unloaded. It's often used to free resources and other things of that sort. You may wonder what the difference is between **finalize()** and **destroy()**. The difference is that unlike **finalize()**, which isn't guaranteed to be invoked, **destroy()** is always invoked.

While You Were Running...

While an applet is running, a lot of things may happen to it: the user may click the graphical output area of the applet, the mouse may enter or leave that area, the user may press different keys, the applet may need repainting, and so on. It's these events and the way you handle them that define the behavior of your applet.

Many of the events are handled by supplying your own implementation to the event-handling methods of the **Applet** class. Such methods are:

```
public boolean lostFocus(Event evt, Object  what);
public boolean mouseDown(Event evt, int  x, int y);
public String getAppletInfo();
```

For a complete listing of the methods you can override, please refer to the API.

Although graphics programming and the AWT are discussed in later chapters, I'd like to introduce one method of the **Applet** class that has to do with graphics:

```
public void paint(Graphics g);
```

The **paint()** method is inherited from **Applet**'s ancestor, **Component**. This method is invoked whenever the applet's surface needs painting. This can happen when the applet is first drawn, when the window displaying the applet is exposed after being obscured by some other window, periodically in animating applets, and other occasions.

The parameter **g** , an instance of the **Graphics** class, is a graphic context supplied to the applet by the application in which the applet is running. The **Graphics** class will be discussed later when we talk about the AWT, but one method of the class:

```
public abstract void drawString(String  str, int  x, int  y);
```

will be used in the following example. This method displays the specified string in the specified **x**, **y** coordinates on the applet's surface.

The following simple applet overrides the paint method to display a greeting message on the applet's surface.

```
import java.applet.Applet;
import java.awt.Graphics;

public class MyApplet extends Applet
{
   public void paint(Graphics g)
   {
      g.drawString("Hello there", 10,10 );
   }

}
```

If you run this applet, you'll see something like this:

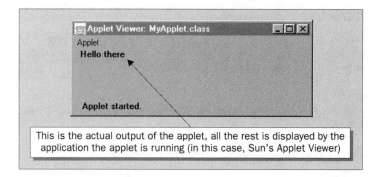

This is the actual output of the applet, all the rest is displayed by the application the applet is running (in this case, Sun's Applet Viewer)

The Applet HTML tag

Applets are embedded in Hyper Text Markup Language (HTML) files. HTML is a simple language used to create web pages. The following section assumes some knowledge of HTML.

> *If you don't know HTML and wish to publish on the World Wide Web, you may want to lean HTML from one of the many online guides found on the web (the web is really very self-contained). Links to HTML tutorials on the web can be found at:*
>
> *http://www.w3.org/pub/WWW/MarkUp/*
>
> *and other places on the WWW. Alternatively, check out the forthcoming Instant HTML from Wrox Press.*

The minimal HTML tag for applets is:

```
<applet code = ClassURL width = InitialWidth height = InitialHeight >
</applet>
```

where **ClassURL** is a quoted string specifying the URL of the applet (absolute path or relative to the HTML file's location). The **InitialWidth** and **InitialHeight** specify the initial width and height of the applet's drawing area.

As you can see, the applet tag is made of two parts. The first denotes the beginning of the applet definition section, and the second denotes its end. Any text, image, or anything else that appears between the opening and losing tag markers (except for applet parameters–which we'll see in the next section), are ignored by Java-aware browsers.

HTML syntax defines that any tag that isn't recognized by a browser is ignored. This, along with the definition of the applet tags, means that you can write a single HTML file that would render differently on Java-aware and Java-challenged browsers. The former would display the applet and the latter anything that comes between the applet tags. Here's a snippet of such an HTML file

```
<applet code = "MyApplet" width = 150 height = 50 >
A Java aware browser would display an applet here.
</applet>
```

Applet Parameters

You can pass parameters to a Java application using the command line. The application could then parse the command line and act according the supplied parameters. However, applets don't run from the command line. How then can you pass arguments to an applet?

The applet HTML tag can also include parameter declarations. These parameters are read along with the rest of the HTML file by the browser, and passed to the applet upon request. The syntax for applet parameters is:

```
<param name= ParameterName value= ParameterValue>
```

where **ParameterName** is the name of the parameter and **ParameterValue** is a quoted string containing the value of that parameter. (Unlike command line parameters, applet parameters have a name, allowing them to appear in any order.)

Here's an example of sending parameters to applets (again, this is only a snippet from the complete HTML file needed by the browser):

```
<applet code = "MyApplet" width = 150 height = 50 >
<param name="Message" value="This is a Java applet">
</applet>
```

An applet can obtain parameters using:

```
public String getParameter(String   name)
```

This method returns the value of the named parameter in the HTML file. The name argument is case-insensitive, meaning that the name of the parameter in the HTML file and the name in your applet may have different capitalization.

The following applet is an extension of the previous one. Instead of printing a hard-coded message, it prints the message specified in the HTML file.

```
import java.applet.Applet;
import java.awt.Graphics;

public class MyBetterApplet extends Applet
{
    public void paint(Graphics g)
    {
        String msg = getParameter("MESSAGE");

        if (msg==null) msg = "Default Message";

        g.drawString(msg, 10,10 );
    }
}
```

When this applet is embedded in this HTML file:

```
<HTML>
<head>
<title "Testing MyBetterApplet">
</head>

<body>
<applet code="MyBetterApplet.class" width=150 height=50>
<param name=message value="This is a Java applet">
<P>
I'm sorry, your browser doesn't support Java, so you can't see this applet.
</applet>
</body>
</HTML>
```

and you view the HTML file using Sun's Applet Viewer, you'll see something like this:

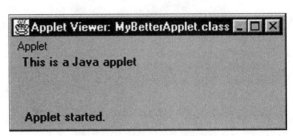

Summary

In this chapter, we've reviewed some of Java's fundamental classes. These include classes from the packages **java.lang** and **java.util** in particular. Remember that you should refer to the API for more details.

We've also discussed the Applet class, and seen how you can put together a basic applet. We'll do more with applets in the AWT chapters (Chapters 7 to 11).

Threads

"Two roads diverge in a yellow wood,
I chose to travel both" **

Multithreading can enhance the performance of Java applets and applications, making them more responsive and interactive. It can simplify the design and implementation of things that are very hard to do in a single threaded program, thus helping the programmer create better programs. When used properly, they are a programmer-friendly feature.

In this chapter we'll cover:

- What threads are and how they are created
- Thread states and priorities
- Synchronization and monitors
- Being thread-safe
- The hazards of multithreading

Understanding Threads

Before we start talking about threads in Java we need to understand the concepts and ideas behind threads.

What Are Threads?

A **thread** is a single sequential flow of execution that runs through your program.

All programmers are familiar with writing sequential programs. These all have a starting point (for example, the very first statement in your **main()** method), a sequence of execution and an endpoint (the very last statement executed in your program). The most important thing about sequential programs is that at any given time there is a single statement being executed.

The program itself only defines a place where things can happen. For a program to actually do something, it must have at least one thread of execution running through it. When you execute a program, Java creates a new thread and runs it through the **main()** method of that program. It's that thread that defines the starting point, the sequence of execution and the endpoint of the program. A thread can't exist on its own, it must have a program to host it.

The thing about threads is that you can potentially have more than one thread running at the *same time* inside a single program. (We'll look at exactly what this means a bit later.)

**Apologies to Robert Frost for altering his poem "The Road Not Taken"*

> **Every program starts executing as the result of Java running a single thread through its main() method. This is true both for single-threaded and multithreaded programs. This thread is called the *main* thread.**

In a multithreaded program, existing threads spawn new threads that run in parallel with them. A thread can spawn another thread to do some work on its behalf, to do something completely independent, or any combination of the two.

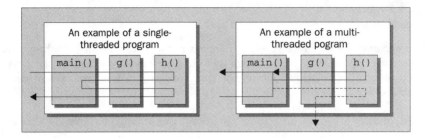

Synchronization mechanisms and thread priorities can be used to control the execution order of independent and collaborating threads.

Why Use Threads?

A single thread offers nothing new. The added value is gained when using multiple threads. This means that your application can seem to do more than one thing at a time. Each thread can do something different (for example, one can load an image over the network while another animates a cloudy sky) or they can all do the same work (e.g. collaborate in rendering a 3D scene).

Threads can help in creating a better application. A good example of threads put to use is a word processor that can print (paginate, lay out and send the output to the printer or spool device) in the 'background'. You can continue editing while the pages are sent to the printer. Imagine writing sequential interleaved code that would perform both tasks at the same time.

Threads can also speed up calculations. By breaking a task down into sub-tasks and then having a different thread execute each sub-task, you can dramatically increase the speed of execution.

This is obviously true if you have a system with more than one processor. Have each processor work on a different task and you get a great improvement in performance. But what about systems with only one processor?

Many tasks can logically be broken down into two phases: compute bound phases and I/O bound phases. The compute bound phases require the full attention of the CPU, utilizing it for various calculations. The I/O bound phases require the attention of various input and output devices (printers, hard-disks, network cards etc.) and in these phases the CPU is mostly idle, waiting for the I/O device to do its stuff.

Speed is gained by the interleaving of phases. While a thread in an I/O bound phase waits for data to be loaded from the hard disk, a compute bound thread can utilize the CPU, and when it arrives at the I/O bound phase, the other thread (having completed the I/O bound phase) can start utilizing the CPU.

Concurrent Execution and Context Switching

Without starting a discussion on hardware issues, it's correct to say that a computer's CPU can only execute one command at a time. Why then did I say earlier that different threads can seem to run at the same time?

Well, what actually happens is that instead of having one thread run through and then another and then another, all the different threads run in an interleaved fashion (one runs for a little while, then another and then another and so on), creating the illusion that they're all running simultaneously. This illusion seems as real as the illusion that the discrete 30 images per second captured by the human eye are actually a continuous stream of images. We poor humans can't notice the difference.

The process of one thread relinquishing the CPU and another thread starting to run is called a **context switch**. In a context switch, the currently running thread is suspended and another thread (that was previously suspended) is resumed. Since a compiled program is actually executed one bytecode instruction after another, and since there's no measure of the time that passes between the execution of one instruction and the next, a thread doesn't know it has been suspended and resumed.

Let's examine the term **context** a little further. When many threads run through the same code, we want each thread to have its own independent point of execution and local variables, otherwise all the threads would do exactly the same thing. When we say that each thread has its own context, we mean that each running thread has its own point of execution and private view of the values of local variables. One point to note though is that while having **separate contexts**, the different threads share the **same memory space**. This means that all the threads see the same objects and values of properties. They can seamlessly share object handles and affect the way other threads run.

Why Not Use Threads?

Context switches cost. It takes time for the CPU to 'freeze' the state of one thread and 'thaw' another. If the concurrent threads run on a single CPU and are all compute bound, then the total execution time will often be longer than the time it would take linear code to return the same result.

More often than not it's better to use threads (even if it slows down your calculations a little) to parallel independent operations, but it makes no sense using threads when there is no need to. For example, to find an element in an array, *don't* spawn a thread for each element and have each thread compare the content of the element with the searched value.

Threading with Java

Now that you understand the concept of a thread, let's see how multithreading is supported in Java.

Java threads are implemented by the **Thread** class which is part of the **java.lang** package. The **Thread** class implements a **system-independent** encapsulation of threads. The actual implementation of threads is often provided by the underlying operating system, and the **Thread** class provides a unified interface for all the systems. However, although the interface is the same, there are some implementation differences that you should take into account when programming your multithreaded application (as you'll see later).

Since the implementation of threads may be different across the various operating systems, and even across different implementations of Java on the same operating system, your multithreaded application might behave differently with each interpreter.

Creating a New Thread

For a thread to be able to execute a class's method, the class has to either:

- Extend the **Thread** class (which implements **Runnable** itself), or
- Implement the **Runnable** interface, an interface every class must support in order to run as a separate thread.

Here's a simple rule of thumb to help you decide what option to use: if your class *must* be derived from some other class (the most common example being **Applet**) then it should implement **Runnable**, otherwise it should extend **Thread**.

Classes that you can instantiate such objects from are called **runnable classes**, and the objects are called **runnable objects**.

Extending the Thread Class

Consider the following class:

```
class MyThread extends Thread {
    public void run() {
        System.out.println ("Hello World!");
    }
}
```

This class extends the **Thread** class and overrides one of its methods–the **run()** method. The **run()** method contains the code that the thread executes. For most ongoing threads this method contains an infinite loop.

In order to start the execution of the **run()** method in a class that extends **Thread**, you first need to instantiate it and then invoke the created object's **start()** method. The **start()** method makes the thread active and subsequently invokes the **run()** method.

Remember–don't invoke run() directly, always invoke the **start()** method which will itself invoke run().

Here's a class that spawns a new **MyThread** thread:

```
class MyTest {
    public static void main(String Args[]) {
        new MyThread().start();
    }
}
```

This code, combined with the **MyThread** class code above, prints "Hello World!" on the screen. What actually happens is this: the **main()** method starts the thread and terminates. The new thread doesn't terminate when the **main()** function is done. It executes its **run()** method independently. The **run()** method simply prints "Hello World!" and exits. When both the thread that runs **main()** and the thread that it created terminate, the run-time system exits.

Note that on some implementations of Java, this program doesn't appear to end. If this happens, just press Ctrl-C to exit.

Implementing the Runnable Interface

The other way to create threads is for a class to implement the **Runnable** interface. Here's an example:

```
class MyThread implements Runnable {
    public void run() {
        System.out.println ("Hello World!");
    }
}
```

A class that implements the **Runnable** interface can extend *any* class. It's the implementation of the **Runnable** interface that makes it runnable. Although creating a runnable entity this way seems very similar to the former way, spawning the thread in this case is a little different:

```
class MyTest {
    public static void main(String Args[]) {
        new Thread(new MyThread()).start();
    }
}
```

Note that this time, we used another constructor from the **Thread** class to instantiate a thread. This constructor requires a handle to a runnable object. (In this example, we use the handle returned by the **new** operator directly).

Other Constructors of the Thread Class

The other constructors in the **Thread** class all use the following prototype:

```
Thread( ThreadGroup, Runnable, String )
```

(all the parameters are optional—for the full list see the Java language API).

Specifying the **ThreadGroup** parameter assigns the thread to a **thread group**: a set of threads that enables all the threads in it to be manipulated as a whole (thread groups are discussed later). The **Runnable** parameter is the source of the new thread's **run()** method (a handle to a runnable object). The **String** parameter supplies a name for the new thread. This name can be used in conjunction with the **Thread** class's method **getName()** for mnemonic reference to the thread.

Daemon Threads

The **Thread** class provides a mechanism that enables you to use a thread for background processing, and have it killed automatically if it's never going to be given any work to do. These threads exist for the purpose of providing a certain service and are known as **daemon threads**.

For example, the HotJava web browser has a daemon thread, named Background Image Reader, that reads images from the file system or network for any object or thread that needs an image.

Being a service provider, the **run()** method for a daemon thread is typically an infinite loop that waits for a service request.

Any thread can become a daemon or return from a daemon mode to a non-daemon mode by invoking the **setDaemon()** method. You can check the state of a thread using the **isDaemon()** method.

When there are only daemon threads running in a program, the run-time environment will terminate its execution.

Parallel Execution of Threads

Even though the examples above don't seem to exhibit any parallelism, they do actually do things in parallel. Once the **Thread.start()** statement finished execution, the instance of **MyThread** started running. It's not unlikely that the "Hello World!" message was printed before **main()** had finished execution. In fact, the printing thread may have ended before the main thread. It all depends on the way the processor's time was allocated to the threads, and whether there is more than one processor.

To demonstrate this principle, consider the following program and its output:

```
class PrintThread implements Runnable {
    String str;

    public PrintThread (String str) {
        this.str = str;
    }

    public void run() {
        for (;;)
            System.out.print (str);
    }
}

class ConcurrencyTest {
    public static void main (String Args[]) {
        new Thread(new PrintThread("A")).start();
        new Thread(new PrintThread("B")).start();
    }
}
```

If you run this program on a Java interpreter where Java threads are implemented using a pre-emptive timeslicing method, the output will look like this, which was taken from a Windows NT machine running SUN's JDK:

AAAAAAAAAAAAAAAAAAAAAAAAAAAAAAAAAAAAAABBBBBBBBBBBBBBBBBBBBBBBBBBBBBBBBBBBBBBBBBBB
AAAAAAAAAAAAAAAAAAAAAAAAAAAAAAAAAAAAAAAABBBBBBBBBBBBBBBBBBBBBBBBBBBBBBBBBBBBBBBBBB
BBBAAAAAAAAAAAAAAAAAAAAAAAAAAAAAAAAAAAAAAAAAAAABBBBBBBBBBBBBBBBBBBBBBBBBBBBBBBBBBB
BBBAAAAAAAAAAAAAAAAAAAAAAAAAAAAAAAAABBBBBBBBBBBBBBBBBB...

The output has fairly equal number of As and Bs.

Other implementations of the Java interpreter which don't use pre-emptive multitasking of threads will have a rather different output. Both types of output are 'correct', but you need to allow for differences between the implementation of threads on different Java interpreters and host systems.

Preemptive vs. Non-preemptive Multithreading

Preemptive multithreading means that a thread may be preempted by another thread with an equal priority while it's running. The Java run time won't preempt the currently running thread for another thread of the same priority. However, the underlying operating system implementation of threads may do so if it supports preemption of equal priority threads.

The output of the previous example program on an implementation of Java for the Solaris operating system is something like this:

AAAAAAAAAAAAAAAAAAAAAAAAAAAAAAAAAAAAAAAAAAAAAAAAAAAAAAAAAAAAAAAAAAAAAAAAAAAAAA
AAAAAAAAAAAAAAAAAAAAAAAAAAAAAAAAAAAAAAAAAAAAAAAAAAAAAAAAAAAAAAAAAAAAAAAAAAAAAA
AAAAAAAAAAAAAAAAAAAAAAAAAAAAAAAAAAAAAAAAAAAAAAAAAAAAAAAAAAAAAAAAAAAAAAAAAAAAAA
AAAAAAAAAAAAAAAAAAAAAAAAAAAAAAAAAAAAAAAAAAAAAAAAAAA...

This is because that implementation doesn't use the preemptive multitasking capabilities of Solaris.

> **Since a system that supports multithreading won't necessarily have a preemption mechanism, you should never rely on preemptive multithreaded scheduling.**

Yielding to the CPU

A thread is supposed to be *well-behaved* and give up the CPU periodically in order for other threads to be able to run. If your thread doesn't give up the CPU by suspending itself, waiting for a condition or sleeping, then it should relinquish the CPU periodically by invoking the **Thread** class's **yield()** method.

Here's a revised version of the **PrintThread** class that yields to the CPU after each letter is printed:

```
class WellBehavedPrintThread implements Runnable {
    String str;
    public WellBehavedPrintThread(String str) {
        this.str = str;
    }
    public void run() {
        for (;;) {
            System.out.print (str);
            Thread.currentThread().yield();
        }
    }
}
```

The statement **Thread.currentThread().yield()** uses a **public static** method of the **Thread** class to get a handle to the currently running thread and then tells it to yield. This is just to show off **currentThread()**–you can do the same thing by invoking the public method **yield()** with no object e.g. **Thread.yield()**. This also causes the current thread to yield.

The output of this example is:

ABABABABABABABABABABABABABABABABABABABABABABABABABABABABABABABABABABABABABABABA

167

BABABABABABABABABABABABABABABABABABABABABABABABABABABABABABABABABABA
BABABABABABABABABABABABABABABABABABABABABABABABABABABABABABABABABABA
BABABABABABABABABABABABABABABABABABABABABABABABABABABABABABAB...

As a rule of thumb, threads should yield whenever possible, to allow others run.

Thread States

A thread can be in various states according to past events. Following is a table that summarizes the different states a thread can be in:

State	Description
A **newly created** instance	The thread's **run()** method isn't being run, so processor time won't be allocated. In order to start the thread, you have to invoke its **start()** method. In this state it's also possible to invoke the **stop()** method, which would kill the thread.
A **running** thread	The thread has been started by invoking the **start()** method. It's the thread that the CPU is currently running. (On MP systems there may be more than one running thread at a given time.)
A **runnable** thread	The thread has been started, but it isn't being run by a CPU at this time. This could be because the thread has given up the CPU by invoking its **yield()** method, or because the scheduling mechanism decided to take the CPU from the thread and give it to some other thread. The thread will become a running thread again when the scheduling mechanism decides so. As long as there's another thread with a higher priority, the thread won't become running. (We'll discuss thread priorities in a moment).
A **non-runnable** thread	The thread can't run for some reason. It may be waiting for an I/O operation to finish; it may have invoked the **wait()**, **sleep()** or **suspend()** methods, or some other thread may have invoked its **sleep()** or **suspend()** method. To become runnable again, whatever happened to the thread must be reversed.

Here's a chart that shows how a thread moves from one state to another:

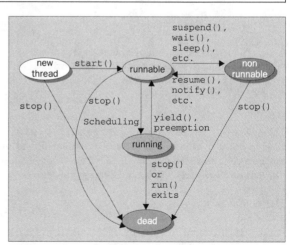

When the **stop()** method is invoked, the thread dies without considering its current state. Applets often use the **stop()** method to kill all of their threads when the Java-enabled browser in which they are running tells them to stop (for example, when the user exits the page in which the applet is embedded).

Thread Priorities

Each thread is assigned a **priority**, ranging from **Thread.MIN_PRIORITY** (equals 1) to **Thread.MAX_PRIORITY** (equals 10). A thread inherits its priority from the thread that spawned it.

> **Remember that you shouldn't use the numbers directly as they may change. Instead, use the constant properties of the Thread class.**

The **scheduling algorithm** always lets the highest priority runnable thread run. If at any time a thread with a higher priority than all other runnable threads becomes runnable, the run-time system schedules it for execution. The new higher priority thread preempts the other threads.

If there are several runnable high-priority threads, the CPU is allocated to all of them, one at a time, in a round-robin fashion.

A lower priority thread can only run when all higher priority threads are non-runnable.

The priority of the main thread (the thread that starts the **main()** method of your program) is **Thread.NORM_PRIORITY** (equals 5).

You can set a thread's priority by invoking the **setPriority()** method and get the thread's priority by invoking **getPriority()**.

Here's an example of using high- and low-priority threads:

```
class LowPriority extends Thread {
    public void run(){
        setPriority(Thread.MIN_PRIORITY);

        for(;;){
            System.out.println("The LOW priority thread is running");
        }
    }
}

class HighPriority extends Thread {
    public void run(){
        setPriority(Thread.MAX_PRIORITY);

        for(;;){

            for (int i=0; i<5; i++)
                System.out.println("The HIGH priority thread is running");

            try {
                sleep(100);
            } catch (InterruptedException e) {
                System.exit(0);
            }
        }
    }
}
```

169

```
class Spawner {
    public static void main( String args[] ) {
        LowPriority  l = new LowPriority();
        HighPriority h = new HighPriority();

        System.out.println("Starting threads...");

        l.start();
        h.start();

        // Let the other threads start running
        Thread.currentThread().yield();

        System.out.println("MAIN is done");
    }
}
```

Notice the **try...catch** statement surrounding the **sleep(100)** statement. A thread that goes to sleep may be interrupted by invoking its **interrupt()** method. This causes the **sleep()** method to throw an **InterruptedException** which must be caught. Other than that the code is pretty simple.

The output from this example look something like this:

```
Starting threads...
The HIGH priority thread is running
The HIGH priority thread is running
The HIGH priority thread is running
The HIGH priority thread is running
The HIGH priority thread is running
MAIN is done
The LOW priority thread is running
...
The LOW priority thread is running
The HIGH priority thread is running
The HIGH priority thread is running
The HIGH priority thread is running
The HIGH priority thread is running
The LOW priority thread is running
...
The LOW priority thread is running
The HIGH priority thread is running
^C
```

Let's examine the output.

The very first line is printed by the main thread. The main thread kicks off the low- and high-priority threads and yields to let them start running. The low-priority thread starts running, sets its priority as low and is immediately made not-runnable as the other threads are of higher priority and can run. The high-priority thread starts running, sets its priority high and thus starts running on its own (the other threads have lesser priorities). After printing 5 lines, it goes to sleep and the main thread is summoned (it's the highest priority runnable thread). The main priority thread prints a goodbye message and terminates. Now the only runnable thread is the low-priority thread.

From this point on the output follows a pattern. The low-priority thread prints its message repeatedly until the high-priority thread wakes up. The high-priority thread starts running, prints its 5 lines and goes to sleep again. The low-priority thread can then run again.

Thread Groups

Each thread belongs to a **thread group**. A thread group is a set of threads (and possibly other thread groups) with mechanisms to perform operations on all the members of the set.

Each newly created thread joins the same thread group that the thread that spawned it belongs to, unless otherwise specified in its constructor. When an application first starts up, Java creates a thread group named 'main', and creates the main thread of your application in it. If you don't specify other thread groups to run your threads in, they are all created inside the main thread group. (If your threads are created inside an applet, it's possible that the initial thread group will be called something other than 'main' depending on the browser the applet is running in.) To find out which group a thread belongs to, you can use the **getThreadGroup()** method.

In order to create your own thread group, you first need to create a **ThreadGroup** object. You can use one of these two constructors:

```
ThreadGroup(String)

ThreadGroup(ThreadGroup, String)
```

The first creates a new **ThreadGroup** with the specified name and the second creates a new **ThreadGroup** with the specified name in the specified thread group. In order to create a thread inside a thread group other than main, you have to specify it when invoking the thread's constructor. The newly created thread group becomes a member of the older one, creating a hierarchy of groups. Note that construction is the only time when you can assign a thread to a specific thread group.

The following code snippet shows how to create a new thread group and assign a thread that runs the **myRunnableObject** to it:

```
ThreadGroup myThreadGroup = new ThreadGroup("A Group of threads");
Thread myThread = new Thread(myThreadGroup, myRunnableObject, "a thread");
```

Now that you have threads organized in a group, you can invoke common operations on all these threads. The main operations used in conjunction with a group of threads are **stop()**, **suspend()** and **resume()**, which have the same meaning as when used with a single thread (for other operations applicable to a thread group see the API).

Using groups can ease operations. For example, when a tree search is executed in parallel, and the hierarchy of groups reflects the structure of the tree, stopping groups of processes instead of one process at a time can save computing resources. You can also use groups collectively to manage different tasks in an application.

Thread Synchronization

If you're using several threads, you often need to be able to synchronize their activities. There are also cases where you need to prevent concurrent access to data structures in the program that are shared among the threads. Java helps you do these things by providing built-in mechanisms for **synchronization** and **mutual exclusion** (allowing only one thread to run through critical code sections in the program).

Consider the following class. This class stores integer data in a private property, and supplies a **store**/ **load** interface:

```java
class MyData {
    private int Data;

    public void store(int Data) {
        this.Data=Data;
    }

    public int load() {
        return this.Data;
    }
}
```

Now suppose there are two threads in the system. The first is trying to store values and the second is trying to fetch the stored values. Here's the code that creates those threads. In order to simulate processing time in a 'real system' (and at the same time create well-behaved threads), we send the threads to sleep after each fetched number.

```java
class Main {    // This class is used to set things in motion.
    public static void main(String argv[]) {
        MyData data = new MyData();
        new Thread(new Producer(data)).start();
        new Thread(new Consumer(data)).start();
    }
}

class Producer implements Runnable {      // The producer thread class
    MyData data;
    public Producer(MyData data) {
        this.data=data;
    }

    public void run() {
        int i;
        for (i=0;;i++) {
            data.store(i);
            System.out.println ("Producer: "+i);
            try {
                // doze off for a random time (0 to 0.5 sec)
                Thread.sleep ((int) (Math.random()*500));
            } catch (InterruptedException e) { }
        }
    }
}
```

```
class Consumer implements Runnable { // The consumer thread
   MyData data;
   public Consumer(MyData data) {
      this.data=data;
   }

   public void run() {
      for (;;) {
         System.out.println ("Consumer: "+data.load());
         try {
            // doze off for a random time (0 to 0.5 sec)
            Thread.sleep ((int) (Math.random()*500));
         } catch (InterruptedException e) { }
      }
   }
}
```

This program consists of two threads: **Consumer** and **Producer**. The producer is 'producing' numbers by putting them into the shared data structure **MyData** using its method. The consumer is 'consuming' those numbers by retrieving them from the shared data structure.

The Problem

At first glance the code seems okay, but this isn't the case as the output shows: (We've arranged the output from the different processes in two columns to make it more readable.)

```
Producer: 0
                        Consumer: 0
Producer: 1
                        Consumer: 1
                        Consumer: 1
Producer: 2
Producer: 3
                        Consumer: 3
Producer: 4
Producer: 5
                        Consumer: 5
Producer: 6
                        Consumer: 6
Producer: 7
                        Consumer: 7
                        Consumer: 7
Producer: 8
Producer: 9
Producer: 10
                        Consumer: 10
```

As you can see, here the numbers 2, 4, 8 and 9 were 'produced', but never 'consumed'. On the other hand, the numbers 1 and 7 were 'produced' once, but 'consumed' twice!

This unfortunate result is due to a 'wrong' execution order. The problem is twofold:

▲ The producer has no way of knowing that the consumer hasn't consumed the data yet, and therefore overwrites it.

▲ The consumer has no way of knowing whether the value it reads is a new value or an old one.

A First Solution

In order to solve the problem we can use ordinary Boolean variables as flags to control data access. The **Ready** flag will signify that new data has been produced and is ready to be consumed, and the **Taken** flag will signify that the data was consumed and it's okay to overwrite it:

```java
class MyData {
    private int Data;
    private boolean Ready;
    private boolean Taken;

    public MyData() {
        Ready=false;
        Taken=true;
    }

    public void store(int Data) {
        while (!Taken);

        this.Data=Data;
        Taken=false;
        Ready=true;
    }

    public int load() {
        int Data;

        while (!Ready);
        Data = this.Data;      // save the value because once
                               // Taken is "true" it may
                               // change at any time.
        Ready=false;
        Taken=true;
        return Data;
    }
}
```

The code above will achieve the expected results: each number is consumed only once and all the numbers are consumed. However, it has a major disadvantage: the **store()** and **load()** methods are using **busy-wait loops**. The threads are constantly checking the flags to see if their value has been changed.

Using a busy-wait loop might prevent this program from working on non-preemptive platforms because the threads in this example don't give up the CPU and so the other thread (that should change the value– releasing them from the loop) might not be scheduled to run (though this specific problem could be easily solved by inserting a **Thread.yield()** in the busy-wait loop).

When using the same code with more than one consumer, another problem that might occur is a **race condition**. Running more than one thread through the **Consumer** class and having the different threads consuming from the same source can lead to a situation where the same value is consumed more than once (this problem can only occur on preemptive platforms). Here's an example of a possible race condition:

```
Consumer 1              Consumer 2              Producer

while (!Ready);
                        while (!Ready);
                                                this.Data=Data;
                                                Taken=false;
                                                Ready=true;
Data=this.Data;
                        Data=this.Data;
Ready=false;
Taken=true;
return Data;
                        Ready=false;
                        Taken=true;
                        return Data;
```

As you can see, the two consumers consumed the same value. This can easily happen if the threads share a single processor, or if multiple processors run the threads at the same time.

A solution to the latter problem is to use a built-in Java synchronization mechanism—**monitors**.

Monitors

Java supports thread synchronization through the use of monitors. A monitor is an inhibitor, like a token that a thread can acquire and release. A monitor is associated with a specific object and functions as a lock on that object. When a thread holds the monitor for an object, other threads trying to access the object in a synchronized fashion are locked out. A thread can acquire the monitor of an object if no other thread currently owns it, and it can release it at will. A thread can re-acquire a monitor if it already owns it.

> *Monitors were first outlined in C. A. R. Hoare's article Communicating Sequential Processes (Communications of the ACM, Vol. 21, No. 8, August 1978, pp. 666-677). They were later implemented in some concurrent programming languages like Pascal-S and Java.*

The code segments within a program that mustn't be accessed concurrently are known as **critical sections**. In Java, you declare a code segment to be a critical section using the **synchronized** keyword.

Declaring a code section synchronized is done like this:

```
void myClass()
{
    // Unsynchronized code
    ...
    synchronized (objectWhoseMonitorIsToBeUsed)
    {
        // Synchronized block
        ...
```

```
    }
    // More unsynchronized code
    ...
}
```

The monitor of the object whose handle is given inside the parentheses is used as a lock on the synchronized section. Only the thread that owns the key (monitor) may enter that section.

You may have any number of synchronized blocks in a method, and the synchronization blocks can also be nested.

You can declare an entire method to be synchronized like this:

```
synchronized myMethod(...)
{
    // Synchronized block
    ...
}
```

The monitor used in this case is the one attached to the object this method is invoked on. If the method is a static method, it uses a global instance that's implicitly created by Java.

If possible, it's better to declare an entire method synchronized (instead of synchronizing a single block inside the method using **this**) as it makes your program easier to understand.

Declaring a code section **synchronized** means that only the thread holding the monitor can run through it in that instance. If no thread owns the monitor, the act of accessing the synchronized section (invoking the method or executing the **synchronized()** statement) causes the thread to acquire it. The monitor acquisition is a single **atomic operation** which guarantees that only one thread will get the monitor. An atomic operation guarantees that once it's started, the processor won't be allocated to any other thread until it's finished.

Synchronization Using Monitors

Following is an example of our **MyData** class using synchronized methods:

```
class MyData {
    private int Data;
    private boolean Ready;
    private boolean Taken;

    public MyData() {
        Ready=false;
        Taken=true;
    }

    public synchronized void store(int Data) {
        while (!Taken);
        this.Data=Data;
        Taken=false;
        Ready=true;
    }

    public synchronized int load() {
```

```
        while (!Ready);
        Ready=false;
        Taken=true;
        return this.Data;
    }
}
```

Notice how declaring the methods **synchronized** removes the need for storing the value of the **Data** variable in the **load()** method. The **load()** and **store()** won't be able to execute at the same time in different threads anymore.

Unfortunately, the code above contains a serious flaw. The problem will occur when one thread engages the busy-wait loop, when it still owns the monitor. The other thread will never be able to execute its code because it can't acquire the monitor. The two threads are in a **deadlock**: one of them waits for the value to change while preventingthe other one from changing it (we'll talk more about deadlocks towards the end of the chapter).

We need to acquire the monitor *after* waiting for the flag. To do this, we use the **synchronized** keyword on a code segment (as opposed to an entire method), thus protecting only the critical code segment that needs mutual exclusion:

```
class MyData {
    private int Data;
    private boolean Ready;
    private boolean Taken;

    public MyData() {
        Ready=false;
        Taken=true;
    }

    public void store(int Data) {
        while (!Taken);
        synchronized (this) {
            this.Data=Data;
            Taken=false;
            Ready=true;
        }
    }

    public int load() {
        while (!Ready);
        synchronized (this) {
            Ready=false;
            Taken=true;
            return this.Data;
        }
    }
}
```

Note that when using the **synchronized** keyword on a code segment, you have to supply an object to synchronize. This is the object whose monitor is to be used for the critical section.

Still, one problem is left unsolved–the busy-wait loop. It's considered bad practice for a thread to use a busy-wait loop: it's processor-expensive on a preemptive implementation, and might cause deadlock on a non-preemptive one.

Waiting for Events

There's a way to avoid the busy-wait loop and, at the same time, dispose of one of the flags we used for the synchronization. The solution is to use the **wait()** and **notify()** methods, which are members of the class **Object** (and thus exist for every object). The **wait()** and **notify()** methods are used for waiting for events and reporting them to waiting threads, respectively. This mechanism works as follows:

The **wait()** method makes a thread release the monitor and shift from the runnable state to a non-runnable state. The thread will stay in a non-runnable state until it's woken up by a call to **notify()**. When a thread stops **wait()**ing, it re-acquires the monitor.

The **notify()** method arbitrarily chooses a thread from those that are **wait()**ing and releases it from its wait state.

Using **wait()** and **notify()** the final version of the **MyData** class is as follows:

```
class MyData {
    private int Data;
    private boolean Ready;

    public MyData() {
        Ready=false;
    }

    public synchronized void store(int Data) {
        while (Ready)
            try {
                wait();
            } catch (InterruptedException e) { }
        this.Data=Data;
        Ready=true;
        notify();
    }

    public synchronized int load() {
        while (!Ready)
            try {
                wait();
            } catch (InterruptedException e) { }
        Ready=false;
        notify();
        return this.Data;
    }
}
```

The above code achieves the desired results, without engaging a busy-wait loop and without any synchronization problem.

> Note that notify() and wait() can only be called from within synchronized methods. This is an integral part of the concept of monitors.

Being Thread-safe

A class is **thread-safe** if its code is protected against the possible hazards of multiple simultaneous access. All of the built-in classes in Java are thread-safe, meaning you can use them in multithreaded code without fear. It's good practice to make your classes thread-safe, even if you don't intend to use them in a multithreaded program right now. Since Java is all about reusing objects, and since you don't know when you'll need to use a class again, it's better to design it as thread-safe from the beginning.

Many Consumers - One Producer

The final implementation of our data storing class is thread-safe. Consider a case where there are many consumers and one producer, and the producer hasn't yet produced anything. The first consumer will acquire the monitor, but then will **wait()** and release it, allowing the second consumer to follow the same path. We will eventually have all the consumers in a **wait()**ing state, and an available monitor.

Now the producer kicks into action. It produces and invokes **notify()**. This causes one of the **wait()**ing threads to try to re-acquire the monitor. Since the producer had just released the monitor, this will cause no problems. The consumer will consume, and **notify()**. The **notify()** will wake up another consumer which will find out nothing is ready for it yet, and will thus return to the **wait()**ing state, releasing the monitor again. The producer will then be able to acquire it and supply another value.

Many Producers - One Consumer

If the situation was reversed and you had many producers and a single consumer, the producers would be **wait()**ing while the consumer woke them up one at a time, allowing them to produce. Because **Ready** is false after the consumer consumes each value, one producer thread can produce a new value. Because the producer thread changes **Ready** to false, the other producers won't overwrite the new value (even if they were woken) until it's consumed.

Barriers

In multithreaded applications there's often a need for several threads to synchronize at a specific point. One example is a parallel phased calculation, where all the threads must finish one phase before moving *all together* to the next one.

A barrier is a mechanism used for synchronizing many threads. A thread that reaches the barrier automatically **wait()**s. When the last of the threads reaches the barrier it notifies all the other threads, resulting in a joint crossing of the barrier. Here's an example implementation of a barrier:

```
import java.util.*;

class Barrier { // A barrier class - synchronize all participation
               // threads to a "single" point in time.

    private int ParticipatingThreads;
    private int WaitingAtBarrier;

    public Barrier(int num){                // Object constructor
        ParticipatingThreads = num;
        WaitingAtBarrier=0;
    }

    public synchronized void Reached() {    // The barrier method
```

```
        WaitingAtBarrier++;
        if ( ParticipatingThreads != WaitingAtBarrier ) {
          // This means this thread is not the last one.
            try {
            wait();                 // This is where all the threads hang until
          // they are released.
            } catch (InterruptedException e) { }
        } else {
          // This was the last active thread
            notifyAll();
            WaitingAtBarrier=0;     // release them all and initialize
        }
      }
    }
```

The barrier is achieved by having all the threads (but the very last one) waiting inside the synchronized method for the very last one to set them all free. As they wake up, they compete for the monitor, one of them gets it and exits immediately (there are no more statements to execute after the **wait()**), thus releasing the monitor. The others keep competing and exiting until the very last one exits and they are all free.

In this example we assumed that the number of participating threads is known in advance. While this is true in most cases, it's not always so. If the number of participating threads isn't known in advance, a registration mechanism can be applied. Every thread that wants to wait at the barrier first has to register itself, increasing the number of threads to wait for.

Waiting for a Thread to End

Sometimes it's necessary to wait for the termination of a thread. For example, a main thread can spawn a secondary thread to do some work on its behalf, go on doing something else, and when it's done wait for the worker thread to finish. Java provides means to monitor the state of another thread and suspend execution until it terminates.

One method you can use is **isAlive()**. This method returns **true** if the thread it's invoked upon has been started but not stopped. This means that we can't differentiate between threads that are new and threads that are dead; nor can we differentiate between runnable and non-runnable threads.

In order to wait for a thread to terminate (without using a busy-wait loop) you can use the **join()** method. This method waits for the thread to stop (with an optional timeout) and resumes execution only after the thread has stopped. You can interrupt a thread waiting for the join by invoking its **interrupt()** method. In this case **join()** would throw an **InterruptedException.**

Here's a code snippet that illustrates one thread waiting for another thread to end:

```
Class MainThread extends Thread {

    public void run() {
        SecondaryThread s = new SecondaryThread();

        s.start();

        // do my job ...

        // wait for the secondary thread to die
```

```
        if (s.isAlive())
            s.join();


        // We're done !
    }
}
```

Other Synchronization Methods

"Okay", you may say, "Java has this great monitor synchronization thing but I want to have my good old semaphores."

No problem. Using monitors you can implement any synchronization object you like: mutexes, semaphores or anything else. Having a single atomic operation in the system enables the implementation of any synchronization mechanism by simulating its behavior inside a critical section.

Here's a possible implementation of a semaphore in Java:

```
class Semaphore {
    protected int value;

    Semaphore( int initialValue ) {
        value = initialValue;
    }

    Semaphore() {
        value = 0;
    }

    public synchronized void Get() {
        while (value<1) wait();
        value--;
    }

    public synchronized void Put() {
        value++;
        notify();
    }
}
```

A thorough discussion of semaphores and other synchronization mechanisms is beyond the scope of this book. However, if you don't know what semaphores are then you probably wouldn't want to implement them in Java as Java offers you integrated synchronization facilities.

A New World of Problems

Writing multithreaded application opens a new bag of problems. Not only do you have to deal with the linear correctness of its code (bugs!, ladies and gentlemen, bugs!), you must consider every possible sequence of parallel execution. The operative word is caution.

Again, a thorough discussion of the hazards of parallel and concurrent programming is way beyond the scope of this book, however, I'd like to mention two of the most important issues in parallel and concurrent programming: deadlocks and starvation.

Deadlock

Deadlock occurs when two or more threads are waiting for some condition to change, while that condition is precluded from changing because all threads that can change the condition are waiting. We've seen how a deadlock can occur if we use a busy-wait loop inside a monitor—we're waiting for another thread to change a condition but never give it the opportunity to obtain the monitor.

We say that threads are in a deadlock if the calculation (or whatever it is the threads are doing) can't continue.

Starvation

The term starvation is used to denote situations where one thread is deprived of a resource (the CPU or access to a monitor). Unlike deadlock, in a starvation situation the calculation can continue in the system, it's just the starved thread that can't go on.

Starvation can occur when a high-priority thread starts running and never relinquishes the CPU. Although the high-priority thread can do a great many things, all the lower priority threads are starved. It can also occur when equally prioritized threads share a resource in a synchronized fashion, and some thread doesn't relinquish the resource for prolonged periods.

Summary

In this chapter we've looked at how multithreading can improve the performance of Java programs.

A large multithreaded application is virtually impossible to test to prove it's correct. I'm not talking about an application made of independent threads each running its own task but rather about an application in which threads collaborate and interact. The reason for this is the explosion in possible paths through the code when threads and timing are taken into account.

The proper way to prove that large multithreaded applications work correctly is to use methods such as code inspection and flow analysis. These topics are, again, well beyond the scope of this book, but if you intend to write serious multithreaded applications, I recommend that you refer to one of the books on these topics.

Input and Output

In Java, as in C and C++, input and output (I/O) are not supported directly in the language; instead an external package is used. The **java.io** package encloses a set of classes that provide a unified interface to the underlying system's input and output facilities.

Java has adopted the UNIX I/O notions of **streams** and **pipes**.

Streams are an abstraction used to denote a continuous one-way flow of data. The programmer isn't concerned with the source of the data (if it's an input stream) or the destination (if it's an output stream). The interface looks the same to the programmer, whether the data source is a file, a network connection, real-time data acquisition hardware or any other data source you can think of. Likewise, the destination can be a file, a modem, a printer, another computer on the other side of the planet or the communication unit of a deep space probe at the far reaches of the galaxy (okay, so maybe that's pushing it a little...).

Pipes are a conceptual abstraction used to denote the channeling of data from one place to another. A pipe is a uni-directional FIFO (first in first out) data connection with two ends: on one end there's someone who sends data into the pipe, and on the other end there is someone who takes the data out of the pipe. (You can think of a pipe as, well... a pipe).

This chapter is logically divided into two parts: the first is an overview of the classes you can find in the I/O package; the second is a collection of examples that show you how to use these classes for various tasks.

The first part is more concerned with showing you what's in the package, providing a broad look at the Java I/O system (after all, if you don't know it's there, chances are you won't use it). It isn't a substitute for the Java API–it only provides an overview. You are encouraged to refer to the API for more details.

The main goal of the second part is to provide you with a starting point for your own application, so a thorough study of the code examples will prove worth the effort.

To sum up, this chapter will cover:

- Input and output streams
- Accessing the file system
- Copying and parsing files
- Using pipes

Streams

At the core of the Java I/O system are the **InputStream** and **OutputStream** classes. These abstract classes are the base classes for pipes, files, filtered streams, I/O to strings, and others. Another basic building block is the **IOException** class that provides exception objects for I/O failures. Almost all the methods in the I/O classes throw an **IOException** (or one of its derived classes) if the desired operation fails.

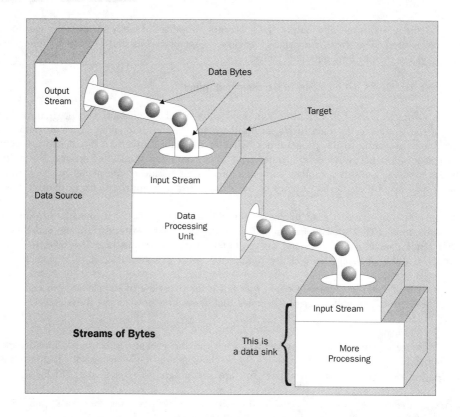

Since **InputStream** and **OutputStream** are the base classes for most other I/O classes, we'll study them in detail. We'll then just briefly describe the other classes (for a full description see the Java API).

InputStream

The **InputStream** class extends **Object** and is the base class for all the input stream classes.

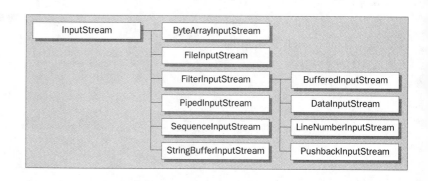

Unless otherwise specified, the methods of this class throw an **IOException** if an I/O error occurs.

Reading

The reading methods are used to obtain data bytes from the stream. If no data is available when they're invoked, they block (wait) until some is available.

Once the end of the stream is reached, any further calls to these methods return –1. This is why the return type is **int**. The value returned for each byte read is a positive value in the range 0 to 255, reserving –1 for reporting that the end of stream was reached. Had the return type been **byte**, reading the value 0x80 would produce a **byte** value of –1, which would be indistinguishable from the end-of-stream mark.

Let's have a look at the different forms of **read()**.

```
public abstract int read() throws IOException;
```

This reads in a byte of data and returns its value.

```
public int read(byte b[]) throws IOException;
```

This reads **b.length** bytes of data into the array of bytes pointed to by **b**, and returns the number of bytes read. If the number of bytes available is less than **b.length**, it reads all the available bytes–in this case the return value will be less than **b.length**. Any further calls after the end of file (EOF) is reached will result in –1 being returned.

```
public int read(byte b[], int off, int len) throws IOException;
```

This reads a maximum of **len** bytes into the array of bytes pointed to by **b** and returns the number of bytes read. The variable **off** is the offset into the array indicating where to start reading them in. If the number of bytes available is less than **len**, it reads all the available bytes and the return value will be less than **len**. Note that if **off** + **len** is not less than **b.length** you might get an **IndexOutOfBounds** exception. Again, any calls after the end of file (EOF) is reached will return –1.

Navigating

If you need to read ahead a little to see what's in the stream, you can use stream marks. When you've identified the content you can 'rewind' the stream and pass it on to someone who can handle its content. Note that not all the stream classes implement the functionality of this method.

```
public synchronized void mark(int readlimit);
```

This marks the current position in the input stream. A later call to **reset()** will reposition the stream at the last marked position so that subsequent reads will re-read the same bytes. The stream allows up to **readlimit** bytes to be re-read but if you read beyond this without calling **reset()**, the mark becomes invalidated (**readlimit** is the size of the internal buffer allocated to hold the data for re-reading).

```
public synchronized void reset() throws IOException;
```

This 'rewinds' the stream to the last marked position. Java throws an **IOException** if the stream hasn't been marked, or if the mark has been invalidated. Not all the stream classes implement the functionality of this method.

```
public boolean markSupported();
```

This returns a boolean value indicating whether this stream type supports mark/reset.

```
public long skip(long n) throws IOException;
```

This method skips **n** bytes of input. The skipped bytes are discarded. It returns the actual number of bytes skipped.

Others

```
public int available() throws IOException;
```

This method returns the number of bytes that can be read without blocking. This can be useful when your application needs a large chunk of data to start its processing stage.

> A word of warning: this method doesn't return a true value in each of the derived classes as it's not always possible to know the number of available bytes in advance.

```
public void close() throws IOException;
```

This method closes the input stream. It must be called to release any resources associated with the stream.

You may have expected the closing of the file to be implicit (like the implicit memory deallocation). "Why not do it in the finalizer?" you may ask. Well, the problem is that while memory is an internal resource, a stream is considered an *external* resource. In many cases a resource can't be used simultaneously (e.g. a file can't be written to by two applications simultaneously) and you can't always wait for the stream object to be garbage collected.

Output Stream

The **OutputStream** class extends **Object** and is the base class for all the output stream classes.

Unless otherwise specified, the methods throw an **IOException** if an I/O error occurs.

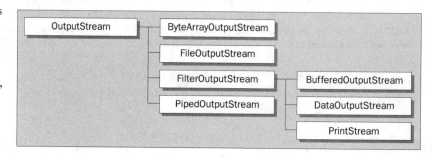

Writing

The writing methods are used to send data bytes to the stream. These methods block until the data is actually written.

```
public abstract void write(int b) throws IOException;
```

This writes the byte **b** to the stream.

```
public void write(byte b[]) throws IOException;
```

This writes the array of bytes pointed to by **b** to the stream.

```
public void write(byte b[],int off, int len) throws IOException;
```

And this writes **len** bytes from **b** to the stream, starting at offset **off**.

Others

```
public void flush() throws IOException;
```

This flushes the stream (writes any buffered output bytes).

```
public void close() throws IOException;
```

This closes the stream. As with **InputStream**, this method must be called to release any resources associated with the stream.

File Streams

Files can be treated as finite streams of data (later in the chapter we'll see other ways to manipulate files). A file can be seen as either an input stream or an output stream.

You can associate an input stream with a file on your local file system or on your Local Area Network (LAN) by using one of the constructors of the **FileInputStream** class:

```
public FileInputStream(File file);

public FileInputStream(FileDescriptor fdObj);

public FileInputStream(String name);
```

As you can see, the source can be specified either using a **File** object, a **FileDescriptor** or a **String** containing the name of the file (**File** and **FileDescriptor** are discussed later in the chapter).

Likewise, an output stream can be associated with a file using one of the constructors of the `FileOutputStream` class:

```
public FileOutputStream(File file);

public FileOutputStream(FileDescriptor fdObj);

public FileOutputStream(String name);
```

Filtered Streams

Filter streams are like wrappers you can put on a stream. They sit on top of an already existing input stream (a.k.a. the *underlying* input stream), manipulate its output in some way, and present the result.

The class **FilterInputStream** itself simply overrides all methods of **InputStream** with versions that pass all requests to the underlying input stream. This is really a 'do-nothing' class that only serves as a common base class for all the 'real' filter classes. Although this is not very useful, you can lay down layers upon layers of **FilterInputStreams**, getting the same output as you would have from the underlying input stream. Each layer would pass down any request to the underlying stream (which is, except for the innermost layer, a **FilterInputStream**) and the very last (inner) layer would pass it to the real input stream. The input stream's reply would then propagate up through the layers and be returned from the outer layer. (As in a true bureaucracy everybody is very busy doing nothing but shuffling the same data from one place to another).

Subclasses of **FilterInputStream** override some of these methods to provide useful filters (they also provide additional methods and fields to help accomplish their goals). These subclasses are as follows:

- **BufferedInputStream**—this allows an application to read bytes from a stream without necessarily causing a call to the underlying stream for each byte read. The buffer is first filled with data so subsequent reads can access the data directly from the buffer. This class is very useful as it helps reduce the overhead of accessing a physical resource (like a hard disk, for example).

- **DataInputStream**—this provides a way to read primitive Java data types from an underlying input stream in a machine-independent way. More often than not you want to read the content of a stream as something other than bytes (doubles, strings, etc.), and this is where this class comes in handy.

- **LineNumberInputStream**—this provides functionality to help keep track of the stream line numbers.

- **PushbackInputStream**—this provides a one-byte push back buffer. This feature allows an application to 'unread' the last byte it read. The next time you try to read from the input stream filter, the 'unread' character will be re-read.

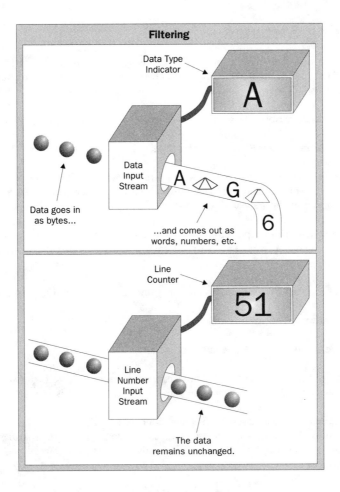

Here's an example of filter cascading:

```
InputStream source = FileInputStream( "MyFile.txt");
LineNumberInputStream lines = new PushbackInputStream( source );
DataInputStream data = new DataInputStream( lines );
```

Of course, we could also have this notation:

```
DataInputStream data = new DataInputStream(
                new LineNumberInputStream(
                new FileInputStream( "MyFile.txt") ) );
```

but then we wouldn't have access to the functionality provided by the **LineNumberInputStream** as we would have no handle to that object.

Byte and String Streams

You can store bytes from a stream into an array of bytes using the **read(byte b[])** and **read(byte b[], int off, int len)** methods of input streams. The **ByteArrayInputStream** class allows you to do the opposite: use an array of bytes as the source of the stream.

```
public ByteArrayInputStream(byte buf[]);

public ByteArrayInputStream(byte buf[], int offset,int length);
```

The constructors create a new byte array input stream which reads data from the specified byte array. The byte array is *not* copied. If **length** and **offset** are both specified then up to **length** characters are read from the byte array, starting at the indicated **offset**.

Invoking **reset()** on a byte array input stream rewinds the stream to the starting position, no matter where the mark was set. Invoking **available()** on such a stream returns the exact number of unread bytes in the stream.

A byte array can also be used as an output stream using the **ByteArrayOutputStream** class.

```
public ByteArrayOutputStream();

public ByteArrayOutputStream(int size);
```

These constructors create a new byte array output stream and associate it with the specified byte array. The buffer's initial capacity is 32 bytes and it grows automatically as data is written to it.

The **StringBufferInputStream** class supplies the same functionality as the **ByteArrayInputStream** class, only using a **String** as the data source. Java strings are in Unicode (with each character represented by a 16 bit value), but only the eight low bits of each character in the string are used by this class.

```
public StringBufferInputStream(String s);
```

Concatenating Input Streams

The **SequenceInputStream** class can be used to concatenate several input streams, thus making them appear as though they were one continuous stream. Each input stream is read from in turn, until the end of the stream is reached. The **SequenceInputStream** class then closes that stream and seamlessly switches to the next one. There is no way of telling when the switch occurs.

```
public SequenceInputStream(Enumeration e);
```

This constructs a new sequence input stream from the specified enumeration of input streams. Each object in the enumeration must be an **InputStream**.

```
public SequenceInputStream(InputStream s1, InputStream s2);
```

This constructs a new sequence input stream where **s1** is read first and **s2** second. You can nest these streams to create longer sequences without using enumeration like this:

```
InputStream in = new SequenceInputStream (
                        new SequenceInputStream( in1, in2),
                        new SequenceInputStream( in3, in42) );
```

Directories and Files

The file system on your computer can be accessed by Java applications in a system-independent fashion using **File**, **FileDescriptor**, **RandomAccessFile**, and the various stream classes. Java applets are restricted by the web browser they run in, and can't access the file system for security reasons (this limitation is imposed by a security manager in the web browser, not by Java itself).

To obtain the properties of a file or a directory you use the **File** class. This class provides an abstraction that deals with most of the machine-dependent variation of files and path names in a machine-independent fashion. You can obtain the underlying system's file descriptor for the file by invoking the **getFD** method which returns a **FileDescriptor** object.

A file is specified by a path name, which can either be absolute or relative to the current working directory. **The path and file names must follow the naming conventions of the host platform**. The static properties **pathSeparatorChar** and **separatorChar** provide the host file system's file and directory separating characters.

(For a full listing of the **File** class methods and properties refer to the API.)

Directories

Here is an example of using the **File** class. This application displays a directory tree, using the supplied argument as a starting point. It also prints the number of files and directories in the tree.

```
import java.io.*;

class PrintTree
{
    static int totalFiles, totalDirectories;

    private static void PrintSubTree( File root, String prefix ) {

        String[] dirList= root.list();
        String    name;
        File      f;

        // Print this directory's name
        System.out.println( prefix + root.getName() );

        // Increase the indention of the prefix
        if( prefix.equals("") )
           prefix = "|-";        // done only at the first time through
        prefix = "| "+prefix;

        // Iterate through the files and directories
        // in the current directory
        for (int i=0; i<dirList.length; i++) {
```

```
            // The full name of the file or directory is the concatenation
            // of the full path of the root, the system specific separator
            // character and the name of the file or directory.
            name =  root.getAbsolutePath() +
                    File.separatorChar +
                    dirList[i];

            f=new File(name);

            if (f.isDirectory()) {
               totalDirectories++;

               // Print the sub-tree of the directory
               PrintSubTree( f, prefix);
            } else {
               totalFiles++;
            }
        }

    }

    public static void main(String args[]) {

        File root;

        // Verify correct number of argumants
        if (args.length != 1) {
           System.err.println("Usage: java PrintTree <root>");
           System.exit(0);
        }

        root    = new File(args[0]);
        totalFiles      = 0;
        totalDirectories = 0;

        if (!root.exists()) {
           System.err.println("Directory " + root + " not found.");
           System.exit(0);
        }

        PrintSubTree(root,"");
        System.out.println("\n******");
        System.out.println("A total of " + totalFiles +
                    " files in " + totalDirectories + " directories.");
    }
}
```

For each subdirectory in the current directory the **PrintSubTree()** method is called recursively, creating the hierarchy you can see in the output. Notice the use of the **isDirectory()** method to distinguish between **Files** that are files and **Files** that are directories.

Here's an example output of this program:

D:>java PrintTree java
java
| |-bin
| |-lib

```
| |-demo
| | |-ArcTest
| | |-BarChart
| | |-Blink
| | |-CardTest
| | |-DitherTest
| | |-DrawTest
| | |-Fractal
| | |-GraphLayout
| | | |-audio
| | |-GraphicsTest
| | |-JumpingBox
| | | |-sounds
| | |-MoleculeViewer
| | | |-models
| | |-NervousText
| | |-SimpleGraph
| | |-SpreadSheet
| | |-TicTacToe
| | | |-images
| | | |-audio
| | |-WireFrame
| | | |-models
| | |-Clock
| | |-SortDemo
| | |-Animator
| | | |-images
| | | | |-SimpleAnimation
| | | | |-Beans
| | | |-audio
| | |-ImageMap
| | | |-audio
| | | |-images
| |-include
| | |-win32
| |-.hotjava
```

```
******
```

A total of 290 files in 38 directories.

Files

Files can be used either sequentially as streams or by using random access. Random access to files is necessary when you need to travel the file in a non sequential order (e.g. when creating your own database system). In all other cases, we recommend that you use stream files as they provide powerful tools in the form of filter classes and others, and are better managed by the system (using sequential access allows data caching and read-ahead, resulting in better performance of your applications and the system).

Copying Files

When you want to copy a file using streams, you first need to open two streams: an input stream (or **source** stream) and an output stream (or **destination** stream). Having opened these streams the rest is trivial: you read from the source and write to the destination.

Copying Byte by Byte

Here's a program which copies a file byte by byte:

```java
import java.io.*;

class ByteCopy
{
    static public void main(String args[]) {

        FileInputStream   in  = null;
        FileOutputStream  out = null;
        int               inByte;

        // Verify correct number of argumants
        if (args.length != 2) {
            System.out.println("Usage: java ByteCopy <in file> <out file>");
            System.exit(0);
        }

        try {
            // Create file input stream
            in = new FileInputStream(args[0]);
            // Create file output stream
            out = new FileOutputStream(args[1]);

            // Read the first byte
            inByte = in.read();
            while(inByte != -1) {
                // Write a byte to output stream
                out.write((byte)inByte);            // must cast inByte to a byte
                // Read the next byte
                inByte = in.read();
            }

        } catch (EOFException eofe) {
            // Do nothing on end of file
        } catch (FileNotFoundException fnfe) {
            // No such file
            System.err.println("File not found: " + args[0] );
        } catch (IOException ioe) {
            // On other exceptions print error message
            System.err.println( ioe.getMessage() );
        } finally {
            // ALWAYS close the file when done with it
            try {
                if (in!=null)  in.close();
                if (out!=null) out.close();
            } catch (IOException e) {}
        }
    }
}
```

Since the **write()** method expects a **byte**, and since we must store the read value in an **int** (because we want to identify the -1 received at the end of the file), we must cast the value in **inByte** to a **byte**.

Copying Line by Line

Copying line by line is almost the same as copying byte by byte, only this time we pass the input stream through a filter that provides the means for reading lines.

Here's the modified source (as a bonus, it also echoes the copied lines to the screen):

```
import java.io.*;

class LineCopy
{
    static public void main(String args[]) {

        FileInputStream    fis  = null;
        DataInputStream    in   = null;
        FileOutputStream   fos  = null;
        DataOutputStream   out  = null;
        String             line;
        int                linesRead = 1;

        // Verify correct number of arguments
        if (args.length != 2) {
            System.out.println("Usage: java LineCopy <source> <destination>");
            System.exit(0);
        }

        try {
            // Create file input stream
            fis = new FileInputStream(args[0]);
            // Redirect stream through a DataInputStream filter
            in  = new DataInputStream(fis);

            // Create file output stream
            fos = new FileOutputStream(args[1]);
            // Redirect stream through a DataOutputStream filter
            out = new DataOutputStream(fos);

            // Read the first line
            line = in.readLine();

            // Obtain the (system dependent) line separator character(s)
            String lineSep = System.getProperty("line.separator");

            while(line != null) {
                // Print the line to the screen
                System.out.println(linesRead++ + " : " + line);
                // Copy it to the output file. The original line had a line
                // separator which was removed by readLine, and so we add
                // it back.
                out.writeBytes(line + lineSep);
                // Read the next line
                line = in.readLine();
            }
```

```
        } catch (EOFException eofe) {
            // Do nothing on end of file
        } catch (FileNotFoundException fnfe) {
            // No such file
            System.err.println("File not found: " + args[0] );
        } catch (IOException ioe) {
            // On other exceptions print error message
            System.err.println( ioe.getMessage() );
        } finally {
            // ALWAYS close the streams when done with them
            try {
                if (fis!=null) fis.close();
                if (in!=null)  in.close();
                if (fos!=null) fos.close();
                if (out!=null) out.close();
            } catch (IOException e) {}
        }
    }
}
```

Note that we had to append the line separator character (or characters) ourselves as the **readLine()** method trims them. To maintain system independence, we obtained the line separator (which is not the same across the different operating systems) by using the **System** class' static method **getProperty()**.

System-independent Properties

Other properties available on all platforms using **System.getProperty()** and other methods are listed in the following table.

Key	Associated Value
file.separator	Operating system file separator ('/' for Unix, '\' for Windows)
java.class.path	The CLASSPATH environment variable
java.class.version	Java' class library version number
java.home	Java' installation directory
java.vendor	Java vendor-specific string (usually the vendor' name)
java.vendor.url	Java vendor's URL (so you know where to find it on the web...)
java.version	Java version number
line.separator	Line separator ('\n' for Unix, '\r\n' for Windows)
os.arch	Operating system architecture
os.name	Operating system name
os.version	Operating system version
path.separator	Path separator (':' for Unix, ';' for Windows)
user.dir	User's current working directory
user.home	User's home directory
user.name	User's account name

Parsing Files

Using the **StreamTokenizer** class, you can easily create applications that parse input files to retrieve information. This class enables you to retrieve the tokens in the file one by one by invoking the **nextToken()** method. This method retrieves the next token from the file, stores it in either **nval** (if it' numeric) or **sval** (if it's a string), and returns the type of the token (it also stores the type in the **ttype** property). Objects of this class can be configured to allow different types of string delimiter (defaulting to double quotes), end-of-line processing (defaults not to be recognized as a token) and other options.

The type of the token returned from the **nextToken()** method and stored in the **ttype** property is one of the following constant properties, or the character that was read in if none of them is appropriate.

Property	Meaning
TT_WORD	The token is a word.
TT_NUMBER	The token is a number.
TT_EOL	The end of line has been read. The field can only have this value if the end of line is significant as governed by the **eolIsSignficant()** method.
TT_EOF	The end of the input stream has been reached.

For a full listing of the class' methods and properties refer to the API.

Using SystemTokenizer

The following sample application is a simple book store utility. If you invoke it with one parameter it prints a full listing of the books in the specified database, and if you invoke it with two parameters it searches for a substring of the title in the database (the search is case insensitive).

Note that we use double quoted strings to enclose the name of the author and book. The strings' type (stored in **ttype**) is the same as the string-delimiter (double quote).

```java
import java.io.*;

class BookList
{
    static public void main(String args[]) {

        FileInputStream    fis   = null;
        StreamTokenizer    in;
        String             author, title;
        double             price;
        boolean            match;

        // Verify correct invocation
        if ( (args.length != 1) && (args.length != 2) ) {
            System.out.println(
                "Usage: java BookList <book file>\n" +
                "          or\n" +
                "          java BookList <book file> <part of title>" );
            System.exit(0);
        }
```

```java
try {

    // Create file input stream
    fis = new FileInputStream(args[0]);

    // Create a stream tokenizer that uses the file stream as input ...
    in = new StreamTokenizer(fis);

    // Read first token
    in.nextToken();

    while(in.ttype != in.TT_EOF) {

        // Store the author's name
        if (in.ttype != '"') {                          // must be a string
            System.err.println("Bad file format!");
            break;
        } else {
            author = new String(in.sval);
            in.nextToken();
        }

        // Store the book's title
        if (in.ttype != '"') {                          // must be a string
            System.err.println("Bad file format!");
            break;
        } else {
            title = new String(in.sval);
            in.nextToken();
        }

        // Store the book's price
        if (in.ttype != in.TT_NUMBER ) {                // must be a number
            System.err.println("Bad file format!");
            break;
        } else {
            price = in.nval;
            in.nextToken();
        }

        match = false;

        // If we should look for a sub-string and the sub-string exists
        if ( (args.length == 2) &&
                        (args[1].length() <= title.length())) {

            // Try to find the search string in the title
            for (int i=0; i <= title.length()-args[1].length(); i++) {

                // If a match is found
                if (title.regionMatches(true, i, args[1],
                                        0, args[1].length())) {
                    // Remember it ...
                    match = true;
                    // and stop the search
                    break;
                }
```

```
                }
            }

            // Print the entry
            if ( (args.length == 1) || match) {
                System.out.println("Author: " + author);
                System.out.println("Title:  " + title);
                System.out.println("Price:  " + price);
                System.out.println();
            }

        }
    } catch (FileNotFoundException fnfe) {
        // No such file
        System.err.println("File not found: " + args[0] );
    } catch (IOException ioe) {
        // On other exceptions print error message
            System.err.println( ioe.getMessage() );
    } finally {
        // ALWAYS close the streams when done with them
        try {
            if (fis!=null) fis.close();
        } catch (IOException e) {}
    }
}
}
```

Given this input file (**data.txt**):

```
"Douglas Adams"     "The Hitch Hiker's Guide to the Galaxy"     4.99
"Douglas Adams"     "The Restaurant at the End of the Universe" 4.99
"Douglas Adams"     "Life, the Universe and Everything"         4.99
"Douglas Adams"     "So Long, and Thanks for all the Fish"      4.99
"Bruce Pandolfini"  "Weapons of Chess"                          9.95
"Isaac Asimov"      "Buy Jupiter"                               4.49
```

the output is:

D:\JAVABOOK\IO>java BookList data.txt
Author: Douglas Adams
Title: The Hitch Hiker's Guide to the Galaxy
Price: 4.99

Author: Douglas Adams
Title: The Restaurant at the End of the Universe
Price: 4.99

Author: Douglas Adams
Title: Life, the Universe and Everything
Price: 4.99

Author: Douglas Adams
Title: So Long, and Thanks for all the Fish
Price: 4.99

Author: Bruce Pandolfini
Title: Weapons of Chess
Price: 9.95

Author: Isaac Asimov
Title: Buy Jupiter
Price: 4.49

D:\JAVABOOK\Part3\IO>java BookList data.txt ch
Author: Douglas Adams
Title: The Hitch Hiker's Guide to the Galaxy
Price: 4.99

Author: Bruce Pandolfini
Title: Weapons of Chess
Price: 9.95

D:\JAVA\WORK\JAVABOOK\Part3\io>java BookList data.txt "r al"
Author: Douglas Adams
Title: So Long, and Thanks for all the Fish
Price: 4.99

The following example also uses a stream tokenizer. This time we use the system's standard input stream (**System.in**) as an input source for a simple arithmetic utility. This utility parses arithmetic expressions given in Reverse Polish Notation (RPN) and returns the results.

RPN is a notation where you first specify the operands and then the operation. The expression is evaluated from left to right and at the end of the calculation the content of the stack is printed on screen. The following table explains how RPN works (the RPN expression to be evaluated is equivalent to $(1+1)*(4-2)$ in normal notation):

Expression Left to Parse	Stack	Remarks
1 1 + 4 2 - *	*empty*	This is the original expression.
1 + 4 2 - *	1	Took 1 from the expression and placed it on the stack.
+ 4 2 - *	1 1	Pushed the next 1 on the stack.
4 2 - *	2	Popped the 1s, added them and pushed the result back on the stack.
2 - *	4 2	Pushed 4 on the stack.
- *	2 4 2	Pushed 2 on the stack.
*	2 2	Popped 2 and 4, subtracted them and pushed the result back on the stack.
	4	Popped 2 and 2, multiplied them and pushed the result back on the stack. This is the result of the expression.

Here's the source for the example:

```java
import java.util.Stack;
import java.io.StreamTokenizer;
import java.io.IOException;

class RPN
{
   public static void main(String args[])
   {
    Stack stack = new Stack();
      StreamTokenizer tokens = new StreamTokenizer( System.in );
      int tokType;
      double l_op, r_op, res = 0;

      tokens.eolIsSignificant(true);
       tokens.ordinaryChar('/');

      try {
         do {
            tokType = tokens.nextToken();

            if (tokType == tokens.TT_NUMBER)
            {
               stack.push( new Double(tokens.nval) );
            }
            else if ( (tokType == tokens.TT_EOL) || (tokType == tokens.TT_EOF) )
            {
               while (! stack.empty() )
                  System.out.println(stack.pop());
            }
            else
            {
               l_op = ((Double) stack.pop()).doubleValue();
               r_op = ((Double) stack.pop()).doubleValue();

               switch(tokType) {
                  case '+':
                     res  = l_op+r_op;
                     break;
                  case '-':
                     res  = l_op-r_op;
                     break;
                  case '/':
                     res  = l_op/r_op;
                     break;
                  case '*':
                     res  = l_op*r_op;
                     break;
               }

               stack.push( new Double(res) );
            }

         } while(tokType != tokens.TT_EOF);

      } catch (IOException e) {
         System.out.println("ERROR : " + e );
```

```
        }

    }

}
```

Here's an example output from this utility (user input is in **bold** type):

D:\JAVA\WORK\JAVABOOK\Part3\io>java RPN
1 2 +
3
4 2 /
2
4 5 *
20
4 1 -
3
3 2 + 4 5 *
20
5
3 2 + 4 5 * /
0.25
25 7 / 2 3 4 * / 6 * 6 + *
25
^Z

This example shows that the standard input is in fact a stream like any other, only it originates from the keyboard. It can be redirected in the operating system and manipulated in any way you like in your application.

Random Access Files

Random access files are accessed using the **RandomAccessFile** class. This class supports both reading and writing to a random access file. It has methods that facilitate the reading and writing of various data elements, including loading the entire contents of the file into an array of bytes in memory (useful for image loading and processing). An application can read and write the elements at the current position in the file and can also modify the position in the file at which the next read or write occurs. The current position in the file is referred to as the **file pointer**.

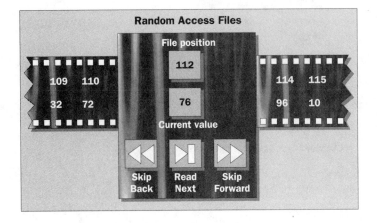

RandomAccessFile Methods

To give you a feeling of what you can expect a **RandomAccessFile** object to do, here's a listing of all the methods found in **RandomAccessFile**, arranged by type. The names are self explanatory (for more details, refer to the API).

Constructors:

```
public RandomAccessFile(File   file, String   mode);
public RandomAccessFile(String   name, String   mode);
```

General methods:

```
public void close();
public final FileDescriptor getFD();
public long getFilePointer();
public long length();
public void seek(long   newPosition);
public int skipBytes(int   n);
```

Reading methods:

```
public int read();
public int read(byte   b[]);
public int read(byte   b[], int   offset, int   length);
public final boolean readBoolean();
public final byte readByte();
public final char readChar();
public final double readDouble();
public final float readFloat();
public final void readFully(byte   b[]);
public final void readFully(byte   b[], int offset, int length);
public final int readInt();
public final String readLine();
public final long readLong();
public final short readShort();
public final int readUnsignedByte();
public final int readUnsignedShort();
public final String readUTF();
```

Writing methods:

```
public void write(byte   b[]);
public void write(byte   b[], int   off, int   len);
public void write(int   b);
public final void writeBoolean(boolean   v);
public final void writeByte(int   v);
public final void writeBytes(String   s);
public final void writeChar(int   v);
public final void writeChars(String   s);
public final void writeDouble(double   v);
```

```
   public final void writeFloat(float  v);
   public final void writeInt(int  v);
   public final void writeLong(long  v);
   public final void writeShort(int  v);
   public final void writeUTF(String  str);
```

Using RandomAccessFile

Here's a simple 'encoding' utility which reverses the bytes in the file to create an 'encoded' version. Run it again on the reversed file and you've got your original file back.

```java
import java.io.*;

class Flipper
{
   public static void main(String args[]) {

      RandomAccessFile in  = null, // Input file
                       out = null; // Output file
      long             pos;        // Points to the next byte to copy

      // Verify correct invocation
      if (args.length != 2) {
         System.out.println(
            "Usage: java Flipper <soucre> <destination>\n\n" +
            "This utility reverses the byte order in a " +
            "file to \"encode\" it.\n" +
            "To \"decode\" it run it through the utility again.");
         System.exit(0);
      }

      try {
         // Open input and output files
         in  = new RandomAccessFile(args[0], "r");
         out = new RandomAccessFile(args[1], "rw");

         pos = in.length()-1; // The offset is zero based,
                              // so the index of the last
                              // byte in the file is length()-1

         // Copy the bytes in reverse order
         while (pos >=0) {

            // Point to next byte to copy
            in.seek(pos--);
            // Read from the source and write to the target
            out.write( in.read() );
         }

      } catch (FileNotFoundException fnfe) {
         // No such file
         System.err.println("File not found: " + args[0] );
      } catch (IOException ioe) {
         // On other exceptions print error message
         System.err.println( ioe.getMessage() );
      } finally {
         // Always close the files when done with them
```

```
        try {
            if (in  != null) in.close();
            if (out != null) out.close();
        } catch (IOException e) {}
    }


    }
}
```

Pipes

We have seen that on a single processor two threads run in an interleaved fashion, first this one, then the other and back again. If these threads need to communicate, then a buffered stream must be used to allow one to write while the other is not reading.

Pipes are thread-safe, **uni-directional** buffered streams that provide the conduit for thread communication. A pipe has two ends: a sending end and a receiving end. The two ends are 'wrapped' by two classes: **PipedInputStream** and **PipedOutputStream**. Once the piped input stream (in-pipe) of one thread is connected to the piped output stream (out-pipe) of the other thread, and the out-pipe of the other thread is connected to the in-pipe of the first, the communication channel is established and you can use the pipes like any other input or output stream.

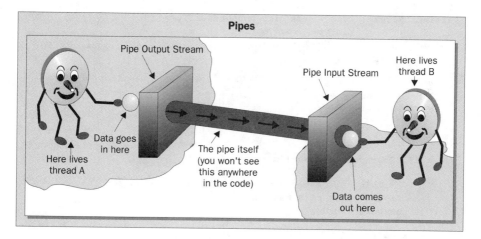

Using Pipes

Here's a program that uses pipes for thread communication. This has two threads that calculate statistics on files. The first is **WordCountThread** which counts the words in the input stream and the second is **LineCountThread** which counts the lines in the input stream. The two are connected using a pipe whose two ends are called **p_in** (the input side of the pipe) and **p_out** (the output side of the pipe).

The example code consists of three classes. The first two classes (**WordCountThread** and **LineCountThread**) implement the threads that calculate the statistics. You will find no reference to pipes in them, because threads see pipes as any other kind of input or output streams. The last class (**FileStat**) is the class that sets the thing in motion. It creates the pipes, connects them and passes them as arguments to the threads. It then starts the threads and waits for them to terminate before printing "Done".

This is a rather long example, but it's worth a thorough study. Start at the bottom—at the **main()** method of the **FileStat** class—and see how pipes are created, connected and used. After you are done with this class, study the first two classes to see how pipes are passed as parameters and used. (The actual functionality of these classes is of little importance as it has nothing do to with pipes – it's the setup and termination that are important.)

```java
import java.io.*;
import java.io.*;

/*
 *
 * WordCountThread
 *
 */

class WordCountThread extends Thread {
    private InputStream  in;
    private OutputStream out;

    public WordCountThread(InputStream in, OutputStream out) {
        this.in  = in;
        this.out = out;
    }

    public void run(){
        DataInputStream    dis = new DataInputStream( in );
        int                inByte, wordCount=0;
        boolean            newWord = true;

        try {

            // Read first byte
            inByte = dis.read();

            while(inByte != -1) {

                if (Character.isSpace((char)inByte))
                {
                    // White space means we should start looking for the
                    // beginning of a new word.
                    newWord = true;

                } else {

                    if (newWord) {
                        // Non-white-space marks the beginning of a new word.
                        wordCount ++;
                        newWord = false;
                    }

                }

                // If there is an output stream then write the byte to it
                if (out!=null) out.write(inByte);
                // Read next byte
                inByte = dis.read();
```

```
        }

    } catch (IOException ioe) {
        // On exceptions print error message
        System.err.println("Error:" + ioe );

    } finally {
        // ALWAYS close streams when done
        try {
            in.close();
            if (out!=null) out.close();
        } catch (IOException ioe) {
            // Print error message
            System.err.println("Error:" + ioe );
        }
    }

    // Print statistics
    System.out.println( wordCount + " words");
    }
} // End of WordCountThread

/*
 *
 * LineCountThread
 *
 */

class LineCountThread extends Thread {
    private InputStream  in;
    private OutputStream out;

    public LineCountThread(InputStream in, OutputStream out) {
        this.in  = in;
        this.out = out;
    }

    public void run(){
        LineNumberInputStream   lis = new LineNumberInputStream( in );
        int                     inByte, i=0;

        try {

            // Read first byte
            inByte = lis.read();

            while(inByte != -1) {
                // If there is an output stream then write the byte to it
                if (out!=null) out.write(inByte);
                // Read next byte
                inByte = lis.read();
            }

        } catch (IOException ioe) {
            // On exceptions print error message
            System.err.println("Error:" + ioe );
```

```java
        } finally {
            // ALWAYS close streams when done
            try {
                in.close();
                if (out!=null) out.close();
            } catch (IOException ioe) {
                // Print error message
                System.err.println("Error:" + ioe );
            }
        }

        // Print statistics
        System.out.println(
            (lis.getLineNumber()+1)  // Numbering is zero based
            + " lines" );
    }
} // End of LineCountThread

/*
 *
 * FileStat
 *
 */

class FileStat {
    public static void main(String args[]){
        WordCountThread   t1;
        LineCountThread   t2;
        FileInputStream   in    = null;
    PipedInputStream    p_in = null;
        PipedOutputStream p_out = null;

        try {
            p_in = new PipedInputStream();
            p_out = new PipedOutputStream(p_in);
            p_in.connect(p_out);

            if (args.length != 1) {
                System.out.println("Usage: java FileStat <file name>");
                System.exit(0);
            }

            // Create file input stream
            in = new FileInputStream(args[0]);

            t1 = new WordCountThread( in, p_out );
            t2 = new LineCountThread( p_in, null );

            System.out.println("File statistics for " + args[0]);
            t1.start();
            t2.start();

            try {
                t1.join();
                t2.join();
            } catch (InterruptedException ie) {
                System.err.println("main thread interrupted !");
                System.exit(1);
            }
```

```
            System.out.println("Done.");

        } catch (FileNotFoundException fnfe) {
            System.err.println("File not found: " + args[0] );
        } catch (IOException ioe) {
            // Print error message
            System.err.println("Error:" + ioe );
        }
    }
}  // End of FileStat
```

Here's an example output of this program:

D:\JAVABOOK\Part3\io>java FileStat pipes.java
File statistics for pipes.java
467 words
176 lines
Done.

In this example you can see again why it is so important to close streams as soon as you're done using them. If we didn't close the output pipe in the word counting thread, the line counting thread would not find the end of the stream. (Try removing the **out.close()** statement from the word counting thread and see what happens).

The word counting thread and the line counting thread can be connected the other way around: the line counting thread to the input file and the word counting thread to the pipe. The only change needed in the source is to change these lines:

```
        t1 = new WordCountThread( in, p_out );
        t2 = new LineCountThread( p_in, null );
```

to

```
        t1 = new WordCountThread( p_in, null );
        t2 = new LineCountThread( in, p_out );
```

and the only difference in the output would be:

D:\JAVABOOK\Part3\io>java FileStat pipes.java
File statistics for pipes.java
176 lines
467 words
Done.

Summary

In this chapter we've given an overview of the classes in the I/O package. We concentrated on the core classes **InputStream** and **OutputStream** and discussed some of the methods they include for reading, writing and navigating streams. We also looked at how the file system can be accessed by Java applications and gave some examples of file manipulation.

We finished by taking a look at pipes and gave an example that uses pipes for thread communication.

The Abstract Window Toolkit and Event-Driven Programming

Like a kick in the butt, the force of events wakes slumberous talents.
Edward Hoagland *(b. 1932), U.S. novelist, essayist. Guardian (London, 11 Aug. 1990).*

By this point, you should be feeling pretty comfortable with Java. You've learned the basics, written small applets and applications, worked with the data types, learned the features of object-oriented programming and how Java is positioned as an object-oriented language. That's a lot of knowledge, but these days, looks are everything, so if you're going to call yourself a Java programmer, you're going to have to be able to develop the kind of windowed user interfaces that people have become used to, and that is where the Abstract Window Toolkit comes in.

The Abstract Window Toolkit, or AWT, as we will call it from this point on, is a collection of classes and interfaces encapsulating text fields, buttons, checkboxes and other user interface controls, along with the classes needed to handle layouts, graphics, text and event management. The AWT contains all the tools you'll need to build fully functional, window-based user interfaces which will run on any Java-enabled operating system or Internet browser. Using the AWT requires an understanding of event-driven programming; its very nature makes AWT programming mostly non-procedural, so that's where we're going to start. This chapter will deal with:

- AWT overview
- Event handling
- Mouse events
- Helper methods

AWT Overview

You've probably realized this already, but you've used the AWT in the applet you developed in Chapter 4. That's why you had to insert the line

```
import java.awt.*;
```

at the start. This tells the Java compiler to look in the AWT package for classes included in your source. Before we can start talking about how the AWT functions we need to define some important terms. We'll be using these throughout the AWT chapters.

Components, Containers, and Layout Managers

While each of these terms is explained in greater depth in later chapters, you need to have an idea of what each is to help you to start putting the together whole picture:

- ▲ **Component**–A user interface element such as a button, checkbox, or menu. You might know it as a control under Windows, or as an X-Windows widget.

- ▲ **Container**–Basically a component which can include other components. For example, a Panel is a container which can contain many components, including other containers.

- ▲ **Layout Manager**–Layout Manager is a class which manages the process of positioning components and containers in a platform-independent manner.

Basically, a Java user interface is a layered collection of **components**. These are laid out within **containers** which might be members of other containers and which are all arranged and positioned by **Layout Managers**. This isn't much different from the 'window within a window within a window' model that is seen in Windows programming, but the concept of dynamic component layout will be new for most of you. Layout managers are basically responsible for the arrangement of components according to criteria defined by the developer, and the attributes of the system that the application is running on. This means that, although components may look different from one platform to another, and they may even be different sizes, the layouts should still look similar. Generally, you will not define specific sizes and coordinates for user interfaces because they may have to change on different platforms.

The AWT Class Hierarchy

We'll look at AWT Class Hierarchy, so that you'll get a feel for the classes included in this package:

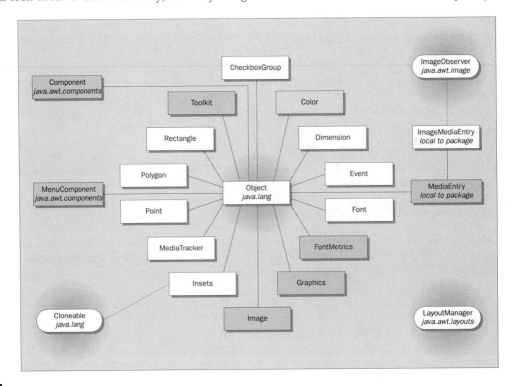

You can see classes for controls, containers, layout managers, and event managers. These classes will allow you to build a user interface which is abstracted from the particular operating system or hardware it runs on.

Of course, there's a price to pay for this abstraction. To some extent, the AWT is a lowest common denominator of components which can be mapped to native peer components on most common platforms. Having stated that, I'll also say that I think you'll find all the features you need to build the user interface you desire. The following diagram should help to illustrate this concept of peers.

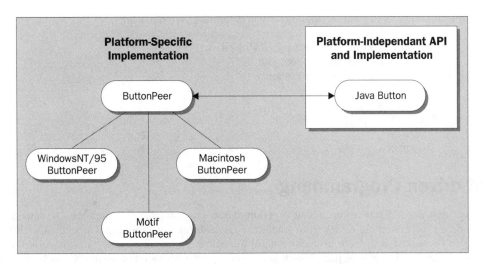

For each platform that Java can be run on, the AWT knows how to map its components (like Canvas, Label, Button, Scrollbar, etc.) to platform-specific 'peer' components. This will allow your applications to look like Windows 95 applications on Windows 95, Macintosh applications on a Mac, etc.

Toolkit Class

To find out some of the specifics of the AWT implementation you're using, you can use the AWT **Toolkit** class.

The following small applet will obtain a **Toolkit** object and query it to obtain the name of the default Toolkit, screen resolution, and the available fonts. We'll print out the information using the standard output stream (which is an instance of the **PrintStream** class) and its **println()** method:

```
import java.applet.*;
import java.awt.*;

public class sysinfo extends Applet
{
    public void start()
    {
        String strTKName = System.getProperty("awt.toolkit");
        System.out.println("System Toolkit: " + strTKName);

        Toolkit myTK = Toolkit.getDefaultToolkit();
```

```
        System.out.println("\n\nScreen Resolution: "
        + myTK.getScreenResolution() + " dots per inch");

        String myFonts[] = myTK.getFontList();
        System.out.println("Fonts available on this platform: ");
        for (int i = 0; i< myFonts.length; i++)
           System.out.println(myFonts[i]);
    }
 }
```

You'll see the following in the output window if you're running Windows 95:

> System Toolkit: sun.awt.win32.MToolkit
> Screen Resolution: 96 dots per inch
> Fonts available on this platform:
> Dialog
> Helvetica
> TimesRoman
> Courier
> Symbol

Event-driven Programming

One concept that the AWT relies on is that of **event-driven** programming. It's important to understand how event-driven programming differs from traditional **procedural** programming. Up until this chapter, the programs you've worked with have been procedural in nature. By that, we mean that the code flow followed a predictable, linear-type path. There was looping and calls to other methods which allowed the code flow to jump around a little, but you always knew what path the code was going to take, and the next instruction to be executed.

In event-driven programming, you don't know what's going to happen next because the next step is going to be decided by the way in which the user interacts with the interface. Certain parts of the code may still be linear, but there's no consistent top-to-bottom flow. For instance, an applet or program will generally execute a specific set of initialization steps when it's invoked, such as constructing objects, laying out the components and initializing values of variables, but upon completing that initialization, it will stop and wait for an **event** to happen.

An event can be defined as a type of signal to the program that something has happened that the program needs to respond to. An event can be generated by a user action such as a mouse movement or key press, or it can be generated by the operating system such as when a timer is fired (an autosave feature for instance) or when a window is told to repaint itself. When writing event-driven programs you will find yourself writing lots of small chunks of code which handle particular events. In the course of an execution of your program, some of the event-handling code may be executed and some may not. In fact, often times, the 80/20 rule will apply: 20% of your code is executed 80% of the time. If you have never programmed this way, it will take some getting used to, but you'll pick it up pretty quick.

> The AWT event-handling techniques will be very familiar for Windows developers.
> An AWT Event object can be thought of as a kind of user-friendly Windows
> message. Instead of dealing with a message loop and the WM_XXXX messages,
> Windows developers will now be overriding functions to handle specific events or
> groups of events.

> For instance, when handling mouse movements, the `mouseMove()` method should be overridden rather than responding to a `WM_MOUSEMOVE` message (if you're using the SDK) or writing an `OnMouseMove` function if you're using the Microsoft Foundation Class library. And there's no Message Map to be concerned with.

The Event Object

When working with the AWT, you'll find that events are the principal means of communication among the your program's components. Any time a significant event happens, an **Event** object is created. The **Event** object will contain descriptive information about that event such as type of event (action, mouse movement or click, key press, etc.), target component, the x, y coordinates where the event occurred, and the state of the modifier keys (*Alt, Ctrl, Shift*) when the event occurred. The event-handling mechanism of the AWT will then route the event to the appropriate component. This component can then respond in any of the four following ways:

▲ It can ignore the event and allow it to be passed up the Component hierarchy.

▲ It can modify the information passed in the Event instance before allowing it to be passed up the Component hierarchy.

▲ It can react in some other non-event related way such as calling a method that processes some data.

▲ It can intercept the event and stop it from being processed any further.

If the component doesn't handle the event, it's passed up the hierarchy tree to the component's parent component which then gets a chance to handle it, and then, if it has still not been handled, the event again gets passed to its parent and its parent until it is handled, or the topmost component is reached. If the topmost component (which is usually the browser or the AppletViewer main window) is reached, the event is handed back over to the peer component. Peer components are at the end of the event chain.

> In the current implementation of Java, the actual start of the event chain is inconsistent. When a key press event occurs, the component for which the event is intended gets the event first. However, for mouse events, the peer is the first to get the event. Also, the peer doesn't necessarily pass all events to the component. For example, Motif text fields don't forward mouse move events.

To give you a feel for the event-handling process, compile and run this small applet. It simply prints out the Event object contents when any event occurs. Don't worry about the specifics, just use it to see some events in action.

```
import java.applet.*;
import java.awt.*;

public class Events extends Applet
{   Graphics g;
    public void init()
    {
        g = getGraphics();
```

```
    }

    public boolean handleEvent(Event evt)
    {
        g.setColor(getBackground());
        g.fillRect( 0,0, size().width, size().height);
        g.setColor(Color.black);
        System.out.println(evt.toString());
        g.drawString(evt.toString(), 10, size().height / 2 );
        return false;
    }
}
```

If you're using the AppletViewer, your screen will look like this:

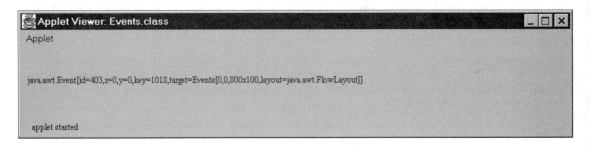

As you can see, when this applet is executed, an event is generated virtually every time you touch your mouse or keyboard. When the mouse is moved, the events are going by so quick you won't be able see them on the screen, which is why we also wrote them to the log. That way you can take a closer look at the different event types being generated.

This applet is about the simplest example of event-driven programming you'll see. Every event is handled in exactly the same manner. Most of your programs will be far more specific in what events they respond to, and how they do it. As we look in more detail at the AWT, we'll come back to discussions of event handling and event objects with every component we talk about because they all rely on the event handling system to work.

Event Handling

Earlier, we stated that almost every user action causes an **Event** object to be created, with descriptive information about the event. In some cases, the system itself will generate an event. In either case, the AWT must then deliver this **Event** object to the appropriate component for handling. Although the specifics of how the event is delivered need not be understood in order to write Java code, it's useful to have an idea about what's going on.

When an event is generated, the AWT will attempt to deliver it to the topmost component of the applet or application by invoking the **container** class **deliverEvent()** method. The **container** **deliverEvent()** method will either pass the event to a subcomponent (which also might be a container) by calling the appropriate subcomponent's **deliverEvent()** method, or handle the event in the container itself by invoking the **postEvent()** method. If the subcomponent isn't a container, the component **deliverEvent()** is invoked which immediately calls **postEvent()**. The event will continue to be passed down the component hierarchy until a **postEvent()** is invoked. The **postEvent()** method will call the component's **handleEvent()** method so the event can be handled. If the **handleEvent()** method returns true, the **postEvent()** method will immediately return true, otherwise the component's parent's **postEvent()** method is called which will perform the same action.

This is a simplified version of the process, but the aim is to give you a feel for how an event is passed down the component tree (and back up). There are two important concepts to keep in mind as we explain events further. First, all these methods follow the rule of returning true if an event has been handled in the method, and false if not. When you override any of these methods you must do the same, return true or false depending on whether the event has been handled. Second, when you return false, the event will propagate up to the parent in the component hierarchy, *not* the superclass. For example, if you subclass a **Button**, and create your own **myButton** class, events posted to **myButton** which aren't handled will be passed to the component which contains **myButton**, not to **Button**. If you want to pass the event to the superclass, you must do so explicitly. We'll talk more about that later.

The handleEvent() method

How events are handled in Java is controlled by the **handleEvent()** method. The **handleEvent()** method acts like a traffic director. Based on the **Event id** value, it calls one of eleven 'helper' methods:

- **mouseEnter()**
- **mouseExit()**
- **mouseMove()**
- **mouseDown()**
- **mouseDrag()**
- **mouseUp()**
- **keyDown()**
- **keyUp()**
- **action()**
- **gotFocus()**
- **lostFocus()**

If you take a look in the actual Java source code at the **Component** class **handleEvent()** method, you'll find this code:

```
public boolean handleEvent(Event evt) {
    switch (evt.id) {
      case Event.MOUSE_ENTER:
        return mouseEnter(evt, evt.x, evt.y);

      case Event.MOUSE_EXIT:
        return mouseExit(evt, evt.x, evt.y);

      case Event.MOUSE_MOVE:
        return mouseMove(evt, evt.x, evt.y);
```

```
        case Event.MOUSE_DOWN:
          return mouseDown(evt, evt.x, evt.y);

        case Event.MOUSE_DRAG:
          return mouseDrag(evt, evt.x, evt.y);

        case Event.MOUSE_UP:
          return mouseUp(evt, evt.x, evt.y);

        case Event.KEY_PRESS:
        case Event.KEY_ACTION:
          return keyDown(evt, evt.key);

        case Event.KEY_RELEASE:
        case Event.KEY_ACTION_RELEASE:
          return keyUp(evt, evt.key);

        case Event.ACTION_EVENT:
          return action(evt, evt.arg);
        case Event.GOT_FOCUS:
          return gotFocus(evt, evt.arg);
        case Event.LOST_FOCUS:
          return lostFocus(evt, evt.arg);
      }
    return false;
  }
```

It's easy to see that this method is one big switch statement which calls all of the helper methods with appropriate parameters or returns false. Each of these methods has a default component implementation which simply returns false to indicate that the event hasn't been handled. These methods are called 'helper' methods because they make it easy to handle the events by overriding the appropriate method in your own class.

To demonstrate how this works, let's examine in detail the mouse events.

Mouse Events

Mouse events are probably the most common events that you'll need to handle in your applications. Because of the available 'helper' methods, the mouse events are very easy to handle; you simply override the method in your class implementation and you're done. Here's a listing of the mouse events that can be intercepted, and the user action that generates them:

▲ **mouseDown(Event, int, int)**–Called when the mouse button is clicked.

▲ **mouseUp(Event, int, int)**–Called when a mouse button is released.

▲ **mouseMove((Event, int, int)**–Called when the mouse moves without any mouse buttons depressed.

▲ **mouseDrag((Event, int, int)**–Called when the mouse moves with at least one button depressed.

▲ **mouseExit((Event, int, int)**–Called when the mouse leaves the component with no buttons down.

▲ **mouseEnter((Event, int, int)**–Called when the mouse enters a component with no buttons down.

As you can see, all these methods are called with the same parameters. The event object which was generated for the event is passed, along with the x, y coordinates of the current mouse position in that order. The x,y coordinates are technically not even necessary. Since you're passed the event object, you could check that object to get the coordinates. They're broken out simply for convenience (I assume, I have never actually spoke to the architects) .

> Since the AWT is designed to be cross-platform, you should always assume that there's only one mouse button. On systems with multiple mouse buttons (such as Windows 95), they will be triggered for *any* mouse button. In the example coming up, we'll show you how to detect which mouse button was actually clicked in that situation.

Mouse Events Example

Let's look at an example which will show all of the mouse events in use. This is an applet which allows a user to 'write' on the screen by dragging with the left mouse button pushed, and to erase lines by dragging with the right mouse button pushed.

Since we don't want to deny Macintosh users the erase functionality just because they have only one button, we also allow erasing by dragging with the left mouse button clicked while holding down the shift key. A double click will clear the screen. Here's what you will see if you run this applet in the AppletViewer: Another 'Hello, World' program of sorts:

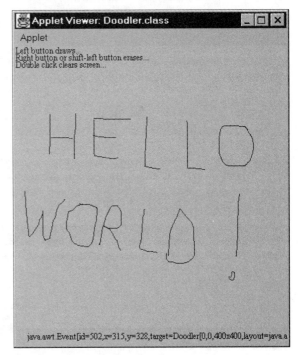

Take a look through the source and then we'll explain it line by line. There's one thing I should make clear right away. The 'constant' type information (foreground color, background color, Circle size) would be better handled as user configurable parameters. We didn't do that because we wanted to keep the applet small and simple. Should you want to, you could easily add that flexibility.

```
import java.applet.*;
import java.awt.*;

public class doodler extends Applet
{
    Point lineStart = new Point(0,0);
    int circleSize = 16;
```

```
    Graphics g = getGraphics();

    public void init()
    {
        setBackground(Color.cyan);
    }

    public void paint(Graphics g)
    {
        g.setColor(Color.blue);
        g.drawString("Left button draws...",1,10);
        g.drawString("Right button or shift-left button erases...",1,20);
        g.drawString("Double click clears screen...",1,30);
    }

    public boolean mouseDown(Event e, int x, int y)
    {
        showStatus(e.toString());
        if ( e.metaDown() || e.shiftDown() )     // right button
            setForeground(getBackground());
        else        // left button
            setForeground(Color.blue);

        if ( e.clickCount == 2 )  // double click
        {
            setForeground(getBackground());
            repaint();
        }
        else
        {
            lineStart.move(x,y);
        }
        return true;
    }

    public boolean mouseDrag(Event e, int x, int y)
    {
        showStatus(e.toString());
        g = getGraphics();
        if ( e.metaDown() || e.shiftDown() )  //right button - erase
        {   // we'll erase with an oval to cut a wider swath
            g.fillOval(x - (circleSize / 2), y - (circleSize / 2 ),
            circleSize, circleSize );
        }
        else
            g.drawLine(lineStart.x, lineStart.y, x, y);

        lineStart.move(x,y);
        return true;
    }

    public boolean mouseUp(Event e, int x, int y)
    {
        showStatus(e.toString());
        return true;
    }
```

```
   public boolean mouseEnter(Event e, int x, int y)
   {
       showStatus("Hello....");
       return true;
   }

   public boolean mouseExit(Event e, int x, int y)
   {
       showStatus("goodbye....");
       return true;
   }

}
```

The first three lines should be familiar by this point, we're just telling the compiler to look in the **applet** and **awt** packages for class definitions, and that our program is an extension of the **Applet** class.

Next, we define some variables we'll need later. Our **Doodler** applet is going to 'write' by drawing lines between the coordinates of the mouse received by each **mouseDrag()** event. This means we'll need to be able to save the starting point coordinates of each line. We could use two integers to hold the x, y values of the starting point, but Java provides a **Point** class which for this purpose will work even better.

The Point Class

The **Point** class is an extension of the object class which encapsulates an x,y coordinate. The x and y values are its only variables and it contains five methods.

▲ **Point(int, int)**—The constructor. Initializes a point to the specified x, y coordinates.

▲ **equals(Object)**—Compares two points.

▲ **hashCode()**—Returns a hashcode for this point.

▲ **move(int, int)**—Moves the point to the specified x,y coordinates.

▲ **toString()**—Returns the string representation of the point.

▲ **translate(int, int)**—Translates the point. This is useful if you want to use an origin other than 0,0, when scrolling for instance.

We'll call our **Point lineStart** and instantiate an instance right away. The constructor requires that we initialize the instance to starting values, so we arbitrarily chose 0,0. This doesn't matter because we'll change the values before we use it anyway. Next, we define an integer, **circleSize**, and a Graphics object **g**.

The init() and paint() Methods

We use the **init()** method to set the background to the color we like (this is one of the items mentioned that might be made user-configurable) and then we implement our override of the default applet **paint()** method.

Our **paint()** method is pretty simple, we set the color we want to write with, and then we use the **drawString()** method to write three text strings to the screen to tell the user how to use the applet.

> The drawString() method is derived from the Graphics class. It uses the current font and color to draw the contents of the str parameter to the location on the screen specified by the x,y values.
>
> ```
> public abstract void drawString(String str, int x, int y)
> ```

The mouseDown Event

The mouse events are more interesting:

```
public boolean mouseDown(Event e, int x, int y)
{
    showStatus(e.toString());
    if ( e.metaDown() || e.shiftDown())     // right button
        setForeground(getBackground());
    else       // left button
        setForeground(Color.blue);

    if ( e.clickCount == 2 )  // double click
    {
        setForeground(getBackground());
        repaint();
        return true;
    }
    else
    {
        lineStart.move(x,y);
    }
    return true;
}
```

In the **mouseDown** handler we start by making a **showStatus()** call to display the contents of the Event object via the **toString()** method.

> The toString() method will return a string representation of an object's contents. We recommend that you override this method in your own classes so it will return something meaningful. Since there's a default implementation in the Object class, and all objects can ultimately trace their roots up to Object, you can use the toString() method on any object and be assured of receiving some result back.

This **showStatus()** call is there purely for illustrative reasons. It will allow you to get a look at the Event object's content while the applet is running.

The next line requires some explaining:

```
if ( e.metaDown() || e.shiftDown())     // right button
```

We mentioned earlier that in this applet you can write by dragging with the left mouse button, and erase by dragging with the right mouse button, or by holding the *shift* key while dragging with the left mouse button. When the applet was originally written, this second type of erasing (*shift*–left mouse button) wasn't available. However, as Macintosh users only have one button we didn't want to leave them without an erase function.

We use a simple technique for erasing here: drawing over the chosen area with the background color. This effectively wipes out the previous contents. The **mouseDown()** indicates that a line is being started. We have to find out if the user is trying to write or erase, so we can set the color appropriately. We use the Event **metaDown()** method to determine whether the right button has been pushed. On most operating systems (this is true for Windows 95 and NT), the right mouse button is mapped to the meta key, so this method will return true if this button is pressed. When you run the applet, watch the event contents to see for yourself. If the **metaDown()** or **shiftDown()** method (which indicates if the *shift* key is pressed) return true, we assume the user wants to erase, and appropriately set the color.

The clickCount Variable

Next, we use another relatively undocumented feature to implement a double-click function. The Event object has a **clickCount** variable which contains the number of consecutive times the mouse was clicked. The Java source code offers only one clue in the comments before the declarations as to how the **clickCount** variable gets set:

```
/* The number of consecutive clicks. This field is relevant only for
 * MOUSE_DOWN events. If the field isn't set it will be 0.Otherwise,
 * it will be 1 for single-clicks, 2 for double-clicks, and so on.
 */

public int clickCount;
```

In Windows 95 and NT, the configurations click speed setting is used for determining consecutive clicks. If you update the setting, the AWT will respond accordingly. When using this variable bear these points in mind:

- It will always be zero for **mouseUp** events.

- Its value seems to have no upper limit.

- For each mouse click, **mouseDown()**, **mouseDrag()**, and **mouseUp()** events will be generated.

- To handle double clicks, you must be prepared to handle those three events for the first click, and then for the second click. This makes sense as the only way the first click could be suppressed would be if the operating system waited after every click to see if there was a second (or third, fourth, etc.). If it had to do this the interface would be very sluggish.

In our applet, if the user has double-clicked, **clickCount** will be equal to two. In the double-click handling code we call **repaint()** to request a screen paint. This wipes out all current lines on the screen. Notice, however, that before we do that, we set the foreground color to the background color. The reason we do this is that a **mouseUp()** event always causes a **mouseDrag()** to be generated, even when the mouse is stationary. Our **mouseDrag()** event will cause a line to be drawn even when the mouse hasn't moved, so a tiny dot will appear on the cleared screen unless the mouse was double-clicked with the right button or while *shift* was held down.

If the **clickCount** isn't equal to two, we assume a new line has been started so we set the **lineStart** object to the current mouse position by calling the **Point move()** method.

The last line in the **mouseDown()** method returns a true value to the AWT. This tells the AWT that this event has been handled and doesn't need to be propagated up the component hierarchy. If you want the event to be propagated up the hierarchy after your code has completed, return **false**.

The mouseDrag Event

In the **mouseDrag** event we actually do the drawing:

```
public boolean mouseDrag(Event e, int x, int y)
{
    showStatus(e.toString());
    g = getGraphics();
    if ( e.metaDown() || e.shiftDown())  //right button - erase
    {   // we'll erase with an oval to cut a wider swath
        g.fillOval(x - (circleSize / 2),
             y - (circleSize / 2 ),
            circleSize, circleSize );
    }
    else
        g.drawLine(lineStart.x, lineStart.y, x, y);

    lineStart.move(x,y);
    return true;
}
```

After the gratuitous **showStatus()** call, we request a new Graphic object which will represent our current environment and color settings. This is one of the neat Java features: you can request a new object without worrying about freeing the last one. The garbage collector will release its memory once it has no current references.

> This isn't entirely true. In production code, it's usually good programming practice to use the **dispose()** method if the class has one. This way you'll reclaim any operating system resources the instantiated object was allocated.

We then determine whether the user is drawing, or erasing. If drawing, we draw a line from the start point saved in the **lineStart Point** object, to the current mouse coordinates. If the user is erasing, we do something different. Since the AWT doesn't provide a way to increase the line width, erasing could turn into a very tedious activity. To make it a little easier, we'll erase by drawing circles so we have a slightly wider erase path. We draw the circle with the Graphics **fillOval()** method. Since the **fillOval()** method works by drawing an oval inside a rectangle specified by the parameters, we have to make some adjustments to center the circle on the current mouse coordinates. We center the circle by subtracting half the circle size from the current x and y values. This moves the rectangle origin higher and to the left of the current mouse position and when the circle is drawn, it's centered.

After drawing the appropriate line or circle, we reset the **lineStart** value to the current position to prepare for the next line.

Loose Ends

The other mouse events are self-explanatory. We wanted to make sure you saw all mouse events in action. This is a fairly simple example, but I think it shows how easy the AWT is to use. Those of you experienced with Windows programming will realize that this application would have been much more complex and lengthy if it were implemented with the SDK or even a Windows class library such as the Microsoft Foundation Class. It's comparable in complexity to a Visual Basic implementation, but, of course, that would not be cross-platform, or embeddable in a Web page.

There may be times when you choose not to use the helper methods. Perhaps the event you need to handle doesn't have an associated 'helper' method, or you want a more centralized event-handling function. Whatever the reason, you can always implement a solution without using any of the helper methods.

Example Applet without Helper Methods

In this next example, **doodler2**, we have implemented the same **doodle** applet, but instead of using the helper methods, we overrode the **handleEvent()** method to catch and respond to the relevant events. Take a look at the code:

```java
import java.applet.*;
import java.awt.*;

public class doodler2 extends Applet
{
    Point lineStart = new Point(0,0);
    int circleSize = 16;
    Graphics g = getGraphics();

    public void init()
    {
        setBackground(Color.cyan);

    }

    public void paint(Graphics g)
    {
        g.setColor(Color.blue);
        g.drawString("Left button draws...",1,10);
        g.drawString("Right button or shift-left button erases...",1,20);
      g.drawString("Double click clears screen...",1,30);
    }

    public boolean handleEvent(Event e)
    {
        showStatus(e.toString());
        switch (e.id)
        {
          case Event.MOUSE_DOWN:
          if ( e.metaDown() || e.shiftDown())      // right button
            setForeground(getBackground());
            else        // left button
                setForeground(Color.blue);

            if ( e.clickCount == 2 )  // double click
            {
                setForeground(getBackground());
                repaint();
            }
            else
            {
                lineStart.move(e.x,e.y);
            }
              return true;

          case Event.MOUSE_DRAG:
```

```
         g = getGraphics();
         if ( e.metaDown() || e.shiftDown())  //right button - erase
         {   // we'll erase with an oval to cut a wider swath
             g.fillOval(e.x - (circleSize / 2),
             e.y - (circleSize / 2 ),
             circleSize, circleSize );
         }
         else
             g.drawLine(lineStart.x, lineStart.y, e.x, e.y);

         lineStart.move(e.x,e.y);
         return true;

     case Event.MOUSE_UP:
         showStatus(e.toString());
         return true;

     case Event.MOUSE_ENTER:
         showStatus("Hello....");
         return true;

     case Event.MOUSE_EXIT:
         showStatus("Goodbye...");
         return true;
     }
     return super.handleEvent(e);
 }

}
```

To handle the events, we created a switch statement, much like the one in the default **handleEvent()** method, where we check for the event ID of the events we're looking for, and implement the code to respond to them.

Notice that in the last line, rather than returning false, we return the result of a call to the superclass **handleEvent()** method. The reason for this is that there are two possible hierarchy chains to follow to look for event handlers. One is up the embedded chain or container tree. For example, a Button embedded within an instance of a Panel that is itself embedded within another instance of a larger Panel, etc. The second possible hierarchy chain is the chain of subclasses. For example, **myAnimationButton** that is a subclass of **myImageButton** that is a subclass of Button, etc. It's usually desirable to have the run-time system transverse the subclass chain first, then go to the enclosing container and check out all of its superclasses. The effect of this call using **super.handleEvent()**, is that the event is first passed up the class hierarchy. If we simply return false, the event will be propagated up to the embedded or container parent, not to the superclass. Since the default **handleEvent()** wouldn't be invoked, other default behavior, such as calling other 'helper' methods like **keyDown()** or **action()**, would be lost. In this applet, it wouldn't matter, but in many cases, it might, so get into the habit of calling the superclass **handleEvent()** whenever you override it.

The Other Helper Methods

Let's go through one more example applet to show some of the 'helper' methods in action:

▲ **keyDown(Event, Key)**–Called when a key is pressed.

▲ **keyUp(Event, Key)**–Called when a key is released.

▲ **action(Event, Object)**–Called when a specific user interface action occurs, such as clicking on a button.

▲ **gotFocus(Event, Object)**–Called when a component gains focus.

▲ **lostFocus(Event, Object)**–Called when a component loses focus.

This applet will display a message when a key has been pressed, focus has been lost or received, and when an Action event has been received. Just type a letter, and the letter will be displayed in the applet. Depending on where the focus is, your input may not be received by the applet without clicking on it first. A command button has been included to generate action events, don't worry about how it was added, we'll cover that in the components section in a later chapter.

Here's the source:

```java
import java.awt.*;
import java.applet.*;

public class helpers extends Applet
{
    String msgStr;

    public void init()
    {
        setFont(new Font("TimesRoman", Font.BOLD, 24));
        msgStr = "Press any key...";
        setForeground(Color.blue);
        add(new Button("make action event"));
        resize(400,200);
    }

    public void start()
    {
        requestFocus();
    }

    public boolean keyDown(Event e,  int key)
    {
        msgStr = "\"" + (char)key + "\"" + " key pressed";
        repaint();
        return true;
    }

    public boolean keyUp(Event e,  int key)
    {
        msgStr = "\"" + (char)key + "\"" + " key released";
        repaint();
        return true;
```

```
    }

    public boolean gotFocus(Event e,  Object arg)
    {
        msgStr = "Got Focus";
        if (arg!= null)
            msgStr = msgStr + " arg: " + arg.toString();
        repaint();
        return true;
    }

    public boolean lostFocus(Event e,  Object arg)
    {
        msgStr = "Lost Focus" ;
        if (arg != null)
            msgStr = msgStr + " arg: " + arg.toString();
        repaint();
        return true;
    }

    public boolean action(Event e,  Object arg)
    {
        msgStr = "Action Event." ;
        if (arg != null)
            msgStr = msgStr + " Arg: " + arg.toString();
        repaint();
        return true;
    }

    public void paint(Graphics g)
    {
        FontMetrics currFM = g.getFontMetrics();
        g.drawString(msgStr, ( size().width -
        currFM.stringWidth(msgStr)) / 2,
        (size().height- currFM.getHeight())/ 2 +
        currFM.getLeading() + currFM.getAscent());
    }

}
```

And here's a screen snapshot of the applet in action:

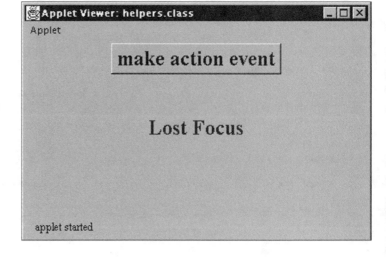

This applet is fairly self-explanatory so we'll skip the line-by-line analysis. When a **keyDown()**, **keyUp()**, **gotFocus()**, **lostFocus()** or **action** event is fired, the **msgStr** String object is set to an informational message about the event being handled, and a repaint is requested. In the **paint()** method, the **msgStr** object is drawn in the center of the screen. To center the string, we use a FontMetrics object to obtain information about the font currently selected. We'll cover fonts in the next chapter, so let's focus on the event-related stuff for now.

There's one note to remember about the **gotFocus()** and **lostFocus()** events, the Object parameter will usually be null, so be prepared. Either check for null before using it or get ready to catch a **NullPointerException**.

You'll find these helper events to be quite easy to use. They will also add a nice structured style to your code which will increase its readability and maintainability.

How Do You Choose Where to Handle an Event?

All of the events mentioned so far could be handled by a helper method or in a **handleEvent()** method override. In the next chapters, the question will get more complex because when components are in a container you can choose to handle them in the component itself or in the container. You'll see that in many cases there's no hard and fast rule which can be applied. Use your judgment to select the method which you believe makes the code most understandable and maintainable.

Summary

In this chapter, we started by explaining the function of the Abstract Window Toolkit (AWT) in Java. We explained why this necessitated a change in approach from traditional procedural programming to event-driven programming. We then looked at how event-driven handling is done in Java, and in particular what events the mouse generates. We looked at a 'doodle' applet which implements each of the mouse events to do its drawing. We then looked at how the **handleEvent()** method could be used to catch mouse events without the relevant helper methods. Finally, we looked at some remaining helper methods in an applet which caught these events and returned information to the user about the event.

In the next chapter, we'll lay the foundation for graphics programming in Java and continue to utilize what we've learned here about events.

AWT Graphics Fundamentals

Now that you have a basic understanding of events, you can put them to good use—and what better use is there than colorful, moving graphics? First, we must start with a concept that is fundamental to all graphical windowing systems: the notion of a graphic context and its attributes. Next, we talk about a second fundamental concept called persistence, which prepares us for our discussion on the three important graphics-related methods. Finally, we cover in detail three common Graphics attributes: color, clipping regions and fonts. By the end of this chapter you'll understand:

 The graphics context and how it affects all drawing

 What persistence is and how windowing systems compensate

 How to keep what you draw on the screen

 The **paint()**, **update()**, and **repaint()** methods, and when to use them

 How to override the **update()** method to avoid screen flicker

 What Graphics attributes are

 The difference between Color Spaces and Color Models

 How to set and change the color of objects

 How to use colors to your advantage

 What a Clip Area is and how to use it

 How to specify and use fonts

The Graphic Context

Fundamentally, the computer screen consists of small discrete picture elements called **pixels** that collectively form an array. All graphic operations ultimately boil down to illuminating the desired pixel in the array with the desired color—be it black, white, gray, or red. Naturally, it would be rather tedious to specify a drawing pixel-by-pixel, so the JDK provides methods to draw higher level objects such as lines, shapes and text. In computer graphics parlance, we call this drawing operation a **rendering** operation. These rendering methods use attributes that determine just how to draw this higher level object on the screen. For example, the font type, as well as style, point size, foreground, and background colors, are all attributes of a string of text. An internal data structure preserves this collection of attributes and forms a context, specifically a graphics context, and all graphics operations refer to this context before rendering any object. As we would expect, a class called Graphics manages this graphics context or set of rendering properties.

You can think of the Graphics class as an abstract device to which the programmer draws or writes text. You can perform graphics operations, which are device-dependent by nature, without a detailed knowledge of the type or capabilities of the underlying video hardware. It not only remembers and maintains all the graphics attributes and properties together in one convenient place, but also allows our drawings to look as predictable as possible on various platforms.

In Java, you can't create a graphics context directly. As an abstract class, the Graphics object isn't instantiated–you must get a new one from an existing Component or Image using the **getGraphics()** method. The following line will generate a compiler error:

```
Graphics myGC = new Graphics(); // ...did this once, it doesn't work!
```

The following code segment is an example of how to obtain a Graphics object directly from another object using the **getGraphics()** method:

```
Image img;                              // an offscreen image
Graphics imgGC;
int w = 250;
int h = 250;

public void int()  {
   resize(w,h);
   img = createImage(w, h);            // first we create an offscreen image
   imgGC = img.getGraphics();    // now get the context from the image

   // now we can change the attributes of this offscreen image

}
```

The **createImage()** method is rather intuitive, so no need to worry about the details now. The important thing to observe here is that we first get the context or Graphics object from another object. Not so obvious is, that the current attributes (background color, font style, and point size, for example) of the original object become the default attributes of the new context. If we just want a copy of an existing context, we use the **create()** method. After we obtain the Graphics object we can later adjust the attributes to suit our needs.

> The use of the Graphics object is analogous to the use of the Device Context in Microsoft Windows programming, the GrafPort in Macintosh programming, or the Graphics Context or GC in X11 Windows programming. We prefer using the term Context since the word Graphics alone is rather overused and leads to ambiguity.

Persistence

Consider a hypothetical windowing system displaying a complicated illustration, painstakingly rendered with radiant colors. Now the user moves another large window on top of the masterpiece and obscures it, then later, returns that large window to its original location. In the frame where we expect to see the colorful drawing, we now see nothing. What happened to our artwork? This graphics system didn't save the original pixel values of the drawing prior to painting the new window on top of it. So, those pixel values are simply lost. In other words, this graphics system isn't **persistent**.

Most modern windowing systems aren't persistent but provide mechanisms to compensate. Typically, a window manager monitors all screen activity. When the user makes a change that damages or exposes part or all of another application, the window manager sends a notification to the embarrassed application. This notification is an **exposure** event and tells the compromised application that part or all of its window needs repainting. It's the application itself that repairs any damage done by the windowing system.

Java implements this mechanism using a combination of an internal system thread called the AWT Callback Thread and three Component methods named **paint()**, **update()**, and **repaint()**. The programmer has no control over this thread–it's part of the Java Virtual Machine. However, it's important to understanding its operation and how it calls these methods. The following diagram illustrates the relationship between these methods and the AWT Callback Thread:

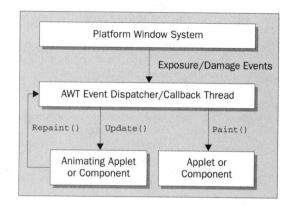

AWT Callback Thread

The AWT Callback Thread is one of the system threads that are always running in the Java Virtual Machine (another similar thread, for example, is the Garbage Collector). This thread calls both the **paint()** and the **update()** methods–but for different reasons or circumstances, as we'll describe in the next two sections. The Java system automatically constructs a default graphics context, a Graphics object, and passes a reference to it as a parameter to these methods. This object reference is local in nature; it's good only for the life of the method, so you can't use it after the method exits. As pointed out in the first section of this chapter, this reference is necessary because all rendering requires a graphics context.

> Remember that there's only one AWT Callback Thread. Consequently, the easiest way to get incomplete or strange-looking screens is to do something in one of these methods that causes this thread to block. If it blocks, it obviously can't call any component method.

paint() Method

The AWT Callback Thread asynchronously calls the **paint()** method when either of two broad situations occur. First, when you haven't overridden the default **update()** method; and second, when the visibility of the applet window has changed. The first one isn't really a separate case. However, it's important to remember, since this is the source of much confusion about the **paint()** and **update()** methods. This should become much clearer in the next section, where we show the source code for the default **update()** method.

The second situation is indeed quite broad. Whenever the visibility of our application or applet window changes, the platform's window manager sends an exposure event to the AWT Callback Thread. This event includes the coordinates of the portion of the application screen where the visibility changed. The AWT Callback Thread determines which of the program's many possible components lie within those coordinates, and then calls the **paint()** method of each exposed component.

What actually constitutes a change in visibility? The following list describes four events that are significant to cause the exposure event and subsequent **paint()** call:

▲ When the window first becomes visible. It's easy to overlook this case.

▲ When you resize the window. It isn't necessary for the actual component within the window to change visibility, just the window. It's easy to see that a component's visibility changes when we make the window smaller than that component. When we make a window larger, the visibility of any component inside that window doesn't really change. Both window changes, smaller and larger, force the call.

▲ When you maximize or de-iconify the window. This one is obvious.

▲ When part or all of the window becomes damaged. This is due to the lack of persistence on the part of the windowing system. When only part of a window becomes damaged, the platform windowing system passes the coordinates of the damaged portion only to the AWT Callback Thread. The AWT Callback Thread then sets what we call a **clipping region** (detailed later in this chapter) prior to calling the **paint()** method.

> Note that the AWT Callback Thread doesn't call the **paint()** method when you simply move a window. In this case, it's the windowing system that clears the old location and paints the window to the new location.

One last point before we leave the **paint()** method. When the AWT Callback Thread calls this method, it first clears the background color. It does this internally. If you're painting a color that's different from the background, the background color will flash momentarily on the screen just before the **paint()** method does its job.

update() Method

One of the best features of Java is its efficient network-centric approach to downloading media. Consider loading a large image, for example, from across the network. Depending on the image size, this operation can take numerous seconds, or even minutes. Consequently, Java does the loading incrementally. After each iteration, the AWT Callback Thread calls the **update()** method. This allows the program to actually update (oh, so that's why they called it update) the screen while the loading is in progress.

If we search the file **src/java/awt/Component.java** in the Java source for the **update()** method, we find that it consists of only four lines of code:

```
public void update(Graphics g) {
    g.setColor(getBackground());
    g.fillRect(0, 0, width, height);
    g.setColor(getForeground());
    paint(g);
}
```

First, look at the last line. **update()** in turn calls **paint()**. (This is why **paint()** gets called when we don't override the **update()** method as stated in the previous section.) The first line sets the current color to the component's background color; the second fills the component's display area with the current color. The third line sets the current color to the component's foreground color. Again, we see that if you fill the background with a different color in **paint()**, you'll see a momentary flash each time the AWT Callback Thread calls **update()**. The difference here is that we can override the method like this:

```
public void update(Graphics g) {
   paint(g);
}
```

Without clearing the default background, this new **update()** method directly calls the **paint()** method which eliminates the screen flicker.

repaint() Method

It's hard enough to keep the above two methods straight when one method calls the other. Now, to muddy the waters: this third Component method, **repaint()**, causes the AWT Callback Thread to eventually call the **update()** method! All should become clearer once we understand the differences between these methods.

There are two things that make the **repaint()** method different from **paint()** and **update()**. First, the **repaint()** method doesn't require a parameter reference to a Graphics object. This isn't a problem because you usually don't have access to one in the routines where you want to use **repaint()**. Second, the call to **repaint()** returns immediately without repainting anything. It's a request to the AWT Callback Thread that it should call the **update()** method as soon as possible, and so the result is asynchronous. It schedules exactly when to act on this request and we have no control over it. In addition, multiple calls to **repaint()** can be collapsed into a single request and subsequently, a single call to **update()**–all at the discretion of the AWT Callback Thread.

Again, if we look at the Java source in **src/java/awt/Component.java**, we find that there are actually four repaint methods:

▲ **public void repaint()**

This is the one you'll probably use most often. It queues a call to **update()** as explained above.

▲ **public void repaint(long tm)**

This will schedule a call to **update()** within **tm** milliseconds. If **tm** milliseconds expire before the AWT Callback Thread can call **update()**, the request is dropped on the floor and forgotten about. Since there's no return value or exception thrown, you never know for sure if the AWT Callback Thread called **update()**, so be careful with this one.

▲ **public void repaint(int x, int y, int width, int height)**

This version likewise schedules a call to **update()**. In this case, however, the request is only for the rectangle region specified by the parameters. In other words, the JVM only repaints the region we explicitly define.

▲ **public void repaint(long tm, int x, int y, int width, int height)**

This is the granddaddy of them all. Each of the first three versions above actually calls this one using appropriate default parameters.

> As a consequence of this calling architecture, there's an indeterminable amount of time between our call to repaint() and when update() actually repaints the Component. This means that you shouldn't use time-critical or state-transitional code in update(). The benefits of this architecture are numerous: more efficient screen management, better mouse tracking and improvements in the overall performance of event-driven software.

When to Use the Component Methods

Now that we've described the three Component methods, **paint()**, **update()**, and **repaint()**, when and how should you use them? The first thing to remember is that you'll never need to call **paint()**–the AWT Callback Thread always calls it for you. The same is usually true for **update()**. The only one you directly call is **repaint()**. Think of it this way: **paint()** and **update()** are for overriding; **repaint()** is for calling.

If you use a static display with just menus and button-like components, you probably won't need to override or call these methods. When you have a dynamic display with things that change, like animation for example, then you typically override the **paint()** method and insert the rendering code, then call **repaint()** after each change. This instructs the AWT Callback Thread to call **update()** which in turn calls **paint()**. A complex animation usually requires that you override **update()** to eliminate screen flicker as explained earlier.

The correct use of these methods is vital to the proper display of all graphics on the screen. As with most things in life, there's an appropriate and inappropriate time to use them. In the section on colors, we develop an applet that should help you get an intuitive feel for this painting mechanism.

Graphics Attributes

We've talked about how to paint on the screen using the **update()**, **paint()** and **repaint()** methods. We've also talked about how to keep things on the screen once painted. Now, our concern is their appearance or how they look on the screen. In this section, we'll talk in detail about three of the graphics attributes. Java isn't very sophisticated when it comes to the richness or extent of attributes provided–our cup isn't exactly overflowing here. However, these core attributes provide enough functionality for most circumstances. Future releases of the Toolkit will no doubt expand and extend the current capabilities. We'll start with a discussion on colors, then proceed to clipping regions, and finally cover fonts.

Colors

Before the color monitor became so ubiquitous, monochrome monitors were the norm. Most people considered color an unnecessary and costly extravagance. Only artistic types could justify a nice color monitor. Now that the street price for color monitors is affordable, all that has changed. Most PC companies don't even advertise monochrome monitors, even if they manufacture them. However, the advantages of using color have always been there. Even during the expensive period, color contributed tremendously to the user-computer experience.

We can simplify the user interface by using color to order and classify menus, associate related icons, and enhance or subdue active and inactive windows. We can more easily understand output data if we use color to help organize complexity. Color can reveal the structure and relationships of information otherwise difficult to decipher. It's more than just a pretty face. Color research has shown the positive effects of color on response time, error rate, and learning.

Since color is one of the first things a user will notice in our applets, we should understand how to use it to our advantage. We'll start by discussing the subtle distinction between color spaces and color models. After that, we'll talk in detail about the Color class before giving some suggestions on color usage. Finally, we conclude this subsection with a couple of applets.

Color Spaces and Models

A **Color Space** is simply a way to represent a given color. These spaces are useful for visualizing the relationships between one color and another. Over the centuries in which scientists have been studying color, they have come up with many different spaces. All of these spaces fall into two basic types: color generation spaces and color perception spaces.

Color generation spaces rely on the additive nature of the three primary colors, red, green, and blue.

> **For the purposes of computer graphics, the additive primary colors are red, green, and blue, in the form of lights, because when these colors are mixed they form a wider range of colors than the primary colors of the artist's palette, red, yellow, and blue.**

We produce a secondary set of colors when we combine these three primaries in pairs; we produce black when we combine all three. No two primaries can produce a third primary. The computer CRT uses this additive technique to generate pixel colors. It uses three different phosphors that glow red or green or blue, respectively, when excited by an electron gun. The amount or intensity of each of the three color phosphors is a direct result of electron gun voltages.

Only within the last 65 years, have color vision research and experimental data resulted in the development of new spaces that rely on color perception. These spaces are useful for visualizing the relationship of subjective psychological aspects of color like hue, saturation, and brightness.

You might be asking yourself why are we using the term **space** instead of **model**. Indeed, we hear model used in this sense more often than space. However, the Java designers used the term model to imply something a little different. In Java, color models describe the screen's pixel-to-color relationship—not the way to specify colors. The **ColorModel** class is part of the AWT image package. It's an abstract class used to encapsulate the different ways to use individual pixel values. This is important because the vision for Java is to extend beyond our familiar PC to support the displaying of images on all sorts of diverse display devices in small appliances. These could include microwave ovens, PDAs, printers, car navigation systems, and cellular telephones, each using a different display technology and pixel usage.

The AWT includes two classes that extend the **ColorModel** class: the **DirectColorModel** class and the **IndexColorModel** class. Each encapsulates a different way to encode image pixel values. Each implements methods to convert their particular pixel representation into the individual RGB components, so the application can manipulate the colors in a familiar way. They even support an additional color component—the alpha color—that is useful in image processing applications. The **DirectColorModel** class encodes the individual color components directly in the bits of the pixel value itself. This is the default model used on the PC. The **IndexColorModel** uses the pixel value as an index into a fixed colormap array. The colormap array itself consists of multiple arrays that each holds the individual color components.

> **The use of the ColorModel object is analogous to the use of the Visual in X11 Windows programming. The Java DirectColorModel object is similar to an X11 TrueColor visual and the IndexColorModel is similar to an X11 PseudoColor visual. X11 supports four other visual types not currently defined in the AWT. However, Java allows us to derive any model type by extending the ColorModel class.**

Color Class

The AWT supports color definition and choice through the **Color** class. This class allows us to use either of two color spaces; one color generation type and one color perception type. However, the class implements support for each space differently.

Specifying a Color

You can characterize a color using the RGB Space by specifying the individual red, green, and blue components that, when combined, produce the desired color. There are three constructors each supporting a different format for specifying the individual RGB components:.

▲ **public Color(int r, int g, int b);**

This one uses a separate integer parameter for each RGB component. Each parameter is in the range 0–255. Only the lower order 8 bits are significant in these integers. A red component specified as 0xFFFFFF01 is the same as 0x00000001.

▲ **public Color(int rgb);**

This one uses a single integer parameter—usually written in hexadecimal to help readability—for all three RGB components. The red component is in bits 16–24, the green component is in bits 8–15, and the blue component is in bits 0–7. For instance, 0xFF0000 is pure red, 0x00FF00 is pure green, and 0x0000FF is pure blue.

▲ **public Color(float r, float g, float b);**

This one is similar to the first constructor above except here we specify each RGB component in a float value in the range 0.0–1.0.

Alternatively, you can use the HSB Space by specifying the hue, saturation, and brightness components of the desired color. In this case, we have to use a static method since the class doesn't provide an HSB space constructor directly. The following illustrates this:

```
Color c;
hue = 0.1f;
sat = 0.7f;
bright = 1.0f;
c = Color.getHSBColor(hue, sat, bright);
```

If you request an unavailable color, Java will either map it to another color or dither it. The actual color returned from the above methods depends on finding the best match between the requested and available colors.

Converting One Color Space to Another

The Color class also provides two methods to convert from one color space to another.

▲ **public static int HSBtoRGB(float h, float s, float b);**

This method returns the RGB value of the color corresponding to the given HSB color components.

 `public static float[] RGBtoHSB(int r, int g, int b, float vals[]);`

This method returns the HSB values corresponding to the color defined by the red, green, and blue components. The float array **vals[]** stores the resulting hue, saturation, and brightness values if we specify this parameter array as non-null. Otherwise, this method returns an array of floats containing the HSB values.

From just a color-usage point of view, there are several things to consider when choosing which color space to use. However, from a practical programming perspective, there are only two: user preference and the importance of computational speed to the application. The methods using the RGB Space are faster than those of the HSB Space. This is because the RGB Space is essentially the same model used by the video hardware and CRT to generate pixel colors. When using the HSB Space, conversion to the red, green, and blue component values for screen display is ultimately necessary.

Retrieving Components from a Color Object

At any time, we can retrieve the individual components from a color object:

```
public int getRed();
public int getGreen();
public int getBlue();
```

These return an integer corresponding to their respective RGB component.

```
public int getRGB();
```

This returns an integer that corresponds to the default RGB ColorModel. Bits 24–31 are hard-coded as 0xFF, bits 16–24 are the red component, bits 8–15 are the green component, and bits 0–7 are the blue component.

Other useful methods in the Color class include the following:

```
public Color brighter();
public Color darker();
```

These return a brighter and darker version of the color, respectively.

As a programming convenience, the Color class defines thirteen final static variables containing common colors. The following table lists these variable names with their respective RGB specification. The values are in a byte hexadecimal format.

Color	Red	Green	Blue
black	0x00	0x00	0x00
blue	0x00	0x00	0xFF
cyan	0x00	0xFF	0xFF
darkGray	0x40	0x40	0x40
gray	0x80	0x80	0x80

Table Continued on Following Page

Color	Red	Green	Blue
green	0x00	0xFF	0x00
lightGray	0xC0	0xC0	0xC0
magenta	0xFF	0x00	0xFF
orange	0xFF	0xC8	0x00
pink	0xFF	0xAF	0xAF
red	0xFF	0x00	0x00
white	0xFF	0xFF	0xFF
yellow	0xFF	0xFF	0x00

Remember that Java is case-sensitive. Consequently, using the variable **Red** or **darkgray** will produce a compiler error. The Color class is a final class, so this is the proper way to use these variables in a **setBackground()** method for example:

```
setBackground(Color.lightGray);
```

Color Guidelines

The following are some guidelines for color selection and usage–they are based on color perception research and can serve as suggestions.

▲ Follow established standards when they are appropriate for an application and maintain consistent color assignments.

▲ Use a minimum number of colors. If we do the math, Java allows us to specify almost 17 million different colors–but we don't have to use them all at once! In reality, we only have access to as many colors as are supported on the underlying video hardware.

▲ If the user needs to remember the meanings of colors, use no more than five colors. The next time you want to use more than seven colors concurrently, consider the resulting confusion if traffic lights at busy street intersections used seven colors instead of three.

▲ Whenever possible, use the default Java colors.

▲ Remember that some users have color vision deficiencies. Most problematic are cyan with white and blue with purple.

▲ Don't use the same intensity of green and red for 'safe' and 'danger'–use colors with differing intensity.

▲ Try to avoid using pure colors that consist of mostly one of the three primary colors. Use colors that consist of two or all three primary colors–they light up the screen more.

▲ Try to avoid saturated blue, especially for extremely small graphics, fonts or images. The reason is that the human eye is less sensitive to blue than to the other two primary colors. Sometimes the eye is unable to focus on images made of pure blue. When using blue shades, mix them with white because white contains equal parts of all three primary colors.

▲ Try to enhance color harmony by using color combinations that are opposite in the color space. In the RGB space, the opposite color combinations are red and cyan, blue and yellow, and green and magenta. Spectrally extreme combinations–like red and blue or red and green–are less harmonious. Adjacent color combinations are also less harmonious. These include the blue and cyan, cyan and green, green and yellow, yellow and red, red and magenta, and magenta and blue combinations.

▲ Remember that different cultures have different associations to colors. In the US, for example, the color yellow usually means caution or cowardice; in Japan, they associate it with grace and nobility; in Egypt, it's happiness and prosperity.

rgbpaint Applet

The following Applet does several things, none very practical, but all very educational.

▲ It ties together a lot of material we have seen up to this point.

▲ It demonstrates both the **Color** class we just covered as well as mouse events that we discussed in the previous chapter.

▲ It's also a perfect example to give an intuitive feel for when the JVM calls the **update()** and **paint()** methods as explained in a previous section.

▲ Finally, it shows how to create a cool color spectrum effect.

If the video card on your PC supports 16 or 24 bit color, it's very instructive to run this applet under those higher color modes. It not only shows a gradually shaded color spectrum, but also illustrates the device independent nature of the Graphics class–no code changes are necessary to view the color spectrum at different color resolutions.

When it's first initialized, **rgbpaint()** shows a blank area with text at the bottom next to the Applet status area. When the user clicks on the mouse button, the **paintColor()** method paints the color spectrum. It will monitor the number of calls to our three paint methods and tell us how long it took to paint the spectrum. This is what it looks like:

Here is the source:

```java
import java.awt.*;
import java.applet.*;
import java.util.Date;

public class rgbpaint extends Applet
{
    int paintCounter = 0;
    int updateCounter = 0;
    int repaintCounter = 0;

    public void init()
    {
        resize(256, 330);
        setBackground(Color.lightGray);
    }
    public void paint(Graphics g)
    {
        g.setColor(Color.black);
        g.drawString("Mouseclick to call paintColor()",1,275);
        g.drawString("Shift-Mouseclick to call repaint()",1,290);
        g.drawString("Paints: " + ++paintCounter + "  Updates: "
            + updateCounter + "  Repaint requests: "
            + repaintCounter, 1, 305);
    }

    public void update(Graphics g)
    {
        updateCounter++;
        g.setColor(getBackground());
        g.fillRect(0,0,size().width,size().height);
        paint(g);
    }

    public boolean mouseDown(Event e, int x, int y)
    {
        if (e.shiftDown())
        {
            repaintCounter += 2;
            repaint();
            repaint();
        }
        else paintColor();
        return true;
    }

    public boolean mouseMove(Event e, int x, int y)
    {
        if (y > 255) y = 0;
        showStatus(
            "Red: = " + x +
            "  Green: = " + (255 - y) +
            "  Blue: " +  y);
        return true;
    }
```

```
public void paintColor()
{
        int x, y;
        long startTime;
        Date date = new Date();
        startTime = date.getTime();
        Graphics g = getGraphics();

        for (y = 0; y <= 255; y+=5)
        {
                for (x = 0; x <= 255; x+=5)
                {
                        g.setColor(new Color(x,(255 - y),y));
                        g.fillRect(x,y,5, 5);
                }
        }

        date = new Date();
        g.setColor(Color.black);
        g.drawString("Paint time(milliseconds): " +
                (date.getTime() - startTime), 1,320);
}
}
```

We define three counters to keep track of the calls made to the **update()**, **paint()**, and **repaint()** methods. In the **init()** method, we resize the applet to 256 by 330 pixels. There is nothing significant about this size except that it will make **paint()** simple later on. The larger y value allows for more room after the color spectrum so we can see our calling reports. Then we set the default background color to light gray, using the predefined **lightGray** color in the Color class.

Our **paint()** method is very simple. We simply draw the user instructions and current counter values to the screen and increment the **paintCounter** variable. We have overridden the **update()** method to do nothing except increment our update counter and call **paint()**. We put in the code to fill the background, but commented it out for now. You should remove the comments at some point to see how it changes the behavior of the painting. Functionally, the **mouseDown()** method will invoke either the **paintColor()** method or two **repaint()** calls, depending on the state of the shift key. We call **repaint()** twice to illustrate that the AWT Callback Thread can collapse the second one into a single request. The **mouseMove()** method writes the RGB values to the status line so we can see the composition of the color at the mouse coordinates.

The last method in our applet is **paintColor()** which paints a color spectrum of sorts to the screen. We produce this effect by dynamically creating colors based on the x and y coordinates. Then we paint small 5 pixel-wide squares to the screen in each created color. We nest a loop within a loop and use the Graphics **setColor()** method to set the current color to a new one. We use the x coordinate for the red component, the y coordinate for the blue component, and 255 minus the y coordinate for the green component to construct the new color. Pure green is in the upper left corner while pure blue is in the bottom left corner. Yellow is in the upper right, purple is in the lower right, and all kinds of combinations are in between. The 5 pixel width of the squares is arbitrary. It results in 2704 different Color objects being created and an equal amount of squares being drawn. We could have used 1 pixel squares but that would have resulted in 65536 colors and draws. While we wanted to pick an example of an intense graphic, we didn't want to go overboard! Visually, you'll see no difference anyway. On most platforms, you don't have near that many different colors. You may want to try modifying the logic to draw larger squares, until you get to the point where you start to see a difference.

Painting this effect is quite time consuming. In the next example, we show how to speed it up, so we have put in some timing logic for comparison purposes. At the beginning of the method, we declare and instantiate a new Date object. The **Date** class is a wrapper for a date that has some useful methods for returning the day, hour, minute, weekday, and many other useful date properties. The **Date()** constructor initializes the new Date object to the current date and time. To get the value we need, we invoke the **getTime()** method that returns the number of milliseconds since the last epoch, and save the result. At the end of **paintColor()** we instantiate a new Date object to get the new time (isn't it nice to not have to worry about deleting the previous date object?). The last action we perform in the **paintColor()** method is to print the elapsed time to the screen.

Take some time and play with this applet in the AppletViewer. Resize it and you'll see the call to **paint()**, but not **update()**. Click the mouse button quickly and you can actually get ahead of the **paintColor()** method. When you stop clicking, it will still be repainting. If you shift-click, you'll notice usually only one call to **update()** even though there are two calls to **repaint()**. You can even see more dropped **repaint()** calls if you shift-click very fast. Also, try covering part of the AppletViewer window and then uncover it. Notice the call to **paint()**, but only for the covered part of the window.

At certain points, the counts may appear garbled on the screen. This is because our **update()** method doesn't clear the screen. When you uncomment the two lines in **update()**, the problem will go away for the call numbers but not for the elapsed time message—we render the time message in the **paintColor()** method. Take note of the paint time detailed on the screen. On a 133 MHz PC running Windows 95, the **paintColor()** method takes about 750 milliseconds. On a 150 MHz PC optimized for 24 bit color, it takes 710 milliseconds. The same machine using 8 bit color took over 1.2 seconds! Play with this applet, add code, modify it, and view the results until you have a good feel for the painting process.

Improved rgbpaint Applet

In the previous example, the most intense section was the process of going through the rows and columns to build the color spectrum. We built the color spectrum every time we called **paintColor()**—even though the result never changed. We could actually see the graphic progressing each time we painted a row. We chose a time consuming process to illustrate how a simple technique will improve the overall performance of our applet.

In this next example, we use a technique called **double buffering** to speed up the apparent screen painting. The term double buffering refers to using two drawing surfaces. One surface is off-screen where we prepare the graphic; the other surface is the actual visible screen. To implement this technique, we create the color spectrum off-screen once, then copy it to the screen only when necessary. This will speed up the **paintColor()** method dramatically, because we don't have the overhead of constructing Color objects and drawing rectangles. In most cases, the double-buffer technique won't speed up the actual rendering. Preparing a graphic off-screen isn't necessarily quicker than building it right on the actual visible display device. It obviously requires more system resources because of the need to store the off-screen graphic. However the overall efficiency of our applet has improved. The new and improved source code reads:

```
import java.awt.*;
import java.applet.*;
import java.util.Date;

public class rgbpaint2 extends Applet
{
    int paintCounter = 0;
```

```
int updateCounter = 0;
int repaintCounter = 0;
Graphics grphScratch;
Image imgScratch;

public void init()
{
      int x, y;
      resize(256, 330);
      imgScratch = createImage(256,256);
      grphScratch = imgScratch.getGraphics();
      for (y = 0; y <= 255; y+=5)
      {
             for (x = 0; x <= 255; x+=5)
             {
                    grphScratch.setColor(new Color(x,255 - y,y));
                    grphScratch.fillRect(x,y,5,  5);
             }
      }
      setBackground(Color.lightGray);
}

public void paint(Graphics g)
{
      g.setColor(Color.black);
      g.drawString("Mouse click to call paintColor()",1,275);
      g.drawString("Shift-Mouse click to call repaint()",1,290);
      g.drawString("Paints: " + ++paintCounter + "  Updates: " +
            updateCounter +
            "  Repaint requests: " + repaintCounter, 1, 305);
}

public void update(Graphics g)
{
      updateCounter++;
      g.setColor(getBackground());
      g.fillRect(0,0,size().width,size().height);
      paint(g);
}

public boolean mouseDown(Event e, int x, int y)
{
      if (e.shiftDown())
      {
             repaintCounter += 2;
             repaint();
             repaint();
      }
      else  paintColor();
      return true;
}

public boolean mouseMove(Event e, int x, int y)
{
      if (y > 255) y = 0;
      showStatus("Red: = " + x + "  Green: = " + (255 - y) +
            "  Blue: " +  y);
```

```
            return true;
      }

   public void paintColor()
   {
         int x,y;
         long startTime;
         Date date = new Date();
         startTime = date.getTime();
         Graphics g = getGraphics();

         g.drawImage(imgScratch,0,0,this);
         date = new Date();
         g.drawString("Paint time(milliseconds): " +
                (date.getTime() - startTime), 1,320);
      }
   }
```

We added declarations for both an Image object and a Graphics object that we need for the off-screen buffer. In **init()**, we create the image using the **createImage()** method. Then we use the **getGraphics()** method from the Image class to obtain a graphics context for writing into the image. This context will only work for off-screen images. Next, we have moved the loop that creates the Colors into **init()** since we only need to go through it once. Inside the loop, we draw the rectangles using the image's graphic context. In **paintColor()**, we modified the logic to use the **drawImage()** method to copy the **imgScratch** object to the applet's graphic object, i.e. the visible screen.

The applet behavior is essentially unchanged except for the speed up. When run on the 133 MHz machine described earlier, the **paintColor()** method runs in under 50 milliseconds compared to 770+ milliseconds in the previous example. Keep in mind that we have added some time to the initialization. The difference will be roughly the same amount of time it took to complete one **paintColor()** method. In this case, the tradeoff is clearly worth it. For other situations, it may be a harder decision.

Clipping Regions

In the previous example, our paint methods operated on the whole screen all the time. This was sufficient for the application. However, when we get to complicated graphics that are constantly changing, like animation for example, this is obviously not the way to go. Why not just paint the part that has changed? Efficient paint methods should only paint the part of the display that has changed since the last time it was painted.

There are two ways to tell the AWT which part of the screen to paint. We can use the **repaint(x, y, width, height)** method instead of the normal **repaint()**.

Alternatively, we can use the **clipRect()** method to set a clipping region. This clipping region is one of the attributes of our Graphics object and it limits the area of the screen that gets painted. The following are the two clip-related methods in the **Graphics** class.

▲   **public abstract void clipRect(int x, int y, int width, int height);**

This one defines a clipping region of the specified rectangle. Graphic operations have no effect outside the clipping area.

`public abstract Rectangle getClipRect();`

This one returns the current clipping region. Note that it will return null if the entire Component or Image is the current clip region.

The use of the Graphics **clipRect()** method is conceptually very easy. This method tells the AWT not to paint anything outside of a specified rectangle. Even though the JVM executes the full **update()** and **paint()** methods, it ignores the portions of the graphics that are outside this newly defined region. All subsequent graphics operations are confined to this area. Repeated use of **clipRect()** creates a rectangle area that is the intersection of the previous area and the newly specified rectangle.

This is a very useful method when you know that only a limited part of the screen has changed, and there is no need to paint the whole thing. Using a clipping region results in quicker paints with less flicker. The trouble is that we have to calculate the rectangle to pass to the method. Complicating the problem further is the fact that not every call to **repaint()** results in a call to **update()** and a subsequent **paint()**, as we explained in a previous section. We not only have to figure out what region has changed since the last time we executed **repaint()** (which isn't too hard), but we have to know what region has changed since the last time the AWT Callback Thread actually executed **paint()**. Ouch!

clipper Applet

In this next example, we demonstrate both techniques just described, where we restrict the paint area. This Applet continuously paints a red circle and increments location variables to make the ball appear like it's moving. Whenever it gets to a window boundary, we switch the direction so that it looks like it's bouncing around inside the applet:

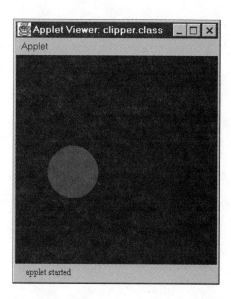

Currently, you'll find that this Applet employs the **clipRect** method, although it's a fairly trivial task to alter it to use the **repaint** method. The source code is as follows:

```
import java.awt.*;
import java.applet.*;

public class clipper extends Applet implements Runnable
{
    int xLoc = 0;
    int yLoc = 0;
    int xSpeed = 3;
    int ySpeed = 5;
```

```java
int circleSize = 75;
int appletSize = 300;
Thread moveCircle=null;
Rectangle clipRect;


public void init()
{
     setBackground(Color.white);
     resize(appletSize,appletSize);
     clipRect = new Rectangle(0,0,0,0);
}

public void paint(Graphics g)
{
     clipRect = new Rectangle(xLoc,yLoc,circleSize,circleSize);
     g.setColor(Color.black);
     g.fillRect(0,0,appletSize,appletSize);
     g.setColor(Color.red);
     g.fillOval(xLoc,yLoc,circleSize,circleSize);
}

public void update(Graphics g)
{
     // comment out the next line to try repaint clipping
     g.clipRect(clipRect.x, clipRect.y, clipRect.width + 1 ,
          clipRect.height + 1);
     paint(g);
}

public void start()
{
     if (moveCircle == null)
     {
          moveCircle = new Thread(this);
          moveCircle.start();
     }
}

public  void run()
{
     while (moveCircle != null)
     {
          xLoc += xSpeed;
          yLoc += ySpeed;
          if ((xLoc < 0) || ((xLoc + circleSize) > appletSize))
               xSpeed = -xSpeed;    // change x direction

          if ((yLoc < 0) || ((yLoc + circleSize) > appletSize))
               ySpeed = -ySpeed;    // change y direction

          clipRect = clipRect.union(new Rectangle(xLoc, yLoc,
                    circleSize,circleSize));
          repaint(); // comment this line out for repaint clipping

          // uncomment the next 2 lines to use repaint clipping
          //repaint(clipRect.x, clipRect.y,
```

```
    //              clipRect.width + 1, clipRect.height + 1);
            try Thread.sleep(50);
            catch (InterruptedException e);
        }
    }

    public void stop()
    {
        if (moveCircle != null) moveCircle.stop();
        moveCircle = null;
    }
}
```

clipRect Method

In the **paint()** method, we set **clipRect** to the rectangle where we are about to draw the red circle. In the **run()** method, we use the **union()** method from the Rectangle class to create a new rectangle that encompasses the old and new circle position. In **update()**, we use the value of the **clipRect** rectangle to call the Graphics **clipRect()** method. The next **paint()** will only paint the background part of the screen and circle within this rectangle. It will then reset the clip rectangle, **clipRect**, to the coordinates of the current circle.

If the AWT Callback Thread drops a call to **paint()**, this applet will still work. The **run()** method will just keep using the **union()** method to add the current circle position to previous one, which may also be the union of two circle positions. A new **clipRect** rectangle will grow until the AWT Callback Thread gets around to calling **paint()**.

repaint Method

To try the repaint-based clipping technique, comment the appropriate lines in or out, recompile and run. It's easier to use the **repaint(x, y, width, height)** version than it's to deal with clipping regions. Just pass the currently invalidated rectangle and it will work fine. The AWT Callback Thread will adjust the area if it drops any previous calls to **paint()**.

> The width and height passed to **clipRect()** or **repaint()** must have 1 added to them. This is because the drawing routines actually draw one pixel right and one pixel down from the coordinates specified.

doubleClipper Applet

The previous example implemented efficient painting techniques. However, you'll have noticed that both methods flickered fairly badly. Look at the following line in **paint()**. It fills or paints the whole applet the current color.

```
g.fillRect(0,0,appletSize,appletSize);
```

This operation—the painting of the background—could be optimized. However, the only way to eliminate the flicker is to use our old friend, double buffering. This next example combines clipping with double buffering techniques to produce a smooth animation. Here is the improved version of this applet:

```
import java.awt.*;
import java.applet.*;

public class doubleClipper extends Applet implements Runnable
{
    int xLoc = 0;
    int yLoc = 0;
    int xSpeed = 3;
    int ySpeed = 5;
    int circleSize = 75;
    int appletSize = 300;
    Rectangle clipRect;
    Thread moveCircle=null;
    Graphics grphScratch;
    Image imgScratch;

    public void init()
    {
        setBackground(Color.white);
        resize(appletSize,appletSize);
        clipRect = new Rectangle(0,0,0,0);
        imgScratch = createImage(size().width, size().height);
        grphScratch = imgScratch.getGraphics();
    }

    public void paint(Graphics g)
    {
        clipRect = new Rectangle(xLoc, yLoc,circleSize,circleSize);
        grphScratch.setColor(Color.black);
        grphScratch.fillRect(0,0, appletSize, appletSize);
        grphScratch.setColor(Color.red);
        grphScratch.fillOval(xLoc,yLoc,circleSize,circleSize);
        g.drawImage(imgScratch,0,0,this);
    }

    public void update(Graphics g)
    {
        g.clipRect(clipRect.x, clipRect.y, clipRect.width + 1 ,
                    clipRect.height + 1 );
        paint(g);
    }

    public void start()
    {
        if (moveCircle == null )
        {
            moveCircle = new Thread(this);
            moveCircle.start();
        }
    }

    public  void run()
    {
        while (moveCircle != null)
        {
            xLoc += xSpeed;
            yLoc += ySpeed;
```

```
            if ((xLoc < 0 ) || ((xLoc + circleSize) > appletSize))
                  xSpeed = -xSpeed; // change x direction

            if ((yLoc < 0 ) || ((yLoc + circleSize) > appletSize))
                  ySpeed = - ySpeed;        // change y direction

            clipRect = clipRect.union(new Rectangle(xLoc,yLoc,
                  circleSize, circleSize));
            repaint();  // comment this line out for repaint clipping

            // uncomment the next 2 lines to use repaint clipping
            //repaint(clipRect.x, clipRect.y,
            //          clipRect.width + 1, clipRect.height + 1);

            try Thread.sleep(50);
            catch (InterruptedException e);
      }
   }

   public void stop()
   {
         if (moveCircle != null ) moveCircle.stop();
         moveCircle = null;
   }
}
```

Now you'll see that there is no more flickering. After our previous explanations, this code should be fairly easy to follow. Take note that we left all the clipping logic in when we added the double buffering code. Even with off-screen buffering, the clipping will make the applet more efficient.

Fonts

One of the most frequently used yet least-understood term is **font**. A font is a collection of all the characters of one size with a unified and consistent design. The term **typeface** refers to the overall design and font refers to a specific size and style of that design. A **typeface family** is a set of typefaces with slight variations on the design theme–all intended to work attractively together. There are actually hundreds of typeface families including such familiar ones as Helvetica and Courier. The style variations within a given family are not quite so numerous. These include italic, bold, extended, condensed, and extra-bold, to name just a few. For example, within the Times family, we have Times Roman, Times Italic, Times Bold, Times Obliqued, and so on. We measure font sizes in **points** generally referred to as 1/72 of an inch.

Traditionally, displaying text has been the most important output operation of computer systems. Users spend enormous amounts of time reading text displayed by applications. Granted, graphical images are rivaling text for the most important slot but we'll cover their usage in the next chapter (when we get there, we may even say Images are the most important). Still, one of the foremost factors governing the look of a Web page is the choice and usage of fonts. In this section, we'll talk about font support in the Graphics class, as well as in both the Font and FontMetrics classes.

Graphics Class Font Methods

Recall we said that a font was an attribute of a Graphics object. When the AWT Callback Thread passes one of these objects to the painting methods, there is a default font already associated with it. However, the only interaction we have with the context when dealing with fonts is to either retrieve font information or set a different font.

`public abstract void setFont(Font f);`

This sets the font for all subsequent text-rendering operations. For example, using `drawString(string, x, y)` would now paint its **string** in the current font and current color from the **x, y** coordinates.

There are two other classes that encapsulate font information: the Font class and the FontMetrics class. Here are two methods from the Graphics class that retrieve the specific font details contained in those font-related classes.

 `public abstract Font getFont();`

This method retrieves the current font. Once obtained, we use Font class methods described next to retrieve the desired font information.

 `public FontMetrics getFontMetrics();`

This method retrieves even more specific information about the font as we'll explain in the section on font metrics.

Font Class

Java guarantees that every port of the JVM will support a minimum set of five universal typeface families. These include the following:

 Dialog—default: if you don't explicitly set a font, this is what you get.

 Helvetica

 TimesRoman

 Courier

 Symbol

Within each typeface family, the Font class supports three style variations: plain, bold, and italic. The class defines three final static variables used to specify these styles: **Font.PLAIN**, **Font.BOLD**, and **Font.ITALIC**. Mixed styles are possible by bitwise ORing them. For example: **Font.BOLD | Font.ITALIC** specifies a combination of the two.

```
public boolean  isPlain();
public boolean  isBold();
public boolean  isItalic();
```

These three methods each return a boolean and are self-explanatory.

```
public  int  getSize();
```

This one returns the size in points.

```
public  int  getStyle();
```

Note that this method returns an integer that represents the style of the font. This return value is then bitwise tested against the static class variables to finally determine the style.

```
public  String  getFamily();
```

This method returns the platform specific family name of the font.

```
public  String  getName();
```

The string returned here is the logical name of the font.

The Font constructor allows us to create a new font with a specified family name, style and point size.

```
Font titleFont = new Font("TimesRoman", Font.BOLD, 48);
g.setFont(titleFont);
drawString("The Beatles", x, y);
```

FontMetrics Class

Remember typewriters? The typewriter font was a **monospaced** typeface; the lowercase m was just as wide as the l or i. The 12-point plain Courier font that is one of the standard Java fonts, is a pretty good reproduction of the pica output from the IBM Selectric typewriter. However, most fonts we use today are what we call **proportional** fonts–the m is wider than the l or i. In addition, there are many variations between the thickness of vertical strokes and the thinness of horizontal strokes.

A difficulty arises when we want to precisely position text and we are dealing with proportional-spaced fonts. The width of any given string depends on the letters within that string. Therefore, we need more detailed font-dependent information. The FontMetrics Class encapsulates this additional information.

This diagram illustrates some common font terminology:

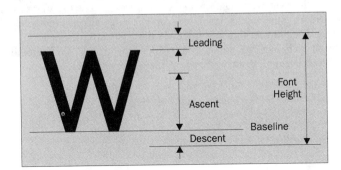

- Ascent–the distance from the baseline to the top of the characters.

- Descent–the distance from the baseline to the bottom of the characters.

- Height–this is the sum of the leading+ascent+descent. Another way to look at it's that the height is the distance between the baseline of adjacent lines of text.

- Baseline–the main bodies of the characters (not counting the descent) sit on this line. Think of this line as the reference point of the font.

- Leading–line spacing is another term for leading. This is because it only becomes important when dealing with multiple lines of text. It's the amount of space reserved between the descent of one line of text and the ascent of the next line.

It should be obvious what the following four methods return.

```
public  int  getLeading();
public  int  getAscent();
public  int  getDescent();
public  int  getHeight();
```

This is perhaps the most used FontMetric method:

```
public  int  stringWidth(String  str);
```

Once we have a FontMetrics object, we can center any string rendered in that font. For horizontal centering, we start with the width of the applet window. Using the **stringWidth()** method, we get the pixel width of the string and subtract that from the applet window width. We divide that result by two and use it for the horizontal coordinate of **drawString()**. Vertical centering is a little trickier. The **drawString()** method will draw from the font baseline, not the font top, so we have to adjust for that. We calculate the vertical coordinate for **drawString()** by subtracting the font height from the applet height and dividing that by two. Finally, we add the font leading and ascent values so the baseline is the center of the applet window.

Summary

In this chapter, we have covered a lot of material and we are still not finished with all the AWT functionality. So far you have learned about graphics contexts and the Graphics class. We have talked a lot about different painting techniques using the **paint()**, **update()**, and **repaint()** methods. We looked at color spaces, color models, clipping regions, and fonts. As with any language, the best way to learn is to start writing code. Hopefully, the examples provide a nice starting point for experimentation. In the next chapter, we continue our discussion of the AWT Graphics class, by learning more about the different rendering methods.

AWT Graphics Rendering

This chapter continues our discussion on the **Graphics** class. With a firm understanding of the graphic context and painting methods under our belts, we're now ready to actually draw or render objects on the screen. We start with the Java coordinate system so that we can precisely position our objects. Then we talk in detail about the many rendering primitives. The Java image model is explained in detail, and then we finally give a couple of nice applet examples. By the end of this chapter, you'll understand:

▲ The coordinate system and its peculiarity

▲ How to position and draw lines, rectangles, and polygons

▲ How to position and draw ovals and arcs

▲ How to design 3D objects

▲ How to use the **translate()** method to scroll

▲ How the Java image paradigm is so distinctive

▲ How to monitor or track image-loading

Coordinate System

The **Graphics** class provides 40 methods: five have to do with context management, four each for colors and fonts, and the rest–the overwhelming majority of 27 methods–deal with graphic operations. Each of these graphic operations uses (either directly or indirectly through another class like Polygon for example) x and y values as method parameters. This coordinate pair identifies the specific location where a line, character, or shape should start or end.

The Java coordinate system has 'x' in the horizontal direction and 'y' in the vertical direction with the origin (0,0) at the upper-left screen corner. x increases to the right and y increases downward. Coordinates are discrete and are in units of pixels. Each Component (image, window, for example) has its own coordinate system. The following diagram illustrates:

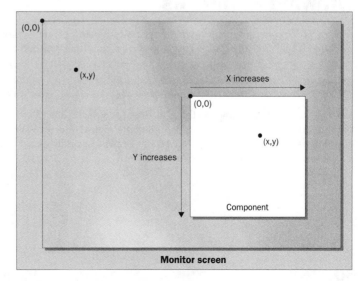

There is an anomaly with most computer graphics systems that is counter-intuitive, and Java is no different. This can cause rendering errors for the impatient programmer and so warrants a brief explanation. This is that the filling and drawing versions of the rendering methods we are about to cover do not draw the same outline if given the same arguments. All of the fill methods render an outline one pixel smaller in width and height than the corresponding method that just draws the primitive.

For example, to draw a regular rectangle 5 pixels high, 7 pixels wide, at x location 0 and y location 0 we need to use the following:

```
g.DrawRect(0,0,6,4);
```

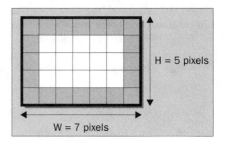

If pixels were square (they are not), we could illustrate this thus:

Here's the fill version with its result.

```
g.fillRect(0,0,6,4);
```

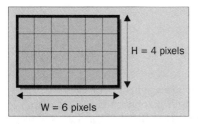

Of course, it's simple to adjust the arguments for the methods so that they both render equivalent outlines. Just add 1 to x and y and subtract 1 from w and h whenever you use the regular or non-fill version. Beware, this is a much more tricky adjustment in the case of ovals and arcs.

Drawing Primitives

The AWT Graphics class includes many basic drawing primitives for rendering lines and shapes in paint methods. You'll find them all fairly easy to use now that you are an expert in painting techniques!

Lines

We will start with the simplest thing to draw: a straight line. The **drawLine()** method draws a line between any 2 points. It requires 4 arguments, the x, y coordinates of the starting location and the x, y coordinates of the ending location. All the drawing primitives use the current graphics color. Here is a simple example that draws lines in an applet:

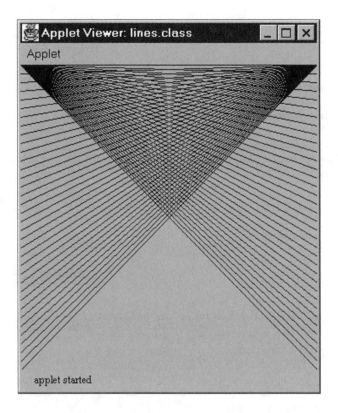

Here is the source:

```
import java.awt.*;
import java.applet.*;

public class lines extends Applet
{
    public void paint(Graphics g)
    {
        for (int i = 0; i <= size().height; i+=10 )
        {
            g.drawLine(0,0,size().width,i);
            g.drawLine(size().width, 0,0, i);
        }
    }
}
```

In this applet, we just draw 2 sets of lines, one set with top-left (0,0) as a starting point, and another with the top-right (width,0) as a starting point. For each line end point, we use the left or right applet border as the x value and the current value of an increasing variable as the y value. Notice the interesting moiré pattern produced by these lines.

Moiré patterns are named after the French water fabrics that create a similar effect. This particular pattern is an interference pattern between the grid pattern of the computer screen itself and the pattern being drawn.

Rectangles

There are three different kinds of rectangles–each has two drawing styles, either an outline or a solid. The first type of rectangle is just a plain, square-cornered rectangle. To draw a rectangle outline, use the **drawRect (int, int, int, int)** method. The first two parameters represent the x,y coordinates of the top left corner of the rectangle, and the next two parameters represent the width and height. To draw a filled rectangle use the **fillRect(int, int, int, int)** method where the parameters are identical to **drawRect()**.

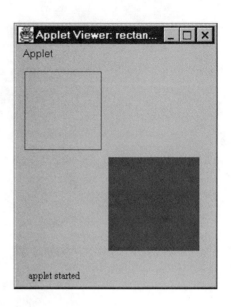

This is a quick applet which uses both **drawRect()** and **fillRect()**:

```
import java.awt.*;
import java.applet.*;

public class rectangle extends Applet
{
   public void paint(Graphics g)
   {
      g.setColor(Color.red);
      g.drawRect(10,10, 100,100);
      g.fillRect(120,120, 120,120);
   }
}
```

The **Graphics** class also provides methods to draw rectangles with rounded edges.

```
public  abstract  void  drawRoundRect(int  x,  int  y,
      int width,  int  height,  int  arcWidth,  int  arcHeight);
public  abstract  void  fillRoundRect(int  x,  int  y,
      int  width,  int  height,  int  arcWidth,  int  arcHeight);
```

These methods are very similar to the previous two methods except they require two additional parameters, **arcWidth** and **arcHeight**. These parameters specify the diameter of the arc at the four corners–in other words, how rounded the corners are. The lower the **arcWidth** and **arcHeight**, the closer the result is to a normal rectangle. At the point where the **arcWidth** and **arcHeight** are equal to the width and the height of the rectangle, you get an oval (or a circle if the width is equal to the height).

Rounded Rectangles

The second type is the rounded rectangle. In this applet, we use **drawRoundRect()** method for five rounded rectangles; all have the same rectangle width and height but different arc width and height. This will show the flexibility available. We then do the same for **fillRoundRect()**.

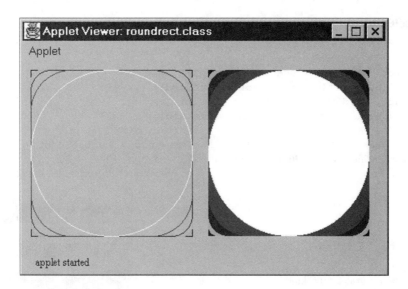

Here is the source:

```
import java.awt.*;
import java.applet.*;

public class roundrect extends Applet
{
    public void paint(Graphics g)
    {
        g.setColor(Color.black);
        g.drawRoundRect(10,10, 200,200,1,1);
        g.setColor(Color.green);
        g.drawRoundRect(10,10, 200,200,25,25);
        g.setColor(Color.blue);
        g.drawRoundRect(10,10, 200,200,50,50);
        g.setColor(Color.red);
        g.drawRoundRect(10,10, 200,200,100,100);
        g.setColor(Color.white);
        g.drawRoundRect(10,10, 200,200,200,200);

        g.setColor(Color.black);
        g.fillRoundRect(230,10, 200,200,1,1);
        g.setColor(Color.green);
        g.fillRoundRect(230,10, 200,200,25,25);
        g.setColor(Color.blue);
        g.fillRoundRect(230,10, 200,200,50,50);
        g.setColor(Color.red);
        g.fillRoundRect(230,10, 200,200,100,100);
        g.setColor(Color.white);
        g.fillRoundRect(230,10, 200,200,200,200);
    }
}
```

3D Rectangles

The third type of rectangle methods draws 3D rectangles.

```
public abstract void draw3DRect(int x, int y,
       int width, int height, boolean raised);
public abstract void fill3DRect(int x, int y,
       int width, int height, boolean raised);
```

Both methods have the same first four parameters as the **drawRect()** and **fillRect()** methods. A fifth boolean parameter specifies a raised (true) or recessed (false) rectangle. There is some bad news about these two methods: for certain background and fill color combinations, the rectangles do not really look 3D!

The next applet demonstrates four kinds of 3D rectangles, so you can see for yourself. Experiment with some other color combinations—in many cases, the 3D effect is nearly unnoticeable. Red background with gray rendering or blue background with light gray rendering tends to appear 3D. Also, **fill3Drect()** with the boolean set false for raised, automatically renders in a darker shade than the current color.

Here is the source code:

```java
import java.awt.*;
import java.applet.*;

public class java3Drect extends Applet
{
    public void init()
    {
        setBackground(Color.red);
    }

    public void paint(Graphics g)
    {
        g.setColor(Color.gray);
        g.draw3DRect(20,20,100,100, true);
        g.draw3DRect(140,20,100,100, false);
        g.fill3DRect(20,140,100,100, true);
        g.fill3DRect(140,140,100,100, false);
    }
}
```

There is nothing magical about 3D effects. Typically, we can make any rectangle look 3D by drawing a white line on the top and left sides, and dark lines on the right and bottom. This simulates a light source from the upper left direction. We will do just that in the next example where we roll our own 3D effects.

Polygons

In addition to four-sided rectangles, the **Graphics** class supports rendering polygons with any number of sides.

```
public abstract void drawPolygon(int xPoints[], int yPoints[],
    int nPoints);
public abstract void fillPolygon(int xPoints[], int yPoints[],
    int nPoints);
```

Both these methods require that we set up two integer arrays, one containing the x coordinates of the points, and the other containing the y coordinates. We call these methods with the x array, the y array, and the number of polygon points. For instance, the following code segment will draw a filled triangle with points at (0,0), (50,0) and (50,30).

```
int x[] = {0,50,50};
int y[] = {0,0,30};
g.fillPolygon(x,y,3);
```

> There is a less obvious difference between these two polygon methods. The
> **drawPolygon()** method will not close the polygon unless we add the starting
> point to the end of the array. The starting point is the same as the ending point but
> each specified separately.

In this next example, we will demonstrate how to use the polygon methods to implement a 3D shadow effect for both regular rectangles and rounded rectangles. The technique we use is very simple. We draw each target rectangle as a combination of one center rectangle and four bordering polygons. The polygons give the center rectangle a beveled look. This diagram exaggerates the effect to illustrate:

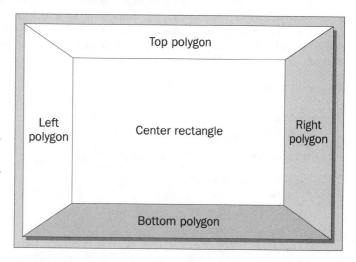

Top polygon

Left polygon

Center rectangle

Right polygon

Bottom polygon

For raised rectangles, we draw the top and left polygons white. We draw the right polygon light gray and the bottom polygon a darker gray. For recessed rectangles, we switch the top polygon color with the bottom color and the right polygon color with the left color. The process is more tedious than difficult.

Creating 3D rounded rectangles isn't quite as simple. The technique used in this example is to draw three rounded rectangles. The first one is white with a width and height slightly less than the target rectangle size. The second one is gray and positioned lower-right of the origin point by the bevel size. Finally, the third one is in the intended color, at the same starting point as the gray one, but with a smaller width and height. The combination of the exposed gray and white areas creates the 3D effect. In this case however, the result isn't quite as effective and, if you raise the bevel over 4 pixels, the result will not look quite right.

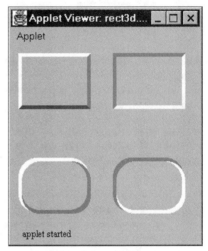

To implement these techniques, we have chosen to create two new classes. The **our3DRect** class is a square-cornered 3D rectangle. The **our3DRoundRect** class extends **our3DRect** and overrides its **draw()** method to create the rounded effect. The **our3DRect** class has one constructor that takes width, height, bevel, and style as parameters. The **our3DRoundRect** class has an identical constructor, and simply uses the **super** operator to invoke the **our3DRect** constructor with the parameters passed in the constructor. The **draw()** method for both of these classes uses the Graphics object, x coordinate and y coordinate passed as parameters to draw the 3D rectangle using the technique just discussed.

To keep this example simple, and because the purpose of this applet is to illustrate graphics techniques, we've left out the normal data encapsulation methods. If we were to implement these classes in a production environment, we would add methods to set and fetch the values for the rectangle properties such as width and height and make them private. A good user exercise would be to enhance these classes to use set and get methods for all data, in addition to validating the values of the properties in the set methods.

Here is the source code:

```java
import java.awt.*;
import java.applet.*;

public class rect3d extends Applet
{
    int width = 100;
    int height = 75;
    int bevel = 5;

    // declare, instantiate rects
    our3DRect raisedRect = new our3DRect(width,height,bevel,true);
    our3DRect sunkenRect = new our3DRect(width,height,bevel,false);

    our3DRoundRect raisedRoundRect = new our3DRoundRect(width,height,
    bevel,true);
```

```
    our3DRoundRect sunkenRoundRect = new our3DRoundRect(width,height,
    bevel,false);

    public void init()
    {
        setBackground(Color.lightGray);
    }

    public void paint(Graphics g)
    {
    raisedRect.draw(g,10,10);
    sunkenRect.draw(g,140,10);

    raisedRoundRect.draw(g,10,150);
    sunkenRoundRect.draw(g,140,150);
    }
}

class our3DRect
{
    int x, y, width, height, bevel;
    Color color;
boolean style;//true = raised, false = indented

    public our3DRect(int w, int h, int b, boolean s)
    {
        width = w;
        height = h;
        bevel = b;
        color = Color.lightGray;
        style = s;
    }

    public void draw(Graphics g, int x, int y)
    {
        // draw center of rect
        g.setColor(color);
        g.fillRect(x+bevel, y+bevel, width - bevel*2, height - bevel * 2);

        // set color for top edge depending on style
        if (style) g.setColor(Color.white);
        else g.setColor(Color.gray);
        int xTop[] = {x, x+width, x+width - bevel,x+bevel};
        int yTop[] = {y,y,y+bevel,y+bevel};
        g.fillPolygon(xTop,yTop,4);

        // set color for left edge depending on style
        if (style) g.setColor(Color.white);
        else g.setColor(Color.gray);
        int xLeft[] = {x, x+bevel, x+bevel,x};
        int yLeft[] = {y,y+bevel,y+height-bevel, y + height};
        g.fillPolygon(xLeft,yLeft,4);

        // set color for right edge depending on style
        if (style) g.setColor(Color.gray);
        else g.setColor(Color.white);
        int xRight[] = {x+width, x+width,x+width-bevel, x+width-bevel};
        int yRight[] = {y,y+height,y+height-bevel,y+bevel};
```

```
        g.fillPolygon(xRight,yRight,4);

        // set color for botton edge depending on style
        if (style) g.setColor(Color.darkGray);
        else g.setColor(Color.white);
        int xBottom[] = {x, x+bevel, x+width - bevel,x+width};
        int yBottom[] = {y+height,y+height-bevel, y+height-bevel,y+height};
        g.fillPolygon(xBottom,yBottom,4);
    }
}

class our3DRoundRect extends our3DRect
{
    public our3DRoundRect(int w, int h, int b, boolean s)
    {
        super(w,h,b,s); // call parent constructor
    }

    // override draw method
    public void draw(Graphics g, int x, int y)
    {
        if (style) g.setColor(Color.white);
        else g.setColor(Color.gray);
        g.fillRoundRect(x,y, width - (bevel / 2), height - (bevel / 2),
        50,50);

        if (style) g.setColor(Color.gray);
        else g.setColor(Color.white);
        g.fillRoundRect(x + bevel ,y + bevel, width - bevel , height - bevel,
        50,50);
        g.setColor(color);
        g.fillRoundRect(x + bevel,y + bevel, width - (bevel * 2), height -
        (bevel * 2),50,50);
    }
}
```

Ovals

The Graphics class supports two methods for rendering ovals or elongated circles.

```
public abstract void drawOval(int  x,  int  y,  int  width,  int  height);
public abstract void fillOval(int  x,  int  y,  int  width,  int  height);
```

Notice that these methods have the same parameters as the rectangle versions. We specify the rectangle into which we want to draw the oval. Consequently, we specify a corner point to draw an oval around a particular center point. This corner point is to the upper-left of the desired center point by a factor of half the width and half the height.

In this simple applet, clicking on the mouse will specify the corner point of an oval. You can draw many ovals:

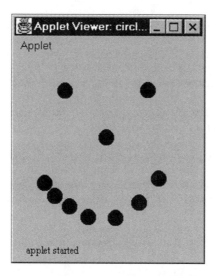

Here is the source code:

```java
import java.awt.*;
import java.applet.*;

public class circles extends Applet
{
    int circum = 20;
    Graphics myG ;

    public void init()
    {
        myG = getGraphics();
    }

    public boolean mouseUp(Event e, int x, int y)
    {
        myG.fillOval(x - (circum/2),y - (circum/2),circum,circum);
        return true;
    }
}
```

Whenever a mouse up button event occurs, the **mouseUp()** callback routine draws a filled circle at the current mouse position. Notice that we had to use the **getGraphics()** method to obtain a Graphics object. We did not get a graphic context passed automatically to us because we are not in either the **paint()** or **update()** methods. Also, since we do not have a paint method, if screen damage occurs, we will lose our artwork.

A good follow-up exercise would be to make the circles persistent using either of the following methods:

- Save the coordinates in a vector and override the **paint()** method to recreate them each time the AWT Callback Thread calls it.

- Whenever you draw a circle to the screen, also draw it to an off-screen double. Then override the **paint()** method to copy the buffer to the screen.

Arcs

An arc is simply part of an oval. Again, the **Graphics** class supports two kinds of arc rendering methods.

```
public abstract void drawArc(int  x,  int  y,  int  width,  int  height,
            int  startAngle,  int  arcAngle);
public abstract void fillArc(int  x,  int  y,  int  width,  int  height,
            int  startAngle,  int  arcAngle);
```

Both methods require the same six parameters. The first four—**x**, **y**, **width** and **height**—specify an oval just like the previous oval methods. This oval is what the rendering methods base the arc on. The last two parameters specify the starting point and extent of the arc, using the 360 degrees of a circle as a basis. Think of it as a clock with 0 degrees at 3 o'clock, 90 degrees at 12 o'clock, 180 degrees at 9 o'clock and 270 degrees at 6 o'clock.

We can specify the extent of the arc as a positive or negative number, allowing us to specify the same arc in two different ways. For example, the follow two method invocations will draw the same arc.

```
drawArc(10, 15, 100, 100, 0, 180)
drawArc(10, 15, 100, 100, 180, -180)
```

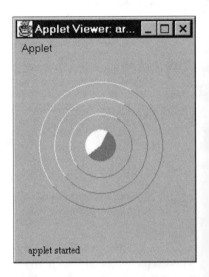

Here is a simple applet to show these two methods in action. Once again, we are creating a poor man's 3D effect.

The source code is as follows:

```
import java.awt.*;
import java.applet.*;

public class arcs extends Applet
{
    public void paint(Graphics g)
    {
        g.setColor(Color.white);
        g.drawArc(30,30,160,160, 60,160);
        g.drawArc(50,50,120,120, 60,160);
        g.drawArc(70,70,80,80, 60,160);
```

```
          g.fillArc(90,90,40,40, 60,160);

      g.setColor(Color.gray);
      g.drawArc(30,30,160,160, 220,200);
      g.drawArc(50,50,120,120, 220,200);
      g.drawArc(70,70,80,80, 220,200);
      g.fillArc(90,90,40,40, 220,200);
   }
 }
```

Scrolling

There may be times when we would like to change the normal (0,0) origin point of the graphics coordinate system. Perhaps we need to give the user the ability to scroll an image or render a figure that does not fit within the size of the view window. The **Graphics** class provides a method that allows us to set the origin to any arbitrary point.

```
public abstract void translate(int x, int y);
```

This method translates the specified parameters into the origin of the graphics context–they become the new origin. All subsequent operations on this context will now be relative to this origin.

To illustrate the use of this method, we have taken the arc applet from earlier in this chapter and added the ability to scroll the figure using the up, down, left, and right arrows. To make this enhancement work, we add a **handleEvent()** method and increment or decrement the origin variables, **originX** and **originY**, in response to the user actions, then request a repaint from the AWT Callback Thread. In the **paint()** method, we use the **originX** and **originY** values to reset the origin appropriately. This is the source code for our scrolling figure:

```
import java.awt.*;
import java.applet.*;

public class scroller extends Applet
{
int originX = 0; // initial origin X coordinate
int originY = 0; // initial origin Y coordinate

   public void init()
   {
      requestFocus();
   }

   public void paint(Graphics g)
   {
      g.translate(originX, originY);
      g.setColor(Color.white);
      g.drawArc(30,30,160,160, 60,160);
      g.drawArc(50,50,120,120, 60,160);
      g.drawArc(70,70,80,80, 60,160);
      g.fillArc(90,90,40,40, 60,160);

      g.setColor(Color.gray);
      g.drawArc(30,30,160,160, 220,200);
```

```
        g.drawArc(50,50,120,120, 220,200);
        g.drawArc(70,70,80,80, 220,200);
        g.fillArc(90,90,40,40, 220,200);
    }

    public boolean handleEvent(Event e)
    {
        if (e.id == Event.KEY_ACTION)
        {
            if (e.key == Event.LEFT)  originX--;
            else if(e.key == Event.RIGHT)  originX++;
            else if(e.key == Event.DOWN)  originY++;
            else if(e.key == Event.UP)  originY--;

            repaint();
            return true;
        }
        System.out.println(originX + e.toString() );
        return super.handleEvent(e);
    }
}
```

Images

Images are perhaps the most important display output of Web pages. Arguably, the current most frequent use of Java is to provide small animation applets to liven up static HTML pages. One common animation technique is to sequentially paint a series of images (usually **GIF** files) to create the illusion of movement. Not much different then the Looney Toons you used to watch as a kid (or still watch). To take advantage of these animation capabilities, we need to learn about how Java deals with images.

Image processing is the modification of images within an application. Java supports a rich set of capabilities that allow access to the pixel values for all sorts of processing in much the same fashion as other development platforms. However, the truly unique contribution of Java is in image loading. The Java image paradigm does not constrain access to the local disk. In other words, we can load an image from across a network just as easily as we can locally (not a bad idea for an Internet technology). In a network environment, this loading will obviously take much longer to complete than if it was from a local hard disk drive. This is significantly different from other windowed applications, and consequently, presents additional issues for the designer. For example, what do we do while loading images? Depending on the application, we may want to wait for an image to finish loading before continuing processing. Alternatively, we could perform some other task while loading image data in the background.

Creating Image Objects

As we would expect, the AWT has an Image class; it's an abstract class and cannot be instantiated with a **new** function. To create a new Image object, we will generally use a method we saw in a previous double-buffering example: **createImage()**. Alternatively, we could use one of two **getImage()** methods. If we are writing an applet, we can use the Applet class **getImage()** method that works with either a fully-qualified URL or a combination of a URL and String object. If we are developing a console application, we will need to use the Toolkit **getImage()** method. This requires a Toolkit object, so it is slightly more complex to use than the applet **getImage()**. In either case, the **getImage()** method will return an Image object for subsequent use.

However, there are some critical things to remember about the Java image paradigm. First, these **getImage()** methods return immediately and do not check whether the image data even exists. Second, the data loading is on demand and only starts when calling either the **getWidth()**, **getHeight()**, **getProperty()**, or **drawImage()** methods. For most applets, the actual loading of image data does not begin until the first time the program attempts to draw the image. Then, Java spawns a new thread of execution and runs that code to load the image from its source. That source may be a local file, or it may be a Web site located halfway around the world. In essence, the AWT **de-couples** the image pixel data from the Image objects that we work with. It's this de-coupling that allows us to continue to send messages to Image methods before we have image data. In other words, we have an available Image object for use—with image rendering routines, for example—even though we do not have the actual pixel data loaded yet.

There is a tendency for C programmers to think of the Image object as a declared pointer, whose initialization will be automatic but will take some time. In a sense, this isn't entirely accurate, because the Image object isn't a container for the pixel data. Instead, we can think of these Image objects as conduits for requesting pixel data from a source and delivering it off to an image consumer.

So, what do we do if image loading is only partially complete and we want to paint the screen? Well, the answer is probably application dependent. Ultimately, it's up to us. Often, if it's a single image, we will elect to display it in its incomplete form, and repaint it every time more image data is available. At other times, if we are doing an animation, we may not want to display any part of the image until all the data is available.

Image-loading Applet

An applet example will help to explain this concept. This applet will simply load a few images (Duke, the Java mascot) and display them in the **paint()** method.

Here is the applet source code (the desired GIF file should be in the same directory as the applet code, if the program is to work as intended):

```
import java.awt.*;
import java.applet.*;

public class imagapplet extends Applet
{
    Image myImg;
    int numPaints = 0;

    public void init()
    {
        resize(390,220);
        myImg = getImage(getCodeBase(),"T1.gif");
        System.out.println(myImg.getSource().toString());
    }

    public void paint(Graphics g)
    {
        numPaints++;
        g.drawString("The vacationing Duke family",5,10);
        g.drawString("Calls to paint: " + numPaints,5,26);

        // duke is originally 55x68 pixels
        g.drawImage(myImg,10,30,121,150,this);// papa Duke
```

```
    g.drawImage(myImg,140,78,83,102,this);  // mama Duke
    g.drawImage(myImg,244,112,55,68,this);  // baby Duke
    g.drawImage(myImg,324,129,41,51,this);  // tiny Duke

      g.drawString("Papa Duke",45,200);
      g.drawString("Mama Duke",150,200);
      g.drawString("Baby Duke",244,200);
      g.drawString("Tiny Duke",320,200);
    }
  }
```

Here is what it looks like in the
AppletViewer:

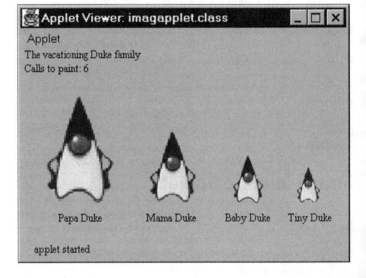

Right up front, we define an Image object we call **myImg**. Also, we declare a counter to keep track of the number of paints it takes to paint all images. In the **init()** method, we issue the **getImage()** method to instantiate the Image object. Therefore, we can use the **getCodeBase()** method to retrieve a URL for the current directory and only hard-code the image file name. We could have hard-coded the whole URL, but that would make maintenance more difficult if we move the files around.

The **Graphics** class declares four **drawImage()** methods, two of which we use in this example.

▲ Public abstract boolean drawImage(Image img, int x, int y, ImageObserver observer);

▲ Public abstract boolean drawImage(Image img, int x, int y, int, w, int h, ImageObserver observer);

▲ Public abstract boolean drawImage(Image img, int x, int y, Color c, ImageObserver observer);

▲ Public abstract boolean drawImage(Image img, int x, int y, int, w, int h, Color c, ImageObserver observer);

All of these methods, of course, need an Image reference to draw. The next two parameters are the x,y coordinates, respectively, of where to draw the image. Next are the width and height of the image and are useful for scaling the image. The **Color** parameter specifies what color to draw underneath the image.

This is sometimes useful if the image contains transparent pixels. The final parameter in each case is the **ImageObserver**. The use of this object allows us to monitor the loading progress and we will examine it in detail in the next section. This parameter can be any object that implements the ImageObserver interface. Since the **Component** class implements that interface, and an applet is a descendent of **Component**, in our example, we pass the applet object, or **this**, as the ImageObserver.

In the **paint()** method, we use a Graphics **drawImage()** method four times to draw the images to the screen. The reason we draw Duke four times is to illustrate the scaling available through the appropriate **drawImage()** method. Note that these **drawImage()** methods all return a boolean value, but we do not use it in our example. It really isn't necessary. If the image is already completely loaded and drawn when we call this method, the return value will be true, otherwise, false. In all but the extreme cases, the use of either the ImageObserver interface or the MediaTracker class is preferable to monitor the status of image loading.

In this example, the image data does not start to load until our first call to **drawImage()**. The component class that implements the ImageObserver interface calls **repaint()** as more and more image data becomes available. The paint counter will show us how many times the AWT Callback Thread invokes **paint()** before we finish the loading.

ImageObserver Interface

The ImageObserver is the key to managing the process of loading the image data. What if we do not like the way the default ImageObserver behaves? We can change the behavior by implementing our own ImageObserver interface. This interface has only one method, **imageUpdate()**, so it's not that intimidating. This method has six parameters, the **Image** object, an **int** holding various informational flags, and the **x, y, width, height** values representing the bounding box of the new pixels (if applicable). We'll look at each of the flags now:

- **ABORT**—An image which was being tracked asynchronously was aborted before production was complete. The image load will be restarted if the Image is accessed, or if there is an attempt to draw it.

- **ALLBITS**—A static image, which was previously drawn, is now complete and can be drawn again in its final form. When this flag is set, the **x, y, width** and **height** parameters are not meaningful.

- **ERROR**—An image which was being tracked asynchronously has encountered an error.

- **FRAMEBITS**—Another complete frame of a multiframe image, which was previously drawn is now available to be drawn again.

- **HEIGHT**—The height of the base image is now available and can be taken from the height argument to the **imageUpdate** callback method.

- **PROPERTIES**—The properties of the image are now available (via the **getProperty()** method).

- **SOMEBITS**—More pixels needed for drawing a scaled variation of the image are available.

- **WIDTH**—The width of the base image is now available and can be taken from the width argument to the **imageUpdate** callback method.

The **imageUpdate()** method is effectively a callback function that gets called every time additional data about the image becomes available. In some cases, this default behavior will be acceptable, other times we will want to modify it. Typically, we override the **imageUpdate()** method in an applet for one of two reasons. One, we want to wait until an Image is complete before displaying, or two, we would like to show a progress indicator as the image is in the process of loading.

ImageObserver Applet

In this next example, we have added our own ImageObserver implementation to a simpler version of a previous example. We then use the **imageUpdate()** method to print out a load percentage complete status indicator.

```java
import java.awt.*;
import java.applet.*;
import java.awt.image.ImageObserver;

public class imgapplet extends Applet implements ImageObserver
{
    Image myImg;
    int numPaints = 0;
    int percentComplete;
    int partLoaded=0;

    public void init()
    {
        resize(200,300);
        myImg = getImage(getCodeBase(),"T1.gif");
    }

    public boolean imageUpdate(Image img, int infoFlags, int x, int y,
    int width, int height)
    {
        if ((infoFlags & ERROR) != 0)
        {
            getGraphics().drawString("Error Loading Image", 5,50);
            return false;
        }
        else if ((infoFlags & ALLBITS) != 1)
        {
            if (partLoaded < img.getHeight(this))
            {
                partLoaded += height;
                percentComplete = (partLoaded * 100) / img.getHeight(this);
            }
            repaint(500);
            return true;
        }
        else return false;
    }

    public void paint(Graphics g)
    {
        numPaints++;
        g.drawString("Duke paint#: " + numPaints + ",  % loaded: " +
        percentComplete,5,10);
        g.drawImage(myImg,5,20,this);
    }
}
```

In order to implement the ImageObserver interface, we have to import it, so we have added a line to do this. We also have added the **implements ImageObserver** modifier to the **imgapplet** class definition. Next is our **imageUpdate()** method override.

There are a couple things to keep in mind when implementing an **imageUpdate()** method. First, remember that more than one flag can be set at the same time. That is why we are using the bitwise AND operator, **&**, to check individual flags. If we had used a conditional test such as **infoFlags == ERROR**, we would have had unexpected results because the **ERROR** flag and **ABORT** flag are often set to true at the same time. In that case, the test just mentioned would return false, even though the **ERROR** flag is true. Second, the method should return true if loading is incomplete, and false if loading is complete or you want to stop loading for some reason. Third, be careful while in the method to avoid endless loop scenarios. For instance, in the first cut at this applet, we had a **repaint()** method call right before the **return false** to stop the image load when an **ERROR** flag was set. Since we had a **drawImage()** in the **paint()** method, the load would be restarted and the same error would be encountered over and over. Also, if you leave out the check for the **ERROR** flag, you can easily get caught in a loop if the image file isn't found or is corrupted.

Our implementation is pretty simple. First, we check the **infoflags** values for two specific values, **ERROR** and **ALLBITS**. The **ERROR** flag indicates that some problem has been encountered during the load process, and the **ALLBITS** flag indicates that the image load is now complete. The most frequent reason for the **ERROR** flag to be set is that the image can't be found. In our implementation, when the **ERROR** flag is set we draw an error message, and return false to halt the image load. If the **ALLBITS** flag isn't set, and the height of the image loaded so far is less then the total height of the image, we increment the **partLoaded** variable with the new data and recalculate the completion percentage. Then, we call for a repaint within 500 milliseconds. You should try different values here to see the effect. With less repaints, the image will actually load quicker. Lastly, we return true to indicate that the loading isn't complete. The only other change made to this applet is a modification to the **paint()** method to display the percent complete.

MediaTracker

In situations where we are waiting for several images to complete loading before initiating some action, the **imageUpdate()** method can be very complex. Fortunately, there is an easier way.

The **MediaTracker** is a class specifically designed for managing the process of tracking image loading, and is extremely easy to use. It has methods for loading images, checking status of images, and for grouping images into logical groups. Although it currently will only track image loading, there are plans to enhance it in future Java versions to also track other media types such as audio or video clips. To use the **MediaTracker**, just create a new instance of it, and use the **addImage()** method to tell it which images to track. There are too many methods in **MediaTracker** to cover all of them, but we'll go through the important ones.

Let's take a look at an applet that uses **MediaTracker** to manage image loading. This applet will load three images of Duke and when complete, cycle through them, one at a time, to make Duke wave and slide right until he disappears off the screen:

Here is the source code for the applet:

```
import java.awt.*;
import java.applet.*;

public class mtracker extends Applet implements Runnable
{
    Image img[] = new Image[3];
    Image buffer;  // for offscreen graphic
    int numPaints = 0;
    MediaTracker trackit;
    Thread painter;

    public void init()
    {
        resize(200,300);
        trackit = new MediaTracker(this);
        img[0] = getImage(getCodeBase(),"T1.gif");
        trackit.addImage(img[0],0);
        img[1] = getImage(getCodeBase(),"T2.gif");
        trackit.addImage(img[1],1);
        img[2] = getImage(getCodeBase(),"T3.gif");
        trackit.addImage(img[2],2);
        painter = new Thread(this);
        buffer = createImage(130,80); // init offscreen image
        // Also note buffer size must be the same size as the gif file
    }

    public void start()
    {
        painter.start();
    }
```

```
public void stop()
{
   painter.stop();
}

public void run()
{
   Graphics gOffScreen, gOnScreen;

   while (trackit.checkAll(true) == false )
   //loop until all images are loaded
   {
      try { Thread.sleep(1000); }
      catch (InterruptedException e) {}
      repaint();
   }

   // let all three display a moment
   try { Thread.sleep(1000); }
      catch (InterruptedException e) {}

   // get Graphic for offscreen and onscreen images
   gOffScreen = buffer.getGraphics();
   gOnScreen = getGraphics();

   gOnScreen.setColor(Color.lightGray);
   gOffScreen.setColor(Color.lightGray);

   for(int loop = 0;loop<3;loop++)
   {
      for(int i = 0;i<30;i++)
      {
         gOffScreen.drawImage(img[i % 3],0,0, this);
// draw buffer to screen. Creep right each time

         switch(loop)
         {
            case 0:
            gOnScreen.drawImage(buffer,i * 5,
            (size().height - 280),this);
            break;

            case 1:
            gOnScreen.drawImage(buffer,i * 5,
            (size().height - 200),this);
            break;

            case 2:
            gOnScreen.drawImage(buffer,i * 5,
            (size().height - 120),this);
            break;
         }

         try { Thread.sleep(200); }
            catch (InterruptedException e) {}
      }
   }
```

```
    }

    public void paint(Graphics g)
    {
        g.drawString("Paint# " + ++numPaints,5,10);
        if (trackit.checkID(0,true))
        {
            g.drawImage(img[0],5,20,this);
        }
        else g.drawString("img0 still loading..",5,25);

        if (trackit.checkID(1,true))
        {
            g.drawImage(img[1],5,100,this);
        }
        else g.drawString("img1 still loading..",5,105);

        if (trackit.checkID(2,true))
        {
        g.drawImage(img[2],5,180,this);
        }
        else g.drawString("img2 still loading..",5,185);
    }
}
```

In this applet, we chose to implement the Runnable interface so we can easily use a separate thread for driving the Image status-checking and **repaint()** calls. We have also added a MediaTracker reference we call **trackit** and a Thread reference called **painter**.

In our **init()** member, we instantiate the **trackit** and **painter** objects. After each **getImage()** call, we invoke the MediaTracker **addImage()** method to tell the object that we want the image added to the list of those being tracked. The **addImage()** method has two parameters, the first is the image you want tracked, and the second is a user chosen ID that will be used afterward for status checking. We haven't done it here, but we can use the same ID for more than one image if we want to track them as a group. That ability can come in handy if we are waiting for a group of images to load before starting some action such as an animation.

In the **run()** method implementation, we declare two Graphics class references for the image buffers and then enter a **while** loop. We want to stay in this loop until *all* images have completed loading, so we use the MediaTracker **checkAll()** method in the **while** condition. This method will return true only when all images it's tracking have completed loading. The true parameter instructs the MediaTracker to start the load if it has not been started yet. Inside the loop, we pause for a second and issue a **repaint()**. In our **paint()** method, we use the **checkID()** method, with the IDs assigned in the **addImage()** method to check the status of each image and, if incomplete, paint a loading message or, if complete, draw the image. Since these images are all the same size, and are being loaded locally, there is a good chance that they will all complete at the same time. Run it a few times however, and you'll probably see cases where one gets drawn while the others are still loading. If you modify the applet to load images from a remote URL, you'll definitely find that the three images will complete loading at different times.

When all three images have completed loading, we perform our animation. To make the animation as smooth as possible, we use the double-buffering technique covered earlier. In an off-screen image, we paint the background to match the applet window, and then use the modulus function (%) to return the index of the next image to draw. Next, we draw the off-screen image to the applet window. Each time we paint to the window, we slide the image right 5 more pixels to make Duke look like he is sliding to the right.

Putting It All Together

Before we close this chapter, we will include two more examples that use the techniques and principles covered here. If you have read this chapter without the added stimulus of late-night television, then most of the code that follows will be easy to understand, since it builds upon the previous examples. In both cases, we first start with an HTML file, explain any underlying theory, show what the applet looks like on the screen, list the source code, then finally, examine it in more detail.

The Aperture Applet

This applet animates a series of rotating polygons. It appears similar to what we would see if looking out the lens from the inside of a camera. Each polygon gets smaller and smaller as it rotates and finally disappears in the middle. After convergence, the color changes. Then it draws multiple circles, each larger than the previous, simulating the effect of coming out the end of a tunnel. The color changes again and the whole process repeats *ad infinitum*. Here is the HTML file:

```
<HTML>
<HEAD>
<TITLE> Aperture </TITLE>
</HEAD>
<FONT SIZE="+5"><CENTER><B> Aperture </B></CENTER></FONT>

<APPLET CODE="aperture.class" WIDTH=300 HEIGHT=300>
<PARAM NAME=pps value=50>
<PARAM NAME=depth value=160>
</APPLET>

</BODY>
</HTML>
```

The parameter **pps** determines how fast the applet draws the polygons–it's actually the number of polygons drawn per second. The **depth** parameter is the number of polygons drawn before the sequence reverses, and circles begin.

This applet does not use the **drawPolygon()** method to render each polygon. Instead, we use the **drawLine()** primitive and calculate each point according to parametric line equations. To describe what is happening, let's use the notation **A(x,y)** to denote a point **A** at position coordinates **x** and **y**. A line segment **AB** connects two points **A** and **B**. For each successively smaller polygon, we need to use new points calculated from the previous polygon's points. Each new point **A'** along line segment **AB** gets closer to point **B**. The following diagram illustrates:

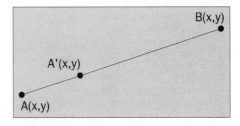

These two parametric line equations show us how to calculate each new point **A'**:

$$x_{A'} = (1 - \lambda)x_A + \lambda x_B$$
$$y_{A'} = (1 - \lambda)x_A + \lambda x_B$$

Note that when $\lambda = 0$, point **A'** coincides with **A**, and when $\lambda = 1$, **A'** is the same as **B**.

Here is what the Aperture applet looks like shortly after it starts:

Here is the source code:

```java
import java.applet.*;
import java.awt.*;
import java.util.Random;

public class aperture extends Applet implements Runnable
{
    int cirx, ciry, cirw, cirh, delay, depth, dInitial;
    float P1x, P1y, P2x, P2y, P3x, P3y, P4x, P4y;
    float P5x, P5y, P6x, P6y, P7x, P7y, P8x, P8y;
    float lambda = 0.1f;
    boolean in = true;
    Graphics bufGC;
    Thread motor;
    Dimension d;
    Image buf;
    Random r;
    Color c;

    public void init()
    {
        // get a couple of parameters from the Applet
        String str = getParameter("pps");
        int fps = (str != null) ? Integer.parseInt(str) : 10;
        delay = (fps > 0) ? (1000/fps) : 100;

        str = getParameter("depth");
        dInitial = (str != null) ? Integer.parseInt(str) : 100;
        depth = dInitial;

        // initialize the (x,y) coordinates for the polygon points
```

```
      d = this.size();
      P1x = (d.width - 1)/3;      P1y = 0;
      P2x = 2*((d.width - 1)/3);  P2y = 0;
      P3x = (d.width - 1);        P3y = (d.height - 1)/3;
      P4x = (d.width - 1);        P4y = 2*((d.height - 1)/3);
      P5x = 2*((d.width - 1)/3);  P5y = (d.height - 1);
      P6x = (d.width - 1)/3;      P6y = (d.height - 1);
      P7x = 0;                    P7y = 2*((d.height - 1)/3);
      P8x = 0;                    P8y = (d.height - 1)/3;


      // seed the random number generator
      r = new Random();

      buf = createImage(d.width,d.height);
      bufGC = buf.getGraphics();

      bufGC.setColor(Color.black);
      bufGC.fillRect(0,0,d.width,d.height);

      c = Color.red;
      bufGC.setColor(c);
}

public void update(Graphics g)
{
   paint(g);
}

 public void paint(Graphics g)
 {
    if (in == true)
    {
       // paint rotating polygons going in
       // draw the current polygon
       bufGC.drawLine((int)P1x,(int)P1y,(int)P2x,(int)P2y);
       bufGC.drawLine((int)P2x,(int)P2y,(int)P3x,(int)P3y);
       bufGC.drawLine((int)P3x,(int)P3y,(int)P4x,(int)P4y);
       bufGC.drawLine((int)P4x,(int)P4y,(int)P5x,(int)P5y);
       bufGC.drawLine((int)P5x,(int)P5y,(int)P6x,(int)P6y);
       bufGC.drawLine((int)P6x,(int)P6y,(int)P7x,(int)P7y);
       bufGC.drawLine((int)P7x,(int)P7y,(int)P8x,(int)P8y);
       bufGC.drawLine((int)P8x,(int)P8y,(int)P1x,(int)P1y);

       // calculate the new points for the next smaller polygon
       P1x = (1.0f - lambda)*P1x + (lambda*P2x);
       P1y = (1.0f - lambda)*P1y + (lambda*P2y);
       P2x = (1.0f - lambda)*P2x + (lambda*P3x);
       P2y = (1.0f - lambda)*P2y + (lambda*P3y);
       P3x = (1.0f - lambda)*P3x + (lambda*P4x);
       P3y = (1.0f - lambda)*P3y + (lambda*P4y);
       P4x = (1.0f - lambda)*P4x + (lambda*P5x);
       P4y = (1.0f - lambda)*P4y + (lambda*P5y);
       P5x = (1.0f - lambda)*P5x + (lambda*P6x);
       P5y = (1.0f - lambda)*P5y + (lambda*P6y);
       P6x = (1.0f - lambda)*P6x + (lambda*P7x);
       P6y = (1.0f - lambda)*P6y + (lambda*P7y);
       P7x = (1.0f - lambda)*P7x + (lambda*P8x);
```

```
                P7y = (1.0f - lambda)*P7y + (lambda*P8y);
                P8x = (1.0f - lambda)*P8x + (lambda*P1x);
                P8y = (1.0f - lambda)*P8y + (lambda*P1y);

                // are we ready to switch over to circles yet?
                if (depth-- < 0)
                {

                    // reinitialize the circle parameters
                    cirw = 50;
                    cirh = cirw;
                    cirx = (d.width/2) - (cirw/2);
                    ciry = (d.height/2) - (cirh/2);

                    depth = dInitial;
                    changeColor();
                    in = false;
                }
            }
            else
            {
                // paint circles getting larger going out
                // draw the cirrent circle
                bufGC.fillOval(cirx,ciry,cirw,cirh);

                // adjust for the next larger circle
                cirw += 20;        cirh += 20;
                cirx -= 10;        ciry -= 10;

                // are we ready to switch over to polygons yet??
                if (cirw > (d.width+(d.width/2)))
                    {
                    // reinitialize the polygon points
                    P1x = (d.width - 1)/3;      P1y = 0;
                    P2x = 2*((d.width - 1)/3);    P2y = 0;
                    P3x = (d.width - 1);          P3y = (d.height - 1)/3;
                    P4x = (d.width - 1);          P4y = 2*((d.height - 1)/3);
                    P5x = 2*((d.width - 1)/3);    P5y = (d.height - 1);
                    P6x = (d.width - 1)/3;    P6y = (d.height - 1);
                    P7x = 0;                  P7y = 2*((d.height - 1)/3);
                    P8x = 0;                  P8y = (d.height - 1)/3;

                    depth = dInitial;
                    changeColor();
                    in = true;
                    }
                }

                // now paint the offscreen buffer onto the visible screen
                g.drawImage(buf,0,0,null);
            }

public void changeColor()
{
    int col[] = new int[3];

    // get the rgb components of the current color
```

```
        col[0] = c.getRed();
        col[1] = c.getGreen();
        col[2] = c.getBlue();

        // adjust each rgb component to define a new random color
        col[0] += r.nextInt();
        col[1] += r.nextInt();
        col[2] += r.nextInt();
        c = new Color(col[0], col[1], col[2]);
        bufGC.setColor(c);
    }

    public void run()
    {
        // before we start the animation, remember the starting time
        long tm = System.currentTimeMillis();
        while (Thread.currentThread() == motor)
        {
            // display the current frame
            repaint();

            // delay depending on how far we are behind
            try
            {
                tm += delay;
                Thread.sleep(Math.max(0,tm-System.currentTimeMillis()));
            }
            catch (InterruptedException e)  { }
        }
    }

    public void start()
    {
        if (motor == null)
        {
            motor = new Thread(this);
            motor.start();
        }
    }

    public void stop()
    {
        if (motor != null)
        {
            motor.stop();
            motor = null;
        }
    }

    public String getAppletInfo()
    {
        String str = "\tAperture\n\n";
        str += "This is an example of an animation using the\n";
        str += "primitive line and circle rendering methods\n";
        str += "and double buffering.\n\n";
        str += "Applet parameters:\n";
        str += "\tpps    - polygons per second; default is 10\n";
```

```
            str += "\tdepth  - number of polygons; default is 100\n";
            return str;
    }
 }
```

First of all, look at the list of declarations where we initialize **lambda**.

```
float lambda = 0.1f;
```

By default, Java thinks all floating point literals are doubles. Consequently, if you combine a **float** declaration with an initialization and leave off the trailing **f** (or **F**), the compiler complains with a confusing and cryptic citation. (My compiler returns the following: '...Incompatible type for double. Explicit cast needed to convert double to float...' Who said anything about a double?)

The **init()** method is straightforward. We use the **getParameter()** method to retrieve the parameters specified in the applet's HTML file, then we explicitly initialize the first polygon's point coordinates. After setting up the random number generator, we clear the screen, then finally set an arbitrary line drawing color. We override the **update()** method to eliminate screen flicker.

The **paint()** method has two parts, one for rendering the polygons and another for rendering the circles. A simple boolean determines which part to enter. The **depth** variable, used as the conditional, determines when it's time to change from polygons to circles, and vice versa. In each case, a primitive draws the graphic then we calculate the new points for the next time **repaint()** (which is in the **run()** method) forces a call to **paint()**. The primitives use an off-screen context in a double-buffer fashion.

The **changeColor()** method extracts the RGB components from the current color. It then uses the **nextInt()** method from the **Random** class to adjust the components for a new pseudo-random color. The intent is random color, so any possible overflow or rollover in the additions just contributes to the randomness.

The only remaining part that may need explanation has to do with how we determine the sleep time in the **run()** method.

```
long tm = System.currentTimeMillis();
        .
        .
        .
    try {
       tm += delay;
       Thread.sleep(Math.max(0,tm-System.currentTimeMillis()));
    } catch (InterruptedException e)  { }
```

Recall that it's the operating system that ultimately allocates precious processor cycles to our Java applet. He/she that gives, can take. Also, the JVM may decide to do some internal housekeeping. If we were to give the **sleep()** method the same, constant value in the loop, each occasion we took a hit we might see a less-than-even performance in our animation. Consequently, **currentTimeMillis()** from the System class and **max()** from the Math class help us adjust–in a dynamic way–when necessary.

The Tweedybird Applet

This applet is a slight variation of a previous animation in this chapter. Here is the HTML file:

```
<HTML>
<HEAD>
<TITLE> Tweedybird </TITLE>
</HEAD>
<FONT SIZE="+5"><CENTER><B> Tweedybird </B></CENTER></FONT>

<APPLET CODE="tweedy.class" WIDTH=640 HEIGHT=350>
<PARAM NAME=fps value=10>
<PARAM NAME=deltaX value=15>
</APPLET>

</BODY>
</HTML>
```

The **APPLET** tag in the HTML file requires both the **WIDTH** and **HEIGHT** parameters. In this case, we set them to the width and height, respectively, of our background image. In a similar fashion as the previous example, the parameter **fps** determines the number of frames we display per second. The **deltaX** parameter is the number of pixels we move each successive frame to the right.

In this animation, we will display a series of frames over a complex background image. Perhaps the most critical factor in multiframe or cell animation, is the frames themselves, or more specifically, the difference from one frame to the next. Look at the following sequence of eight GIF images of a bird in flight. The sequence proceeds from left to right.

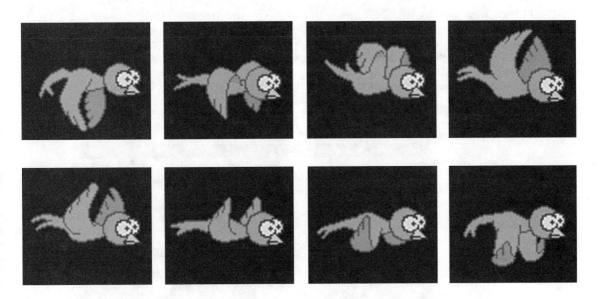

This material has been reprinted with the permission from, and under the copyright of, Kinetix - www.ktx.com.

Notice the difference between each successive frame. Four frames are used to show the total upward movement of the wings; likewise for the downward movement. Also, note that the wings are never straight but curved just the right amount as a result of air resistance. Obviously, a skilled animator with an understanding of bird flight and the laws of physics drew these frames. Animators call these frames **in-betweens**, and if they are correct, the animation will look natural and life-like.

Each of the eight **GIF** images above is in the 1989 version of the **GIF** file format commonly referred to as **GIF89a**. This version has the ability to set a bit flag in one of the file's control blocks. This flag indicates that the control block contains a color map index called the Transparency Index. When this index is present, and Java is about to display a pixel with that index's color, the rendering mechanism skips that pixel and processing goes on to the next pixel.

What this means is that we can effectively add one image to another. Typically, we add or superimpose a smaller image (our bird frame) on to a larger image (our background image). We save each of the bird frames in the **GIF89a** format, with the Transparency Index set to the index of the background color of that frame; in this case, the index of the color blue. We do not use that background color elsewhere in the image. Our larger image—the one used for the overall applet background—needs no such preparation. This allows us to draw each bird frame on top of, or over, the background image with the resulting composite: the background plus just the bird. Another way to look at it is the result will be the background image plus every pixel of the bird frame not set to the transparent index.

> Beware! Most GIF files are in the GIF87a format, which does not support this transparency feature. Currently, only a few of the mainstream bitmap image editors allow you to save a GIF image in the GIF89a format with a specified transparent color. A shareware package that does support transparency is Paint Shop Pro and is available at the URL http://www.jasc.com/psp.html. It's important to remember that the GIF89a format only allows one transparent color. Consequently, a dithered background can't be transparent. Dithering is a technique that uses more than one color to fool the eye into thinking it sees a color shade not directly supported by the underlying hardware color palette. These multiple colors are slightly different enough to give the desired effect but actually not equal. In such cases, convert the background to exactly one color. Be sure to pick an unused color.

Here is a snapshot of what the Tweedybird Applet looks like after image loading is complete:

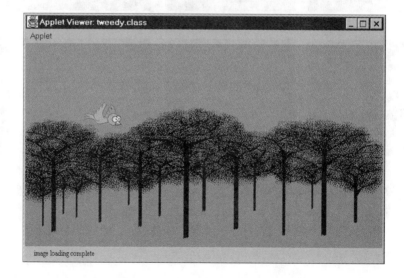

Here is the source code:

```java
import java.applet.*;
import java.awt.*;
import java.awt.image.*;

public class tweedy extends Applet implements Runnable
{
    int x, y, w, h, i, delay, delta;
    int frame = 0, prog = 0, n = 0;
    Image frames[], bk, buf;
    boolean loaded = false;
    MediaTracker tracker;
    Graphics bufGC;
    Thread motor;
    Dimension d;

    public void init()
    {
        // get a couple of parameters from the Applet
        String str = getParameter("fps");
        int fps = (str != null) ? Integer.parseInt(str) : 10;
        delay = (fps > 0) ? (1000/fps) : 100;

        str = getParameter("deltaX");
        delta = (str != null) ? Integer.parseInt(str) : 12;

        // setup all the image tracking stuff
        tracker = new MediaTracker(this);
        frames = new Image[8];
        for (i = 0; i < 8; i++)
        {
            frames[i] = getImage(getCodeBase(),"tweedy"+(i+1)+".gif");
            tracker.addImage(frames[i],i);
        }
        bk = getImage(getCodeBase(),"trees.gif");
        tracker.addImage(bk,i);

        w = 85;          // width of the tweedybird images
        h = 78;          // height of the tweedybird images
        x = -w;          // starting x position wrt bk; start off screen
        y = 100;         // starting y position wrt background

        d = this.size();
        buf = createImage(d.width,d.height);
        bufGC = buf.getGraphics();
    }

    public void update(Graphics g)
    {
        paint(g);
    }

    public void paint(Graphics g)
    {
        // if images are loading, paint an expanding progress bar
        if (loaded == false)
        {
```

```
            g.setColor(Color.blue);
            g.fillRect(0,d.height-14,prog,14);
            prog += 2;
            return;
        }


        // paint a clean background into the offscreen buffer
        bufGC.drawImage(bk,0,0,null);

        // paint the current frame onto the clean offscreen buffer
        bufGC.drawImage(frames[frame],x,y,null);

        // now paint the offscreen buffer onto the visible screen
        g.drawImage(buf,0,0,null);
}

public void run()
{
    for (i = 0; i < 9; i++)
    {
        while (tracker.statusID(i,true) == MediaTracker.LOADING)
        {
            showStatus(
            "loading image #" + (i+1) + ", one moment please...");

            try
            {
                Thread.sleep(10);
            }
            catch (InterruptedException e)  { }

            // paint a loading progress bar
            repaint();
        }
    }
    loaded = true;
    showStatus("image loading complete");

    // before we start the animation, remember the starting time
    long tm = System.currentTimeMillis();
    while (Thread.currentThread() == motor)
    {
        // display the current frame
        repaint();

            // delay depending on how far we are behind
            try
            {
               tm += delay;
               Thread.sleep(Math.max(0,tm-System.currentTimeMillis()));
            }
            catch (InterruptedException e)  { }

            // update the new (x,y) position and next frame in sequence
            x += delta;
            if (x > d.width) x = -w;
            y = 100 + (int)(20 * Math.sin(((++n % 24) * Math.PI)/12));
```

```
                       frame = ++frame % 8;
        }
    }

    public void start()
    {
        if (motor == null)
        {
            motor = new Thread(this);
            motor.start();
        }
    }

    public void stop()
    {
        motor.stop();
        motor = null;
    }

    public String getAppletInfo()
    {
        String str = "\tTweedybird\n\n";
        str += "This is an example of an animation over a\n";
        str += "complex background using double buffering.\n\n";
        str += "Applet parameters:\n";
        str += "\tfps    - frames per second; default is 10\n";
        str += "\tdeltaX - change in x-direction in pixels; ";
        str += " default is 12\n";
        return str;
    }
}
```

The core of this applet is very similar to the previous example. In the **init()** method, we first retrieve two parameters specified in the HTML file, then load the eight bird images and the background image. By using the **MediaTracker** class, we can monitor the loading progress of each image.

Both the **paint()** and the **run()** methods have two parts, an image loading or tracking part and the main animation part. In **run()**, we enter a **for** loop and make periodic checks on the loading progress of each image. When loading the **GIF** files, we use the **showStatus()** method to display a message in the applet's status area. Repeated calls to **repaint()** in this loop eventually force calls to **paint()**. Our **paint()** method uses **fillRect()** to display a small, horizontal bar graph. This graphic increases from left to right and gives a visual indication that things are happening–we are making progress.

The following clip is a snapshot of the lower left corner of the applet during image tracking:

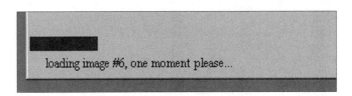

A simple boolean, **loaded**, differentiates between the image loading state and the free-running animation state. Again, we use calls to **currentTimeMillis()** to smooth out any timing inconsistencies that would result in uneven performance. In the animation loop, we calculate the **x** and **y** position coordinates for the next bird frame. The **sin()** method from the Math Class allows us to give some variation to the **y** coordinate which makes the flight look a little more interesting.

Summary

In this chapter, we have expanded on what we learned about the AWT Graphics class in the previous chapter, and we still have more to cover on the AWT. The different rendering methods we learned about here construct the foundation for all subsequent graphics work. We talked about the unique image paradigm that Java introduced, and how to load and display multiple images. In the next chapter, we'll show you how to handle components and give you some good examples of how to put it all together.

AWT Components

Whether you're running UNIX, NT, Windows or some other windowed system, you will be familiar with user interface components. On some platforms they are called controls, on others, widgets, but we're talking about the same thing, the buttons, checkboxes, listboxes and other objects which make up your interface. In this chapter we'll introduce you to the standard components that come with the AWT, show you how you might use them, and then show you how you might 'roll your own' custom component from scratch. The main topics in this chapter will be:

- The nine AWT components
- A sample applet which utilizes all nine components
- The Container, Panel and Window components
- A Custom Slider class

Platform-specific Components

The AWT architects had an important decision to make early in their design. Should they create a group of AWT controls which would be consistent in appearance and behavior across all platforms, or should they create an interface for communicating with the native controls that already exist on each platform that Java is ported to? Ultimately, they chose the latter, and as you would expect, that decision produces both benefits and drawbacks for the toolkit.

The main effect of this decision on the programmer, is that the components will look and behave slightly different on each platform, because the components are slightly different on each platform. Depending on opinion, these platform differences can be seen as a positive thing or a negative thing. In any case, when you run a Java application on Windows 95, it will look like a Windows 95 application. When you the same application on a Macintosh, it will look like a Macintosh application, etc.

These platform differences are also probably the main reason that the concept of a Layout Manager has been implemented in the AWT. A Layout Manager is a set of methods which dynamically size and position components at run time. We'll be talking in depth about the layout managers in the next chapter so don't worry about it right now.

As a Java programmer, you are abstracted away from the platform-specific differences by 'peer' classes which act as translators between the AWT components and their corresponding native controls. In order for the AWT to be ported to a new platform, only these 'peer' classes need to be rewritten (and the Java virtual machine, of course).

The Nine AWT Components

The AWT includes nine basic components which can be used for building user interfaces:

- ▲ Button
- ▲ Canvas
- ▲ Checkbox
- ▲ Choice
- ▲ Label
- ▲ List
- ▲ Scrollbar
- ▲ TextArea
- ▲ TextField

These components are all subclasses of the abstract Component class which provides common functionality needed by all components such as sizing, event handling and enable/disable methods.

Now let's take a look into each of the AWT components in a little more detail. We will not cover all the details, just the important ones. You should consult the Java documentation for a list of all methods and variables for each component.

Button

The Button is a simple component, generally used to allow the user to initiate some action. It generates an **ACTION_EVENT** event when it's released, *not* when pressed. The **Event.arg** variable contains the button's label.

A Button

The Button component has two constructors:

- ▲ **Button(String)**–Constructs a button with the specified label
- ▲ **Button()**–Constructs a button with no label.

Canvas

This is a component which does nothing! Actually it can be quite useful in many situations. Although it has no default drawing or event handling functionality, it can be subclassed to paint itself and handle any type of user interface action such as mouse movements and key presses. It works well as a base for implementing your own custom components.

It has one default public constructor:

```
Canvas()
```

Checkbox

This is a simple component which is generally used to allow a user to make some true/false choice. The Checkbox component will generate an **ACTION_EVENT** event when it's clicked and the event **arg** variable will be set to true or false indicating the new state.

Checkboxes can be logically grouped together with a **CheckboxGroup** object to make them mutually exclusive. When the **CheckboxGroup** is used, the checkboxes will look and behave like radio buttons.

A regular non-grouped checkbox looks like this:
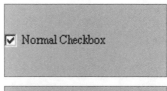

A checkbox which is part of a group looks like this:
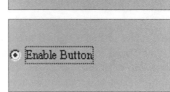

The checkbox component has three available constructors.

- **Checkbox()**–Simple non-grouped checkbox with no label.
- **Checkbox(String)**–Simple non-grouped checkbox with a label.
- **Checkbox(String label, CheckboxGroup group, Boolean state)**–A grouped version of the previous constructor. All checkboxes with a common CheckboxGroup value will behave like radio buttons, only one will be allowed to be set to true at any point. When a checkbox in the group is clicked, the checkbox which is currently set to true will be set to false.

You can use the **getState()** and **setState()** methods to check or set the boolean state of the checkbox, and the **getLabel()** and **setLabel()** methods to check or set the text of the checkbox label.

Choice

The Choice control is used to give the user a drop-down list of choices to select from. It can't be set to allow multiple selections.

You can use the **addItem(String text)** method to add selections to the control. The **getSelectedIndex()** and **getSelectedItem()** methods can be used for querying the index and/or item text, and the **select(int index)** or **select(String text)** methods can be used for programmatically selecting a value.

This is the Choice control as it normally appears:

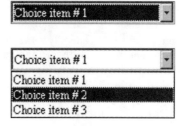

When selected, the choices will drop down:

It has one default constructor:

```
Choice()
```

Label

The Label component displays a single line of text in a container, with a left, right or center justification. You could create the same visual effect with the **drawString()** Graphics method, but using the Label component is generally more desirable since the text will then be positioned and sized dynamically by the container's Layout Manager. The text can be retrieved or modified programmatically with the **getText()** and **setText()** methods but can't be modified by the user.

The Label component has three public constructors:

▲   **Label()**–Constructs a new Label object with left justification.

▲   **Label(String label)**–Constructs a new Label object initialized to the specified string, and left justified.

▲   **Label(String label, int alignment)**–Constructs a new Label object initialized and justified as specified. The alignment value must be one of **Label.LEFT**, **Label.RIGHT**, or **Label.CENTER** or an **IllegalArgumentException** will be thrown.

List

The List component is similar to the Choice control. The List component however creates a scrollable list of choices and supports single or multiple selection.

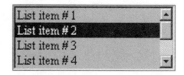

You can use the **addItem(String text)** or **addItem(String item, int index)** method to add selections to the control. The first one will add the selection to the end of the list, the second one will add the item at the specified index. Use the **getSelectedIndex()** and **getSelectedItem()** methods for querying the index and/or item text when in single select mode. Use the **getSelectedIndexes()** (will return an array of **int**) and **getSelectedItems()** (will return an array of strings) methods when in multiple select mode. The **select(int index)** method can be used for programmatically selecting a value. There are many other methods available for clearing items, deleting items, checking selections, etc.

There are two public constructors:

▲ `List()`–Will create a new single select List control with no visible lines.

▲ `List(int Rows, boolean multipleSelections)`–Will create a new List control with the number of visible lines specified by `Rows` and multiple selections `if` `multipleSelections` is true.

Scrollbar

The Scrollbar is used to allow the user to select a value from a continuous range between a minimum and maximum value. It's usually used for values which a user would perceive as analog, such as sound volume or the click speed of a mouse. Of course, it's not really analog, the position of the scrollbar handle is always rounded into a numeric value. You commonly see scrollbars used for allowing users to scroll text or pictures. AWT scrollbars can be positioned vertically or horizontally.

A user can adjust a Scrollbar's value by dragging the 'thumb', clicking on the arrow on either end, or clicking on the space between the thumb and the end point. Programmatically the value can be set with the `setValue()` method.

Scrollbar is the one component that does not generate an `action()` event. To react to a change in a scrollbar value you will need to use the `handleEvent()` method. The event `arg` variable will contain the new value of the control so it's a fairly easy event to handle. The following code fragment from an applet we'll review next shows a sample `if` clause from a `handleEvent()` method.

```
if (e.target == theScrollbar)
{
   theTextArea.appendText("\nScrollbar value: "
   + ((Integer)e.arg).intValue());
   return true;
}
```

The Scrollbar has three public constructors:

▲ `Scrollbar()`–Constructs a new Scrollbar with a vertical orientation.

▲ `Scrollbar(int orientation)`–Constructs a new Scrollbar with the orientation specified. Use the `Scrollbar.HORIZONTAL` and `Scrollbar.VERTICAL` constants to safely specify the orientation. This constructor will throw an `IllegalArgumentException` if an invalid orientation value is passed to it.

▲ `Scrollbar(int orientation, int value, int visible, int minimum, int maximum)`–Constructs a new Scrollbar with the specified orientation, initial value, visible area, and minimum and maximum values.

Unique Scrollbar Behavior on Windows 95... Bug or Feature?

In Windows 95, the Scrollbar has some unique behavior which we believe (hope) is a bug. All the events generated while you are sliding the scrollbar tab are stacked up and delivered to the `handleEvent()` method at once, when the scrollbar tab is released. The desired behavior would be to receive the events as they are generated. An acceptable alternative to that would be to receive one event when the tab is released.

Receiving all the events after the fact is probably never what one would want. According to the user group ramblings about this issue, the component does behave correctly on other platforms. Later in the chapter, we'll implement a slider control which generates events as it's 'slid' on all platforms.

TextArea

The TextArea is a plain text, multiline edit control. It's generally used to allow a user to enter a text description of something. It has scrollbars so the line length is not limited. A new-line character **\n** in the text will cause a new line to be started.

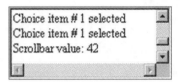

TextArea has four public constructors:

- ▲ **TextArea()**—Constructs a new TextArea.
- ▲ **TextArea(int, int)**—Constructs a new TextArea with the specified number of rows and columns.
- ▲ **TextArea(String)**—Constructs a new TextArea initialized with the text specified.
- ▲ **TextArea(String, int, int)**—Constructs a new TextArea initialized with the text, rows and columns specified.

TextField

The TextField control is a plain text single line edit field. It's usually used to allow the user to enter simple text such as name, address etc. It includes a **setEchoCharacter** method which can be used for masking entry of sensitive information such as a password (or for some people, age and/or weight!).

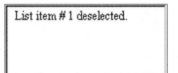

The TextField has four public constructors:

- ▲ **TextField()**—Constructs a new TextField.
- ▲ **TextField(int)**—Constructs a new TextField initialized with the specified number of columns.
- ▲ **TextField(String)**—Constructs a new TextField initialized with the specified text.
- ▲ **TextField(String, int)**—Constructs a new TextField initialized with the specified text and number of columns.

The AWT Sample Applet

We'll now take a look at an applet which contains all of the basic AWT components. This will enable you to see what they look like on your system and check out the code for creating an interface and handling events. This applet contains an instance of each control, added to the applet screen in alphabetical order. Yes, it is ugly right now, but in the next chapter we'll show you how it can be laid it out better using a Layout Manager.

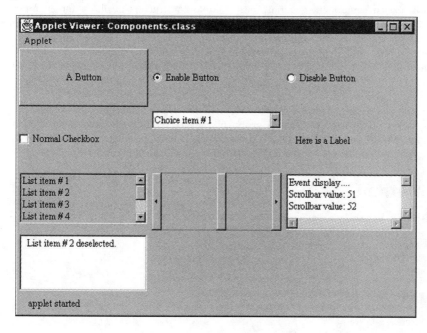

Since there is a fair amount of code in this example, we are going to break it up, and describe it section by section.

In building an interface with the AWT , there are a few standard housekeeping tasks you'll always implement. You will declare instances of some (or all) of the components, add them to the interface in the proper position, and implement the code for handling the events generated by the components when the user makes an action such as clicking a button, or selecting a listbox item. We'll explain more as we review each section:

Declaring References

```
import java.awt.*;
import java.applet.*;

public class Components extends Applet
{
    Button        theButton = new Button("A Button");
    CheckboxGroup   CBG1 = new CheckboxGroup();
    Checkbox      checkbox1 = new Checkbox("Enable Button", CBG1, true);
    Checkbox      checkbox2 = new Checkbox("Disable Button", CBG1, false);
```

```
Checkbox     checkbox3 = new Checkbox("Normal Checkbox");
Choice       theChoice = new Choice();
List         theList = new List(4,true);
Scrollbar    theScrollbar = new Scrollbar(Scrollbar.HORIZONTAL);
TextArea     theTextArea = new TextArea(10,10);
TextField    theTextField = new TextField(20);
```

The first thing we do is declare references for all our components, and construct an instance of each one. As you saw earlier, each component generally has multiple constructors available for creating new instances. The Button component, for instance, has two constructors available, one which takes a **String** object as a parameter specifying the caption, and one with no parameters. In our applet, we use the constructor which allows us to define the caption. In this case, it's simply a matter of convenience—we could have almost as easily used the default constructor and then used the **setLabel()** method to add the caption.

The only non-component object created in this section is the CBG1 CheckboxGroup instance. A CheckboxGroup is an object used to make a group of checkboxes mutually exclusive. This, in effect, makes them radio buttons and they even look different when the CheckboxGroup is used. We have included both kinds of checkboxes in this applet so you can see the difference.

The init Method

```
public void init()
{
    setLayout(new GridLayout(0,3,5,5));
    add(theButton);


    add(checkbox1);
    add(checkbox2);
    add(checkbox3);

    theChoice.addItem("Choice item # 1");
    theChoice.addItem("Choice item # 2");
    theChoice.addItem("Choice item # 3");
    theChoice.addItem("Choice item # 4");
    add(theChoice);

    add(new Label("Here is a Label"));

    theList.addItem("List item # 1");
    theList.addItem("List item # 2");
    theList.addItem("List item # 3");
    theList.addItem("List item # 4");
    theList.addItem("List item # 5");
    theList.addItem("List item # 6");
    theList.addItem("List item # 7");
    add(theList);


    theScrollbar.setValues(50,5,0,100);
    add(theScrollbar);
```

```
        theTextArea.setText("Event display....");

        add(theTextArea);

        theTextField.setText("Yes, this is a TextField");
        add(theTextField);
    }
```

In the `init()` method we create the user interface by adding each component to the applet using the **add** method that the applet class inherits from the **container** class.

This is where we see the fundamental difference between building user interfaces with the AWT, and building them with other development environments such as Visual Basic, Visual C++, or PowerBuilder. In those environments, controls are positioned explicitly with a drag and drop type interface builder, and an intermediate file is used to store the layout of the window (although controls can still be added dynamically). With the AWT, the interface is built entirely by Java code. Even in the Java Development Environments becoming available which feature 'drag and drop' interface builders, the end result is Java code which will construct the interface at run time. Unfortunately, so far, these tools all construct the interface by using a NULL Layout Manager, and explicitly sizing and positioning the components. While this may ease development of the interface, it will also increase the possibility of your interface looking horrible when run on platforms other than the one you developed it on. In the next chapter, we'll discuss Layout Managers and we think you'll find that, when used correctly, they are a much more effective solution for building platform-independent interfaces.

In this example, we have chosen to use the **GridLayout** Layout Manager, one of the simplest. As we'll be discussing Layout Managers in the next chapter, you only need to know that **GridLayout** causes the components to be laid out in a grid formation defined by the programmer in the constructor. Here we're asking for 0 rows and 3 columns. The last two parameters in the constructor are the inset values, which define the horizontal and vertical space between components. As components are added to the applet, they are positioned from left to right, top to down. You may be wondering why we requested zero rows. Zero is a special value which means 'any number'. The result will be three columns of components and as many rows as needed to hold them (by the way, you can also specify the opposite–a fixed number of rows and as many columns as necessary).

Although we have declared and instantiated components at the beginning of the class, Java does not force you to do that. You'll often see code where a component is instantiated when it's added to a container. To demonstrate this, we have used this technique for the Label component in this applet.

Keep in mind that, when this technique is used, you have no reference to that component. In this applet we don't need a reference to this component but if you do this with a component for which you will be processing events, this will increase the complexity and maintainability of your event handling code as you will have to use some other technique for determining which component is the target. If your code is relying on checking the text or caption of the component, you will have to modify the code if (or should we say *when*) the label changes.

Also in the `init()` method, we're using some of the other component methods to add or change properties of the components. The List and Choice components, for example, require the use of the **addItem()** method to add entries to the control.

The action Method and the handleEvent Method

```java
public boolean action(Event event, Object arg)
{
    if (event.target == theButton)
        theTextArea.appendText("\nButton clicked");

    else if (event.target == checkbox1)
        theButton.enable();

    else if (event.target == checkbox2)
        theButton.disable();

    else if (event.target == theChoice)
        theTextArea.appendText("\n" +
            theChoice.getSelectedItem() +  " selected");

    else if (event.target == theList)
        theTextArea.appendText("\n" +
            theList.getSelectedItem() +  " selected");

    return true;
}

public boolean handleEvent(Event e)
{
    if ((e.id == Event.LIST_SELECT )
        && (e.target == theList))
    {

        theTextField.setText(theList.getItem(((Integer)e.arg).intValue())
        + " selected.");
        return true;
    }

    else if ((e.id == Event.LIST_DESELECT )
        && (e.target == theList))
    {

        theTextField.setText(theList.getItem(((Integer)e.arg).intValue())
        + " deselected.");
        return true;
    }

    else if (e.target == theScrollbar)
    {
        theTextArea.appendText("\nScrollbar value: "
        + ((Integer)e.arg).intValue());
        return true;
    }

    return super.handleEvent(e);
}
}
```

The next method in this example is our **action** method override. The **action** method is the 'helper' method which gets invoked for all **ACTION** events. We can do most of our event handling here, although we'll still need a **handleEvent()** method for some events that do not generate **ACTION** events. The first thing the **action** event must do is determine which of its components should handle this event. Since we have references to all the components (except the **Label**, which we know won't have any events), we just check the event target variable to determine which component it belongs to.

The **handleEvent()** method override handles the List class **LIST_SELECT** and **LIST_DESELECT** events which are generated when an item is selected or deselected from a List control. We also check for scrollbar events and add a note to the TextArea component when any are received.

At the end of our **handleEvent()**, if the event wasn't one of the ones we're looking for, we call the superclass **handleEvent()** to ensure that the proper 'helper' methods get invoked. If we had not done this, the **action()** method we wrote would never be called.

Containers

This isn't the end of our look at components–we still need to consider where we place our components. This is where another type of component comes in: the **Container**.

Put simply, a container is a non-displayable component which can contain other components (or Containers) and treat them as a group. A Container will usually have a Layout Manager associated with it that manages the process of sizing and positioning the contained components.

The Container subclass hierarchy looks like this:

The Container has two subclasses, Panel and Window.

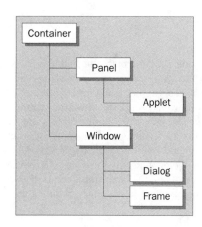

Panel

Let's talk about Panel first. If you come from a Windows development background, do not confuse an AWT Panel with a Windows panel. The AWT Panel is invisible (although it can be subclassed to have a **paint()** override) and is generally used just to group a set of components together within a parent Frame or other Panel, and lay them out according to the constraints of the assigned Layout Manager. Many times, a Frame or applet Window will be broken up into separate sections, with different Layout Managers. The Panel class is ideal for this. You have seen a lot of examples in this chapter that added components directly to an applet window. As you can see from the class hierarchy, the **applet** class is actually a subclass of Panel with lots of additional methods.

Panel has one constructor: **Panel()**

Window

The Window class is a borderless, menuless window. Although it can be used directly, usually its subclasses Dialog and Frame are used instead. All three classes are containers to which components can be added. In the next chapter we will cover the Window, Dialog and Frame classes in detail.

At this point, you know all you need in order to develop simple user interfaces, and respond to the events generated by it. But we still need to cover one more component. This time, however, it's going to be a custom component, written completely in Java. Because it's implemented entirely in Java and has no native 'peer', this custom control will look and behave exactly the same on every platform Java runs on.

Custom Slider Class

In this section we are going to implement a 'Slider' control. This example was chosen because it requires us to write code to paint the control, respond to user events such as mouse clicks and drags, and to generate events when the controls value has changed. In summary, it will demonstrate just about every AWT topic we have covered so far.

After going through this example, you will know all of the basics of creating a custom component.

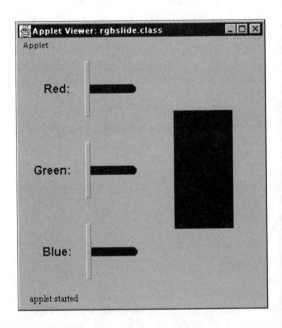

The source code contains both the Slider class, which encapsulates the component, and a small applet to demonstrate it. The applet is a simple interface of three 'Slider' controls which represent the three primary colors: red, green, and blue. As the sliders are moved, **ACTION** events are generated. The applet has an **action()** method override which gets the new values, creates a new Color, and sets the Canvas to the new color. The Canvas immediately repaints itself in the new color, so the effect is dynamic. Here's a snapshot of the applet:

The applet itself is called **RGBSlide**, and it uses two other classes called **swatchCanvas** (a simple subclass of canvas) and **Slider** (a custom control which implements a type of 'slider' control seen in products such as Visual Basic 4.0). There's a lot going on in this applet, so let's take it one class at a time.

RGBSlide

```
import java.applet.*;
import java.awt.*;
import java.lang.*;


public class RGBSlide extends Applet
{
    Slider sldrRed, sldrGreen, sldrBlue;
    int vRed, vGreen, vBlue;
    Panel pnlColors, pnlDisplay;
    swatchCanvas canSwatch;
    Font font = new Font("Helvetica", Font.BOLD, 16);

    public void init()
    {
        sldrRed = new Slider(0,255);
        sldrGreen = new Slider(0,255);
        sldrBlue = new Slider(0,255);

// Layout in two equal sections,
        setLayout(new GridLayout(1,2,10,10));
        pnlColors = new Panel();
        pnlDisplay  = new Panel();

        canSwatch = new swatchCanvas(Color.black);

        //layout colors in 3 by 2 grid for Labels and Sliders
        pnlColors.setLayout(new GridLayout(3,2,20,10));
        pnlDisplay.setLayout(new GridLayout(1,1));

        pnlColors.setBackground(Color.lightGray);
        pnlColors.setFont(font);
        pnlColors.add(new Label("Red:",Label.RIGHT));
        pnlColors.add(sldrRed);
        pnlColors.add(new Label("Green:",Label.RIGHT));
        pnlColors.add(sldrGreen);
        pnlColors.add(new Label("Blue:",Label.RIGHT));
        pnlColors.add(sldrBlue);
        pnlDisplay.add(canSwatch);

        add(pnlColors);
        add(pnlDisplay);

    }

    public void start()
    {
        sldrRed.setVal(0);
        sldrGreen.setVal(0);
        sldrBlue.setVal(0);
        vRed = sldrRed.getVal();
        vGreen = sldrGreen.getVal();
        vBlue = sldrBlue.getVal();
        canSwatch.setColor(new Color(vRed, vGreen, vBlue));
    }
```

```
    public boolean action(Event e, Object arg)
    {
        if (e.target == sldrRed)
  vRed = ((Integer) e.arg).intValue();
        else if (e.target == sldrGreen)
            vGreen = ((Integer) e.arg).intValue();
        else vBlue = ((Integer) e.arg).intValue();
            canSwatch.setColor(new Color(vRed, vGreen, vBlue));
        return true;
    }
}
```

This is a fairly simple class which lays out the user
interface components, initializes their values and
handles events generated by them. We haven't
covered the various layouts yet, but this applet uses
two simple 'grid' layouts to create the interface. First
a grid layout is used to split the applet window into
two vertical halves, then another grid is used to
further divide the left half into two columns and
three rows like this:

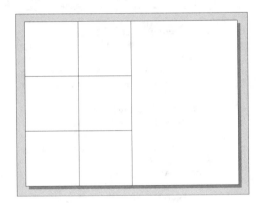

Don't worry if you are confused by the layout code. You'll understand it more clearly once we've covered
Layout Managers in the next chapter.

The Slider control has one constructor which requires that you pass the minimum and maximum values
for it as parameters. Since the sliders will each represent an RGB value, each is constructed with a
minimum of 0 and a maximum of 255. Then we create our interface by adding the components to the
Panels, and the Panels to the applet.

In the **start()** method we initialize all the sliders to zero, set the **vRed**, **vGreen**, and **vBlue** integers to
the current slider values, and set the color of our 'swatch' to a new Color object which has been created
with the current Red, Green and Blue values. An action method override is all we need to handle the
events. The Slider generates **ACTION_EVENT** events when its value changes. We check to see which Slider
posted the event, update the current value, and set the swatch color with a Color object created with the
new values.

The swatchCanvas Class

```
*****************************************************************
* The swatchCanvas class will paint a solid color rectangle *
* in its center with a width and height half the size of    *
* of the canvas.                                            *
* It has one constructor:                                   *
*     swatchCanvas(Color color)                             *
*****************************************************************/
```

```
class swatchCanvas extends Canvas
{
    Color currColor;
Dimension    dimSwatch = new Dimension();
    Point inset;

    public swatchCanvas(Color color)
    {
        currColor = color;
    }

    public void setColor(Color color)
    {
        currColor = color;
        repaint();
    }

    public void paint(Graphics g)
    {
        g.setColor(currColor);
        g.fillRect(inset.x, inset.y, dimSwatch.width, dimSwatch.height);
    }

    public void update(Graphics g)
    {
        paint(g);
    }

    // The only reliable way to detect a window resize is to
    // override the reshape() method.
    public void reshape(int x, int y, int width, int height)
    {
        dimSwatch.width = width / 2;
        dimSwatch.height = height / 2 ;
        inset = new Point(width / 4, height / 4);
        super.reshape(x, y, width, height);
    }
}
```

The **swatchCanvas** class is a simple subclass of **Canvas**. It has one constructor, one accessor method and three method overrides. This class will paint a solid rectangle, half its width and height, in its center. We use a **Dimension** object to hold the size of the rectangle, and a **Point** object to hold the position. It's all fairly self-explanatory except for the **reshape()** method override.

In order to paint the rectangle correctly, we need to know the current dimensions of the component. Usually the dimensions will not change, but they could. The **reshape()** method will be called if the dimensions change, so it's a good spot to reset the position variables. Notice that we are careful to call the superclass's **reshape()** method in case it has some tasks to take care of.

An alternative implementation would have been to call the **size()** method in the **paint()** method to dynamically determine the dimensions, but since that would always be done, and the dimensions are unlikely to change very often, it would be very inefficient. We also wanted to include the tip about using **reshape()** for detecting a change in the window size!

The Slider Class

```
/****************************************************************
* The slider class implements a custom slider control.         *
* It has one constructor:                                      *
*         Slider(int min, int max)                             *
* It posts a ACTION_EVENT with current value as the argument   *
* whenever the value changes                                   *
****************************************************************/
class Slider extends Canvas
{
    int minVal, maxVal, minPos, maxPos, valRange, posRange;
    int curVal, curPos, curWidth, curHeight;
    int sliderWidth, sliderHeight, sliderInset;
    int slotHeight, slotTop, handleWidth, handleTop,
        handleHeight, handleStart;
    boolean setValInProgress = false;
    boolean setPosInProgress = false;
    Image scratchImage;
    Graphics scratchGraphic;

    public Slider (int iMin, int iMax)
    {
        setMin(iMin);
        setMax(iMax);
        valRange = maxVal - minVal;
        setVal(1);
    }

    public void setMin (int iVal)
    {
        if ( iVal < maxVal )
        {
            minVal = iVal;
            setVal(curVal);
        }
    }

    public void setMax (int iVal)
    {
        if  ( iVal > minVal )
        {
            maxVal = iVal;
            setVal(curVal);
        }
    }

    public int getVal()
    {
        return curVal;
    }

    void setVal (int iVal)
    {
        if ( setValInProgress == true )
        {
```

```
        return; // avoid endless looping
    }
setValInProgress = true;
if (iVal < minVal)
    curVal = minVal;
else if (iVal > maxVal)
    curVal = maxVal;
else
    curVal = iVal;
    valRange = maxVal - minVal;
    setPos(
        (int) (Math.round((double) (curVal - minVal)
        / (double)valRange
        * (double) posRange)
        + minPos)
        );
    repaint();
    setValInProgress = false;
}

void setPos(int x)
{
    if ( setPosInProgress == true )
    {
        return; // avoid endless looping
    }
    setPosInProgress = true;

    double relPos;
    if ( x < minPos)
        curPos = minPos;
    else if ( x > maxPos )
        curPos = maxPos;
    else curPos = x;

    relPos = (double)(curPos - minPos) / posRange;

    setVal((int)(Math.round(relPos * (double) valRange))
    + minVal);
    repaint();
    setPosInProgress = false;
}

public void paint(Graphics g)
{
    scratchGraphic.setColor(super.getBackground());
    scratchGraphic.fillRect(0, 0, curWidth, curHeight);
    scratchGraphic.setColor(Color.black);
    scratchGraphic.fillRoundRect(0, slotTop, curWidth,
    slotHeight ,slotHeight ,slotHeight);
    scratchGraphic.setColor(Color.lightGray);
    scratchGraphic.fill3DRect(curPos - handleStart, handleTop,
    handleWidth, handleHeight, true);
    g.drawImage(scratchImage,0,0,this);
}

public boolean mouseDown (Event e, int x, int y)
```

```
    {
        return mouseDrag(e,x,y);
    }

    public boolean mouseDrag (Event e, int x, int y)
    {
        setPos(x);
        Integer I=new Integer(curVal);
        Event evtSlide = new Event(this,Event.ACTION_EVENT, (Object) I);
        postEvent(evtSlide);
        return true;
    }

    // update() is overridden to eliminate the background paint
    // which we do not need, and causes flicker
    public void update(Graphics g)
    {
        paint(g);
    }

    // The only reliable way to detect a window resize is to
    // override the reshape() method.
    public void reshape(int x, int y, int width, int height)
    {
        curWidth = width;
        curHeight = height;

        try
        {
            scratchImage = createImage(width,height);
        }

        catch (IllegalArgumentException e)
        {
            super.reshape(x,y,width,height);
            return;
        }

        scratchGraphic = scratchImage.getGraphics();
        scratchGraphic.setColor(getBackground());
        sliderInset = width / 20;
        minPos = sliderInset;
        maxPos = width - sliderInset;
        posRange = maxPos - minPos;
        slotHeight = height / 8;
        slotTop = ( height / 2 ) -
        ( slotHeight / 2 );
        handleWidth = width / 10;
        handleStart = handleWidth / 2;
        handleTop = height / 8;
        handleHeight = (int) (Math.round(height * .75 ));

        super.reshape(x,y,width,height);
    }
}
```

The **Slider** class is the big one. It's actually not that difficult to write a custom component such as this one. In the interests of clarity, we've tried to keep this control very simple. When you implement one of your own, you will most likely want to add some additional functionality to make it more versatile. For instance, in a control such as this one, you might want to add a few more constructors and make the color and orientation configurable. While designing a custom control, you should always be sure to think about ways to make it more configurable and reusable.

The complexity of this particular control lies in the painting code and the synchronization of the visible position with the control's 'value'. In order to facilitate these processes, we use a number of variables to contain values which would otherwise have to be calculated dynamically. This simplifies the code, as well as increasing its efficiency. Take a look at the first few lines of the class and you'll see variables defined to represent the current dimensions of the control's graphic components and other values.

The constructor requires that the minimum and maximum values to be chosen when the control is instantiated. As an exercise, you may want to add a constructor which also allows the initial value to be set when the control is created.

The **setMin()**, **setMax()** and **getVal()** methods are all pretty simple.

The **setVal()** and **setPos()** methods are also fairly simple, but they both contain a common piece of code which might need explaining.

Because the control's value and its visible position must be kept in synch, and the control's value can be modified either by the user or programmatically, we always update the value when the physical position is changed, and update the physical position when the control's value is updated. This creates the possibility of getting into a call loop between these two methods.

To eliminate that possibility, we have a variable for each method which is used to detect when the method is in progress and avoid calling it again until the current call is completed. We don't want to use the **synchronize** method modifier because we do not want to queue up the requests–we just want to throw them out if there is an execution already in progress.

The lines:

```
if ( setValInProgress == true )
{
    return; // avoid endless looping
}
setValInProgress = true;
```

cause the method to return immediately if an execution is already in progress, and to set the 'in progress' object otherwise.

The **paint()** method uses the dimension and positional values to draw the control in three steps, using the double buffering technique described in Chapter 8: first the background is painted in the current background color of the superclass. This ensures that the control blends into the container, no matter what color it is (unless it is black, since the slot is drawn in black). The second step is to paint the slot using a black, filled, rounded rectangle. The third step is to paint the 'handle' or 'thumb' in its new position as a light gray, filled 3D rectangle. The reason that the starting x coordinate is not the current position is that we need to center the rectangle on the current position. To do that we use the offset in the **handleStart** variable. The fourth, and last, step is to copy the completed off-screen image to the applet window.

We have implemented two mouse methods in this applet: **mouseDown()**, and **mouseDrag()**. Since these methods do the same two things (update the position using the **setPos()** method, and post an **ACTION_EVENT** with the current control value as an argument), we simply call the **mouseDrag()** method from **mouseDown()**. This eliminates the need to have the same code in two places, and eases the maintenance if you need to change it.

Depending on what control behavior you want, you may choose to eliminate the **mouseDown()** method entirely. A **mouseUp()** event will cause a **mouseDrag()** event to be generated, even if the mouse hasn't moved. Comment out the **mouseDown()** event and watch what happens. The control 'thumb' will no longer be repositioned when you depress the mouse button, but it will still be repositioned when you release the button, since that will generate a **mouseDrag()** event. Since we call **setPos()** in the **mouseDrag()** method, there is no way to not reposition the control once you have depressed the button. For that reason, the behavior is probably more natural if you leave the **mouseDown()** method in.

The last method we'll talk about is the **reshape()** override. For the same reasons we cited in the **swatchCanvas()** explanation, the **reshape()** method is a good spot to perform any code you want to execute in response to a window resize event. We have chosen to implement the slider so that it will always be sized proportionally to the size of the component. There are cases where you may want to develop a control which is a fixed size, but we have chosen not to do that in this example.

In our **reshape()** method, we create a new **Image** object and a new **Graphic** object to paint to it, and modify several values based on the new dimensions. Then we call the superclass **reshape()** event so that it may do any necessary processing it has to.

That's all there is to it! We have not reviewed every line of code, but the rest should be fairly self-explanatory. If you are unsure about what it's doing, add some print statements so you can see what is happening.

> *One word of warning—since there is lot going on in this applet, you will find that if you slide the control back and forth very quickly, you will get ahead of it, and it will take a little while to catch up once you have stopped moving it.*

Take your time with this example and play with the code a little bit. You may come up with a visual image you like better than the one presented!

Summary

This chapter gave you a quick but fairly comprehensive look at the AWT components. We also gave you an example of how to develop a moderately complex custom component using the Canvas component.

At this point you are ready to do some exploring on your own. Read through the Java documentation and try some of the more obscure methods out. You may be surprised by what you can and can't do.

If you can't find a control that does what you need, write your own! If you do, however, take our advice. Try to imitate the structure and interface of the standard controls as much as possible. It will make your application much more maintainable.

AWT Layout Managers

In Java, (at least currently) there's no concept of a resource file, or an explicit design-time layout of the window components and positions. A user interface is built dynamically at run time by adding components to containers. Usually this done in the **init()** method of an applet, or the constructor of a frame or dialog. The layout manager is responsible for the task of dynamically sizing and positioning the components within a container, according to the current properties of the components and window that the applet or application is running in. The layout manager is what ensures your user interface will have a consistent appearance across different platforms, with different size components, etc. Unless you explicitly request that the Container does *not* use a layout manager, it will have one associated with it, either by default, or by an explicit request.

In this chapter, we'll look at:

▲ The five layout managers in the AWT

▲ Windows

▲ Frames

▲ Menus

▲ Dialogs

▲ A sample applet: the GridBag viewer

AWT Component Handling

While it's possible to explicitly handle the positioning of the components yourself, it isn't recommended. Since the AWT uses the native controls for the platform that the application is running on, there'll be differences in the size and appearance of the controls from platform to platform. This could result in controls overlapping or being misaligned on platforms other than the one they were developed on. The use of layout managers will take care of many of these platform inconsistencies, and will also take care of resizing and repositioning the components when a container is resized. Unless you know that the user interface is going to be deployed on one particular platform, or you are going to test on *all* possible platforms, you probably should stay away from explicit positioning of controls.

There are a number of layout managers available for use in the AWT. Once you become familiar with them, you'll find that you can almost always implement the layout you want either by using one layout manager, or by nesting containers with different layout managers. If you're ambitious, you can even develop your own layout manager, but we aren't going into the mechanics of creating your own here.

The layout managers currently included with the AWT in the Java Developers Kit are FlowLayout, BorderLayout, CardLayout, GridLayout, and GridBagLayout. We will give you an overview of each one, then we'll go through an example which demonstrates all of them.

Add() and Remove() Methods

Let's get started by talking about something which is common to all the layout managers, the **add()** and **remove()** methods.

All the layout managers use one or more of the three **add()** methods inherited from the **Container** class for adding a component to a particular layout, and the **remove()** method for removing a component from the layout:

- ▲ **public Component add(Component comp)**—Adds the specified component to the end of the container's layout. The component argument is returned.

- ▲ **public Component add(Component comp, int pos)**—Adds the specified component to this container at the given position. A **pos** value of −1 indicates that the component should be added to the end of the layout. The **Component** argument is returned.

- ▲ **public Component add(String name, Component comp)**—Adds the specified component to the end of this container with a **String** tag understood by the layout manager. The **Component** argument is returned.

- ▲ **public synchronized void remove(Component comp)**—Removes the specified component from the container.

You'll be seeing much more of these methods as we go along. Now let's talk about the specific layout managers.

FlowLayout

The FlowLayout is the simplest layout manager, so we'll cover it first. It's also the default layout manager for the **Panel** class, so you will inherit it when you work with applet-derived classes. The FlowLayout layout manager simply lays the components out, left to right, top to bottom, starting new rows when necessary, and aligns the controls left, right or center, as in the following example:

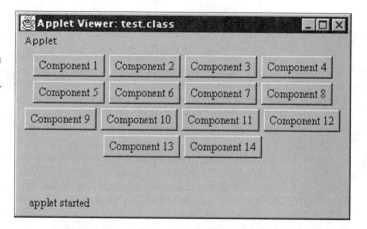

If you resize the window, you'll see how the number of components per row changes. Here we've just added 14 buttons to a panel. Since test extends Applet which extends Panel, we have a FlowLayout by default. No **setLayout()** is needed.

```
import java.awt.*;
import java.applet.Applet;

public class test extends Applet
{
    public void init()
    {
        for (int i = 1; i < 15; i++)
        {
            add(new Button("Component " + i));
        }

    }
}
```

The FlowLayout has three public constructors:

- ▲ **public FlowLayout()**–Constructs a new FlowLayout with 5 pixel horizontal and vertical gaps between components and centered alignment.

- ▲ **public FlowLayout(int align)**–Constructs a new FlowLayout with 5 pixel horizontal and vertical gaps between components and the alignment specified. To specify alignment, use the constants **FlowLayout.LEFT**, **FlowLayout.RIGHT** and **FlowLayout.CENTER**.

- ▲ **public FlowLayout(int align, int hGap, int vGap)**–Constructs a new FlowLayout with the specified alignment, horizontal gap and vertical gap. To specify alignment, use the constants **FlowLayout.LEFT**, **FlowLayout.RIGHT** and **FlowLayout.CENTER**.

Components can be added to this layout using the **add(Component comp)** method which will add the component to the end of the layout, or the **add(Component comp, int pos)**, which will add the component at the location specified. The **add(Component comp, int pos)** will throw an **IllegalArgumentException** if an invalid position is given (such as a position greater than the number of components).

BorderLayout

The BorderLayout is the default for all windows (when writing applications). This layout manager will lay out five components according to a North, South, East, West, and Center attribute that the programmer specifies. The North and South components are sized so that their width is maximum, the East and West components are sized so their height is maximum, and the Center component is given whatever space is left. The result isn't always symmetrical, the East component may have different dimensions to the West component, and the North may be different to the South:

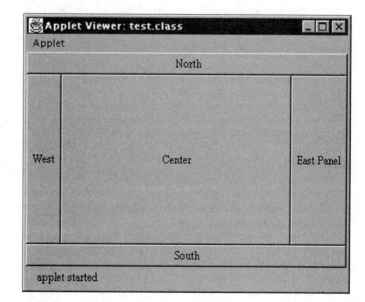

This example sets up the BorderLayout as described.

```java
import java.awt.*;
import java.applet.Applet;

public class test extends Applet
{
    public void init()
    {
        setLayout(new BorderLayout());
        add("East", new Button("East Panel"));
        add("West", new Button("West"));
        add("South", new Button("South"));
        add("North", new Button("North"));
        add("Center", new Button("Center"));
    }
}
```

The BorderLayout has two constructors:

▲ **public BorderLayout()**–Constructs a new BorderLayout with no space between components.

▲ **public BorderLayout(int hGap, int vGap)**–Constructs a new border layout with the specified horizontal and vertical gap between the components (in pixels).

Components are added to a BorderLayout using the **Container** class **add(String, Component)** method. The **String** parameter is expected to be either North, South, East, West or Center indicating the desired location. If an invalid **String** is passed as a parameter, or one of the other **add()** methods is used, the component will not be visible, although it will be added to the container. If multiple components are added using the same location, only the last one will be visible, although all will still exist within the container. You can verify this using the **getComponents()** method which will return an array of all components in the container.

Components may be removed using the container **remove()** method mentioned previously. If multiple components have been added to the same location, removing the visible one will *not* make one of the other components visible. That location will be empty until a component is added again.

CardLayout

The CardLayout is kind of a special type of layout manager. It will only display one component at a time. It is almost always used to manage the display of several containers which contain other layouts. Functionally, it is very much like the 'tab' control in Windows programming.

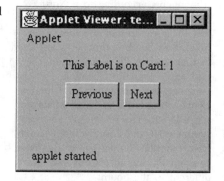

Click the Previous and Next buttons to see the component change. Usually, the component displayed would be a Panel, or some other container. In this example, 4 cards are created and the components are displayed on a Panel:

```java
import java.awt.*;
import java.applet.*;

public class test extends Applet
{

    Panel cardPanel = new Panel();
    CardLayout cards = new CardLayout();

    public void init()
    {
        cardPanel.setLayout(cards);
        add(cardPanel);
        add(new Button("Previous"));
        add(new Button("Next"));

        for (int i = 1; i < 5;i++)
        {
        cardPanel.add(new Label("This Label is on Card: " + i));
        }

    }

    public boolean action(Event e, Object arg)
    {
        if ("Previous".equals(arg))
            cards.previous(cardPanel);

        else if ("Next".equals(arg))
            cards.next(cardPanel);

        return true;
    }

}
```

The CardLayout has two public constructors:

▲ **CardLayout()**–Constructs a new card layout.

▲ **CardLayout(int hGap, int vGap)**–Constructs a new card layout with the horizontal and vertical gaps specified. Since this layout will only display one component at a time, the gaps are less evident that with other layout managers.

Particular components can be made visible using the **next(Container)**, **previous(Container)**, **first(Container)**, **last(Container)** or **show(Container, String)** methods.

Components can be added to this layout using either the **add(Component)** or **add(String, Component)** method. The second form, associates a String tag name with the component. In order to display a component using the **show(Container, String)** method, it must have been added using the **add(String, Component)** method. Otherwise, there is no tag name to request.

> Note that when running under the Windows 95 toolkit, the previous() method does not seem to work correctly if it is invoked immediately after initialization.

GridLayout

The GridLayout will lay the components out in a grid formation, with the number of rows and columns defined by the programmer in the constructor. As components are added to the applet, they are positioned from left to right, top to bottom. A GridLayout can be created with zero for the number of rows, in which case the layout manager will create as many rows as are needed to layout the current components with the number of columns specified. It can also be created with a value of zero for the column value, in which case the layout manager will use as many columns as necessary for the current components and the specified number of rows:

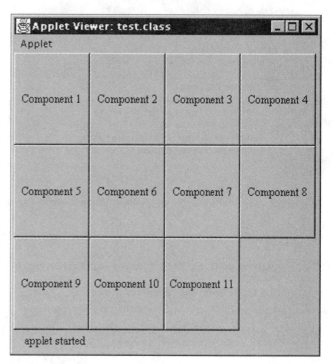

In this example, we create a simple three row, four column layout:

```java
import java.awt.*;
import java.applet.Applet;

public class test extends Applet
{
    public void init()
    {
        setLayout(new GridLayout(3,4));

        for (int i = 1; i < 12; i++)
        {
            add(new Button("Component " + i));
        }

    }
}
```

The GridLayout has two public constructors. Both will throw an **IllegalArgumentException** if the number of rows and columns are both zero:

- ▲ **public GridLayout(int rows, int cols)**—Constructs a grid layout with the specified number of rows and columns.

- ▲ **public GridLayout(int rows, int cols, int hGap, int vGap)**—Constructs a grid layout with the specified number of rows and columns, and the specified horizontal and vertical gap between components.

Components can be added to this layout using the **add(Component comp)** method which will add the component to the end of the layout, or the **add(Component comp, int pos)**, which will add the component at the location specified. The **add(Component comp, int pos)** will throw an **IllegalArgumentException** if an invalid position is given (such as a position greater than the number of components). If the number of components added does not match the number of rows and columns specified, the number of columns (and sometimes number of rows) will be adjusted by the layout manager.

GridBagLayout

"The devil is in the detail"

"No, it is in the GridBagConstraints object" - frustrated Java programmer

The GridBagLayout is the most flexible, as well as the most complex layout manager in the AWT. We will explain it as thoroughly as possible, but it's a layout that you will not feel comfortable with until you have some experience. At some point, after reading the explanation, reviewing the examples, making some changes and observing the effect, it will all come together. Even after that, you'll still be surprised at times by its behavior. Hopefully, though, our explanation and tips will enable you to get comfortable with this layout manager quicker than we were able to.

Like the GridLayout, the GridBagLayout layout manager will divide the container into a grid of rows and columns. Unlike the GridLayout however, the rows and columns may not all be the same size, and a component may occupy more than one grid cell. The criteria for deciding how to size and position a component is primarily dependent on the component and the component's parent's minimum size and preferred size and also the **constraints** associated with the component.

The GridBagConstraints Object

Every component in a GridBagLayout has constraints associated with it, either explicitly, or by default. Generally, these constraints are defined by the programmer in a **GridBagConstraints** object. This is then associated with a specific component using the GridBagLayout **setConstraints** method. A copy of the **GridBagConstraints** object is made during the **setConstraints** call so you can change the contents of the object afterwards without affecting components that used the object previously.

In our examples, you will see that we reuse the same **GridBagConstraints** object over and over. Many programmers choose to create a new **GridBagConstraints** object for each component in their layout. The effect is the same in either case, so do whatever you feel is more maintainable.

You will find that the complexity of the GridBagLayout is all in setting the variables in the **GridBagConstraints** object. Once you have done that, you just use the GridBagLayout **setConstraints** method to associate the object with a specific component, and then use the

add(Component) method to add the constrained component to the layout. The **add(Component comp, int pos)** method may also be used to add a component at a specific position in the layout order. However, as you will see shortly, the constraints associated with a component affect not only that component, but other components surrounding it, and sometimes, all components in the layout. To avoid an increase in the complexity of your layout, you may want to stay away from the positional **add()** method.

The GridBagConstraints Variables

Before we go on, we'll talk about the **GridBagConstraints** object in more detail.

The **GridBagConstraints** object has eleven variables which control the component's positioning and sizing. It also contains fifteen constants which can be used for setting the contents of the variables in a clear, readable manner. We'll discuss each of the eleven variables in turn.

> Where the **GridBagConstraints** constants are used in the explanation, we will be using the constant name only. The class name is always **GridBagConstraints**.

anchor

Depending on the size of the component, the size of its container, and the constraints of other components in the container, the size of a grid cell may be larger than the size of some of the components. You can tell the layout manager how you would like the component justified by setting the contents of this variable. The default value is **CENTER**. Other legal values are **EAST**, **NORTH**, **NORTHEAST**, **NORTHWEST**, **SOUTH**, **SOUTHEAST**, **SOUTHWEST** or **WEST**. Any other value will throw an **IllegalArgumentException**.

fill

This value specifies how the component should be resized if the component's display area is larger than the component's requested size. The legal values are

- ▲ **NONE**–Do not expand this component at all.
- ▲ **VERTICAL**–Make this component tall enough to fill its display area, but do not expand its width.
- ▲ **HORIZONTAL**–Make this component wide enough to fill its display area, but do not expand its height.
- ▲ **BOTH**–Make this component large enough to completely fill its display area, vertically and horizontally.

The default value is **NONE**. This value will have no effect if the corresponding **weightx** or **weighty** constraints are set to zero.

gridheight

The **gridheight** variable specifies the height, in grid cells, of the component. It is important to remember that, depending on the number and constraints of other components, the relative height of the component compared to the container may vary greatly. While the number of rows in the container is less than or equal to the value of **gridheight**, the actual height of the component will be equal to the height of the container (minus some inset, defined later). When the number of rows is more than the **gridheight** value, the component's relative height will be roughly proportional to the ratio of **gridheight** to grid rows. Since the rows don't all have to be the same height, the ratio may not be perfectly proportional. It also means that two components with the same **gridheight** may not have the same actual height in pixels if they are positioned in different rows.

There are two particular values for this variable that will cause some special behavior. The constant **REMAINDER** indicates that the component should be the last one in its column and receive any remaining space in that column. The constant **RELATIVE** indicates that this component should be next to the last component in the column.

gridwidth

The **gridwidth** variable specifies the width, in grid cells, of the component display area. The comments made in the **gridheight** description in regard to relative size also apply to **gridwidth**.

The constant **REMAINDER** indicates that the component should be the last one in its row, and receive any remaining space in that row. The constant **RELATIVE** indicates that this component should be next to the last component in the row.

gridx

Specifies the zero based, horizontal grid cell placement of the control. Use the constant **RELATIVE** (the default value) to request that the component be placed to the right of the component previously added.

gridy

Specifies the zero based, vertical grid cell placement of the control. Use the constant **RELATIVE** (the default value) to request that the component be placed below the component previously added.

insets

Specifies, in pixels, the top, left, bottom and right margins between the components and the display area edges. The default is no margins.

ipadx and ipady

Specifies how much the component should be padded, vertically and horizontally, beyond its minimum size. These values will be multiplied by two and added to the minimum size to determine the pixel size of the component.

weightx and weighty

These values determine how the layout manager will distribute extra vertical and horizontal space. The default value for both is zero, which indicates that no extra space should be received.

When the layout manager is determining the distribution of extra space, it will calculate the weight of a row to be the maximum weight of the components in that row, and the weight of a column to be the maximum weight of all components in that column.

In other words, specifying a higher weight for one component will increase the amount of extra space that other components in the row or column receive.

GridBagLayout Example

Once you see an example, it will make more sense. We'll create an example using GridBagLayout. In this example, we'll display four buttons with this layout manager. Button 1 will be twice as tall as Buttons 2 & 3, and Button 4 will be twice as wide as Buttons 1, 2, and 3. We'll demonstrate how this can be done by breaking the code down into sections, so you can add the requisite lines and then execute it a section at a time, with the additions you have made. The first section of the code simply defines variables for the four buttons and the Panel and CardLayout managers.

```java
import java.awt.*;
import java.applet.Applet;

public class test extends Applet
{
    Button button1 = new Button("Button 1");
    Button button2 = new Button("Button 2");
    Button button3 = new Button("Button 3");
    Button button4 = new Button("Button 4");
```

Once in the **init** method, we'll create a **GridBagLayout** and a **GridBagConstraints** object and set the layout to the **GridBagLayout** object.

```java
public void init()
{
    GridBagLayout gridBag = new GridBagLayout();
    GridBagConstraints gbc = new GridBagConstraints();
    setLayout(gridBag);
```

Next, we set up the **GridBagConstraints** object for the first component.

```java
gbc.fill = GridBagConstraints.BOTH;
gbc.insets = new Insets(5,5,5,5);
gbc.weightx = 1;
gbc.weighty = 1;
gbc.gridheight = 2;
```

The **fill** property is set to **BOTH** because we want the component to expand to the full display size of the component. We also set the **weightx** and **weighty** variables because, otherwise the **fill** property would have no effect. Finally, we set the **gridheight** to 2. The **gridwidth** is 1 by default. If this were the only component in the layout, the fact that the **gridheight** and **gridwidth** are different would have no effect, because the component would expand to fill the whole display area of the container.

Using the **setConstraints** method, we associate the **GridBagConstraints** object with the component, and add the component to the layout:

```java
gridBag.setConstraints(button1, gbc);
add(button1);
```

If we stopped at this point and executed the code so far, the layout would look like this:

Now we'll modify the **GridBagConstraints** object for the next component. Remember, nothing we do will affect the first component's constraints because it already has its own copy. Adding another component will affect the actual sizing of the first component, however, because it will no longer be able to fill the whole display area.

We'll set the **gridheight** to 1 and the **gridwidth** to **REMAINDER**. **REMAINDER** tells the layout manager to use the remaining width for this component and then start a new row. We then set the constraints and add the component to the layout.

```
gbc.gridheight = 1;
gbc.gridwidth = GridBagConstraints.REMAINDER;
gridBag.setConstraints(button2, gbc);
add(button2);
```

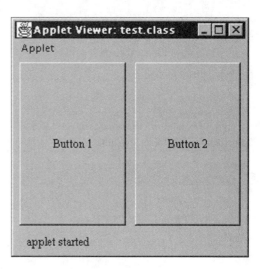

If we executed the program at this point, the layout would look like this:

You might be surprised (we were!) to find that these components end up with the same height, even though the first **gridheight** is 2, and the second is 1. This is how the layout manager behaves–Button 2 will expand to fill the remaining vertical space.

Next, we'll add another component with the exact same constraints.

```
gridBag.setConstraints(button3, gbc);
add(button3);
```

Now the layout would look like this:

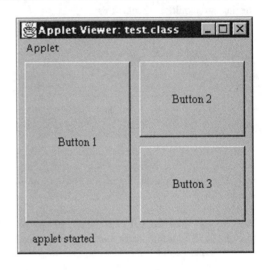

Here you see that the difference in **gridheight** takes effect. Since Button 1 has a **gridheight** of 2, it effectively gets the height of 2 rows. Since Button 2 had a **gridwidth** of **REMAINDER**, the next component gets put into row 2.

Now we'll add one last component, again with the exact same constraints.

```
gridBag.setConstraints(button4, gbc);
add(button4);
    }
}
```

The final layout looks like this:

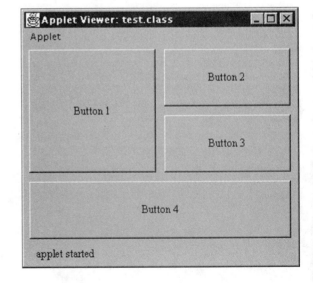

Button 3 had a **gridwidth** of **REMAINDER**, so Button 4 goes into a new row. It also has a **gridwidth** of **REMAINDER**, so it receives the width of the whole row. Since we end up with 3 rows, Button 1 ends up with $^2/_3$ of the height of the container display area. If we added one more component, with the same constraints, it would also go into a new row and be as wide as the whole container display area. This would actually reduce the height of Button 1 to $^2/_4$ or $^1/_2$ of the full container display area.

Although this is a fairly simple example, it is an interesting one because it shows how components with the same constraints can end up with very different actual dimensions and positions. This is something that isn't necessarily intuitive.

Altering the Component Size

Let's make the label of Button 3 longer and observe the effect.

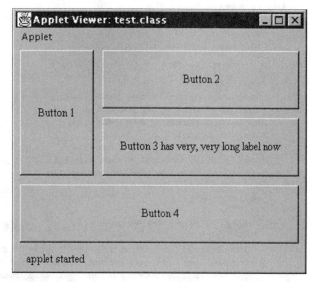

By giving Button 3 a longer label, we have changed the size of both Buttons 2 *and* 3. The layout still has two columns, but they have very different widths. Because Button 3 needed more room, all components in that column are enlarged.

To reiterate what we said earlier, the best way to learn this layout manager is by playing with it and observing the results. There is an example GridBag Viewer applet in Appendix A called **GridBagger** which will help increase your understanding of the GridBagLayout manager (as it makes use of concepts we haven't covered yet, it will be explained later in the chapter). It allows you to add and remove components to or from a GridBagLayout, change the constraints of individual components or all components and observe the effect of the changes you make immediately. It would be a good exercise to modify the **GridBagConstraints** parameters of individual components in this applet until you are comfortable with how they all interrelate.

A Layout of Layouts

We'll now take a look at an applet which demonstrates the use of all the layout managers mentioned previously. This applet uses a CardLayout manager to allow the user to select a 'card' which is actually a panel, with a specific layout manager, and a number of components to illustrate the sizing and positioning.

To clearly illustrate the sizing of the components, we are using a Button control for everything. It is interesting to use other controls and see the difference in the layout. Even changing the captions of the Buttons will cause changes in the way the controls are laid out.

Components within a container can have their own layout manager for components contained within them. In fact, you will often see a user interface laid out into several main panels which are positioned and sized by one layout manager, with each panel managed by a different layout manager.

```java
// This applet will demonstrate the use of the CardLayout,
// FlowLayout, BorderLayout, GridLayout and GridBagLayout
// The CardLayout will be the controlling Layout Manager
// which displays the other four examples

import java.awt.*;
import java.applet.*;

public class Layouts extends Applet
{

    Panel cardPanel = new Panel();
    Panel buttonPanel = new Panel();
    Panel flowPanel = new Panel();
    Panel borderPanel = new Panel();
    Panel gridPanel = new Panel();
    Panel gridBagPanel = new Panel();
    Panel gridBagSubPanel = new Panel();
    CardLayout cards = new CardLayout();

    public void init()
    {
        setLayout(new BorderLayout());

        buttonPanel.setLayout(new GridLayout(2,4,5,5));
        buttonPanel.add(new Button("FlowLayout"));
        buttonPanel.add(new Button("BorderLayout"));
        buttonPanel.add(new Button("GridLayout"));
        buttonPanel.add(new Button("GridBagLayout"));
        buttonPanel.add(new Button("First"));
        buttonPanel.add(new Button("Last"));
        buttonPanel.add(new Button("Previous"));
        buttonPanel.add(new Button("Next"));

        cardPanel.setLayout(cards);
        add("Center", cardPanel);
        add("South", buttonPanel);

        //set up flowlayout panel
        flowPanel.setLayout(new FlowLayout());
        for (int i = 1; i < 11; i++) // add some buttons
        {
            flowPanel.add(new Button("Flow: " + i));
        }
        cardPanel.add("FlowLayout", flowPanel); //add to card layout

        //set up borderlayout panel
        borderPanel.setLayout(new BorderLayout());
        // add some buttons
        borderPanel.add("North",new Button("North Panel"));
```

```
borderPanel.add("South",new Button("South"));
borderPanel.add("East",new Button("East Panel"));
borderPanel.add("West",new Button("West"));
borderPanel.add("Center",new Button("Center"));
cardPanel.add("BorderLayout", borderPanel); //add to card layout

// set up GridLayout panel
gridPanel.setLayout(new GridLayout(3,3));
for (int i = 1; i < 10; i++) // add some buttons
{
    gridPanel.add(new Button("Grid: " + i));
}
cardPanel.add("GridLayout",gridPanel); // add to card layout

// set up GridLayout panel and sub-panel
// both will use GridBagLayouts
GridBagLayout gridBag = new GridBagLayout();
GridBagLayout gridBag2 = new GridBagLayout();
GridBagConstraints gbc = new GridBagConstraints();//reuse same one
gridBagPanel.setLayout(gridBag);
gridBagSubPanel.setLayout(gridBag2);

gbc.fill = GridBagConstraints.BOTH;
gbc.insets = new Insets(5,5,5,5);
gbc.weightx = 1;
gbc.weighty = 1;
// sub-panel will have two vertical buttons
addButton(gridBag2, gbc,gridBagSubPanel,"Button 1");
addButton(gridBag2, gbc,gridBagSubPanel,"Button 2");

gbc.insets = new Insets(2,2,2,2);
gbc.fill = GridBagConstraints.BOTH;
gbc.gridx = 0;
gbc.gridy = 0;
gbc.gridheight = 3;

gridBag.setConstraints(gridBagSubPanel,  gbc);
gridBagPanel.add(gridBagSubPanel);
gbc.gridx = GridBagConstraints.RELATIVE;
gbc.gridy = GridBagConstraints.RELATIVE;

gbc.gridheight = 1;

addButton(gridBag, gbc,gridBagPanel,"Button 3");

addButton(gridBag, gbc,gridBagPanel,"Button 4");
gbc.gridwidth = GridBagConstraints.REMAINDER;
addButton(gridBag, gbc,gridBagPanel,"Button 5");
gbc.gridwidth = 1;
addButton(gridBag, gbc,gridBagPanel,"Button 6");
gbc.gridwidth = GridBagConstraints.REMAINDER;
addButton(gridBag, gbc,gridBagPanel,"Button 7");
gbc.gridwidth = GridBagConstraints.REMAINDER;
addButton(gridBag, gbc,gridBagPanel,"Button 8");
addButton(gridBag, gbc,gridBagPanel,"Button 9");

cardPanel.add("GridBagLayout",gridBagPanel); // add to card layout
```

```
          }

          public boolean action(Event e, Object arg)
          {
             if ("First".equals(arg))
                cards.first(cardPanel);

             else if ("Last".equals(arg))
                cards.last(cardPanel);

             else if ("Previous".equals(arg))
                cards.previous(cardPanel);

             else if ("Next".equals(arg))
                cards.next(cardPanel);

             else if (e.target instanceof Button)
                cards.show(cardPanel,arg.toString());

             return true;
          }

          // This method is used to simply the process of adding buttons to
          // to a GridBagLayout
          protected void addButton(GridBagLayout gbl,GridBagConstraints gbc,
          Container parent, String caption)
          {
             Button button = new Button(caption);
             gbl.setConstraints(button,  gbc);
             parent.add(button);
          }
       }
```

We start off the **init()** method by setting the layout manager to a **BorderLayout** using the **setLayout()** method.

Examining the BorderLayout Manager

As we mentioned earlier, the **BorderLayout** allows components to be laid out in a North, South, East, West and Center orientation. As we also mentioned, the Center always gets all the remaining space, after sizing the other components. While a **BorderLayout** with all components at all orientations looks like this:

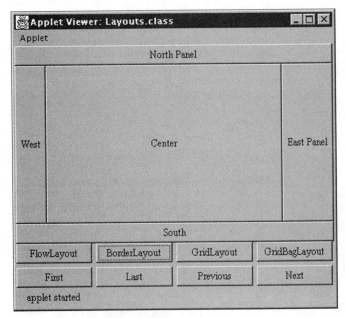

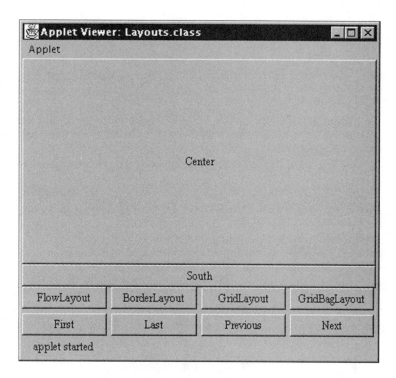

If only the Center and South components are actually added to the layout, the layout looks like this:

This makes it perfect for separating the main window into a main section and a Button row section, as we have done here. In our applet, we use a panel for each section: **buttonPanel** to hold the button row and **cardPanel** for the main section.

To lay out the button row, we set the **buttonPanel** layout to a GridLayout with two rows, four columns and insets between components of 5 pixels. We add all the navigational buttons to the **buttonPanel**, and then add the **buttonPanel** to the BorderLayout.

The code is all pretty straightforward, so we will not go through it line by line. If anything is unclear, see the earlier explanations of the various layouts and read through the Java documentation.

Windows, Frames, Menus, and Dialogs

So far in this section, we have been working mainly with applets. An applet actually runs within an embedded frame in a browser or the AppletViewer. The AWT allows you to create your own Windows, Frames, and Dialogs as well, whether you are writing an applet or application.

If you look at the AWT-Components class hierarchy, you'll see that Panels, Applets, Windows, Frames, and Dialogs are all derived from the Container class. An Applet is a subclass of Panel, and Frames and Dialogs are subclasses of Window.

In the AWT, a window may be a little different to what you expect if you are used to other systems. The AWT window has no border and no title bar. Most of the time (maybe all of the time) you will want to work with the Frame or Dialog subclasses.

Frames

A frame is a window with a title bar, resizable border and menu bar. It is probably what you have in mind when you think of a window. It will use a **BorderLayout** by default, and will receive all mouse, keyboard and focus events that occur over it. Typically, you will derive your own subclass from it so you can give it the behavior you want.

Let's take a look at a simple example. Since we've been working only with applets so far, we'll write this one as an application.

Unlike applets where the AppletViewer or Internet browser provide a main window for your applet, you have to do the work yourself for a stand-alone application. Usually a frame is used as the main application window. In this example, we derive a new class from **Frame** called **simple**, and make a new instance of it in the application **main()** method. The application will look like this:

Here's the code:

```java
import java.awt.*;

public class simple extends Frame
{
    public simple(String title)
    {
        super(title);
        add("Center",new Label("This is my frame"));
        add("South",new Button("Close"));
        resize(200,200);
        show();
    }

    public boolean action(Event e, Object arg)
    {
        if ("Close".equals(arg))
        {
            hide();
            show();
            dispose();
            System.exit(0);
            return true;
        }
        return false;
    }
    public boolean handleEvent(Event e)
    {
        if (e.id == Event.WINDOW_DESTROY)
```

```
      {
        dispose();
        System.exit(0);
        return true;
      }
      else return super.handleEvent(e);
   }

   public static void main(String args[])
   {
      new simple("My Test Frame");
   }
}
```

The layout of the frame is done in the constructor which is passed a string containing the requested title for the frame. The **super** keyword is used to invoke the superclass constructor. The components are laid out, and the frames made visible by invoking the **Window** class **show()** method. The **move()** method is used to position the frame

In this example, we gave the user two ways to explicitly close a **myFrame** instance. The **myFrame** Close button will invoke the **hide()** method (inherited from **Component**) which makes the frame invisible, and the **Frame   dispose()** method which cleans up all the window's resources allocated to that frame. The **hide()** method does not have to be invoked before the **dispose()** method, but it is generally a good practice. After the **dispose()** method, the **System.exit(0)** method is called which shuts down the Java virtual machine.

We also wanted the user to be able to close the frame by clicking the standard system Close button. To do that, we overrode the **handleEvent** method so we can catch the **WINDOW_DESTROY** event and close the frame. If we had not done that, the system Close button on the title bar would not have done anything. Once again, notice that when we do not handle an event in the **handleEvent()** method–we are careful to call **super.handleEvent()**. If we had not, the **action()** method would never be called, and the Close button would stop working. As you can probably sense, it is a lesson we learned the hard way.

> The standard maximize and minimize buttons work without adding any code.

Frames and Stand-alone Applets

Now let's look at another good use for a frame. Suppose you have an applet that you would also like to run as a stand-alone application. You can do that by adding a **main()** method, instantiating a frame to contain the applet, and calling the applet's **init()** and **start()** methods.

Let's take the Components applet example from the previous chapter. By adding the following code to the **Components** class:

```
   public static void main(String args[])
   {
      Applet theApplet = new compAppl(); // create applet instance
      appletFrame theFrame = new appletFrame(); // create Frame
      theFrame.add("Center", theApplet); //add applet to center
      theApplet.init(); // call applet init
      theFrame.resize(500,300);
```

```
        theFrame.show(); // invoke show AFTER init to not see components
        // being added
        theApplet.start();
}
```

and the following new class derived from Frame:

```
class appletFrame extends Frame
{
    public boolean handleEvent(Event e)
    {
        if (e.id == Event.WINDOW_DESTROY)
        {
            this.hide();
            this.dispose();
            System.exit(0);
            return true;
        }
        else return super.handleEvent(e);
    }
}
```

we now have an applet that runs as a stand-alone Java application.

What is happening is that the **main()** method is called when the class is run as a stand-alone application, and will open a frame to host the applet. The **init()** and **start()** methods are called to start the applet running. The reason we made our own Frame subclass was so that we could close the frame when the user clicks on the Close button. If we hadn't done that, the application would start, but the user would not be able to shut it down. The **System.exit(0)** method is what closes down the Java Virtual Machine. When we run this as an applet, the **main()** method and **appletFrame** class are simply ignored.

Dialogs

While a frame is used for a top-level window, there are times when you want a simple window to pop up to receive some information from the user, or provide notification that some event has occurred, and then go away. The **Dialog** class can be used for temporary windows.

A dialog is very similar to a frame, but it can't be a top-level window, and can't have a menu bar. Like the **Frame** class, a dialog will receive all mouse, keyboard and focus events that occur over it.

To illustrate a typical instance where you would use a dialog, we'll take the previous example and add a "Are you sure?" confirmation to the close process. We'll also make some other small changes that we'll explain as we go along. The confirmation dialog will be displayed when a user attempts to close the **myFrame** window, either by clicking the system close button or the Cancel button.

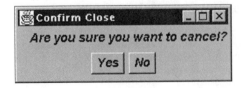

If Yes is clicked, both the confirmation dialog and the **myFrame** window will be closed. If No is clicked, the confirmation dialog will be closed, but the **myFrame** window will remain. The code for the new version follows:

```java
import java.awt.*;
import java.applet.*;

public class Win_dlg extends Applet
{
    Component comp;
    Frame frameref;
    public void init()
    {
        add(new Button("Make Frame"));

        add(new Button("Make Window"));

        comp = this;
        while (true)
        {
            if (comp instanceof Frame)
            {
                frameref = (Frame) comp;
                break;
            }
            comp = comp.getParent();
        }
        ((Frame)comp).setCursor(Frame.CROSSHAIR_CURSOR);

    }

    public boolean action(Event e, Object arg)
    {
        if ("Make Frame".equals(arg))
            myFrame frame = new myFrame("My Test Frame");

        else if ("Make Window".equals(arg))
        {
            Window myWindow = new Window((Frame) comp);
            myWindow.show();
        }
        return true;
    }

}
class myFrame extends Frame
{
    static int xy = 50;
    Dialog confirmDlg;

    public myFrame(String title)
    {
        super(title);
        add("Center",new Label("This is my frame"));
        add("South",new Button("Close"));
        resize(200,200);
        move(xy,xy);
```

```
      if (xy > 600) xy = 100;
      else xy+=50;
      show();
   }

   public boolean action(Event e, Object arg)
   {
      if ("Close".equals(arg))
      {
         confirmDlg = new Confirm(this,
            "Are you sure you want to cancel?",
            "Confirm Close");
         return true;
      }
      return false;
   }

   public boolean handleEvent(Event e)
   {
      if (e.id == Event.WINDOW_DESTROY)
      {
         confirmDlg = new Confirm(this,
            "Are you sure you want to cancel?",
            "Confirm Close");
         return true;
      }
      else return super.handleEvent(e);
   }
}
class Confirm extends Dialog
   {
      Font fontBoldItalic = new Font("Helvetica", Font.BOLD + Font.ITALIC,
      14);
      Panel pnlButtonRow = new Panel();
      Button btnYes = new Button("Yes");
      Button btnNo = new Button("No");
      Frame frame;

      public Confirm(Frame parentFrame, String message, String title)
      {
         super(parentFrame,title,false);
         frame = parentFrame;
         setFont(fontBoldItalic);
         setLayout(new BorderLayout());
         add("South", pnlButtonRow);
         add("Center", new Label(message));

         pnlButtonRow.add(btnYes);
         pnlButtonRow.add(btnNo);
         pack();
         Dimension scrSize = getToolkit().getScreenSize();
         Dimension dlgSize = size();
         move((scrSize.width - dlgSize.width) / 2,
         (scrSize.height - dlgSize.height) / 2 );
         show();
      }
```

```
    public boolean action(Event e, Object arg)
    {
        Class theClass;

        if (e.target == btnYes)
        {
            this.hide();
            this.dispose();
            frame.hide();
            frame.dispose();
            return true;
        }
        else if (e.target == btnNo)
        {
            this.hide();
            this.dispose();
            return true;
        }

        else return false;
    }

}
```

The code is very similar to the **myFrame** code, but we have added some additional features to keep it interesting.

In the Confirm constructor, we use **super** to call the superclass constructor. The main application frame must be passed to the constructor, as well as an optional title and a boolean representing the modality.

The frame passed to the constructor is saved in a variable because it is needed in the **action()** method. Instead of displaying the dialog in the default location, we have chosen to display it in the center of the screen. To do that, we use the Toolkit **getScreenSize()** method to obtain the screen dimensions, the **size()** method to obtain the dialog's dimensions, and them both to center the window.

```
        Dimension scrSize = getToolkit().getScreenSize();
        Dimension dlgSize = size();
        move((scrSize.width - dlgSize.width) / 2,
        (scrSize.height - dlgSize.height) / 2 );
        show();
```

In the **action()** method, when the Yes button is clicked, we use the frame reference to dispose the parent frame (as well as destroying the dialog, of course).

For purely illustrative reasons, we have changed the applet cursor from the default to the crosshair one. Many people think that the cursor can not be changed in an applet, because there is no method in the **Applet** class. There is however, a **setCursor** method which is part of the **Frame** class. If you climb the applet parent chain up high enough, however, you will eventually find a frame. This holds true in the AppletViewer as well as browsers. We added the following code in the **init()** method to find the frame, and used the frame reference and the **setCursor** method to change the cursor. You can also use this technique for opening a dialog from an applet since dialogs also require a frame reference.

```
        comp = this;
        while (true)
        {
```

339

```
        if (comp instanceof Frame)
        {
            frameref = (Frame) comp;
            break;
        }
        comp = comp.getParent();
    }
    ((Frame)comp).setCursor(Frame.CROSSHAIR_CURSOR);
```

We also added a Make Window button, which does nothing but create a generic window so you can see what one looks like. It is completely useless and can't even be closed. It will be closed when the parent Frame is closed.

Menus

There is one last important windowing component we have not yet covered: menus. There are three menu classes you'll need to be familiar with to implement menus: **MenuBar**, **Menu** and **MenuItem**.

Menubar Class

A **MenuBar** is basically a group of menus which is bound to a frame with the frame **setMenuBar()** method. As a **MenuBar** can only be implemented on frames, an applet can't have one. Actually, that isn't quite true. Earlier in the chapter, we presented a technique for finding the frame in which an applet is running. This technique does allow you to add a menu to an applet. The problem is that when an applet is run in a browser, the menu may not be visible. When running in AppletViewer menus will work fine. Unless you are planning on always running from the AppletViewer, you may want to stay away from applet menus. Of course, adding a menu to a frame opened by an applet is fine.

The **menuBar setHelpMenu()** method will allow you to make one menu the help menu. This has different behavior on different platforms. On some, it causes the menu to be displayed on the far right side of the frame.

When a user is navigating through the menu, the application will not receive any events until a lowest level **MenuItem** selection is made. At that point, the application will receive an **action** event so it can respond in an appropriate way.

The **MenuBar** class has one constructor:

```
public MenuBar()
```

Menu Class

The next level down from the menubar is the menu. Each menu is a group of menu items and/or other lower level menus. A **Menu** object has two constructors:

   public Menu(String label)—Constructs a new menu with the specified label.

   public Menu(String label, boolean tearOff)—Constructs a new menu with the specified label and **tearOff** boolean. If the **tearOff** argument is true, the menu can be torn off: it can remain on the screen after the mouse button has been released. The default is a non-tearoff menu. TearOff menus behave no differently then normal ones on the Windows 95 AWT.

Menu objects are added to a **MenuBar** with the **MenuBar   add(Menu m)** method.

MenuItem Class

The **MenuItem** is the lowest level of the menu structure. It has one constructor:

```
MenuItem(String label)
```

which creates a new menu selection with the specified label. The **MenuItem** class includes methods for enabling, disabling and getting/setting text. By default, menu items are enabled. Menu separators can be added with the **addSeparator()** method or by passing a label of '-'.

There is one variation of **MenuItem**: **CheckboxMenuItem**, which can be created for a menu selection. **CheckboxMenuItem** is a subclass of **MenuItem** which adds a boolean state to the MenuItem, and displays a check when its state is true. It has one constructor:

```
CheckboxMenuItem(String label)
```

which creates a new menu selection with the specified label, and a state of false (no check displayed).

Example Applet

We'll now look at a short example which shows a typical menu structure on a frame:

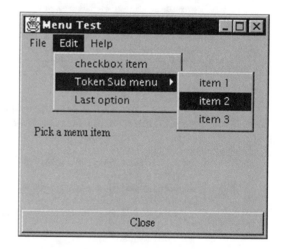

The code is as follows:

```
import java.awt.*;
import java.applet.*;

public class MenuTest extends Applet
{
    public void init()
    {
        add(new Button("Make Frame"));

    }

    public boolean action(Event e, Object arg)
    {
```

```java
            if ("Make Frame".equals(arg))
                menuFrame frame = new menuFrame("Menu Test");

        return true;
    }
}

class menuFrame extends Frame
{
    static int xy = 50;
    Dialog confirmDlg;
    Label lblMenu = new Label("Pick a menu item");

    public menuFrame(String title)
    {
        super(title);
        add("Center",lblMenu);
        add("South",new Button("Close"));
        resize(200,200);
        move(xy,xy);
        if (xy > 600) xy = 100;
        else xy+=50;
        MenuBar mb = new MenuBar();
        this.setMenuBar(mb);
        Menu menuFile = new Menu("File");
        Menu menuEdit = new Menu("Edit");
        Menu menuHelp = new Menu("Help");
        Menu subMenu  = new Menu("Token Sub menu", true); // is tear off

        mb.add(menuFile);
        menuFile.add(new MenuItem("New"));
        menuFile.add(new MenuItem("Open"));
        menuFile.add(new MenuItem("Close"));
        menuFile.addSeparator();
        menuFile.add(new MenuItem("Save"));
        menuFile.addSeparator();
        menuFile.add(new MenuItem("Print"));
        menuFile.addSeparator();
        menuFile.add(new MenuItem("Exit"));

        mb.add(menuEdit);
        menuEdit.add(new CheckboxMenuItem("checkbox item"));
        menuEdit.add(subMenu);
        subMenu.add(new MenuItem("item 1"));
        subMenu.add(new MenuItem("item 2"));
        subMenu.add(new MenuItem("item 3"));
        menuEdit.add(new MenuItem("Last option"));

        mb.add(menuHelp);
        menuHelp.add(new MenuItem("Search Help"));
        menuHelp.addSeparator();
        menuHelp.add(new MenuItem("About"));
        mb.setHelpMenu(menuHelp);

        show();
    }
```

```
    public boolean action(Event e, Object arg)
    {
        if (e.target instanceof Button)
        {
            if ("Close".equals(arg))
            {
                confirmDlg = new Confirm(this,
                    "Are you sure you want to cancel?",
                    "Confirm Close");
                return true;
            }
        }
        else
        if ( e.target instanceof MenuItem )
        {
            lblMenu.setText("You selected menu item: " + (String)arg);

        }
        return false;
    }

    public boolean handleEvent(Event e)
    {
        System.out.println("x");
        if (e.id == Event.WINDOW_DESTROY)
        {
            confirmDlg = new Confirm(this,
                "Are you sure you want to cancel?",
                "Confirm Close");
            return true;
        }
        else return super.handleEvent(e);
    }
}
class Confirm extends Dialog
    {
        Font fontItalic = new Font("Helvetica", Font.ITALIC, 14);
        Panel pnlButtonRow = new Panel();
        Button btnYes = new Button("Yes");
        Button btnNo = new Button("No");
        Frame frame;

        public Confirm(Frame parentFrame, String message, String title)
        {
            super(parentFrame,title,false);
            frame = parentFrame;
            setFont(fontItalic);
            setLayout(new BorderLayout());
            add("South", pnlButtonRow);
            add("Center", new Label(message));

            pnlButtonRow.add(btnYes);
            pnlButtonRow.add(btnNo);
            pack();
            Dimension scrSize = getToolkit().getScreenSize();
            Dimension dlgSize = size();
            move((scrSize.width - dlgSize.width) / 2,
```

```
                      (scrSize.height - dlgSize.height) / 2 );
        show();
    }

    public boolean action(Event e, Object arg)
    {
        Class theClass;

        if (e.target == btnYes)
        {
            this.hide();
            this.dispose();
            frame.hide();
            frame.dispose();                    return true;
        }
        else if (e.target == btnNo)
        {
            this.hide();
            this.dispose();
            return true;
        }

        else return false;
    }
}
```

Most of the code is housekeeping for the frame creation and destruction. The menu creation is all done in the frame constructor. We have implemented a simple **action()** method which just displays the menu selection, but it could easily be modified to initiate a more complex process.

GridBag Viewer

Earlier in the chapter, while explaining the GridBag layout manager, we mentioned the GridBag viewer applet. This applet began as a typical quick and dirty program intended only to help the author understand how this layout really works. Later, we realized that it might also assist others in understanding the GridBag layout manager, and it also turns out to be a good example of the AWT in action. The full code for this applet can be found in Appendix A.

Conceptually, this applet is a pretty simple demonstration of how the **GridBagConstraints** settings will affect the layout of multiple components. To keep it simple, we only use buttons as components but we could easily use other types. It starts up with a single **GridBagLayout** component and a button to add others.

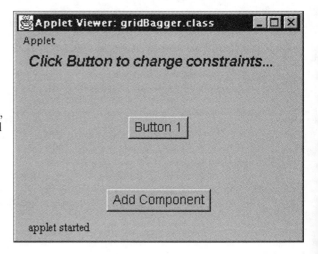

When a component is clicked, the Constraints dialog is opened.

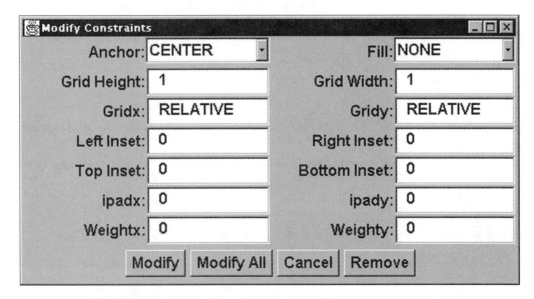

The user can modify the constraints for the component chosen, the constraints for all components, or remove the component. As this applet contains over 400 lines of code, we will not review every line, just the main points of interest. By this point, you will understand nearly all of the code anyway.

Subclassing the Text Control

One technique that we have not discussed so far and that is used in this applet is the subclassing of a text control to give it unique behavior.

```
class gbcTextField extends TextField
{
    public static final int INT_ONLY = 0;   // just allows digits
    public static final int INT_RELATIVE = 1;   // allows digits; shows
    RELATIVE for others
    public static final int INT_REL_REM = 2; // allows digits; else toggle
    RELATIVE-REMAINDER
    public static final int DOUBLE = 3; // allows digits and "." to enter
    precision
    boolean strSwitch = false;
    boolean is_String = false;
    int gbcType;
```

Let's discuss what we have done. The **Modify Constraints** dialog requires that the user be allowed to edit several numeric values. The question is, how can we best assist the user in entering valid data.

The cleanest way to do accomplish this is to not allow bad data to be entered into the **TextField** in the first place. With a subclassed **TextField**, one can easily prevent the entry of non-numeric data. Our case is a little more complex however. Some of these constraints are typically set by assigning a constant such as **RELATIVE** or **REMAINDER**. We don't want the user to have to know the numeric values for these constants (to do so, they'd have to wade through the Java source), but we don't want free form entry because we would then have to write validation code for what is entered. Eventually, we came up with a user-friendly solution. We allow numbers to be entered, and when a non-numeric key is entered we set the contents of the list box to one of the valid constants, and cycle through the others as other non-numeric keys are entered.

There are four different types of numeric data entry fields we need to support:

▲　　**Integer**–This is the easiest one, just filter out everything except 0–9

▲　　**Integer–Relative**–This TextField must allow 0–9 keys and display the word **RELATIVE** when anything else is entered.

▲　　**Integer-Relative-Remainder**–This TextField must allow 0–9 keys and toggle between the word **RELATIVE** and **REMAINDER** when anything else is entered

▲　　**Double**–Allows numbers and the decimal character.

We decided to implement this with one control that can be constructed with four different styles.

There is one public constructor for our new class which invokes the superclass constructor and sets the control type:

```
public gbcTextField(int type)
{
    super();
    gbcType = type;
}
```

handleEvent Method

The other main item of interest is how the applet deals with events. As there is a lot going on in the **handleEvent()** method, we'll break it up into sections and discuss each section.

```
public boolean handleEvent(Event e)
    {
        if ( e.id != Event.KEY_PRESS && e.key != '.') return
        super.handleEvent(e);

        // In case KEY_PRESS event period behavior gets "corrected"
        if ( e.id == Event.KEY_PRESS && e.key == '.')
        return  super.handleEvent(e);

        String s = this.getText();
```

First, if the event is anything other than **KEY_PRESS**, and the key isn't the period, we call the superclass **handleEvent()** method. We had to make the distinction for the period because, for some reason, you do not get a **KEY_PRESS** event when a period is entered. This prevents us from screening it out of the integer style **TextFields**. We do get a **KEY_RELEASE** event, however, so we pull the period back out when we receive that event.

This raises a question though. Isn't it kind of strange that a **KEY_PRESS** isn't received for a period. That could be a bug. So what happens if it's a bug, and then they fix it? Obviously, we'd like our code to keep working, so we add another line so that if **KEY_PRESS** events start to arrive for periods, we just call the superclass **handleEvent()** method, effectively mimicking the current behavior.

```
boolean is_int_char;

if (e.key >= '0' && e.key <= '9') is_int_char = true;
else is_int_char = false;

if ("REMAINDER".equals(s) ||"RELATIVE".equals(s)) is_String = true;
else is_String = false;
```

Next we set two boolean variables, **is_int_char** and **is_String** in order to simply the style switching logic. In the switch, we do some style dependent actions.

```
switch (gbcType)
{
    case INT_ONLY:
        if (is_int_char) return super.handleEvent(e);
        if (e.key == '.')
        {
            int pos = s.indexOf('.');
            if ( pos != -1)
            {
                s=s.substring(0,pos) + s.substring(pos + 1);
                this.setText(s);
                this.select(pos,pos);
            }
        }
        else return true;
```

If the style is **INT_ONLY**, and we already know it's a numeric key, we simply call the superclass **handleEvent()**. If the key is a period, we invoke the logic needed to pull it out of the string. Otherwise we return true which indicates that it has been handled, so all other keys will do nothing.

```
case DOUBLE:
    if (is_int_char) return super.handleEvent(e);
    else return true;
```

If the style is **DOUBLE** and we already know it's a numeric key, we also call the superclass **handleEvent()**. Otherwise we return true. We do not strip out periods in this case because the user may want to enter a decimal.

```
case INT_RELATIVE:
    if (!is_int_char)
    {
        this.setText("RELATIVE");
        is_String = true;
    }
    else if (is_String)
    {
        this.setText((char)e.key + "");
        is_String = false;
    }
```

```
            else return super.handleEvent(e);

        return true;
```

If the style is **INT_RELATIVE** and it's not an integer character, we set the text to **RELATIVE**. If it is an integer and the current contents is a string, we set the contents to the key value. Otherwise, we just call the superclass **handleEvent()**.

```
        case INT_REL_REM:
            if (!is_int_char)
            {
                if (strSwitch) this.setText("RELATIVE");
                else this.setText("REMAINDER");
                is_String = true;
                strSwitch = !strSwitch;
            }
            else if (is_String)
            {
                this.setText((char)e.key + "");
                is_String = false;
            }
            else return super.handleEvent(e);

            return true;

    }
    return super.handleEvent(e);
}
```

The **INT_REL_REM** style is basically the same as **INT_RELATIVE** but we toggle the strings. We have also added and overridden accessor methods so that **setText** will appropriately set the constant names when needed, and the correct integer values will be queried even when the text is set to a constant.

To implement this class took a fair amount of work, but it was a good learning exercise, and the result is a maintainable piece of code. If you do not like the behavior as we implemented it, you can easily modify it. You only need to make changes in this one class, not throughout the whole program.

Summary

This was quite an ambitious chapter. We've covered all of the layout managers, not to mention windows, frames, dialogs and menus. You'll probably agree, however, (with the possible exception of the GridBag layout manager) that the classes and methods are pretty simple to use. As a result, we looked in greater detail at the GridBag layout manager, because while being the most complex of the layout managers, it also offers the most flexibility. We looked at the unique way in which the sizing of components can affect the surrounding components and then looked at this manager within the context of a couple of sample applets. We then considered how frames, dialogs and menus can all be used to enhance the user interface. Finally, we looked at a viewer which allows the user to directly alter the variables of the GridBag layout manager via a dialog and then observe the effect they have.

You'll want to keep referring to this chapter until you've written a few applications, and gotten familiar with all the techniques. You should get comfortable with all the layout managers, so you can take advantage of their power when building user interfaces.

With this chapter, we've completed our overview of the AWT. While at times, it might appear restrictive and difficult to master, we hope that we've shown you how to get the most out of it when doing anything from simple line-drawing to complex animations and user-interfaces.

Networking

One of the powerful features of Java is the networking capabilities that were built into the class library. Java was conceived in the Internet era and was designed to take a place of honor when it comes to network programming.

In this chapter, we will look at:

- ▲ The different types of socket
- ▲ Java's networking classes
- ▲ Different types of communication
- ▲ Some examples of networking with Java

Sockets

Network communication in Java is done using sockets (Java sockets are very similar to UNIX sockets). Using hardware and operating system independent protocols, sockets provide a near perfect solution for network communication. Used in conjunction with Java's stream classes (the very ones you've used with file I/O), they make it one of the easiest languages for writing network applications.

> *Most socket communication systems—in most operating systems—are implementations of the socket interface known as Berkeley Sockets. This networking interface was first introduced in a version of the UNIX operating system named BSD UNIX (Berkeley Software Distribution UNIX).*
>
> *BSD UNIX was developed by the Computer Systems Research Group of the University of California at Berkeley. Bill Joy ran the BSD UNIX development team. He later co-founded Sun Microsystems, bringing 4.2BSD with him as the foundation of SunOS.*

Since the protocols that are supported by sockets (TCP/IP and UDP/IP being the most common) are so widespread, Java is ideal for writing modern front-end applications for legacy systems.

Utilizing Java's cross-platform compatibility, you can write a new front end for your old UNIX-based data management system that runs in the exact same manner on the UNIX machine in the Accounting department, the newly bought Pentiums in Sales, and the Macintoshs in the Design department.

What are Sockets?

A **socket** is an abstraction that represents a terminal for communication between processes across a network. Unlike pipes, sockets are bi-directional and are not necessarily a First In First Out (FIFO) transport. Socket implementation is provided by the host operating system. Java provides a networking package whose classes encapsulate the system's socket implementation.

Each socket has two characteristics that identify it.

The first is the **IP address** of the computer the socket resides in. This is a network unique number that identifies the computer (like an address for a building: every building has a unique address defined by its country, city, street, and house number).

Note that it's possible for a computer to have more than one IP address.

The second characteristic is a **port** number. There are often several network-based services provided by a single computer. These could include File Transfer Protocol (FTP), Hyper Text Transfer Protocol (HTTP–used in the WWW), electronic mail, and more. Each of the services is assigned a well known port number–an address inside the computer that everyone knows of (like an apartment number in a building)–and everyone who wishes to use a service connects to the port for that service. For example, the port number assigned for the FTP services is 21. All the ports are the same. The port numbers are only allocated for software convenience, and have no deeper meaning. Ports with numbers below 1024 are considered reserved for the system, and not available for use by 'normal' programs. You should use port numbers above 1024 for your applications (and it's better to avoid 1234 and other 'easy' numbers, otherwise your application is sure to collide with others).

There are two types of socket: **stream sockets** and **datagram sockets**.

Stream Sockets vs. Datagram Sockets

Stream sockets are the end points of a connection-oriented, reliable communication protocol. In a connection-oriented protocol, such as Transmission Control Protocol (TCP), the applications are required to establish a virtual circuit before data transfer can take place. The virtual circuit is a software mechanism that simulates a physical connection from one point to another.

Stream sockets provide a sequenced and unduplicated flow of data. What goes in one end comes out the other, and in the same order as it went in.

Datagram sockets are the end point of a connectionless fast protocol. In a connectionless transport protocol, such as User Datagram Protocol (UDP), there is no need to establish a virtual circuit in order to transfer data. To transmit, an application only needs to open a socket and send the data. To receive data, an application needs to open a socket and bind it to the port it wishes to listen to.

Datagram data is sent in discrete packets that may arrive out of order (i.e. if packet A was transmitted before packet B, there is no guarantee that A will be received before B). Incoming datagram packets may possibly be duplicated, but you will never get a broken packet.

Datagram packets hold in them the data to send and the destination for the data. They are routed by the computers and other network devices (hubs, bridges, routers, etc.) on the path from the source to the target.

Different packets may be routed differently, and thus may arrive in any order.

Datagram sockets are appropriate when you don't mind losing a packet now and then, and you know how to overcome duplication. Because datagram sockets implement a send-and-forget protocol, they are faster than stream sockets. If your application can use this kind of socket, it probably should.

An example for such an application is a central time synchronization application. Each computer keeps its local time, but every now and then it has to make sure that it's in synch with some central computer. The time synchronization algorithm can compensate for losing a packet now and then, and ignores duplicate packets.

Stream sockets are appropriate for applications that require guaranteed delivery of information. Most applications fall into this category:

- Terminal session applications
- File transfer applications
- Mail applications
- And many more...

Streams sockets are slower than datagram sockets. One of the reasons for this is that the sender needs confirmation that the data it sent arrived safely.

To communicate over the network the two parties must establish a connection. First, a listening socket is bound to a specific network address, then another socket is connected to the listening socket. Once the sockets on both sides are connected the parties can engage in communication. A new socket is needed for every session, which means that not only do you need a new socket for every computer you wish to communicate with, but also that several sockets may be required to communicate with different services on a single computer.

Server Sockets

You can view most communication as either peer-to-peer communication or client/server communication. In peer-to-peer communication the two parties are of the exact same status. They both agree to connect to each other and the connection is the result of that common agreement. In client/server communication, the client initiates a service call, and the server complies to that call. The server is the passive side in this type of attachment. In fact, unlike peer-to-peer communication, the server doesn't even know that there is a client out there until the client actually tries to establish a connection.

How does a server know the address of the client? How does a server even know that a client wishes to attach to it? It's obvious that an ordinary socket wouldn't do here.

Unlike clients and peers, servers use a special connection mechanism called a **server socket**. Server sockets are bound to a specific port on the **host** machine. They listen for incoming connection requests and when a client tries to establish a connection they sprout a new, *ordinary,* socket attached to the client's computer. That socket can be used for further communication with the client.

> A server socket is used solely for accepting incoming connection requests, not for actual communication. The server communicates with the clients using ordinary sockets.

We'll look at server sockets in more detail later in the chapter.

Java's Networking Classes

The networking classes are all in the package **java.net**. Following is a short description of the main methods in the most useful classes in the package.

The classes presented in this chapter are the most useful networking classes. You will rarely use the others.

For a complete description of all the methods and properties in the classes described below, as well as other classes, interfaces and exceptions contained in the package, see the API.

InetAddress

This class encapsulates an Internet Protocol (IP) address. The class has no public constructor and can't be instantiated directly. To obtain an **InetAddress** object you should use the class's **static** methods **getLocalHost()**, **getByName()**, or **getAllByName()**. These methods are called **factory methods** as they 'manufacture' objects upon request. The **getLocalHost()** method returns the **InetAddress** of the local host, and the other two methods determine the **InetAddress** (one or more) of a remote computer given its name. The name can be specified either as a machine name, such as 'java.sun.com' or in 'dotted quad' format (a string representing an IP address), such as '206.26.48.100.'

Other interesting methods are:

```
public byte[] getAddress();
```
The raw IP address as an array of 4 bytes. The highest order byte is in **byte[0].**

```
public String getHostName();
```
A string that holds the specified host name.

DatagramPacket

This class encapsulates a datagram packet, either incoming or outgoing. Each packet is routed from the sender to the receiver based solely on information contained within that packet.

```
public DatagramPacket(byte buffer[], int packetLength);
```

This constructor creates a **DatagramPacket** for receiving packets of **packetLength** bytes. The **packetLength** argument must be less than or equal to **buffer.length**.

```
public DatagramPacket(byte buffer[], int packetLength, InetAddress
hostAddress, int portNumber);
```

This constructor creates a **DatagramPacket** that contains the first **packetLength** bytes of **buffer** that are to be sent to the specified port number on the specified host. The **packetLength** argument must be less than or equal to **buffer.length**.

The other methods in this class are:

```
public InetAddress getAddress();
```
The IP address of the source or intended destination of this package.

```
public byte[] getData();
```
The data in the package as a byte array.

```
public int getLength();
```
The length of the package.

```
public int getPort();
```
The source port or intended destination port of this package.

DatagramSocket

This class encapsulates a socket used for sending and receiving datagram packets. Since the routing information is contained in the packets themselves, the constructors are:

```
public DatagramSocket();

public DatagramSocket(int  port);
```

where the first is used for sending packets and the second is used for receiving packets from the specified port on the host computer. A sending socket doesn't need to be bound to any specific port. A receiving socket is bound to port number **port**.

The other public methods of this class are:

```
public void send(DatagramPacket p);
```
Sends the specified datagram to its destination.

```
public void receive(DatagramPacket p);
```
Waits for a datagram. The received data is stored in the specified datagram.

```
public int getLocalPort();
```
Returns the number of the port on the host computer to which a sending socket is bound.

```
public void close();
```
Closes the socket.

Socket

This class encapsulates a socket. Stream sockets can be created using one of the following constructors:

```
public Socket(String  host, int  port);

public Socket(InetAddress  address, int  port);
```

The host is specified either using its name or by using an already existing **InetAddress** object.

The following constructors create either a stream socket or a datagram socket depending on what you specify:

```
public Socket(String  host, int  port, boolean stream);

public Socket(InetAddress address, int port, boolean stream);
```

Other public methods of this class include:

```
public InputStream getInputStream();
```
Returns an input stream for reading bytes from the socket.

```
public OutputStream getOutputStream();
```
Returns an output stream for writing bytes to the socket.

```
public int getPort();
```
Returns the port number on the remote computer to which this port is connected.

```
public int getLocalPort();
```
Returns the number of the port on the host computer to which the socket is bound.

```
public InetAddress getInetAddress();
```
Returns the IP address of the remote computer to which the port is connected.

```
public void close();
```
Closes the socket.

ServerSocket

This class encapsulates a server socket. Server sockets are constructed using one of these constructors:

```
public ServerSocket(int port);

public ServerSocket(int port, int count);
```

Both constructors require the port number on the host computer to bind the socket to. If **port** is 0, the socket is created on any free port.

Incoming connection requests (sometimes also called 'connection indications') are placed in a waiting queue until they are served. The second constructor allows you to declare a maximum queue length for incoming connection requests. If a connection request arrives when the queue is full, the connection is refused. This is useful if you want to ensure your system doesn't overload with incoming requests.

Other methods in this class are:

```
public Socket accept();
```
Waits for a connection indication and returns a new socket bound to the requester's address.

```
public int getLocalPort();
```
Returns the port number on the local computer to which this port is bound.

```
public void close();
```
Closes the socket.

URL

This class encapsulates a Uniform Resource Locator (URL). A URL is a description of a 'resource' on the Internet such as a World Wide Web (WWW) page, a directory, a single file, an image, or anything else you can find out there in the Internet.

Most URLs are made of 3 parts: the protocol name, the host name, and the resource's name on the host. Take for example the following URL:

```
http://www.wrox.com/index.html
```

The protocol to be used for this resource is **http** (HyperText Transport Protocol, the protocol used for transmitting WWW pages written using HyperText Markup Language–HTML). The host is a computer whose name is **www.wrox.com** and the resource's name is **index.html**.

The resource itself could either already be there when you try to access it (like a file) or be generated on the fly as a result of you trying to access it (like the result of a search engine's query).

The exact meaning of the resource's name on the host depends on both the protocol used and the host machine.

Notice that the URL did not contain the port number to connect to. This is because most protocols have a default port that serves them (for example, the default port for HTTP, is 80). If you wish to connect to a different port, you can specify it by appending a colon and the port number to the host's name. For example, if for some reason the port for HTTP on the host is 8080 (a commonly used port for a caching and/or proxy HTTP server), the URL would be:

```
http://www.wrox.com:8080/index.html
```

More information on URLs and other Internet related topics can be found on the WWW at:

http://www.yahoo.com/Computers_and_Internet/Internet/

URLEncoder

This service class contains a single utility method that converts a string into a MIME format called 'x-www-form-urlencoded' format. (For further details on MIME see the links in the above URL.)

```
public static String encode(String  s)
```

The output of the conversion is:

- ▲ The ASCII characters 'a' through 'z', 'A' through 'Z', and '0' through '9' remain the same.
- ▲ Space characters are converted to plus signs (+).
- ▲ Other characters are converted to the hexadecimal representation of the lower 8-bits of the characters. The notation used for each character is '%XY' where XY are the two-digits of the hexadecimal representation.

If you've ever filled in a form (e.g. a search engine's query) on a WWW browser, you might have seen that the data you typed in was sent to the HTTP server encoded in this manner.

Peer-to-Peer Communication

Peer-to-peer communication (P2PC) is a networking concept. It doesn't reflect the status of the participants in any way. For example, on one end there could be a simple temperature gauge, and on the other end a complex environmental control system. The two parties are considered peers because both ends use simple sockets.

Many applications that use P2PC use datagram sockets as it sidesteps the need for the sender and receiver to establish a virtual circuit.

The following distributed application keeps track of remote computers. A small application on the remote computer uses datagram sockets to send 'I'm alive' messages to a monitoring computer. The monitoring computer logs each remote computer when it first makes contact. It then keeps track of seconds that elapsed since the last time that computer reported in.

The sending application requires the address of the monitoring computer as a command line parameter. It creates a datagram packet containing its address and sends it repeatedly to the monitoring computer. It doesn't verify that the monitoring computer actually receives the messages (we could have the monitoring computer reply to each message, but for this simple application it's not necessary).

Here is the code of the sender. We've highlighted the important networking statements.

```java
import java.net.*;

class SendLifeSigns
{
    public static void main(String args[])
    {
        InetAddress     localAddress=null;
        DatagramSocket  outSocket=null;
        InetAddress     hostAddress=null;
        boolean         verbose = false;

        // Verify correct invocation
        if ( (args.length != 1) && (args.length != 2) )
        {
            System.err.println("Usage: java SendLifeSigns "+
                            "<monitoring computer name> [-v]");
            System.exit(0);
        }

        // Check if we are in verbose mode
        if ( (args.length==2) && (args[1].equals("-v")) ) verbose = true;

        // Get the address of the monitoring computer
        try {
            hostAddress = InetAddress.getByName(args[0]);
        } catch (UnknownHostException e) {
            System.err.println(
                "The specified monitoring computer could not be found.");
```

```
        System.exit(0);
    }

    // Get the address of the local computer
    try {
        localAddress = InetAddress.getLocalHost();
    } catch (UnknownHostException e) {
        System.err.println(
            "Could not determine the address of the local computer.");
        System.exit(0);
    }

    // Store the data to send (the local address) in a byte array
    byte myAddressAsBytes[] = localAddress.getAddress();

    // Continuosly send data out
    for (;;)
    {
        try {
            // Create a new outgoing datagram socket
            outSocket = new DatagramSocket();
            // Send the address in a new datagram packet
            outSocket.send( new DatagramPacket(myAddressAsBytes,
                                               myAddressAsBytes.length,
                                               hostAddress,
                                               2829) );
            outSocket.close();
            if (verbose)
            {
                System.out.print(".");
                System.out.flush();        // force display update
            }

            // wait 5 sec. before sending again
            Thread.currentThread().sleep(5000);
        } catch(Exception e) {
            System.err.println(e);
            e.printStackTrace();
            System.exit(1);
        } finally {
            outSocket.close();
        }

    }
    }
}
```

Please note that this implementation of the sender class was devised to overcome a flaw found in some operating systems' networking services. These platforms do not allow a packet to be re-sent after one transmission, or a datagram socket to be used more than once. To overcome these problems, this implementation creates a new socket and a new packet on each iteration. Normally, there's no need to do this; a packet and a socket can be used again and again.

On platforms that don't have this flaw (Windows NT, for example), you can use the code found in Appendix B. This example uses one socket and one packet. It is generally better because:

▲ *It uses less resources: mainly the memory allocated to every new socket opened—although this memory will be reclaimed when the CG runs.*

▲ *It is faster: fewer method calls inside the loop.*

▲ *It utilizes the system less: every socket operation results in a call to the underlying operating system, and since I/O operations are generally 'expensive' in terms of time and system resources, the less you use them the 'nicer' your applications are to the system.*

The monitor application is made of two classes. The first, **MonitorPanel**, implements the graphical user interface and the time keeping. The second, **Monitor**, first spawns a **MonitorPanel** and then endlessly accepts incoming reports. For each message received, it updates the connection display.

Here is the code for the monitor. Most of it has to do with the user interface and the time keeping. The networking statements are highlighted.

```java
import java.awt.*;
import java.net.*;

class MonitorPanel extends Frame implements Runnable
{
    List       connectionList;
    Button     clearList;
    Thread     thisThread;

    public void init()
    {
        // Create graphic controls
        connectionList = new List();
        clearList = new Button("Clear connection list");

        // Lay them out in the frame
        this.setLayout(new BorderLayout());
        this.add("North", new Label("Connection list:", Label.CENTER));
        this.add("South", clearList);
        this.add("Center", connectionList);

        // Adjust frame and display it
        this.resize(300,300);
        this.setTitle("Connection Monitor");
        this.show();

        // Create a new thread to update the display periodically
        thisThread = new Thread(this);
        thisThread.setPriority( Thread.MAX_PRIORITY );
        thisThread.start();
    }

    public boolean handleEvent(Event e)
    {
        if (e.target==clearList)
        {
```

```
        // The "Clear" button was pressed
        connectionList.clear();
        return true;

    }
    else if (e.id == Event.WINDOW_DESTROY)
    {
        // User chooses Close from the system menu.
        dispose();
        System.exit(0);
        return true; // this is here so the compiler won't complain
    }
    else
    {
        // Default
        return super.handleEvent(e);
    }
}


public void run()
{
    String    itemAddress;

    for (;;)
    {
        // Delay one second
        try {
            thisThread.sleep(1000);
        } catch (InterruptedException e) { }

        // Update the time display for the elements in the list
        synchronized(connectionList)
        {
            int       i, numberOfElements = connectionList.countItems();

            // Iterate through the elements in the list
            for (i=0; i<numberOfElements; i++)
            {
             // Check element i
             itemAddress = connectionList.getItem(i);

             // Increment seconds since last update
             int seconds  = Integer.parseInt(
                            itemAddress.substring(
                                itemAddress.lastIndexOf(' ')+2,
                                itemAddress.length()-1 ) );
            seconds++;

             // Update the string displayed
             itemAddress = itemAddress.substring( 0,
                                    itemAddress.indexOf(' '));

             connectionList.delItem(i);
             connectionList.addItem(itemAddress + " (" + seconds +")", i);
            }
        }
    }
}
```

```java
    public void processMessage(byte msg[])
    {
        // Java treats the raw bytes as signed, so we juggle the data
        // a bit (pun very much intended) to display it as a number in
        // the range 0 to 255.
        String   senderAddress = new String (
                        (msg[0]>0 ? msg[0] : msg[0]+256) + "." +
                        (msg[1]>0 ? msg[1] : msg[1]+256) + "." +
                        (msg[2]>0 ? msg[2] : msg[2]+256) + "." +
                        (msg[3]>0 ? msg[3] : msg[3]+256) );
        String   itemAddress;
        int      i, numberOfElements = connectionList.countItems();

        synchronized(connectionList)
        {
          // Try to find the sender's address in the list
          for (i=0; i<numberOfElements; i++)
          {
          // Check element i
          itemAddress = connectionList.getItem(i);
          itemAddress = itemAddress.substring( 0, itemAddress.indexOf(' '));

          if( senderAddress.equals(itemAddress) ) break;
          }

          if (i<numberOfElements)
          {
             // Address found !
             // Update current element by removing it -
             // the next statement will add it again with zero seconds
             connectionList.delItem(i);
           }

           // Add element where it should be
           connectionList.addItem(senderAddress + " (0)", i);
        }
    }
}

class Monitor
{
    public static void main(String args[]) throws Exception
    {
      MonitorPanel p = new MonitorPanel();
      DatagramSocket s = new DatagramSocket(2829);
      byte msgBuffer[] = new byte[128];
      DatagramPacket msg = new DatagramPacket(msgBuffer, msgBuffer.length);

      p.init();

      // Endlessly process incoming messages
      for(;;)
      {
          s.receive(msg);
          p.processMessage(msg.getData());
      }
    }
}
```

Clients and Servers

Client/server communication is a paradigm in which a single provider (the server) services many requesters (clients).

The server often serves as a gateway to a sharable resource. Such servers include centralized database engines, print servers, Internet proxy servers, and many more. It could also internally hold a resource that wouldn't exist if not for the server. Examples of this kind of server include mail servers, Internet chat servers, and time telling servers.

The client and the server use the same kind of sockets to communicate with each other, but the server also uses a special kind of socket (a server socket) to accept incoming connection requests. It's this special socket that spawns the communication socket. The spawned socket is automatically connected to the client's socket.

Most servers are multithreaded. They spawn a new thread to handle each new connection.

> *Only very simple servers–the kind that don't hold any sessions with the client–are single threaded. We could have created such a server by implementing the monitor application in the previous example using server sockets.*

The following diagram depicts what must happen for a client to communicate with a server:

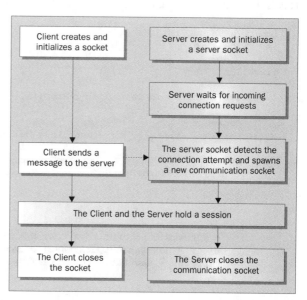

The server can accept other incoming connection requests while it communicates with the client if the session is held in another thread.

The Client/Server Model Put to Use

The remainder of the chapter is devoted to developing a simple distributed application called 'JavaChat'. This is a rather long example in which you will see two non-trivial applications: an Internet Chat client and an Internet Chat server (hosting a single discussion group). I chose to use this example because chat applications are the foundation for many applications in which users interactively communicate with each other to perform a task. This basic chat server is intended to be a starting point for you to develop your own:

▲ Fully fledged chat applications with separate discussion groups

▲ Network enabled interactive games

▲ White Board applications

▲ And many more...

Both the client and the server you are about to see are multithreaded. They use stream sockets to communicate through port 4554. The port number has no special meaning and you may change it–but remember that the change has to take place both in the client and in the server, or else they won't be able to communicate.

Most of the code handles thread synchronization and other activities. The statements that handle the actual client/server communication are highlighted.

The Client

The chat client uses two threads to communicate with the server. The main thread opens the communication socket, spawns a listener thread (a thread that listens for incoming messages), and starts sending the user's messages to the server.

This is the code for the main class in the chat client:

```java
import java.net.*;
import java.io.*;

class ChatClient
{
    public static void main(String args[])
    {
        Socket                  s;
        DataInputStream         user_in = null;
        DataOutputStream        s_out = null;
        String                  stringToSend;
        ChatClientListenThread  listeningThread;

        try
        {
            // Create a new socket and obtain its input and output streams
            s = new Socket("PUT YOUR HOST NAME HERE", 4554);
            s_out = new DataOutputStream( s.getOutputStream() );
            user_in  = new DataInputStream( System.in );

            // Spawn the listening thread
```

```
        listeningThread = new ChatClientListenThread(s);
        listeningThread.start();

        // Send user information to the server
        System.out.print("Enter your name: ");
        System.out.flush();

        stringToSend = user_in.readLine();
        s_out.writeUTF(stringToSend);
        stringToSend="";

        // Send the user's input to the server
        while (!stringToSend.equals("bye"))
        {
            stringToSend = user_in.readLine();
            s_out.writeUTF(stringToSend);
        }

        // Terminate the session - stop the listening thread
        listeningThread.stop();
        try {
            // Wait for the listening thread to stop
            Thread.currentThread().sleep(500);
        } catch (InterruptedException e) { }
    } catch (IOException e) {
        System.err.println("Error while writing : " + e);
        System.err.flush();
    } finally {
        try {
            s_out.close();
            user_in.close();
        } catch (IOException e) { }
    }
    }
}
```

A single object of the next class runs as a separate thread on the client and listens for incoming messages. This thread runs in an endless loop and only stops when the **ChatClient** implicitly stops it by invoking its **stop()** method (inherited from its base class, **Thread**).

```
import java.lang.Thread;
import java.io.*;
import java.net.*;

class ChatClientListenThread extends Thread
{
    private DataInputStream    s_in;
    private Socket             s;

    ChatClientListenThread(Socket s)
    {
        this.s = s;

        try {
            s_in = new DataInputStream( s.getInputStream() );
        } catch (IOException e) {
            System.err.println("Error while constructing " +
                "ChatClientListenThread : \n" + e );
            System.exit(1);
```

```
        }
    }

    public void run()
    {
        String inString;

        try {
            while (true) // This thread is stopped from the outside
            {
                // Wait for incoming message
                inString = s_in.readUTF();
                // Print it to screen
                System.out.println( ">>>" + inString );
            }

        } catch (ThreadDeath td){

            // This thread was stopped by the main thread
            System.out.println("Connection closed!");
            throw td;

        } catch (IOException e) {

            System.err.println("Error while reading : " + e);
            System.err.flush();

        } finally {

            try {
                s_in.close();
                s.close();
            } catch (IOException e) { }

        }
    }
}
```

The two threads are using a single socket, and that socket needs only to be closed once. I chose to close it in **ChatClientListenThread**, but it could also be closed by **ChatClient**.

The Server

The chat server uses two threads to communicate with *each* client. Another thread (the 'main' thread) is used to initiate client sessions. The main thread opens a server socket and waits for incoming connection requests. When a connection request is accepted, it spawns two threads to handle the communication with the client and goes back to listen for more requests.

The thread that handles incoming communication from a client is an instance of **ChatListenThread**. The thread that is responsible for echoing every message sent by any client is an instance of **ChatEchoThread**. The server uses a single object instantiated from **ThreadSynchronizer** to synchronize all the echo threads.

Here is the code of the main server class:

```
import java.net.*;
import java.io.*;
```

```java
public class ChatServer
{
    public static void main(String args[]) {
        ServerSocket        s = null;
        Socket              clientSocket;
        ChatListenThread    listen;
        ThreadSynchronizer  echoSynchronizer= new ThreadSynchronizer();

        System.out.println("JavaChat Server\nA WROX Press service\n" +
                        "by Shy Cohen\n1996(c)\nVersion  1.0\n");

        try {
            // Create the server socket
            s = new ServerSocket(4554);
            System.out.println("JavaChat Server is up and waiting " +
                            "for connections...");

            while (true) {

                // Wait for a new connection
                clientSocket = s.accept();
                System.out.println("SERVER: Contacted by " +
                                clientSocket.getInetAddress() );

                // Spawn a listener and an echo threads for the new connection
                listen = new ChatListenThread ( clientSocket);
                listen.start();
            }

        } catch (IOException e) {
            System.err.println("ERROR IN SERVER : " + e);
        } finally {
            try {
            s.close();
            } catch (IOException e){}
        }

        // The server runs in an endless loop and stops only if an
        // exception is thrown.
        System.out.println("You will never see this message !");
    }
}
```

The next class is **ChatListenThread**. An object of this class listens for incoming messages from a single client. **ChatServer** spawns an instance of the class for each client. If the client says 'bye', it stops listening and stops the echo thread attached to the client ('bye' is the session termination message).

```java
import java.lang.Thread;
import java.net.*;
import java.io.*;
import java.util.Hashtable;
import java.util.Enumeration;

class ChatListenThread extends Thread
{
    static Hashtable clientMap = new Hashtable();
    static long IDSource = 0;

    static synchronized long newID()
```

```
{
   return ++IDSource;
}

static synchronized void addToMap(long id, ChatListenThread client)
{
   clientMap.put(new Long(id), client);
}

static synchronized void removeFromMap(long id)
{
   clientMap.remove(new Long(id));
}

static synchronized void broadcastMessage(String msg)
{
   Enumeration e = clientMap.elements();
   while(e.hasMoreElements() == true)
   {
       ((ChatListenThread)e.nextElement()).send(msg);
   }
}
```

```
private Socket           s;
private DataOutputStream s_out;
private static int       userCount=0;
private long ID;

ChatListenThread(Socket clientSocket){
  ID = newID();
  s     = clientSocket;
}

public void run() {
   DataInputStream        s_in = null;
   String                 inString = "dummy", userName = null;

   // Increase user count
   userCount++;

   try {
      s_in = new DataInputStream( s.getInputStream() );
      s_out = new DataOutputStream( s.getOutputStream() );
     addToMap(ID, this);
      userName = s_in.readUTF();

       // Send greetings and connection count to the new user
       send("JavaChat");
       send("=========");
       send("A service of WROX Press");
       send("by Shy Cohen, 1996(c)");
       send("Version 1.0");
       send("");
       send("SERVER : Hello " + userName + ".");
       send("SERVER : There are " + userCount +
       " users connected to JavaChat at the moment.");
       send("");
```

```
        // Notify all users of the joining
        broadcastMessage( userName + " connected." );

        // Send the user's messages to all the others
        while (!inString.equals("bye")) {
            inString = s_in.readUTF();
            broadcastMessage( userName + " : " + inString );
        }

        // Stop the echo thread and wait for it to finish

        try {
            sleep(500);
        } catch (InterruptedException e){}

        // Notify all users of the disconnection
        broadcastMessage( userName + " disconnected.");

    } catch (EOFException e) {

        // The socket was unexpectedly closed on the other side
        System.err.println( userName + " closed socket");

    } catch (IOException e) {

        // Some other error while reading
        System.err.println("ERROR while reading from " +
                           userName + " : " + e);

    } finally {

        try {
        removeFromMap(ID);
            s_in.close();
            s.close();
        } catch (IOException e){}

    }

    // Decrease user count
    userCount--;
}

private synchronized void  send(String msg)
{
    try{
        // Send the message to a single client
        s_out.writeUTF(msg);

    } catch(IOException e) {
        System.err.println("ERROR: Could not send data: " +e);
    }
    }
}
```

The last two classes are **ThreadSynchronizer** and **ChatEchoThread**. **ThreadSynchronizer** is the object whose associated monitor is used to synchronize all of the **ChatEchoThread** threads. **ChatEchoThread**'s class-wide property **message** holds the message that needs be sent to all the clients.

```java
import java.lang.Thread;
import java.io.*;
import java.net.*;

class ThreadSynchronizer
{
   synchronized void newMessageArrived()
   {
      notifyAll();
   }

   synchronized void waitForMessage()
   throws InterruptedException
   {
      wait();
   }
}

class ChatEchoThread extends Thread
{
   private static String        message;
   private ThreadSynchronizer   synchronizer;
   private Socket               s;
   private DataOutputStream     s_out;


   ChatEchoThread( Socket clientSocket,
                  ThreadSynchronizer commonThreadSynchronizer)
   {
      s =           clientSocket;
      synchronizer = commonThreadSynchronizer;
   }


   void sendAll(String msg)
   {
      // Update shared message and print it on the console
      message = msg;
      System.out.println(">>> " + msg);
      System.out.flush();

      // Notify all the waiting threads that a new message had arrived
      synchronizer.newMessageArrived();
   }


   void send(String msg)
   {
      try{
         // Send the message to a single client
         s_out.writeUTF(msg);

      } catch(IOException e) {
         System.err.println("ERROR: Could not send data: " +e);
      }
   }
```

```
        public void run()
        {
            try {
                s_out = new DataOutputStream( s.getOutputStream() );

                while (true) // This thread is stopped from the outside
                {
                    // Wait on the common object's monitor
                    // for the next message to arrive
                    synchronizer.waitForMessage();

                    // Send it to the client
                    s_out.writeUTF( message );
                }

            } catch (IOException e) {

System.err.println("ERROR while echoing message: " + this + " : " + e);

            } catch (InterruptedException e) {

                // Do nothing

            } finally {

                try {
                    s_out.close();
                    s.close();
                } catch (IOException e) { }

            }
        }
    }
```

Reading Files from a Web Server

To read the content of a file on a web server use the **URL** and **URLConnection** classes. Here's how to do it:

```
import java.net.*;
import java.io.*;

class DownloadFile
{
    public static void main(String args[])
    {
        byte byteBuffer[];
        int  bytesRead;

        byteBuffer = new byte[4096];

        try
        {
            // Establish a connection
            URL sourceURL = new URL(args[0]);
            URLConnection connection = sourceURL.openConnection();
            connection.connect();
```

```
        // if the file does not exist, the following will throw an exception:
        InputStream in = connection.getInputStream();

            // Read it
            bytesRead = in.read(byteBuffer);
        }
        catch (Exception ex)
        {
            System.out.println("Couldn't open the specified file");
            System.exit(1);
        }

        // Print content to screen
        System.out.println("contents of " + args[0] + " :\n" +
                            new String(byteBuffer, 0, 0, bytesRead));
    }
}
```

This class reads the content of the file as a stream of bytes, regardless of its actual content.

For a complete description of **URL** and **URLConnection** see the API.

Summary

In this chapter, we have looked at Java's networking capabilities. We have discussed sockets and looked at peer-to-peer communication and client/server communication. You have also seen some examples of networking in practice.

One of the many uses for Java networking is interfacing existing applications such as:

- POP mail servers
- Simple Network Management Protocol (SNMP) enabled machines
- SQL and other database servers

In order to implement the interface, you need to know the communication protocol with the application. You can find links to information on the exact protocols for many popular applications (DNS, FTP, HTTP, NNTP, NTP, SMTP, SNMP, and many others) on the web at:

```
http://www.yahoo.com/Computers_and_Internet/Software/Protocols/
```

Building Your Own Libraries

CHAPTER 13

In this, and the next, chapter, we'll be looking at what is required to develop a class library in Java. We'll be discussing library design in this chapter, and then we'll look at its implementation in Chapter 14.

Topics will include:

- Developing a model
- API design
- Class design
- Coding
- Packaging
- Reliability and performance issues

Introduction

In general, a class library is a collection of related classes developed for the purpose of providing building blocks for a variety of applications. Applications covered by a class library are often limited to a particular domain. A class library may implement a family of algorithms, useful programming components, a set of user interfaces, etc.

The main motivation for developing a class library is reusability. Typically, a class library is developed by experts and distributed to others, thereby eliminating the need to reinvent the wheel when dealing with certain problems. In other words, a programmer does not have to spend his/her time understanding how problems are solved in a specialized area.

Class libraries are also ideal for assembling prototypes and applications in a short time. A well-designed and reliable class library can reduce the product development time considerably.

Class Libraries in Java

Developing class libraries in Java has tremendous potential significance because of Java's platform independence. In theory, a class library developed in Java will run on any hardware/software platform that has the Java Virtual Machine. In practice, however, class libraries may not run in the same way on all platforms; for example, class libraries involving graphical user interfaces. Since Java makes use of the native user interface components, it's hard to achieve the same behavior across all platforms; for instance, a wait cursor in Window NT may not behave in the same way as the wait cursor on a Sun Sparc machine.

Despite this drawback, developing a class library in Java is a great improvement over developing it using other languages, where tedious porting may be necessary. As Java covers a wide spectrum of platforms and users, a class library developed in Java will be useful to a large audience. Developers of a successful class library can reap huge benefits because of this enormous exposure. However, with benefits come responsibility. As memory and speed requirements vary widely across platforms, a cautious design approach needs to be adopted. Because of the cross-platform nature of Java, optimization must focus on efficient algorithms and data structures, instead of how quickly a particular Java Virtual Machine instruction is executed, since that will vary between platforms.

Java has a number of excellent features to help you build and use class libraries. These include the Java language constructs, **package**, **import**, **interface**, and so on. The Java environment allows the applications to use classes directly from uncompressed zip files. So, an entire class library comprising of classes can be delivered as a zip file.

You can distribute your library without source code, or charge extra for the source if you desire. As the Java compiler provides ways to separate sources from class files, source files can be separately archived and delivered if required. The Java environment has an excellent document generator called **javadoc** which generates HTML-style documents. This tool extracts text from the source files and automatically creates a set of documents. These documents provide cross references and different levels of detail about publicly available classes, interfaces, methods, and variables.

Before we delve into the development of class libraries, it's necessary to discuss how class libraries are organized in Java. The next section will explain what a class library contains and the way it's laid out.

Anatomy of a Class Library

In Java, a class library is a collection of packages. Understanding packages is key to constructing a class library. Packages, just like classes, can be organized as a hierarchical tree. Typically, classes that interact to perform some task or tasks, or solve a problem, are put together in a package. In general, we can say a package enables a grouping of classes along functional lines. The interaction between classes requires visibility among classes, which packages provide. Packages also hide classes from the outside world. Classes and interfaces in a package may belong to a class or interface hierarchy outside that package.

We will discus here how a class library is organized in Java.

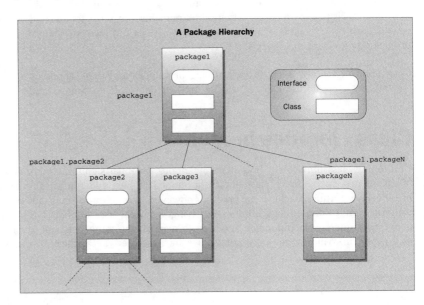

The previous figure shows a package hierarchy. A Java package may contain the following:

- Interfaces
- Classes
- Exceptions

Some of the classes in the package implement the interfaces. The exceptions could be either the extensions of Java built-in exceptions or the specially developed exceptions. The **javadoc** documents will show the package hierarchy and the class hierarchy within a package. If you comment your source code properly, these documents provide a complete layout of the class library. One can easily navigate through the class tree structure using these documents, rather as one would through the class browsers that come with Café and VJ++.

User's Perspective

Application writers are the users of the class libraries. Henceforth in this chapter, we will refer to application writers as users. We will refer to actual users of applications which use class libraries as application users. We also use the word application in a general way, it can mean an applet or a stand-alone application.

Users of class libraries aren't expected to know its actual implementation details. A class library from a user's perspective is much more than a set of related classes. It also includes interfaces to interact with applications and documentation to explain how to use the class library, and provide some example code. Applications interact with a class library through a set of well defined interfaces called APIs (Application Programming Interfaces). An Application Programming Interface is a window to the outside world from a library. Through this window, applications typically pass data and/or commands to perform certain operations and then retrieve the resulting data. Although implementations of a class library may change over time, APIs should seldom need to change. This is because a change to an API would mean modification and recompilation of all the applications that use it. With a set of APIs defined, however, there can be several implementations of a class library.

What do users expect from a class library? As implementation details are hidden from the users, the only thing users need worry about is how to get the required functionality with the least amount of programming. Consistency, both in API definitions and design, is one of the key factors that is essential in making a class library easy to use.

A class library also needs to be flexible and extensible. A flexible class library will provide different ways of achieving a desired result; for example, you might have several APIs which provide debugging information and a consolidated one for the final compilation. This should not detract from the APIs clear interface. Extensibility is essential, because it's often necessary to extend the existing functionality of a class library. From the implementation point of view, users expect a class library to be very reliable and efficient.

Because class libraries should be reusable, developing them can be more complicated than developing application software. It's often necessary to design and publish APIs in advance. In the following sections, we will discuss what it takes to develop a class library.

Development Life Cycle

Just as in any other software development process, development of a non-trivial class library will involve a complete software cycle. Although the development methodologies may vary, a software life cycle will have the following basic phases:

- Requirements
- Design
- Coding
- Testing

Development of a class library involves the above phases, but is quite different from other types of software development.

The creation of a class library usually involves iterating through the design cycle several times. Testing and feedback from alpha and beta users changes the requirements which changes the design and requires more coding. These iterations from prototype to finished class library are valuable because the most useful parts of the library are expanded. Developing an application in parallel with making the class library also makes the class library more useful.

The requirements of a class library may be very broad, but must also focus on particular requirements to be ready on time, and reduce complexity. Requirements need to be formulated anticipating a class library's future use. This may involve assuming some imaginary applications. Having a cookbook for the library, as a result of this testing adds to the usefulness of the API documentation.

In the design phase, requirements are not directly turned into a class library design. Instead, requirements are the basis for API design. The class libraries are then designed to meet the API specifications. Implementation of a class library needs to be very stringent in terms of performance, memory use, and space. Application software can be tested by performing actual actions, such as typing commands, clicking buttons, and so on. A class library can only be tested by a simulator or a test suite.

Design

Before we explore various design issues, we'll briefly discuss our goals. In other words, we'll formulate what is expected of a class library.

An ideal class library should be:

- General enough to cover a large variety of applications.
- Specific enough to achieve the desired functionality in a given application without complex intertwining of APIs.
- Simple enough for users to learn the underlying concept or model.
- Flexible enough to achieve a desired functionality in different ways, and to be extended to tasks not envisaged when the library was first designed.

Achieving the above is very challenging, especially when a large and complex class library is being developed. There is no right way to design a class library, as each library is different. However, there can be certain guiding principles. Experience plays a very important role in the design.

The design framework for a class library may include:

- Developing a conceptual model.
- Designing APIs and deciding how much of the internal workings of the library should be exposed to users.
- Designing the library to implement the APIs.

The above steps may be interdependent. For instance, as APIs are designed, the underlying model may need to change, resulting in changes in the library design. There will be several iterations before a good design emerges.

In the subsequent sections, we'll explain the issues involved in the development of the concept, design of APIs and class libraries. In order to illustrate various design aspects, we'll have a lot of implementation examples. During the course of our discussion, we will also design a class library for the interactive drawing of shapes.

Developing a Concept

A well defined concept or model is essential for a class library that is large and complex. For example, the `java.awt.image` library follows a **Producer-Consumer** model. The APIs are closely linked to this model. So it's essential to specify the underlying conceptual model before a class library is designed. The model on which a class library is based needs to be simple. A complicated model will mean a steep learning curve for users, defeating the very purpose of class libraries.

In general, object orientation is the broad framework for developing a conceptual model for a Java class library. A model is expected to capture the structure and behavior of the class library from the user's point of view. A class library may be providing solutions to certain problems. The model for such a class library needs to capture the problem pattern and its solution. The problem to be solved by the class library may follow a well known design pattern, in which case, the model can be developed using that pattern. If the problem domain is complex, developing a model may entail the development of new software architecture. A complex problem can always be divided into more manageable pieces, each of which is well understood. Software architecture can put pieces into the right places to solve a complex problem.

A model is also expected to capture the protocols that are followed by applications to interact with a class library. In general, a model is a user's view consisting of class organization, the relationship between classes, communication between classes and protocols to interact with the class library.

Our next question is, how do we go about developing a conceptual model? This is a topic of great interest in the world of object-oriented programming. There may be several approaches to developing a model. Interested readers may want to refer to the literature that discusses this topic in detail.

> **An excellent reference is *Design Patterns* by Erich Gamma *et al.*
> (ISBN 0-201-63361-2)**

We'll adopt a common sense approach here; the right place to start is with the requirements. The application domain itself will provide clues. First, we specify the requirements from the application user's point of view. We'll then translate them into requirements of the application writer. These requirements will become the basis for developing the underlying model. We'll discuss the development of a model using an example that draws shapes.

Shapes Model

We'll start with the model's requirements.

Requirements

Before defining any classes, the designer must understand what problem the application user is trying to solve. For example, in a drawing package:

- Is the user doing collaborative drawing over the network?
- Is the user making flow charts?
- Is the user doing engineering drawings?

Figuring out the target audience for the class library and helping them solve their problems will obviously improve the usefulness of the library.

We assume that users of the application will choose one or more of the following three shapes:

- Box–a rectangle.
- Ellipse–an oval.
- Arrow–a line with an arrowhead at one end.

The main objective of the shape class library is to enable the drawing of a shape interactively.

Each shape has a different type of representation–a box is represented by its four corners and an ellipse by its bounding box. Whatever the shape, there will be a starting position which is used as the anchor of the shape. In the case of a box, the starting position can be one of the corners of the box. The shape will also have a current position determined from the position of the cursor. A shape will need its starting position and a current position in order to be drawn. While the starting position remains the same throughout, the current position will keep changing.

With the shape anchored at the starting position, the size of the shape is expected to follow the current position. In the case of a box, the current position can be the opposite corner to the starting position. For an ellipse, where there are no corners, the starting position will be the center of the bounding box surrounding the ellipse, and the current position will be one of the corners of the bounding box.

We'll assume the following requirements for the application user's point of view:

- Choice of shapes–**Box**, **Ellipse**, **Arrow**
- Interactive drawing
- Permanent drawing

380

We'll now specify the requirements from the application writer's point of view.

If we carry out an object-oriented design, we will have three separate classes, one for each of the shapes, **Box**, **Ellipse**, and **Arrow**. Each will provide two functions, **draw** and **interactiveDraw**.

The **draw** function is simple, as a shape is drawn once shape points have been provided. **interactiveDraw** is a little more complicated, but we can erase the previous drawn shape and replace it with a new shape, to give the appearance of the shape changing.

How can an application writer use the solution provided by the class library? To erase a shape, the object would need to remember its location and its size or shape points. To draw a new shape, the objects needs the same information. So interactive drawing needs to be accomplished through a sequence of method calls. The sequence can be as follows:

- Initialize shape
- Set the starting position
- Set the current position

When drawing interactively, we must:

- Erase the previous shape
- Draw the new shape

Since a sequence of operations are involved in draw interactive, the object needs to remember its state. In other words, it's necessary for a shape to be an instance of a class, and each shape instance will have instance variables to store its state. All the three classes will need to perform these operations. As the application user changes the shape on the fly, the application will also need to instantiate a new shape on the fly. This is the **dynamic binding** problem, which is one of the tenets of object-oriented programming. An application writer should be able to design their application in such a way that the method calls to initialize, access attributes, and draw are the same, irrespective of type of shape. This would enable the application user to change the shapes on the fly, and application writers would not necessarily have to write programs to check the shape type whenever a shape type is changed. For example:

```
Shape curShape;
curShape.draw(...);
```

where **curShape** can be any one of the shapes and can be instantiated dynamically. **curShape.draw()** will draw the type of shape the **curShape** is instantiated to when this statement is called.

In summary, the underlying concept in the shapes library is quite simple. It follows three basic OO principles: **inheritance**, **encapsulation**, and **polymorphism**.

API Design

Designing a well-defined and easy to use API is a critical step in developing a class library. APIs are the links through which applications interact with the components of a class library. Ideally, given an interface to a class library, there can be multiple implementations of that interface. API designers, however, need to be aware of the implementation for a variety of reasons.

One of the important guiding principles in designing APIs should be the ease of use. Users prefer the straightforward use of APIs to accomplish a functionality. APIs should be simple and unambiguous. Flexibility is another aspect designers must keep in mind. It's often required to obtain partial or intermediate results. It may be necessary sometimes to cascade APIs to achieve a desired outcome. While designing APIs, API designers may need to consider a number of factors. APIs based on sound OO design is certainly desirable, but a good design may not necessarily result in an efficient implementation in terms of memory use, speed, and code size. So API designers may have to make some compromises.

How do we go about designing APIs? Obviously, the application writer's requirements are the starting point. API design doesn't entail the complete OO design of the class library, as the basic OO design is done while developing the model for the library. So the API design will be based on that design.

There are two approaches to this OOP analysis; the first is more top-down (requirements first, objects last), while the second approach is bottom-up (objects first, relationships last). In the real world, you combine both analysis styles. The user interface and overall behaviour is derived by studying the requirements and mapping them into methods, and then seeing what objects encapsulate these methods. System level (utility or support class level) design often begins with the fundamental objects like an IP data packet object, and then defines what relations other modules must have to that fundamental unit of behavior. The objects come first and interrelations are defined later.

Here's how you might combine the two approaches:

- Define system requirements.

- Define low-level objects and technical requirements.

- Map user requirements to user interface and subsystems.

- Define functionality of each subsystem.

- Map functionality to methods.

- Encapsulate methods into objects. Common methods are bundled together into discrete objects that don't duplicate the properties of any other object.

- Ensure coupling between objects is minimised. This makes sure the minimum amount of data is transferred between each object. If an object must communicate too much information, or 'know' too much about another object, then the object breakdown is not orthogonal or optimal.

- Make sure each object has high internal strength or cohesion. A low-cohesion object is a mixed combination of several functions. Ideally, each module or object should perform only one function, and all methods and data members should relate to that one function.

- Define all relationships including messages and APIs between objects and class libraries.

Once a design is complete, the API specifications are published and interested parties will review the design. The design process may go through a few iterations before a finished design emerges.

API design involves designing publicly available classes, interfaces, methods, and variables. We'll go through the design issues involved in each of this categories.

Translating Requirements into APIs

With an underlying concept or model in mind, the requirements need to be converted into a set of APIs. Typically, a class library solves some problem and there may be several tasks to be performed to accomplish an outcome. The main issue here is how to map these tasks to APIs.

The application writer wants to be able to choose shapes dynamically, and make use of some functionality for each shape. This functionality can be split into:

- Initializing the shape
- Setting the shape's attributes
- Setting the starting position
- Setting the current position
- Drawing the shape permanently
- Drawing the shape interactively

We'll try to map shapes requirements to APIs. As we can see from the above requirements, some may translate into variables and some into methods, which will be encapsulated in classes or interfaces.

Designing Class Level APIs

In this section, our discussion will focus on designing classes from the perspective of an API designer. While designing APIs, it isn't necessary to know the entire class library design. The actual class design may even change over time.

An interface that captures a higher level of abstraction is needed in most designs. This abstraction will encapsulate the common behavior. It should be designed in such a way that the users are shielded from the low level design and implementation details. Abstract classes and interfaces are the likely candidates for such a design.

An interface behaves like a class as far as the users are concerned. But for a library, an interface is like a specification of a class, the body of which will be implemented by the library. Abstract classes, though, behave more or less in the same way. Let's discuss the differences.

To recap, classes that implement the functionality defined in the abstract class need to extend that abstract class. In other words, the relationship between the abstract class and the implemented class is through inheritance. In our shapes example, the implementation of **Box** may want to reuse an existing AWT class, say a **Rectangle**. As we know, this can be achieved by the **Box** class extending **Rectangle**. If we use an abstract class, say **Shape**, to capture the common behavior of shapes, then the **Box** class would be a subclass of **Shape**. Since Java doesn't support multiple inheritance, the **Box** class can't extend both **Rectangle** and **Shape**.

Now, let's us see whether interfaces satisfy this requirement. We will define an interface called **Drawable** to capture the common behavior of the shapes. We know that Java allows a class to extend another class and implement one or more interfaces. So, the **Box** class is allowed to extend **Rectangle** and implement **Drawable**.

Using Interfaces

Interfaces don't allow variables (except **static final**) whereas abstract classes do. This will also have a bearing on the application design. Let's illustrate this with an example:

```
Drawable curShape;
```

Suppose we need the width and height of the box shape. **curShape.width** won't work because **curShape** is of type **Drawable**, an interface. So how do we access the data if we use interfaces? There are two ways.

First, type casting, where the following will work, assuming **Box** has a variable called **width**. It's always wise to perform an **instanceof** check first.

```
if (curShape instanceof Box) {
    ((Box)curShape).width;
    ...
```

Alternatively, you can use explicit set and get methods. For example, **Drawable** can have the **getWidth** and **getHeight** methods. These can be dummy methods in some classes, for instance the **Arrow** class. This can be annoying, if a class has to implement a number of such dummy, or access, methods. They can, though, be very useful for keeping the internal implementation independent of the interface. Suppose you started using measurement as a double, then decided it was inefficient, and long was a better choice? With access methods you can re-implement your internals but maintain a consistent interface to users.

Using Abstract Classes

Abstract classes do allow the declaration of variables. Their subclasses can inherit the variables and use them as instance variables. For example,

```
abstract public class Shape {
    public int width, height;

    //  Methods...

}
```

In the application code,

```
Shape curShape;
```

curShape.width will now work. This may not be desirable. The reasons are explained in the section on accessing data.

Working with an Interface

For this example we'll choose an interface over abstract classes, as this is more extensible. So, next, we'll discuss how instantiation and dynamic binding can be achieved when we use an interface.

It's obvious from the class library model that we need three classes which are **Box**, **Ellipse**, and **Arrow**. We also need to implement dynamic binding. We need a class that encapsulates the common behavior. We'll define an interface called **Drawable** which encapsulates that behavior.

Because of the multiple shapes we want to draw, there has to be some selection mechanism to choose between them. Whenever the application user selects a shape, we can say:

```
Drawable curShape = new Box(...);
```

The problem with this is that the shape selection may be through a component like a button, where the selection of a shape is detected by an event. The event handling program will have to know about the **Box**, **Ellipse**, and **Arrow** class constructors and its arguments. In order to avoid that, we'll represent shape types by integer constants, say **BOX**, **ELLIPSE**, **ARROW**, and so on, although the **instanceof** operator is an alternative. This representation can be a part of **Drawable**. The Java implementation of shape types can look like this:

```
public static final int NONE=0;
public static final int BOX=1;
public static final int ELLIPSE=2;
public static final int ARROW=3;
```

Representing shape types as integer constants will be useful when choosing shapes using a switch statement. Although using **switch** statements is not considered good OO programming practice, it works well in this case. But, where should this **switch** statement be coded? Should it be in the application or in the class library? If the application has to implement the selection, then it needs to know the design and implementation details. Moreover, if the library adds a shape or changes the name of a shape, the application will have to change in all the places where the above switch statement has been implemented.

An application implementing the shape selection mechanism needs more maintenance because it isn't extensible. What is needed is a mechanism in the class library itself to choose and create shapes as requested by the application. The shape object is then sent to the application. In other words, this means that the application passes the shape type, and an object in the class library creates a shape and passes that shape over to the application. In this way, the application doesn't need to be aware of the actual implementation of the shape classes.

We can therefore define a **ShapeProducer** interface to implement the shape selection mechanism. This is the abstract factory beloved of the pattern community.

ShapeProducer can be either a class or an interface. To decide between the two, we note that the method used to select a shape can be static, because it isn't specific to any of the shapes. If we declare **createShape**, as shown below, then it can't be a part of the **interface**.

```
static public Drawable createShape(int shapeType);
```

An implementation of **createShape** might look like this:

```
static public Shape createShape(int shapeType){
    switch(shapeType){
        case Drawable.BOX:
            return(new Box());
        case Drawable.ELLIPSE:
            return(new Ellipse());
        case Drawable.ARROW:
            return(new Arrow());
        default:
            return null;
    }
}
```

*An alternative to the **switch** statement would be Java's 'dictionary', the **hashtable**.*

The methods in an interface are implicitly abstract, hence a class can't implement them by **static** methods. Implementing the above method as an instance method would mean extra overhead and affect code size and speed. Moreover, users will need to instantiate the class. In conclusion, **ShapeProducer** needs to be a class and **createShape** needs to be a static method.

Encapsulating Data

We already know from Chapter 2 that classes encapsulate attributes and behavior. Data is stored in variables, and methods implement behaviors. In the next section, we will discuss the design issues related to designing data access APIs.

Designing Data Access APIs

API designers need to decide a number of things regarding public access of data.

What's the most efficient way to represent data? This is a data structure question. A designer must consider a number of factors before deciding on a data structure. Some of these factors are:

- Intended use.

- Memory restrictions. For example, declaring a variable as an array of images. Each image may be a pixel map of 512x512 pixels. If the array contains 16 images, it would requires at least 4Mb to hold all these images.

- Performance overhead. A designer would have to weigh the benefits of a data structure against its overhead. For example, Java has a number of utility data structures like **Vector**, **Hashtable**, and **Stack**. Though these are easy to use, they may not exactly fit users requirements.

- Who can access the data? A class may have a number of variables, but not all of them may need to be public. Some variables are needed only by the subclasses and some by the classes within the package. This involves the access modifiers dealt with in Chapter 3.

- How to access the data?

The following section will address this last question—should data be directly accessible or only through set and get methods?

Direct Access vs. Method Access

In Java, a publicly declared variable can be accessed directly, that is, from outside the class. Is this a good thing? The following are some of the arguments for accessing instance variables in a class library through set and get methods.

- The access method can add a level of security for accessing data. Accidental and malicious destruction of data can be prevented in this way.

▲ It's safer from a multithreading point of view. A public variable can be modified by another program, even if it's in a method which is locked by the synchronized construct. On the other hand, if it's only accessible through a method, that method can be synchronized. This will prevent more than one method trying to modify a variable at the same time.

▲ A publicly accessible variable may be tied to other variables in the class. When an instance variable is modified by direct access, the dependent variables will remain the same. The next example illustrates the point.

▲ Protecting external users from internal implementation changes.

Let's define a component for displaying images:

```
class ImageCanvas extends Canvas{
    public int width, height;
    private dim cursorPosBox;

    public ImageCanvas(int wid, int ht){
        setWidth(wid, ht);
    }

    public void setWidthHeight(int wid, int ht){
        width = wid;
        height = ht;
        cursorBoxPos = new Dimension(width/10, height/10);
    }
    ...
    // other methods.
}
```

An advantage of direct by accessing variables is that it's faster. If a variable is used as read-only, direct access of data is preferable. However, the read-only access can't be enforced in Java, except in the case of **static final** variables

Shape objects have attributes. In our example, we will use just one attribute, i.e. color. This attribute may not change during the course of drawing shapes, so it's advantageous to set the color of the shape in advance. In order to enable interactive drawing, a shape object has to save the starting position. As interactive drawing progresses, it would also need to save the current position. Thus, the shape attributes, starting position, and current position are candidates for instance variables. In general, data that is specific to an object and which needs to saved and reused can be stored in instance variables.

We will apply our data access philosophy to the shapes example. The requirements specification regarding the access of starting position, current position, and shape attributes translate into the following APIs.

▲ init(int x, int y)—the init API combines the initialization and the setting of the starting position.

▲ setCurPos(int x, int y)—sets the current position of the shape.

▲ setAttribute(Color cl)—sets the Color attribute.

Encapsulating Behavior

The design of actual APIs will depend on a number of factors such as the underlying model, interactions between APIs, and so on. In this section, we will discuss the issues involved in designing API methods.

Designing API Methods

A method is described by its name, type (static, instance, etc.), arguments, return type, and exception specifications. When an API method is designed, all these associations need to be decided. Our discussion will focus on the following:

- Method arguments
- Return types
- Method overloading

Method Arguments

Deciding the method arguments largely depends on the underlying model and the method requirements. API designers have to decide the following:

Argument Type

There can be several choices of type available for certain arguments. Designers need to weigh a number of factors such as performance and memory; for example, when choosing between a vector and an array type. The vector data structure is an elegant way of implementing a collection or a linked list. But it comes with baggage and is slower to access. If performance is the main criterion, and you can cope with using a static data structure, it's obvious that the array data type is the right choice.

Number of Arguments

In certain cases, there may be a large number of arguments. An API with a large number of arguments is unlikely to be user-friendly, and may well indicate a flawed design. An option, in such cases, is to combine the arguments into a class. For example, we might need to pass a set of statistics to a class method. This may include a large number of parameters, say minimum, maximum, average, median, standard deviation, and so on. Instead of passing individual parameters as arguments, we can create a class called **Statistics** and pass it as an argument.

When it isn't possible to combine arguments, there can be trade-offs between the number of arguments and the number of APIs. If a parameter in an API seldom changes, it can be set by a method. Thus, to accomplish a functionality there can be several APIs to set the parameters and several to perform that function. We'll explain this with a detailed example.

Let's say we need to implement an API to magnify images. This API can be used in any application in different ways. We will discuss what parameters the **magnify** API requires. It's obvious that it should have the image and the magnification factor as input parameters. Typically, when an image is magnified, only a portion of the original image is shown on the screen. So we need to specify what part of the magnified image is to be displayed. This can be done by providing a point on the image which can be the center of the magnified image. A version of the **magnify** API might be:

```
magnify(Image image, double magFactor, Point magCenter)
```

We can assume that **image** won't change frequently. The object that magnifies the image may already know the image upon which it's operating. So the **magnify** API doesn't need the **image** argument. The **magCenter** can also be set separately. By default, this can be the center of the image. So the **magnify** API can be split as follows.

```
setImage(Image image);
setMagCenter(Point center);
magnify(magFactor);
```

The application that zooms an image will invoke the **setImage** and **setCenter** APIs first. The **magnify** may be invoked in real-time by an event caused by say a scroll bar movement. The splitting of APIs makes an application writer's job simple.

However, it may not be safe in a multithreaded environment. The variables in the above examples can be modified by different threads, and the behavior of the method implementing the API may not be as expected. This problem can be circumvented by using the **synchronized** construct. The section on multithreading issues discusses this solution in detail.

Return Types

The caller of a method may receive the following:

▲ A value returned by the called method.

▲ An exception if that methods throws one.

We'll deal with each of these separately.

Return Value

The issue here is whether a method should return a result through the **return** statement or its arguments. Let's discuss the pros and cons. As we know, when the parameter to be passed is a basic data type, the parameter passing mechanism is **by value,** and Java doesn't support pointers. If the result returned is a basic data type such as an integer, a double, etc., there is no way that the result can be passed back to the caller through arguments. However, it can be indirectly passed if it can be made a variable of a class. But this is overkill if that object is not used in the called method. In this case, therefore, using the **return** statement to pass back the result is advantageous. Suppose more than one value needs to be returned. There are then a couple of choices:

▲ Create an array, if the parameters are of the same type.

▲ Create a class, if parameters are of different types.

Again, we need to choose whether the result is to be returned through an argument or return statement.

The **computeMinMax** example in the previous section illustrates returning the result through an array argument. We'll implement the same method using the second option, i.e. passing the result using the **return** statement.

```
static  public int[] computeMinmax(int inp[]){
    if(inp == null) return null;
    int minmax[] = new int[2];
    minmax[0] = Integer.MAX_VALUE;
```

```
        minmax[1] = Integer.MIN_VALUE;
        for(int i=0;i<inp.length;i++){
            if(inp[i] < minmax[0]) minmax[0] = inp[i];
            if(inp[i] > minmax[1]) minmax[1] = inp[i];
        }
        return minmax;
    }
```

The **return** statement is our choice, because users don't have to worry about who allocates memory for the array.

An important benefit of using **return** to pass back the value is that they can be embedded in other statements. This makes recursion possible. It also reduces the number of local variables, and thus the size of the code.

In summary, if a method needs to pass data back to application, it's preferable to do this through the **return** statement.

Exceptions

The designer of APIs should decide whether a method can throw an exception. This is important because an application writer needs to be aware of whether an exception should be caught. The topic of exceptions was dealt with in detail in Chapter 3.

Flexible Design through Method Overloading

We have described in the previous section just one way of designing a magnification API. In fact, there are several ways of providing such an interface. As mentioned before, flexibility is desirable in a class library. In other words, a class library should provide users with a lot of choice to achieve a desired functionality. As we saw in Chapter 1, the OO paradigm provides a mechanism, called **overloading,** to make this possible. The Java language allows overloading of methods–several methods have the same name, but are different in argument types and number of arguments.

Coming back to the **magnify** API example, let's explore an alternative way of implementing it. Magnification can also be done by prescribing a rectangle over the image. If we follow this mechanism, then the **magnify** API would need the dimension and location of the rectangle. This means that a **Rectangle** object itself can be passed as the parameter. Do we then need the magnification factor? Not if the magnified image is expected to fit the screen or window exactly. So our new version of the **magnify** API would then be:

```
magnify(Rectangle magRect)
```

Suppose that the magnification weren't tied to the size of the window or screen. Then the API would be:

```
magnify(double magFactor, Rectangle magRect)
```

The rectangle input is well suited in applications where a user draws a rectangle over the image to zoom the portion of the image enclosed by that rectangle.

Multiple Constructors

Constructors are often overloaded. This provides the class library's users with a lot of flexibility in instantiating an object at any stage with the information available at that time. The following example will illustrate this point.

The **ScreenImage** class stores information about a loaded image, including its pixel values. As we know, image loading in Java is asynchronous. The image parameters may not all be available when the **ScreenImage** object is constructed. One solution to this problem is to defer the construction until all the image parameters are available. Since some image operations do not require all the parameters, deferring the **ScreenImage** construction will delay these operations. For example, an image can be drawn without grabbing its pixels values explicitly. If we wait until the pixels have been grabbed, we will be postponing the image drawing operation. The alternative is to design multiple constructors.

In the code below, there are three constructors. The appropriate constructors can be invoked depending on the loading status. Once constructed, the remaining parameters can be set using the set methods, as and when the parameters are available.

```java
public class  ScreenImage extends Object{
    static public final int ERROR = -1;
    static public final int EMPTY = 0;
    static public final int FETCHED = 2;
    static public final int HT_WID_KNOWN = 4;
    static public final int PIXELS_AVAILABLE = 8;

    // Image object
    public Image image;
    // Width and height of the image
    public int width, height;
    // Original pixels of the image
    public int origPixels[];
    // Image load status mask. It is EMPTY initially.
    public int loadStatus = EMPTY;
    // Color model of the image
    public ColorModel cm;

    // Constructor when image is fetched
    public ScreenImage(Image im){
        image = im;
        loadStatus |= FETCHED;
    }

    // Constructor when image is fetched and height and width are known
    public ScreenImage(Image img, int wid, int ht){
        image = img;
        width = wid;
        height = ht;
        loadStatus |= (FETCHED | HT_WID_KNOWN);
    }

    // Constructor when all parameters are available.
    public ScreenImage(Image im, int rwIm[], int wd, int ht,
                    ColorModel colmod){
        image = img;
        width = wid;
        height = ht;
        origPixels = rwIm;
        cm = colMod;
        loadStatus |= (FETCHED | HT_WID_KNOWN| PIXELS_AVAILABLE);
    }

    // Other methods which include the methods to set various parameters.

}
```

Multiple constructors may provide flexibility to the application developer, but they increase the code size. A large number of constructors are not desirable for this reason. In addition, they clutter the API space.

Multithreading Issues

Multithreading is an important factor in the API design. If API methods or variables are expected to be used by more than one thread at a time, a proper synchronization mechanism will have to be defined. In such cases, API designers will have to identify the potential critical regions. A method that forms a critical region can be specified as a **synchronized** method. This will allow only one thread to execute such a method at any time. If a variable is prone to modification by multiple threads, then the corresponding block of code will have to reside in a **synchronized** method. A method that implements proper synchronization will use the **wait()** and **notify()** methods. Further details on synchronization can be found in Chapter 5.

When designing a method, one consideration is the performance of synchronized methods. A synchronized method is considerably (in the current implementation, six times) slower than the corresponding non-synchronized method. For this reason, unnecessary use of **synchronized** construct should be avoided. If performance is the major criterion for the design, API designers should focus on specifying fewer **synchronized** methods.

Designing Asynchronous Methods

Asynchronous methods take advantage of Java's multithreading. An asynchronous method does not perform its action immediately. It only makes a request to the system, and is actually performed when the system finds it convenient to run that task. In other words, a separate thread will execute the body of that method. An observer class is essential, if synchronization is required. The observer class can monitor the progress of the execution through a callback method, which can be invoked by the called object at regular intervals. The Abstract Window Toolkit has several asynchronous methods. These include **getWidth**, **getHeight**, **drawImage**, and so on. The **imageUpdate** method, in the **ImageObserver** interface, keeps track of the image operations.

A class library can also have asynchronous methods. If a task takes a long time to finish calling it with a synchronous method will tie up the CPU for that duration. The task could be waiting for something–say some resource over the network. A lot of CPU cycles may be wasted while waiting. With an asynchronous method working in a separate thread, though, the CPU will be available for other tasks. For example, **computeHistogram** will compute the histogram from an array. If the array is large, it will take a long time to return the result.

The synchronous implementation could be as shown:

```
public class ImageUtility {

    // Other methods
    public Histogram ComputeHistogram(int values[]){
        Histogram histo;
        //Code to compute histogam...
        return histo;
    }

    //Other methods
}
```

The corresponding asynchronous method (which would spawn a thread) is shown below:

```
public boolean computeHistogram(int values[], Histogram histo,
                                HistogramObserver observer){

   // Code to compute histogram

}
```

HistogramObserver can then be an interface with one method:

```
histoUpdate(int percentComplete)
```

histoUpdate is a callback method which will be called by the **ImageUtil** object at regular intervals in the application code,

```
if(!(aImageUtil.computeHistogram(pixels, histo,  this)) {
   histoUpdate = true;
   percentComplete = 0;
}
else percentComplete = 100;

public void histoUpdate(int percent){
   percentComplete = percent;
}
```

histoUpdate can be used for monitoring the histogram computation.

Callbacks

This is a good moment to look at callback mechanisms, in which a client object registers to receive a service from a service provider object, which in turn renders the requested service at a later point by 'calling back' the client object. With the callback mechanism, client objects can proceed with their other tasks while waiting for service. Callbacks thus enable asynchronous operation.

Although the callback mechanism can be used in any context, it's generally identified with event-handling. In event-handling callback, a client object initially registers itself with the event-handling object and when the desired event occurs, the event handler invokes an appropriate method in the client object.

We'll now look at how the callback mechanism can be implemented in Java. Let's start with an obvious approach in which the service provider class defines an instance variable whose data type is client class itself. This instance variable is set when the client object is directly passed as the parameter.

The example below illustrates this approach. For simplicity sake, we won't show the callback from an event-handling method. The **main()** routine creates the **ServiceProvider** and the **Client** objects. The **Client** object registers with the **ServiceProvider** object during the construction of the **Client** object. The main routine triggers the callback by invoking the **notifyClient()** method. In actual applications, an event handler method invokes this callback method.

```
import java.io.*;

   // The main routine that creates Client and ServiceProvider
   // objects and simulates callback
```

```java
public class DirectCallback{
    static public void main(String args[]){
        ServiceProvider sp = new ServiceProvider();
        Client ClientObj = new Client(sp);
        String str = new String(Long.toString(System.currentTimeMillis()));
        //Perform a callback
        sp.notifyClient(str);
    }
}
```

```java
    // Provides service to the registered client.
    // In this example, only one client can register with the
    // ServiceProvider.
```

```java
class ServiceProvider{
    Client clientObj;

    public void registerForCallback(Client client){
        clientObj = client;
    }

    public void notifyClient(String str){
        if(clientObj != null) clientObj.performCallback(str);
    }
}
```

```java
    // An example client class.
```

```java
class Client{
    ServiceProvider server;

    public Client(ServiceProvider sp){
        server = sp;
        registerCallback();
    }

    public void registerCallback(){
        server.registerForCallback(this);
    }

    public void performCallback(String str){
        System.out.println("Time stamp " + str);
    }
}
```

The above approach works very well as long as the type of the callback object doesn't need to be changed at run time. If such a change is required, one option would be to have a number of instance variables, each representing a different client class. A drawback with this option is that the service provider object needs to know all the client classes that require its service. In other words, all the actual client classes have to be present for compiling the **ServiceProvider** class. When a client class is to be compiled separately and loaded dynamically, we can't use this callback mechanism.

The direct callback approach often results in a circular dependency. As can be seen from the above example, the **ServiceProvider** class needs the **Client** class to compile and the **Client** class needs the **ServiceProvider** class to compile. Circular dependency does pose a problem for some compilers.

Using interface

In light of the above discussion, what is desirable is a mechanism that de-couples the **Client** and the **ServiceProvider** classes, and allows the changing of callback object data type during run time. Such a mechanism can be implemented in Java through the use of **interface**. In this scheme, an interface, say **Callback**, specifies the callback methods and the client classes implement those methods. In the **ServiceProvider** class, the callback instance variable will be of the type **Callback**. This instance variable can be set to any of the classes that implement the **Callback** interface.

In the example below, the **Callback** interface has just one method, **performCallback()**. There are two client classes, **ClientOne** and **ClientTwo**, which implement the **Callback** interface. In the **ServiceProvider** class, notice the data type **ClientObj** which is of type **Callback**. An object that implements the **Callback** interface can be assigned to **ClientObj**.

The **main()** routine creates the **Client1** object first and then triggers a callback. It then creates **Client2** and triggers its callback. This illustrates that two different types of classes which implement the same callback interface can be registered with the **ServiceProvider** class.

```java
import java.io.*;

public class UsingInterface{
    static public void main(String args[]){
        ServiceProvider sp = new ServiceProvider();

        ClientOne Client1 = new ClientOne(sp);
        // Simulate callback
        String str = new String(Long.toString(System.currentTimeMillis()));
        sp.notifyClient(str);

        ClientTwo Client2 =  new ClientTwo(sp);
        str = new String(Long.toString(System.currentTimeMillis()));
        sp.notifyClient(str);
    }
}


    // Provides an interface for performing callbacks.

interface Callback{
    public void performCallback(String str);
}

class ServiceProvider{

    //Notice that the ClientObj is of type Callback
    Callback ClientObj;

    public void registerForCallback(Callback client){
        ClientObj  = client;
    }

    public void notifyClient(String str){
        ClientObj.performCallback(str);
    }
}
```

```
class ClientOne implements Callback{
    ServiceProvider server;

    public ClientOne(ServiceProvider sp){
        server =sp;
        registerCallback();
    }

    public void registerCallback(){
        server.registerForCallback(this);
    }

    public void performCallback(String str){
        System.out.println("Client One "+ str);
    }
}
```

```
class ClientTwo implements Callback{
    ServiceProvider server;

    public ClientTwo(ServiceProvider sp){
        server =sp;
        registerCallback();
    }

    public void registerCallback(){
        server.registerForCallback(this);
    }

    public void performCallback(String str){
        System.out.println("Client Two " + str);
    }
}
```

What did we achieve here by using interfaces? The first gain is that the **ServiceProvider** class can be compiled without the presence of any client classes. It needs only the **Callback** interface. Furthermore, the creation of new client classes will not need the recompilation of the **ServiceProvider** class. The second gain is that any class that implements the **Callback** interface can be passed as an argument to the **registerForCallback()** method. This will enable any client object that implements the **Callback** interface to be set as the callback object at run time.

Multiple Callbacks

In the above example, only one callback is allowed at a time. Often, this may not be the case. When an event occurs, the service provider may have to render services to a number of clients. In order to accomplish this, the service provider will have to maintain a collection of registered clients. If a client is not interested in receiving a service, it has to remove itself from this collection.

In the example below, the **ServiceProvider** class maintains the registered client list by using the **Vector** class. When a client registers, it's added to the client callback list, and when it 'unregisters', it's removed from that list.

The **main()** routine simulates event generation by generating some sample events and delivering them to the service provider. In actual applications, the service provider class can be a subclass of an AWT component, such as **Canvas**, **Panel**, **Frame**, and so on. In that case, it will receive events directly from the system through the **handleEvent()** or other event handling methods.

```
import java.io.*;
import java.util.*;
import java.awt.*;
```

```java
public class MultipleCallbacks{
    // The main routine that creates all the
    // objects and simulates events
    static public void main(String args[]){
        //Create all the objects
        ServiceProvider sp = new ServiceProvider();
        ClientOne client1 = new ClientOne(sp);
        ClientTwo client2 = new ClientTwo(sp);

        //Create your own event
        int eventCount =0;
        Event e = new Event((new String("Event "+
                            Integer.toString(eventCount))),
                            eventCount++,
                            Long.toString(System.currentTimeMillis()));
        // Deliver event
        sp.handleEvent(e);

        // Simulate the next event
        e = new Event((new String("Event "+ Integer.toString(eventCount))),
                    eventCount++,
                    Long.toString(System.currentTimeMillis()));
        sp.handleEvent(e);

        client2.unregisterCallback();

        //Simulate the next event
        e = new Event((new String("Event "+ Integer.toString(eventCount))),
                    eventCount++,
                    Long.toString(System.currentTimeMillis()));
        sp.handleEvent(e);
    }
}
```

```java
    // The callback interface. This has just one method.
    // In real-life it can have more.
```

```java
interface Callback{
    public void performCallback(String str);
}
```

```java
public class ServiceProvider{
    Vector clientObjs = new Vector();

    // Client registers itself for callback
    public void registerForCallback(Callback client){
        clientObjs.addElement(client);
    }

    // Client removes itself from callback
    public void unregisterCallback(Callback client){
        clientObjs.removeElement(client);
    }
```

```
    // Notify the client objects
    public void notifyClient(String str){
        for (Enumeration e = clientObjs.elements(); e.hasMoreElements();) {
            ((Callback)(e.nextElement())).performCallback(str);
        }
    }

    // A simulated handleEvent method
    public boolean handleEvent(Event e){
        //Creates a string from the event
        String str = new String((String)(e.target) + " Time stamp "
                                +(String)(e.arg));
        //sends it to registered clients
        notifyClient(str);
        return true;
    }
}
```

```
    // Example Client Classes
```

```
public class ClientOne implements Callback{
    ServiceProvider server;

    public ClientOne(ServiceProvider sp){
        server =sp;
        registerCallback();
    }

    public void registerCallback(){
        server.registerForCallback(this);
    }

    public void unregisterCallback(){
        server.unregisterCallback(this);
    }

    public void performCallback(String str){
        System.out.println("Client One "+ str);
    }
}
```

```
public class ClientTwo implements Callback{
    ServiceProvider server;

    public ClientTwo(ServiceProvider sp){
        server =sp;
        registerCallback();
    }

    public void registerCallback(){
        server.registerForCallback(this);
    }

    public void unregisterCallback(){
        server.unregisterCallback(this);
    }
```

```
        public void performCallback(String str){
            System.out.println("Client Two " + str);
        }
    }
```

Shapes API

In the shapes example, **draw** and **drawInteractive** are the behaviors which can be mapped to corresponding APIs. The **draw** method can have two arguments: the shape's points and the graphics context in which to draw the shape:

```
draw(int shapePoints[], Graphics g)
```

But, in the shapes model, points of the shapes are saved by the shape object. Therefore, the **draw** method doesn't need the shape point arguments, and we'll have the following APIs:

▲ **draw(Graphics g)**–draws a shape permanently. Computes new shape points and draws the shape.

▲ **drawInteractive(Graphics g)**–the graphics context is provided by the caller. This method will use the **startPosition** and the **curPosition** to compute the shape points.

The **Drawable** interface will have all the constants and the method APIs as shown below:

```
public interface Drawable{
    public static final int NONE=0;
    public static final int BOX=1;
    public static final int ELLIPSE=2;
    public static final int ARROW=3;
    public abstract void init(int x, int y);
    public abstract void setCurPos(int x , int y);
    public abstract void drawInteractive(Graphics g);
    public abstract void draw(Graphics g);
    public abstract Shape saveCurShape(Graphics g, int shCnt);
}
```

Now that the shapes APIs have been defined, we can see how these APIs can be used in an application:

```
    Drawable curShape;
    int shType;

    shType = Drawable.BOX;
    curShape =  createShape(shType);
```

A typical sequence to draw a shape interactively using the API calls would be:

```
    curShape.init(x,y);
    setCurPos(x,y);
    drawInteractve(Graphics g);
```

The **drawInteractive** API makes use of **startPos** and **curPos**. If it's called before setting these variables, no shape is drawn because the default values of **startPos** and **curPos** can be set to 0,0. Why not add the current position argument to the **drawInteractive** API? The reason is that the **drawInteractive** method is normally expected to be called from a **paint** or **update** method. The current position will be typically generated from an event. If the current position argument is added, then the user will have to save the current position.

Extending Functionality

It's impossible for a class library to cover all the functionality desired by the users. But the classes and interfaces can be extended by applications to introduce a new functionality.

Let's deal with the shapes example again. Suppose the users need the ability to move shapes; we can create a new interface extending the **Drawable** method to **Movable**.

Firstly, we extend the **Drawable** interface:

```
public interface Movable extends Drawable {
    public void move(Graphics g, Point displacement);
}
```

We then implement that new method in an **MovingBox** class that is derived from **Box**:

```
public class MovingBox extends Box implements Movable {
    public void move(Graphics g, Point displacement){

        // The actual code here

    }
}
```

MovingEllipse and **MovingArrow** can be implemented similarly.

How can we select the shapes now? The **ShapeProducer** will return the **Box** object if **BOX** is selected. Remember, **ShapeProducer** is an interface, so an application must implement that interface.

```
class shapeCreator implements ShapeProducer {
    public void  createShape (int shapeType){
        switch(shapeType){
            case Drawable.BOX:
                return(new MovableBox());
            case Drawable.ELLIPSE:
                return(new MovableEllipse());
            case Drawable.ARROW:
                return(new MovableArrow());
            default:
                return null;
        }
    }
}
```

In order to extend a functionality, it's necessary for the user to know the classes and methods that are extensible. So, this information also forms a part of the API. In Java, a class or method can be declared as **final** to prevent users extending that class or method. Declaring a class or method **final** will help enhance its performance. The compiler won't need to make any provisions for checking method overrides when the method is run, and the code will consequently be smaller. The compiler will also inline the method code if compiled with optimizer switch **-O**. This may increase the size, but improves the performance. The designers should decide, with suitable reticence, which classes and methods can be declared as **final**, if they think there is no chance of them being extended.

A class library will not remain the same over time. User feedback will prompt the developers to add, delete, or modify classes. But this change shouldn't affect existing applications. The API should therefore be designed in such a way that they are extensible. Since extensibility is one of the virtues of the OO paradigm itself, making a Java class library extensible is not very hard. An API designer has to anticipate the future use of the class library and make appropriate provisions in their design.

Library Design

The previous section dealt with the design of interfaces to the class library. The current section, library design, deals with the design of the actual class library. This design has to conform to the API specifications. The library design will involve the following two steps:

▲ Class design

▲ Package design

Class Design

It's clear from the shapes example that **Drawable, ShapeProducer, Box, Ellipse, Arrow** and their methods are all that a user needs to know about the shapes class library. The user isn't aware that there may be a super class of all shapes called **Shape**. By designing interfaces in such a way that the class design is hidden from the users, class developers can delay the class design or modify the design at a later date. With APIs fixed, designers can choose a design that takes into consideration issues of performance, memory use, class numbers, code size, and so on.

Shape Classes

Object-oriented design can be implemented in several different ways. Note, though, that each of the **Box**, **Ellipse**, and **Arrow** classes can implement the **Drawable** interface. Do we then need a superclass? Yes, a super class is convenient and fits into the OO design framework. The common instance variable such as **startPosition, curPosition, drawingColor** can be part of the superclass. From the set methods, we can see that **setCurPos** can be common to all the classes. The drawback of having a superclass is that the shape classes can't extend another shape class, say **Box** extending **Rectangle**.

One of main criteria in designing the library is extensibility. Once a class library is being used, the **change requests** from users will start pouring in. This often leads to modified or new class methods. Occasionally, it may even result in design changes.

> As we have repeatedly pointed out in previous sections, changing the class library API isn't acceptable. What is acceptable is changing the design and implementation without affecting the existing APIs.

We need, therefore, to see whether our shapes design is extensible. We'll use the example of adding move functionality again here. Our aim is not to change the **Drawable** and **ShapeProducer** interfaces, so that existing applications needn't be modified. For those applications which need the move functionality, the interface **Movable** can be defined as in the previous section. Is there a need to define the new classes, **MovableBox, MovableEllipse**, and **MovableArrow**? The answer is no. This is because the **Box, Ellipse**, and **Arrow** class can all be modified to implement **Movable**.

```
public class Box implements Movable{
    public class move(Graphics g, Point displacement){
        // Appropriate code
    }
}
```

Since we didn't change the names of the classes, **ShapeProducer** will remain the same. The applications that use only **Drawable** will work since **Movable** inherits **Drawable**.

Suppose we need to add two more features:

▲ Filling **Box** and **Ellipse** with a given color.

▲ Adding the new shape itself.

Let's discuss how we can add the fill functionality to the class library. Adding the fill method to **Drawable** will not be appropriate, because **Arrow** can't be filled. So, we will define a new interface called **Fillable** which can be an extension of **Movable**.

The **Fillable** API can be defined as:

```
public interface Fillable extends Drawable {
    abstract public void fill(Graphics g, Color g);
}
```

Fillable can be implemented by **Box** and **Ellipse**. The **Box** code is shown below:

```
public class Box implements Fillable{
    public class fill(Graphics g, Color clr){
        // Appropriate code
    }
}
```

The existing applications will work without a problem. If we need to use **fill** in an application, though, there's a problem. The application user is expected to draw all the three shapes, but fill only **Box** and **Ellipse**. **curShape** can't be of type **Fillable**, because the **Arrow** does not implement **Fillable**. How can we make **curShape** execute **fill**? The answer lies in the Java casting mechanism, which enables **curShape** to be cast to **Fillable** interface.

Here's how it's done in the application code:

```
if((curShape instanceof Box) || (curShape instanceof Ellipse)){
    ((Fillable)curShape).fill(offScrGc, Color.white);
}
```

> *Note that you could also create a **canFill()** method to determine which shapes are candidates for the **fill** method.*

Let's now discuss adding a new shape. In the shapes library, suppose it's required to add the ability to draw text. Text isn't really a shape, but it may behave like a shape in many aspects. The text shape is created by sending the individual character. We need an API to set the current character, which can be appended to the string that is being constructed.

We can, therefore, extend the **Drawable** interface to **Typeable**.

```
public interface Typeable extends Drawable{
   public void setCurChar(int key);
}
```

We can call the text shape as **AnnoText** (annotation text), defined in the following way:

```
public class AnnoText implements Typeable{
   protected char curChar;
   // All the Drawable methods
   public void setCurChar(int charKey){
      curChar = key;
   }
}
```

curShape can remain the same. The following code has to be added to the application code to extend the current shape drawing to text as well:

```
// Code to detect the Key press
...
// Enable the Key Press event and obtain the current key pressed.
...
// This is the only code we need to add from the shapes point of view.

if((curShape instanceof AnnoText)){
   ((Typable)curShape).setCurChar(key);
}
```

As new functionality becomes available, the implementation and design need to be changed.

The following figure shows the shapes design with extended functionality.

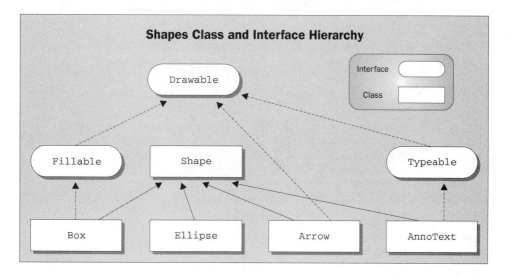

Package Design

As we already know, class libraries are a collection of packages. Packages aren't program units, i.e., they don't produce executables. Packages aren't a part of the OO design or implementation. But they do provide a mechanism to bundle classes into a library, and they are what the end-user will see. So part of any good class library design should be the creation of a complete and consistent package.

Visibility and the grouping of classes along functional lines are the main factors that determine the organization of a package hierarchy. Organizing packages as a hierarchical tree makes the delivery of class libraries easy.

Creating a package tree reduces cluttering, hides the detail of the package and provides a neat way for interaction between packages. This is significant when several teams are working on separate portions of a large and complex library. The teams may then use each other's packages.

Designing the package tree is therefore an important aspect of a class library design. A lot of attention needs to be paid to the naming of packages. The name has to reflect the functionality a package provides. The design of a package should focus on:

- Grouping of classes
- Granularity of the package
- Where it fits in package hierarchy

As mentioned before, a package is a functional grouping of classes. If the functional grouping results in too many classes, it becomes unmanageable. In such cases, the related functionality can be further divided and bundled in sub-packages. Creating sub-packages will not result in any apparent advantages or disadvantages as far as the visibility goes. A sub-package is always visible from the root of the package hierarchy.

Summary

In this chapter, we've looked at the following issues:

- The underlying model needed to design a large and complex class library

- How the application user's requirements are converted to requirements of the application writer.

- How the application writer's requirements are translated into APIs.

- Interfaces are preferable to abstract classes for implementing a higher level of abstraction.

- The data access mechanism should be through set and get methods.

- There can be trade-offs in choosing method arguments.

- If a method is expected to take a long time to execute, provide for asynchronous design.

- Actual library design involves two steps—class design and package design.

- Classes are designed to conform to API specifications.

- Class libraries are wrapped in packages which are organized as a hierarchical tree.

In the next chapter we'll look at what we should consider when implementing a class library. We'll also look briefly at the applet and application that are included in this book's source code and which make use of the **shapes** library.

Implementing a Framework

In the last chapter, we discussed the intricacies of class library design in Java. Our emphasis then was on how to go about creating a class library and how to start on the API and class designs. The result was the **shapes** library, with which we can draw various shapes.

Now we need to look at the issues of implementation, first generally and then practically, using another class library, **viewport**. The design and implementation details are covered for this library, this time from the point of view of implementing an efficient and useful class library.

In order to see these two class libraries in action, the final part of the chapter introduces an applet and application, both having the same look and essential behavior. These show off the features of **shapes** and **viewport** to good effect.

> This chapter complements the last. The full source code for both is available from the Wrox web site: `http://www.wrox.com.`

Implementation normally follows the design phase, though sometimes you may start implementing a prototype before the design of a class library is complete. A prototype certainly tries out unproven concepts or architectures. However, whether it is a prototype or a real product, there are a number of steps involved in constructing a class library.

Constructing a Class Library

Construction of a class library may involve the following general steps:

- Coding
- Packaging
- Compilation
- Documentation
- Archiving

We'll discuss the above topics and some related issues—reliability and testing, and the type of Java programs (applets or applications) that will use the library.

Coding

The coding phase involves writing programs to implement the class library design. Ideally, implementation needs to be optimized with respect to execution speed, memory, code size and maintainability. In practice, though, this isn't possible. You will have to make trade-offs depending on the targeted applications, for example, you may decide to use more memory in order to achieve better speed.

Memory

One of the greatest advantages of Java is its platform independence. A class library is expected to run on a wide variety of hardware and software platforms. But availability of primary memory varies widely with machines and platforms. This poses problems for class library developers as no assumptions can be made about the memory availability. An implementation that is adaptable to wide variations in memory is certainly desirable. An easy solution would be to assume a minimum memory configuration and design the data structures accordingly. This would slow down the execution, however, as more processing would be needed to compensate for the lower memory use. The other solution would be to get information about the underlying architecture using methods of the **System** class. A list of all the properties can be obtained by the **getProperties()** method. Once a property name is known, then the corresponding property value can be obtained by the **getProperty()** method. The method below illustrates how the property names and its values can be printed out:

```
public void getPlatformDetails(){
    Properties prop = System.getProperties();
    Enumeration en= prop.propertyNames();
    //Lists all the property names
    for(int i=0; en.hasMoreElements();i++){
        String next = (String)en.nextElement();
        System.out.println(i+ " "+ next+ " "+ prop.getProperty(next));
    }
    // A property can also be obtained by using System class.
    // An example that gets the underlying architecture.
    System.out.println("The architecture is " System.getProperty("os.arch"));
}
```

It's also possible to obtain information about the amount of free memory available at run time. First, though, we'll discuss garbage collection.

Garbage Collection

We had a brief look at garbage collection back in Chapter 1. As you already know, memory can't be explicitly deallocated in Java as in languages like C and C++; Java employs an automatic memory reclamation mechanism known as **garbage collection** to free unusable memory. Automatic garbage collection makes programming simpler and reduces the risk of introducing memory management defects, but it also poses some problems. Since a low priority thread performs garbage collection at run time, memory reclamation may not catch up with the memory use in some memory intensive applications. Although, there may not be a perfect solution to this problem, we can expedite memory reclamation.

*Sun are still investigating their garbage collection strategy. The current implementation actually has two parts, a 'run **now** because there is none or very little memory free' and the 'low priority collection thread'.*

Here are some tips:

▲ Set objects to **NULL** when they become unusable. This tells the garbage collector to sweep that object. Setting an object to **NULL** reduces a pointer to that object. When an object has no more pointers, that object is marked for garbage collection.

▲ When an object is no longer needed, perform cleanup explicitly. Some of the techniques mentioned in the section on cleanup below may indirectly result in memory reclamation. A good example is the cleanup of an image object by the **flush()** method.

Forced Garbage Collection

Garbage collection can also be forced by using methods in the **System** and **Runtime** classes:

▲ **System.gc()** method forces garbage collection.

▲ **System.runFinalization()** will run **finalize()** methods in objects that are no longer used.

Both the above methods call the corresponding methods in the **Runtime** class. They can be useful in avoiding an unlimited use of memory on operating systems like UNIX where the size of the process isn't limited by the main memory.

The **Runtime** class also provides a number of methods to extract information about the underlying architecture. The **freeMemory()** method returns the amount of memory available for use. Similarly, the **totalMemory()** returns the amount of memory available to the Java interpreter. Note, though, that these methods may not provide accurate information on some platforms.

The utility method shown below performs garbage collection and returns the amount of free memory. It first checks the total memory available to the Java application or applet. It also obtains the free memory available for use before and after garbage collection. The application writer can make use of this information to define data structures. We used this information to compute how many images of size (256x256) can fit in. Although this is rather an optimistic number, it does provide some basis for defining data structures.

```
public long runGc(){
    Runtime rt = Runtime.getRuntime();
    long mem = rt.totalMemory();
    System.out.println("Total memory is "+ mem + "  bytes");
    mem = rt.freeMemory();
    System.out.println("Before garbage collection "+ mem +
                        " bytes are free");
    System.gc();
    mem = rt.freeMemory();
    System.out.println("After garbage collection " + mem +
                        " bytes are free");
    int numImages = (int)(mem/(256*256));
    System.out.println(numImages + " can be cached");
    return mem;
}
```

A note of caution: the `freeMemory` method currently doesn't return accurate information on some platforms. The above method should therefore be used as a debugging help and not in the actual class library.

Speed

One of the complaints about Java (JIT execution environments aside) is that it is slow. This is especially noticeable in number crunching operations. Here are some tips which may help improve performance:

- ▲ Declare classes and methods as **final**, if there is no chance of them being overridden.

- ▲ Declare local methods as **private** and **final**.

- ▲ Use simple data structures where speed matters. Using built-in data structures such as **Vector**, **Stack**, **Hashtable**, etc. may simplify programming, but will affect performance.

- ▲ Have fewer classes. As linking takes place at run time, having fewer classes will make increase the program's speed.

- ▲ Use the optimizer **-O** switch while using the JDK compiler. Be aware, though, that the best optimization is almost always done at a higher level, such as in the choice of algorithms. Producing 'clever' code to shave a few percent off execution time can produce a maintenance nightmare. Be warned that premature optimization is therefore not recommended.

- ▲ Clean up explicitly. As an example, killing an unnecessary thread will save some CPU cycles. Refer to the section on cleanup below for more details.

*JIT execution environments normally compile a class the first time it is called, and then 'cache' the compiled code in case it's needed again. Note this is **not** the same as distributing an executable, as the class is still all Java bytecode when execution commences. The effect of JITs is dramatic, and a claim of 10x JDK is not unjustified for the execution of most programs.*

Code Size

As Java is used extensively in Internet related applications, code size is an important issue.

When code size matters, consider the following:

- ▲ Remove all the debugging information before a class library is shipped.

- ▲ Only use exceptions where necessary. Although exceptions are an elegant way to handle and report errors, they increase the code size. Traditional error handling, i.e. returning a value from the method, is often sufficient to handle errors and exceptions.

- ▲ Have fewer classes and methods. Although, this may not be good programming practice, consolidating classes and methods will reduce the overhead.

Here are some other issues that may help in implementation.

Cleanup

When an object is no longer needed, it should be cleaned up before it's ready for garbage collection. Although there are no destructors, the **Object** class provides the **finalize()** method to the perform cleanup tasks such as closing open files and network connections. This method is called by the system before the garbage collector sweeps the object. Classes that use system resources should override the **finalize()** method.

Some classes explicitly provide methods to free up resources. Here's a list of such classes:

- The **Graphics** class has the **dispose()** method. When a **Graphics** object that was created explicitly is no longer required, it can be disposed of using the **dispose()** method.

- The **Frame** class also has the **dispose()** method and it's important to execute this method when a **Frame** is no longer needed. A **Frame** object can be made invisible by executing its **hide()** method. If **dispose()** isn't executed, several 'hidden' **Frame** objects may exist, of which the users may not be aware.

- The **Image** class has a **flush()** method which releases all resources. These include pixel data cached for rendering purposes.

Threads also consume resources. If a thread is no longer needed, it should be killed explicitly. The code shown below kills a live thread.

```
if(aThread != null){
    if(aThread.isAlive()){
        aThread.stop();
    }
}
```

Visibility

A **public** variable or method is accessible to programs outside the package. Methods and variables should not be declared as **public** unless they are part of the API.

A protected variable is both accessible to other classes within the package and to its subclasses anywhere. If you are not sure of the usage of a variable or method, it's safer to declare it as **protected**.

Distributing Functionality

When APIs are defined, functionality is distributed on class and method levels. However, a method that implements an API may be large. In such cases, it's advisable to break the functionality into a number of manageable methods. These methods may be used by other APIs as well. For example, the **setPolygonVertices** method in the **Box** class is used by several APIs. Having a number of private methods may not affect performance, since the **private** and **final** methods can be in-lined with the **javac** compiler's **-O** option.

Robust Coding

The class library coding needs to be robust since application writers will not be able to debug it. The library designer needs to anticipate failures and add adequate protection by using error and exception handling code. In addition, the following defensive programming tips may help:

Check for validity of the arguments wherever appropriate. An argument may be out of range or **NULL**. Checking all pre-conditions, such as valid parameters, is essential in an API method.

 Inside a method, check for **NULL** objects or use appropriate exceptions when objects are instantiated or returned through a method call. There may be several reasons why an object does not get created. Inadequate memory is one of them. Users need to know immediately when an object isn't instantiated or created.

Packaging

We discussed creating packages in Chapter 3. Here we'll look at creating subpackages. A common mistake in defining the subpackages is that the parent package name isn't included in the subpackage declaration, as shown below.

```
package packageTwo;
public class classTwo{
   ...
```

If **packageOne** uses **packageTwo**, then in **packageOne** you need:

```
import packageTwo.*;
```

If the **packageTwo** file is placed in a directory under **packageOne** and **packageOne** is compiled, there will not be any compile time errors. Based on the package declarations, the compiler treats **packageOne** and **packageTwo** as siblings. This would generate a compile time error because **packageTwo** isn't at the same directory level as **packageOne**, *except* that the **CLASSPATH** is set to the current directory (**packageOne**) and the compiler looks in the current directory and finds **packageTwo**.

The error will be caught, though, at run time as a **classDefNotFound Error : packageOne/ classTwo.class** exception whenever the program tries to access the **classTwo** class.

The correct way to define **packageTwo**, as a sub-package of **packageOne**, is given below.

```
package packageOne.packageTwo;
public class classTwo{
   ...
```

In **packageOne**, the sub-package **packageTwo** can be imported like this:

```
import packageOne.packageTwo.*;
```

Documentation

An important part of a class library is the documents that are published with it. Class library documentation typically consists of the following:

 Overview of the class library. This document is essential when a class library is large and complex or when implementing a novel idea. It may include the underlying concept, design approach and a overall view of the class library organization.

▲ **API manual.** Typically, this document is published before the class library implementation. It's very useful as a reference manual. The document needs to be accurate and complete in all respects. The explanation for class/interface APIs may include their purpose and an example of how they are used. In case of methods, the documentation should describe what they are doing, and also give a description of their arguments, limitations, etc. If a reference type (e.g. objects, arrays) is passed, then the responsibility for the memory allocation should be clearly specified.

▲ **Application writers manual.** This could include a step by step approach to building applications. Sample applications and tips and tricks can be a part of this document. It can also include a list of known defects and workarounds–it is unrealistic to expect a large class library to be defect free. If a defect is known and a workaround exists, users need to be informed about this fact.

Using javadoc - The Java Documentation Generator

In Java, API documents can be automatically generated from comments in the source code. The document generator extracts comments from only the public and protected variables, methods and classes.

Comment Syntax

As you know, a comment block is defined by **/**** and ***/**. Anything within the block is ignored by the compiler. However, the document generator **javadoc** understands some special prefixes such as **@** and **#**. It can also parse some HTML tags such as **<PRE>** and **<TT>**.

Some of the useful **@** commands are:

▲ **param**–method parameters.

▲ **return**–return value.

▲ **exception**–exception.

▲ **see**–cross reference. It can be followed by a **#** command to indicate the cross referenced API or document.

The example below shows the use of the **javadoc** features mentioned above. This example is taken from the **Shapes** library.

```
/*
 * @(#) Box.java 1.0 96/07/24 Larry Rodrigues
 *
 */

package shapes;
import java.awt.*;
import java.lang.Math;

/** Box Class.
 * @version 1.0   24   July 1996
 * @author Larry Rodrigues
 * Although, the Box shape is a rectangle, it is drawn as a polygon
 * in this implementation. The drawing of a rectangle requires the
 * upper left hand corner coordinates as the starting position.
 * So the drawRect will draw the rectangle from
```

```
 * top to bottom and left to right. If the current position
 * moves up or right with respect to the starting position,
 * the rectangle will not be drawn because the width and height
 * values become negative. So there are two options.
 * 1. Switch the starting and current positions whenever
 * the rectangle is drawn from bottom to top or right to left.
 * 2. Use the drawPolygon method.
 * We chose the second option.
 **/
public class Box extends Shape implements Fillable{

    /**
     * xp the x coordinates of the Box corners
     */
    protected int xp[] = new int[5];

    /**
     * yp the y coordinates of the Box corners
     */
    protected int yp[] = new int[5];

    /**
     * Initializes the Box parameters.
     * The arguments provide the starting point of the box
     * which may be the upper left hand corner or lower right hand
     * corner coordinates of the Box.
     * @param  x   the x coordinate of the starting position
     * @param  y   the y coordinate of the starting poistion
     **/
    public void init(int x , int y) {
        st.x = x; st.y = y;
        cur.x =x; cur.y =y;
        setPolygonVertices();
    }

    /**
     * Sets the current position.
     * @param  x   the x coordinate of the current position
     * @param  y   the y coordinate of the current poistion
     *
     **/
    public synchronized void setCurPoint(int x , int y) {
        cur.x = x; cur.y = y;
    }

    /**
     * Draws interactively on a Graphics context g.
     * This API does not check whether the Box overflows
     * the borders of the component.
     * This  method uses the XOR paint mode. It erases the
     * previously drawn shape and draws a new shape in its
     * place.
     * @param g the graphics object on which the shape is to  be drawn.
     **/
    public void drawInteractive(Graphics g) {
        g.setColor(Color.black);
        g.setXORMode(drawingColor);
```

```
        g.drawPolygon(xp, yp,5);
        setPolygonVertices();
        g.drawPolygon(xp, yp,5);
    }


    /**
     * Draws on a Graphics context g.
     * This API does not check whether the Box overflows
     * the borders of the component.
     * @param g the graphics object on which the shape is to be drawn
     **/
    public void draw(Graphics g) {
        g.setPaintMode();
        g.setColor(drawingColor);
        setPolygonVertices();
        g.drawPolygon(xp, yp,5);
    }


    /**
     * Draws and returns itself.
     * shCnt is set by tha caller.
     * Returns itself.
     * @param g the graphics object on which the shape is to  be drawn
     * @param shCnt the shape count
     * @return Shape itself
     **/
    public Shape saveCurShape(Graphics g, int shCnt) {
        g.setPaintMode();
        g.setColor(drawingColor);
        setPolygonVertices();
        g.drawPolygon(xp, yp,5);
        shapeCount = shCnt;
        return (Shape)this;
    }


    /**
     * Fills with a given color.
     * @param g the graphics object on which the shape is to  be drawn
     * @param color the filling color.
     **/
    public void fill(Graphics g, Color color){
        g.setPaintMode();
        g.setColor(color);
        g.fillPolygon(xp, yp,5);
    }
}
```

A sample HTML page for the **Box** is shown on the following page.

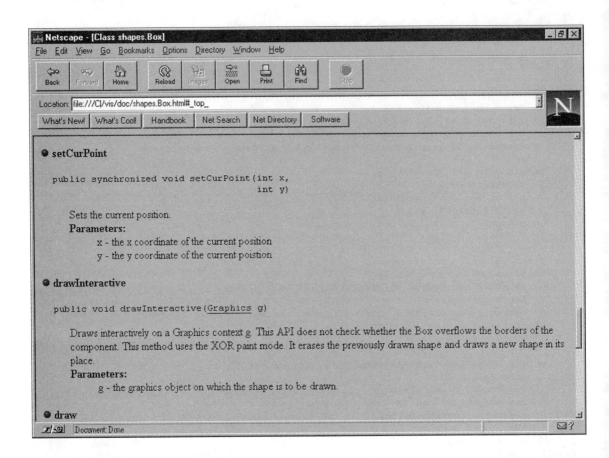

Usage

The **javadoc** command comes in two flavors: it can generate documents for the entire package or for a file. **javadoc** also has three options,

- ▲ **-classpath <new path>**
- ▲ **-d <directory for generated HTML>**
- ▲ **-verbose**

The **-classpath** option, like that of **javac**, will override the current **CLASSPATH**. The **-d** option specifies the target directory in which the generated documents are stored. The **-verbose** option prints out detailed messages during document generation.

As an example,

```
javadoc -d docDir shapes
```

will generate the complete HTML documentation for the **shapes** package and place the document files in the **docDir** directory relative to the **CLASSPATH**.

If more than one package is involved, the package names can be listed on the command line:

```
javadoc -d docDir shapes viewport viewport.util
```

javadoc does not create directories corresponding to the package hierarchy. All the HTML documents are placed under one directory. It does, though, require an **images** subdirectory for the GIF files which are required for any special icons and letters you may want to use. **javadoc** does not automatically create this image directory or load the GIF files. The GIF files we have used are available from the Java API documentation directory.

Compilation

To compile a package, the **CLASSPATH** needs to be set properly. The JDK compiler uses a dependency tree to compile files. In a class library package, it's unlikely that a dependency tree will cover all the files. In the case of a **shapes** library, for example, **javac Shape.java** will produce a **Shape.class** only. If the **Box** class is a subclass of **Shape**, **javac Box.java** will generate **Shape.class** and **Box.class**. The other Java files need to be compiled separately to generate corresponding class files.

During class library development, it's often necessary to compile a package separately. An easy way of compiling a package is by using the wild cards. **javac *.java** will compile all the **java** files. You can use wild card compilation and then remove unnecessary files from the directory.

The JDK compiler has a simple built-in dependency checking mechanism between classes. There is no need to compile an entire package when a few files are changed. However, it does not compile a changed file automatically when that file isn't directly dependent on the file that is being compiled.

Take the following example: **a.java** depends on **b.java** and **b.java** depends on **c.java**. Let's say we modified **c.java**. Now if we compile **a.java**, using **javac a.java**, the **c.java** file won't be compiled automatically. Therefore, it's advisable to compile a file directly whenever that file is modified.

The **javac** compiler comes with a few options.

```
javac -d aDir -O filename.java
```

This will place the class files under **aDir**. If it involves a package hierarchy, **aDir** will be the root of the hierarchy. The **-d** switch will automatically separate the source code and the class files. The **-O** option enables optimization of the class library in terms of performance.

> *Using optimization may actually increase the size of the classes as the **static**, **final** and **private** methods will be compiled inline so they execute faster. This is offset, though, by the fact that optimization also prevents the addition of any debugging information to the class.*

Archiving

Since class libraries are shipped as a single entity, they need to be archived in the form of a zip file. The zip file can be used as is. The **CLASSPATH** variable should include the path to the zip file. If the class library is available as **myclasses.zip** and resides in **somedir**, then set the **CLASSPATH** variable (for Windows) as shown on the following page.

```
set CLASSPATH=.;c:\somedir\myclasses.zip;
```

One caution here, the JDK compiler does not decode the compressed zip files. Therefore, while archiving a class library, the 'no compression' option should be selected.

Reliability Issues

Defects (also knows as bugs) are a reality in software engineering. Even when you take a lot of precautions during coding, it's almost impossible to make a software system defect free. To make a class library reliable, defects need to be kept to a minimum.

You'd think defects could be best found through extensive and rigorous testing. That's a good idea, but also an expensive one. Design reviews and code inspections are much more effective (cheaper per bug found) than testing. A rule of thumb is that there is a factor of ten increase in cost per stage the bug is found. So, finding a bug in the design/code stage may cost X dollars, 10X dollars if the same bug isn't caught until the final test, 100X if a customer reports it, and so on.

Unlike application software, class libraries can't be tested by performing actual actions. The best way to test a library is to develop a simple application that uses all aspects of the class library while actually doing as little as possible—a testing suite or testbed, which can also be used to show users how to utilize the library. The testing of class libraries must be rigorous and regressive. The quality of a class library is dependent upon the amount of testing performed. A defect found in the later stages of the development cycle is expensive to fix. The testing of a class library should start early in the development cycle. However, it's often difficult to foresee the testing requirements before applications based on the class libraries are developed. As people start using the applications, there will always be defects, requests for API changes, etc. With good feedback from users, class libraries tend to get better over time.

Fixing defects in a class library needs great care and caution. When a defect is fixed, it may often introduce several new defects without the library's developers being aware of it. It's very hard to catch such defects because it's not easy to test a class library for all the applications which may use that class library—a gap that automated regression testing aims to fill. The correct way to fix a defect is to find its root cause. This isn't easy when development of a software system involves a number of programmers.

A software development project, therefore, would require a defect tracking mechanism. This must be able to relate bugs to software versions—basically, you need source code control software, like RCS. This will not only bring about some discipline among programmers, but also provide a lot of information about the defects. Experienced programmers can often determine the root cause of a defect by browsing through relevant code and the history of the defect.

Applets and Applications

A class library can be used as part of an applet or a stand-alone application. And an applet can be used on the Internet or Intranet. Here are some of the issues of the target software type that a developer needs to consider when implementing a class library.

Applets for the Internet

Because of network downloading, a class library targeted for applets should be compact in terms of code size. Having fewer classes is better from the point of view of performance. This is because in Java the class linking takes place during run time. Security is a major concern when using applets, and so, if a class library is targeted for applets, the following may not be available:

▲ File I/O

▲ Ability to create processes

▲ Some system properties

A class library is required to provide ample security checks. It's good practice to avoid the use of Java features that have the potential for malicious use. Using security checks is bound to increase the code size and slow down the execution, and you may want, in part, to rely on the security measures residing in the applet viewer.

Applets for an Intranet

Intranets are generally faster than the Internet, as they have higher bandwidth and available server performance per user. Security may also be a less of a issue in an Intranet because Intranets can be completely shielded from the outside. A custom made browser can allow file I/O or provide the ability to create a process. The issues to be considered when using Intranets are therefore the provision of more functionality, flexibility and reliability.

Applications

Java is a fully fledged programming language, so large and complex class libraries can be built using it. Since Java's security restrictions generally don't apply to applications, the main issues to be considered are performance and platform independence:

▲ Java's performance can be poor, especially in number crunching operations. This is offset somewhat by Just-in-Time (JIT) environments.

▲ Java isn't yet fully platform independent in a number of areas, the most noticeable being the user interface. As applications tend to be larger and more complex than applets, it's harder to adjust the Java code run in the same way on all platforms.

You can either work within these constraints or abandon platform independence in order to make use of native methods.

A Practical Example

In this section, we'll discuss a complex class library that is designed for Image Visualization, Manipulation and Analysis applications.

Vis - A Class Library for Image Visualization and Analysis

The goal of this library is to provide useful functions and user interfaces required by image visualization and analysis applications. Let's first list the requirements:

▲ Load images.

▲ View images on a window of given size.

▲ Manipulate images, magnify, rotate, and scroll.

- Draw shapes over images.
- Compute image statistics.
- Draw plots and histograms.

Concept and APIs

Drawing shapes and viewing images are independent of each other. A **viewport** that displays images, text and plots is central to the whole design. It should provide the basic functionality to draw images or graphics. If an AWT component like **Canvas** or **Panel** is used directly, then the application writer will have to implement double buffering. The **viewport** needs to provide this functionality.

For an application writer, the **Vis** class library will have to provide at least the following basic functionality:

- Image viewing and manipulation
- Plotting
- Utility functions
- Interactive drawing of shapes
- User interface

We will discuss each functionality briefly. You should refer to the **Vis** class library API documentation for a comprehensive list of APIs.

Image Viewing and Manipulation

The image viewing and manipulation interface is:

```
ImageManipController
```

It's obvious from the requirements that we need the following functionality:

- Magnify
- Scroll
- Rotate

So, we will have the corresponding APIs:

```
Magnify( int magfactor)
scroll()
rotate( int degrees)
```

Let's look at the classes:

Viewport

This class provides the basic functionality for drawing images, graphics and text. It's the base class for viewing applications. A viewport is like a board on which anything can be drawn. A viewport should be capable of displaying images, tables, plots or plain text. The viewport class provides an off-screen image for double-buffering. Its **paint()** and **update()** methods implement default double-buffering. It can be subclassed to implement any particular type of drawing.

ScreenImage

This class helps in image loading. Images are normally loaded using the **getImage()** method (Applet or Toolkit). The loading is asynchronous, so when **getImage()** is executed, it returns an image object. This means that a request has been made to load that image. Some applications/applets need the width and height of that image; these can be obtained by the **getWidth()** and **getHeight()** methods respectively. These methods again are asynchronous. Some applications/applets may need the actual pixel values, however. When an image is loaded in Java, its image pixel values are not available directly. Pixels are grabbed using the **pixelGrabber** class. Image visualization and analysis applications need all the above information. So, there are three stages of image loading which are:

- Image Object created
- Height width available
- Pixels available

The **ScreenImage** class encapsulates image information, including the loading status and its pixels values. It has multiple constructors which enable the creation of **ScreenImage** at any stage of image loading. If the image parameters (width, height, pixels, etc.) are not immediately available, an application can create the **ScreenImage** without any parameters. This would enable the other tasks to be performed while waiting for the image to load.

ImageViewport

The **ImageViewport** class is a subclass of **Viewport** and implements the **ImageManipulator** interface. This class will have APIs to render images. The **scnImage** instance variable holds the current image displayed on the viewport. The **ImageViewport** class maintains a transform matrix **xMat** to keep track of the rotation and translation. It will also have a number of boolean variables to manage manipulation of images. **ImageViewport** can be subclassed to implement any image visualization applications. The manipulation methods such as **magnify()**, can also be overridden to implement different algorithms. The **magnify()** method currently exploits the AWT's scaling mechanism. Applications may require better quality images. In such cases, **magnify()** can be overridden to implement a different kind of interpolation.

Plotting

Plotting uses the following interfaces:

PlotController

A number of parameters are required to draw an XY plot or a histogram. The common parameters for both XY plots and histograms are:

- Title string
- X and Y label strings

▲   Setting the X and Y tick spacing

▲   Creating a basic template

The **PlotController** interface will provide the interface methods to set these parameters.

Next, let's list some of the parameters specific to XY plots and histograms.

XYPlotController

Some of the XY plot specific parameters are:

▲   Color of the plot

▲   Range of X and Y values.

▲   Maximum number of plots.

The **xyPlotController** interface will be a subclass of **PlotController** and will provide APIs to set the above parameters. In addition, it will have an API to draw the actual plot **plotXYPlot(int x[], int y[])**.

HistoController

Some of the histogram-specific parameters are:

▲   Maximum number of bars or bar width

▲   Color of the bar

The **HistoController** interface will be a subclass of **PlotController** and will provide APIs to set the above parameters. In addition, it will have an API to draw the actual histogram, **plotHistogram(int data[])**.

The plotting part has the following class:

PlotViewport

PlotViewport extends **Viewport** and implements both the **HistoController** and **xyPlotController** interfaces. This class enables the drawing of plots on a viewport. A plot can be a regular XY plot or a histogram. The plot is drawn on the offscreen image. It uses the viewport's painting mechanism. The **PlotController** interface will have a number of methods to set the plot parameters. If nothing is set, it's expected to have a default set of parameters. However, the data to be plotted has to be provided. It will not have any instance variables to hold the image or any other data. **PlotViewport** can also be subclassed to override certain methods. The **createTemplate()** method creates the plot template i.e. the style of the X and Y axes, the fonts of X and Y labels, etc. This can be overridden to suit users requirements.

Utility Functions

Some of the utility functions that are needed in this class library are:

- ▲ Matrix multiplication
- ▲ Matrix copy
- ▲ Computing histogram

The utility functions will be provided by three classes.

Util

This will have plotting related methods such as, **computeHistogram()** and **getMinmax()**.

Matrix

This will have methods to perform some matrix operations such as copy, multiply, etc.

Statistics

This will have methods to compute statistics.

Interactive Drawing of Shapes

The API design for shapes was discussed in detail in the design section of the last chapter.

User Interface

A basic user interface needs to be provided. This will include a window that can embed viewports as well as the command panels. The user interface will also provide different cursors. Only the **Frame** class supports cursors in the current version of AWT. Furthermore, a **Frame** can also be used as a container for viewports and command panels. So, this class library provides a class that extends **Frame** as the basic container for UI objects.

First, we look at the **CursorController** interface:

CursorController

This will have APIs to implements the different cursors. Some of them are:

- ▲ Wait cursor
- ▲ Move cursor
- ▲ Hand cursor
- ▲ Default cursor

FramePanel

This class extends **Frame** and implements the **CursorController** interface.

Summary of Library Design

The basic requirement is that the viewport needs to be a component on which images, graphics and text can be drawn. We chose **Canvas** over **Panel** as the superclass of the viewport. The basic reason is that **Canvas** is a component whereas **Panel** is a container. It's likely that **Panel** may involve more overhead. As per the API design, **PlotViewport** and **ImageViewport** are subclasses of the **Viewport** class. The **ImageViewport** class uses the **ScreenImage** class.

From the above requirements, it's obvious that the **shapes** classes and **viewport** classes are independent of each other. Hence, they can belong to a different package hierarchy. By this logic, we collect **shapes** classes in one package and the **viewport** classes in another. We also have the utility classes used by the **viewport** classes. Should they belong to **viewport** or should they be separate? Since utility functions can be used by any other package, they can all be grouped into one package. The **util** package which combines all the utility classes can be the third package in our class library. Although, **util** can be an independent package, we made it as a subpackage of **viewport**. By doing so, we are hiding the details and reducing clutter at the top. In our case, this advantage is trivial as it involves only three packages.

The figure below shows the class and interface hierarchies in the viewport package.

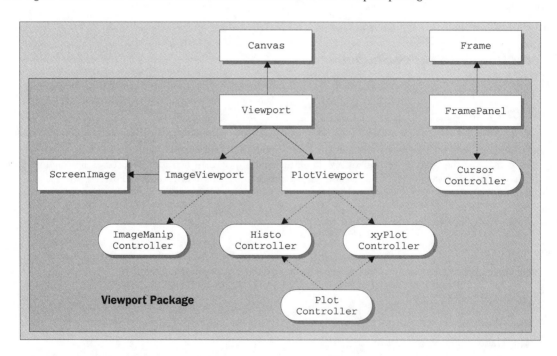

We have already discussed the shape library in the previous chapter. The class diagram of **util** library is trivial as it involves three classes with only static methods.

Using the Vis Library

The **vis** class library has been built to conform to the design discussed above. The source code listing can be downloaded from the Wrox website.

Create a directory called **vis** and copy all the source, classes and documentation under **src**, **lib** and **doc** respectively. Each of the **src** and **lib** directories will have two directories, shapes and viewport. The viewport will have a subdirectory called **util**.

Finally, add the location of the **vis** library's **lib** directory to your **CLASSPATH** variable.

Viewing Documentation

The documents generated using **javadoc** have already been placed in the **doc** directory. To view the class and package hierarchies, you need an HTML browser.

An Example Applet/Application

We assembled an applet and an application using the **shapes** and **viewport** libraries. They implement the same functionality and share most of the code.

Compiling

The source code for the applet and application is available in two separate directories, **<pathname>\vis\applet** and **<pathname>\vis\application**, respectively. Both these directories need an **images** subdirectory. Before executing the applet or application, copy all the images to the **images** directory.

In order to compile and execute both the applet and application, set the **CLASSPATH** first. It should point to the directory in which the **vis** class library files reside. Assuming the class library directory is **c:\vis\lib**, set **CLASSPATH** by entering the following (in Windows):

```
set CLASSPATH=.;c:\vis\lib
```

In the applet or application directory, compile the code by using the following command.

```
javac ImageViewer.java
```

This will generate all the necessary class files.

Running

Before executing the applet or application, make sure the **CLASSPATH** is set correctly. It should be same as the one described in the previous section.

Applet

An HTML file is needed to run the applet. We have provided a sample HTML file called **viewer.html** in the **applet** directory. Run the applet by typing the following command in the **applet** directory.

```
appletviewer viewer.html
```

Application

The application can be executed by the following command in the application directory:

```
java ImageViewer
```

Using the Applet/Application

Whether it's the applet or application, once the above commands are executed, they behave the same way. The applet/application spawns a frame which contains a command panel and an image viewport. The command panel has three sub panels. The top panel is used to select and render images, the middle panel to draw shapes interactively and the bottom panel to manipulate images.

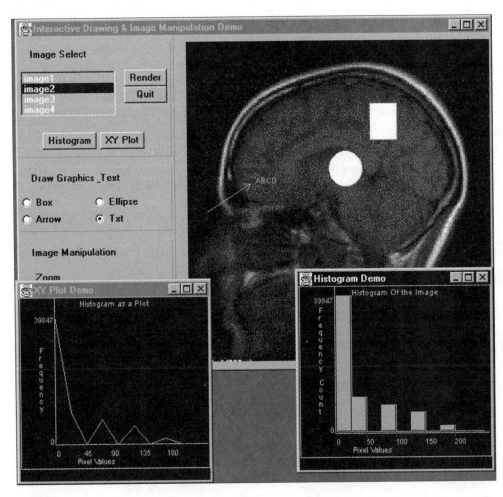

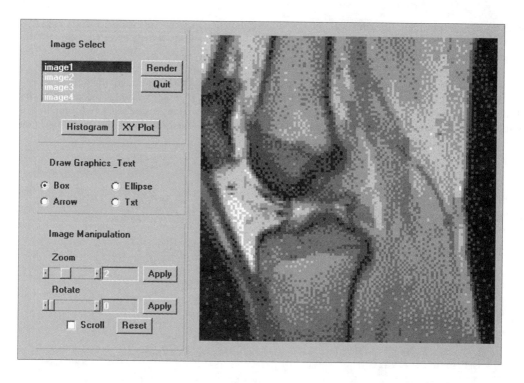

The applet/application will take some time to load all the images. In order to draw a shape, select an appropriate shape on the Shapes panel. In the case of a **Box**, **Ellipse** or **Arrow**, move the cursor over the image and drag it to form the shape outline. In the case of text, move the cursor to an appropriate position and click the mouse button, and then type in the desired characters. The text string will get appended as you type in the characters.

In the Image Manipulation panel, sliders are provided to choose the magnification factor and the rotation angle. When the Apply button is clicked, the appropriate functionality is applied. The rotation of images is very slow. The scroll button provides the image scrolling feature. A magnified image can be scrolled to view the entire image. The Reset button will bring the viewport to the default state.

We also added a Histogram and XY Plot buttons in the Image selector panel. Although, these two buttons do not belong there, we added this to illustrate the use of **PlotViewport**. If you click the histogram button with an image displayed, it will spawn a separate Frame displaying the histogram of the image rendered on the viewport. Similarly, on clicking the XY Plot button, the same histogram will be displayed as a plot on a separate Frame. The histogram or plot will not be displayed if the images are in the process of being loaded.

Some Implementation Details

Loading Images

While loading an image, the applet/application creates a corresponding **ScreenImage** object and updates its loading status as loading progresses. Meanwhile, the applet/application can continue with other tasks.

In order to merge the shape drawing with image viewing functionality, we've created a class called **Screen** as a subclass of **ImageViewport**. The event handling methods in this class take care of the mouse events.

To enable the interactive drawing of shapes, the **paint()** and **update()** methods of the **ImageViewport** class are overridden in the **Screen** class. In the interactive mode, the graphics object supplied in the **update()** method is passed as an argument to the **drawInteractive()** method in the **Shapes** class. When interactive drawing is completed, the **draw()** method draws the shape permanently over the image.

Here is the code for the **update()** method.

```
public void update(Graphics paintGc){
    if(paintGc == null){
       return;
    }
    Rectangle  border = bounds();
    int wid = border.width;
    int ht = border.height;
    paintGc.setColor(Color.black);

    if(fullPaintOn){
       if(offScrImage!= null){
          paintGc.drawImage(offScrImage,0,0,wid,ht, this);
       }
       fullPaintOn = false;
    }
    if(graphicsOn){
       curShape.drawInteractive(paintGc);
       graphicsOn = false;
    }
    requestFocus();
}
```

In the above code, the boolean variables, **fullPaintOn** and **graphicsModeOn** maintain the drawing state. When **graphicsOn** is true, the shape is drawn on the graphics context. For normal display, the **fullPaintOn** has to be true.

In case of histogram, we make use of the **PlotViewport** class directly. An object called **histoVp** is created as an instance of **PlotViewport** class. The histogram drawing parameters like X and Y axis labels, maximum number of bars, X and Y tick spacing, etc., are set before the histogram is drawn. The RGB image data is converted to intensity levels using the **colorToIntensity()** method in the **util** package and then passed to the **plotHistogram()** method.

```
public void plotHistogram(){
    int wid= 256,ht= 256;
    histoframe = new FramePanel(wid,ht);
    histoframe.setTitle("Histogram Demo");
    histoVp = new PlotViewport(wid,ht);
    histoframe.setBackground(Color.black);
    histoframe.add(histoVp);
    histoframe.resize(wid,ht);
    histoframe.show();
    histoframe.waitCursor();
    histoVp.createOffScrImage();
```

```
        if(scnImage[curImageNum] == null){
           showStatus("Image is not yet loaded");
           System.out.println("Image not loaded");
        }
        else{
           int[] pixValue = scnImage[curImageNum].origPixels;
           int[] pixV = Util.colorToIntensity(pixValue);
           histoVp.setTitleString("Histogram Of the Image");
           histoVp.setXLabelString("     Pixel Values");
           histoVp.setYLabelString("Frequency Count");
           histoVp.setBarColor(Color.green);
           histoVp.createPlotTemplate();
           histoVp.plotHistogram(pixV);
        }

        histoframe.done();
     }
```

The **plotXYPlot()** method will also have similar code.

Summary

We discussed the steps involved in the construction of a class library. This includes coding and packaging to implement the class and package designs respectively. We focused our discussion on some of the coding issues.

The other steps involved in class library construction are documentation and archiving. We explained the need for good documentation and described the Java environment tool called **javadoc**.

We then briefly looked at archiving Java class libraries by zipping them and using them in applications and applets. In addition to the class library construction steps, we also discussed some reliability issues and factors to be considered when targeting applets and applications. The chapter ended with an illustration of a practical example of a class library used both by a simple applet and an application.

Interfacing Java and C++

Having spent the last fourteen chapters talking about everything Java can do, let's take time out and discuss what happens when you can't see how to do it in Java.

In its pure form, Java can't yet utilize a printer, play music that isn't in the grainy **.au** format, or display images beyond the ubiquitous **GIF**s and **JPEG**s that litter the Internet. Execution speed taxes programmers' minds, too. A word processor will never challenge the CPU to any great extent because the majority of its time is spent waiting for the infinitely slower user to press a key. Raytracers are an entirely different story. Graphically intensive programs push a system to the edges of its abilities, and an interpreted language will not cut it when alternatives that run twenty times faster are available as freeware today.

Finally, what happens to the millions of lines of C++ code that live in the archives of software companies? If the transition to Java as a major language of development is to take place, those libraries will have to be forfeited—unless some way can be found to seamlessly intertwine Java and C++.

That is the subject of this chapter. The all-wise and all-knowing Java team realized this and put considerable effort into the interface between these two languages. This frees the developer to decide whether they want to create a C++ program that uses threads, or a Java program that plays music.

In this chapter, we'll look at:

- ▲ Why you need native methods
- ▲ How to implement a simple Java/C++ interface
- ▲ Under the hood—what's happening
- ▲ Helper functions—calling Java methods from C++

Who Needs Native Methods?

Native methods open the door to the computer's guts—the specific capabilities that exist on every platform. Java, with its lowest-common-denominator philosophy, hides them away. While Java brings to the table easy multithreading and intelligent GUI components, C++ fires back a compelling shot in the form of joysticks, graphics, sound, speed and, for the short term at least, greater maturity, better and more abundant engineering tools, wide availability of third-party libraries, and a larger mind-bank of trained programmers.

All of these things will eventually come to Java, but for now, programmers are going to have to turn to C++, in extremis. It's also important to point out that Java and C++ solve fundamentally different problems. The principal advantage of native methods is to enhance Java applications with platform-specific stuff.

Advantages

The advantages of adding C++ to Java are clear and need no explanation. The 'best-of-both-worlds' approach gives you the greatest possible control over your programs. Anything that can be accomplished by C++ can be referenced by Java, and some of Java's unique qualities can be applied to programs written mainly in C++.

> Both C and C++ can be used to write native methods. While this chapter arbitrarily uses C++, all statements refer to C also, unless explicitly noted.

Drawbacks

The trade-offs that come tied to using the attractive capabilities of C++ warrant far more discussion. "Look before you leap" is sound advice, and programmers need to ask themselves several questions before they jump:

▲ **"Do I need an applet?"** Applets are not allowed to communicate with C++. Java imports the compiled functions as a dynamically-linked library, which violates the applet security restrictions. This automatically removes a huge resource from the programmer's arsenal–the Internet. If applet capabilities and worldwide accessibility are no great loss, then ask the next question.

▲ **"Will my program appeal to other platforms?"** If so, then every effort should be made to retain the luxuries of platform independence and universal code readability. The overhead of developing routines for 5 different operating systems probably exceeds the time it would take to find a suitable solution using Java's built-in libraries. Obviously, this does not apply to areas where Java is deficient. Such occasions make a strong case for resorting to C++, because a word processor that can't print will never sell many copies.

▲ **"Do I really want to return to the land of pointer arithmetic?"** The question has to be asked. After working with Java, it becomes easy to expect smooth development everywhere, but by the time you realize you are mistaken, so much time has been invested you can't turn back. Also, clean code goes right out the door when two languages combine to make a single program. This seems trivial at the moment, but in large applications (the ones most likely to require C++), spaghetti code is responsible for millions of Excedrin headaches.

The (Deceptive) Need For Speed

At this point, a traditional illusion must be shattered. The most common reason cited by Java programmers for resorting to C++ is execution speed. Without any evidence that a program suffers under interpretation, developers automatically assume that Java performs too slowly for their needs.

The fact of the matter is, in most cases Java's capabilities exceed their expectations. Running on a local computer, animation written in Java plays at up to ten frames per second–a highly respectable figure. GUIs spend most of their time waiting for input, giving the interpreter time to catch up on other operations in the background. Java's compiler produces highly optimized programs, and advanced multithreading further enhances the language's perceived speed.

The Just-In-Time compiler phenomenon that has recently swept the realms of Java strengthens the argument that Java runs fast enough to compete on a commercial level with platform-specific languages. A JIT works with the interpreter, caching translated bytecode for future execution. The next time a particular fragment of code is needed, it is run from this native-code cache, rather than passing through the interpreter again. Practical evidence shows that Java actually rivals compiled C++ code using a JIT—up to a 2000% increase in execution speed!

Such utilities are only available commercially; the current release of the JDK lacks them, although they will be included in the future.

> *The goal of the JOLT project (***http://www.redhat.com/linux-info/jolt//***) is to provide a freely available and redistributable implementation of Sun's Java language and tools including a JIT.*

Symantec's Café contains a JIT, as does Microsoft's Jakarta and Borland's forthcoming Latte. Even Web browsers like Netscape's Navigator and Microsoft's Internet Explorer have incorporated JITs for use with applets.

Without these IDEs, however, the use of native methods is very attractive when speed becomes a problem. Mathematically intensive calculations often benefit from native compilation, too. Raytracers and fractal generators place a premium on speed and to preserve the patience of the user, C++ is the best solution for these cases.

The Quick Tour

If C++ has not yet been overruled as a solution, it's safe to say the desired task can't be accomplished under Java alone. Obviously, this decision requires much thought, as do all design elements that fundamentally affect a program. Native methods offer much in the way of program enhancement, but only under the proper circumstances. They are not a panacea for every Java woe.

Now it's time to pull out the C++ compiler that has been gathering dust up to this point of the book. The next few listings move rather quickly through the process of linking Java with C++. After that, you will be able to create basic C++ functions and call them from Java—the technical details and advanced concepts will come later.

Step 1: Write the Java program

Whenever Java and C++ are used together, the program execution must begin in Java. Therefore, 'main' isn't a valid name for a native method. This somewhat limits how much emphasis can be placed on C++, and makes it more convenient for the programmer to implement the front end in Java, saving C++ for background functions.

Native methods are declared just like any other method, except the 'native' keyword is thrown into the modifier list. By convention, it appears after the visibility modifier and before the return type. Instead of appending a bracket and a method definition, just terminate the declaration with a semicolon. This works identically to forward function declarations in C++, so it should ring a bell.

Java programs that use C++ contain a unique block of code. Independent of any method, the following statements must be present to import the dynamic library that will be created later.

```
static {
    try {
        System.loadLibrary ('add');
    }
    catch (UnsatisfiedLinkError e) {
        System.out.println (e);
        System.exit (1);
    }
}
```

Although quite foreign in this specific application, **static** means the same thing here as it does when applied to methods. Everything enclosed in the brackets is executed once, upon creation of the class, and all instances will benefit from it. The only practical purpose for this special statement is to load dynamic libraries.

Line 3 of this example calls **loadLibrary**, a method defined by the **System** class. The single argument passed to it is the name of the library. Keep in mind that platform-specific prefixes and extensions like **.dll**, **lib** and **.so** are added by Java, and only the name itself should be specified. If the library is undefined or unloadable for some reason, an **UnsatisfiedLinkError** is thrown. Because this is a subclass of **java.lang.Error**, it does not need to be caught; it will automatically stop the program's execution. For learning purposes, however, the library-loading code is enclosed in a **try-catch** block to demonstrate exactly where an error might occur.

The following class, **DemonstrateNative**, defines a native method that takes two integers and returns their sum. Admittedly, this example is simple, but the dearth of code allows the focus to rest on the sequence of steps that lead to a working program.

```
public class DemonstrateNative {
    public static void main (String argv[]) {
        DemonstrateNative dn = new DemonstrateNative();
        System.out.println (dn.add (1, 2));
    }

    public native int add (int a, int b);
    static {
        try {
            System.loadLibrary ('add');
        }
        catch (UnsatisfiedLinkError e) {
            System.out.println (e);
            System.exit (1);
        }
    }
}
```

Everything here is straightforward. Line 3 instantiates the class in order to access the dynamic library (remember, all native methods are dynamically linked into the class). Line 4 calls the native method just as if it were a plain-vanilla Java method. Line 6 declares the C++ function, and lines 7–14 are exactly reproduced from the previous example.

In its present form, the program will not run, because the library **add** doesn't exist yet! It will compile without errors, however, and in order to move on to the next steps, it is necessary to do so now. The resulting file is named **DemonstrateNative.class**, and it serves as the argument to Java's tools in the next two steps.

Step 2: Produce the C Header File

Java's thoughtful designers provided tools that automatically generate header files to include in the C++ implementations. This is done quickly and easily, by running the **javah** command-line utility on the class. The command line looks like this:

```
javah DemonstrateNative
```

The output is a file named **DemonstrateNative.h**, which must be included using a preprocessor directive when it comes time to write the corresponding C++ functions. Java provides numerous helper functions and macros, and this header file helps C++ understand them. If **DemonstrateNative** were contained within a package named **my.programs**, then the header file would be named slightly differently. In this case, it would become **my_programs_DemonstrateNative.h**.

> Note that in version 1.0.2 of the JDK, **javah** mangles the first entry of the **CLASSPATH** variable, causing it to report that the desired class doesn't exist. There are two possible solutions to this. The first is to manually duplicate the first entry. This doesn't bother the other command-line tools. Otherwise, the **-classpath** switch must be added to the command line:
>
> **javah -classpath .;c:\java\lib\classes.zip DemonstrateNative**.

The header file, reproduced below, contains the function signature as the C++ file must define it. It looks a little different here than it did in Java; for one thing, there is an extra argument of type **HDemonstrateNative *** ! This will all be explained in good time; just bear in mind that this must be reproduced *exactly* when it comes time to work in C++.

Perceptive readers will notice that this step is entitled 'Produce the C header file', while everything else refers to C++. The file itself explains the inconsistency: the declaration is enclosed in an **extern "C"** statement if C++ is the language in use. In JDK releases prior to version 1.0.2, the modifier had to be added manually in order to allow inclusion into C++ programs.

Below is our second listing, **DemonstrateNative.h**:

```
/* DO NOT EDIT THIS FILE - it is machine generated */
#include <native.h>
/* Header for class DemonstrateNative */

#ifndef _Included_DemonstrateNative
#define _Included_DemonstrateNative

typedef struct ClassDemonstrateNative {
char PAD; /* ANSI C requires structures to have a least one member */
} ClassDemonstrateNative;
HandleTo(DemonstrateNative);
```

```
#ifdef __cplusplus
extern "C" {
#endif
extern long DemonstrateNative_add(struct HDemonstrateNative *,long,long);
#ifdef __cplusplus
}
#endif
#endif
```

The actual function signature, defined by line 16 may cause some concern, because it looks nothing like the Java declaration! Considerable effort is applied to native methods to make them conform to C++ standards, and this is the result of those behind-the-scenes maneuvers.

C++ functions produced by **javah** follow a strict naming convention in which the entire package name, including the class name, is prepended to the function name. Underscores separate the terms. Therefore, the **String** class would appear to C++ as **java_lang_String**. Remember that case-sensitivity is observed as strictly here as elsewhere.

Discrepancies exist between the sizes of Java and C++ primitives. For instance, Java's **int** is most closely compatible with C++'s **long**. To remove the headaches of converting the size of parameters and returns, Java's **int**, **short** and **boolean** are all mapped onto **long**s from the perspective of C++. When writing C++ functions, treat all integral values from the world of Java, whether explicitly passed to the function or read from the class itself, as **long**s.

Finally, an extra argument is always passed to native methods. Analogous to the **this** pointer, it provides a reference to the Java class making the function call. Through it, the C++ function can access Java member variables. The automatic argument's name follows a pattern, too; it begins with 'H' (denoting 'handle'), followed by the package and class names again separated by underscores.

For the purposes of this example, the handle to the Java class is superfluous and will be ignored. It becomes quite useful, however, in more complex, real-life applications.

Step 3: Generating the Stubs File

One more task remains before the road connecting Java and C++ can be considered smoothly paved. **javah** also has the capability to produce a small file of C functions that define the interface between the two languages. Simply invoke the **-stubs** switch to produce a file named **DemonstrateNative.c**. Upon compilation of the C++ function, this must be linked in as part of the project.

> The same **CLASSPATH** concerns apply here as in the previous step.

The contents of the output file mostly resemble gibberish, but rest assured, they mean something to Java.

Below is the **DemonstrateNative.c** listing:

```
/* DO NOT EDIT THIS FILE - it is machine generated */
#include <StubPreamble.h>

/* Stubs for class DemonstrateNative */
/* SYMBOL: "DemonstrateNative/add(II)I", Java_DemonstrateNative_add_stub */
```

```
__declspec(dllexport) stack_item *Java_DemonstrateNative_add_stub(stack_item
*_P_,struct execenv *_EE_) {
    extern long DemonstrateNative_add(void *,long,long);
    _P_[0].i = DemonstrateNative_add(_P_[0].p,((_P_[1].i)),((_P_[2].i)));
    return _P_ + 1;
}
```

Step 4: Write the C++ Implementation

At this point, let's jump over to the C++ portion of the program and write the function definition. There are two salient points that must not be forgotten:

▲   **#include   DemonstrateNative.h**

▲   Copy the signature as it appears in that file

The signature, as contained in the header file, is:

```
extern long DemonstrateNative_add (struct HDemonstrateNative *,
                                   long,long)
```

Each of the arguments needs a name for reference in C++. Although the first parameter functions like the **this** pointer and is sometimes called such, many compilers consider **this** a reserved keyword. For purposes of clarity, it's better to choose a name, like **java**, and apply that to all native methods. That way, while working in C++, **java** will come to associate automatically with the calling class. All other arguments should bear the same name in C++ as they did in Java; although nothing enforces this, it prevents confusion.

The listing below, **addnative.cpp**, contains only one line of code; concentrate on the fact that the function works exactly the same way as an independent C++ program.

```
#include "DemonstrateNative.h"

extern long DemonstrateNative_add(struct HDemonstrateNative * java,
                                  long a,long b) {
    return (a + b);
}
```

Clearly, this function performs the task Java expects, returning the sum of the two parameters. Save this as **addnative.cpp** for now, but wait to compile it, because there are several issues that must be resolved first.

Step 5: Produce the Dynamic Library

Creating the dynamic library itself is an involved task that certainly warrants the creation of a project file. The target must correspond to the library name given in listing 1. For the current example, name the target 'add'.

Observe all conventions dictated by the operating system. Windows 95 users will end up with a file named **add.dll**, UNIX users with **libadd.so**. Java takes care of stripping these prefixes and suffixes.

At least two files must be included in the project. The first, obviously, is the file containing the native method implementation. Unlike everything else involved in implementing native methods, its name does not matter; **addnative.cpp** works as well as anything else. The second is the stubs file, **DemonstrateNative.c**. If calls to Java's helper functions are made from C++, the file **javai.lib** must be added, as well. As this project does not use the helper functions, the library can be omitted.

> Be careful never to explicitly make **javai.lib**, as this will cause some compilers to overwrite it!

Look back at the second listing, **DemonstrateNative.h**. Line 2 contains an **#include** directive, but the filename is completely foreign to C++ compilers. Yet it's enclosed in brackets, indicating that it's in the default include path! Java makes the assumption that its own header files (which detail the functions that translate between itself and C++) are located in this project entry. Two additions must be made to it in order for the project to compile. The first is usually **java\include**, and the second is a subdirectory of the first, named to reflect the operating system under which Java runs. The library file path requires a similar addition, **java\lib** on most installations of Java.

Now that the compiler knows where to find the required files, it's time to compile and link the library. Be sure to specify that the target is a dynamically linked library—the default is usually an executable, and libraries can be both statically and dynamically linked. First, compile **addnative.cpp**. There shouldn't be any errors; if there are problems at this stage of the process, typing mistakes and programming errors in the C++ implementation itself are the most likely culprits. Then simply link the library, and you are ready to run the program!

Command-line compiler lovers can still produce the library. Specify the switch that indicates a dynamically linked library, then manually set the include and library paths (remembering to include the compiler's paths as well as the Java paths). Finally, type the names of the files to be linked.

Step 6: Run the Program

To help the interpreter out, it's best to put the library in the same directory as **DemonstrateNative.class**. This way there will be no problems locating either file. When attempting to load a library, Java searches the **CLASSPATH**, and on some systems it will search the **PATH** also. Putting everything in one place prevents all possible hassles, though.

DemonstrateNative is invoked in the same manner as any other Java class; communication between Java and the library takes place behind the scenes. At the command line, type:

```
java DemonstrateNative
```

There can be two possible outputs. The first is simply the number '3'. This means that everything works as it should. Congratulations! You have, in a long and drawn-out process, used C++ to perform simple addition. More importantly, the entire journey from Java to C++ has been explained, and that knowledge can be applied to any situation requiring the use of native methods.

If the program malfunctioned, the screen is probably filled with errors. The most likely cause is that the library was misnamed, so that it does not correspond with the file Java is trying to load. Otherwise, the library may be located somewhere other than the **CLASSPATH** and Java can't find it. Move and/or rename it and try again.

Should errors persist, typographical mistakes are probably at fault. If the function definition varies even slightly between Java, the header files, and the C++ implementations, communication will break down entirely. In a situation like this, it's always best to proofread code at least once.

Finally, some compilers have trouble exporting C++ functions in a way that means Java can recognize them. Unfortunately, no workaround for this exists at the time of writing.

At this point, you possess the ability to link any pure C++ function in with Java programs. Anything you do in C++ can be utilized in Java now. Later, you will learn how C++ functions can see back into the Java class that called them, but for now, let's take a look inside native methods and the utilities that produce them.

Under the Hood

What we have covered so far is enough to start writing simple native methods, without knowing anymore about what happens in the background. However, the curious are never satisfied with understanding how to do something; they always want to find out how it works, too. A more substantial reason exists for perusing this section as well, though: much of the knowledge contained here is required to utilize more advanced features like throwing exceptions and synchronizing threads from within a native method.

Parameters and Return Types

DemonstrateNative only scratched the surface of all the possible situations a programmer could conceivably run into. The native method accepted only primitive values and returned another primitive. When working with C++, primitives function as they always do–they are passed by value, and any modifications made to them from within the function are not reflected in their Java counterparts. Aside from the fact that all of Java's integral data types must be treated as longs in C++, nothing is different.

Objects are a completely different story. They can be passed as arguments and C++ functions can return them, but they undergo considerable mangling along the way, from the perspective of the programmer. Because they exist as references, object parameters can be modified permanently by C++ functions, unlike primitives. The automatic parameter is an object, but it looks nothing like the class we wrote in Java.

The object naming convention, discussed briefly earlier, is quite simple. The entire package name is prepended with the letter **H**. This is easy to understand; if two classes shared the same name and were both present in the same function, C++ would have no way to tell them apart.

The **H** that precedes any Java object, be it a class or an array, stands for 'handle', and describes Java's method of organizing data. A handle holds the address of one of the members of a table of pointers. Each pointer itself references an object. Therefore, in a roundabout way, each handle points to a specific object.

Java uses handles, rather than pointers, for this purpose both to make memory allocation easier, and to prevent you, the programmer, from directly accessing the object and harming it. This is as much a security mechanism as a means to prevent bugs. Once the address of an object is known, a good programmer can circumvent all of Java's security controls through manipulation of pointers and other nasty devices.

> Never, under any circumstances, alter the location to which a handle points! Java's garbage collector uses handles to determine whether an object still exists. If the pointer no longer refers to the beginning of the object, it's considered dead and Java destroys it!

With objects so shielded from the programmer's reach, the question then becomes: how can those layers of misdirection be removed so that legal interaction between native methods and Java classes can take place? As always, the omniscient designers from Sun devised a solution.

The unhand() Macro

Defined in **interpreter.h**, one of Java's numerous header files, the **unhand()** macro takes as its argument any handle to an object. Its name, though bringing to mind thwarted thefts, really means that it returns a pointer to a **struct** representing that object. Created when **javah** was run on the class in question, this **struct** contains data fields identical to those in the Java object itself. Keep in mind, however, that primitives named **int** in Java must be treated as **long**s in C++; Java automatically renames them, and it's up to you to notice the change.

Using the macro is simple. For instance, assume a native method takes an argument of type **java.awt.Point**, and names it **Location**. In order to set the x value of **Location** to 3, use the following syntax:

```
unhand (Location)->x = 3;
```

As this illustrates, the **unhand()** macro returns a pointer to the **struct** containing **Location**'s data. Furthermore, Java will see the altered value of **x**, just as if the change had been made from within a normal method.

Perhaps the most common use of **unhand()** is to get data from the class that contains the native method. Using the macro on the automatic parameter allows access to class data. Keep in mind that visibility restrictions apply to native methods as well as Java methods; all fields of a class, including private and static variables, are available to its C++ functions. Otherwise, the rules governing private and protected variables determine whether they are accessible.

Arrays: A Special Case

Java treats arrays as objects, which complicates their transition to C++. Instead of simply creating a pointer to the salient data, **javah** converts arrays passed as parameters to a special handle type. Arrays may contain any object or primitive.

As is the usual case with Java, names matter. An array of **int**s becomes an **HArrayOfInt   *.** In general, **HArrayOf** begins the name, and the type of data is appended to it. For primitives, simply the name will do. Classes are treated in the same way as when they are passed as parameters; the package name precedes the class. Therefore, **String[]** in Java becomes **HArrayOfjava_lang_String   *** in C++.

In this form, arrays are of absolutely no use to C++, because it does not know how to read them. A pointer to the body must be created from within the function. To initialize it, set it equal to **unhand (arrayName)->body**. Now the data can be treated as any other C++ array.

Java-generated Header Files

The function signatures created by **javah** have been thoroughly explained; the rest of its output deserves some attention now.

Each class containing native methods requires its own header file. While all the function stubs can be combined into a single C file, doing this to the headers will give the compiler a fit.

No matter what, the first line of a header file created by Java is a warning not to edit the contents. Heed this well–it's there for your own protection! Much of the interface between Java and C++ is cryptic, entirely hidden from view. Seemingly innocent changes can wreck an entire project.

Next, appears the line **#include   <native.h>.** This is one of Java's header files; like the point of a pyramid, it contains only top-level **#include** statements. To see what lies below, one must follow the trail of inclusions into the heart of Java. This is covered in detail later.

The header file then checks, in standard C++ fashion, whether it has been previously read. To prevent conflicts, the defined constant is named according to the pattern **_Included_package_name_ClassName**.

Immediately below this, Java objects contained as member variables of the class in question receive a type declaration, in preparation for their own declaration. If **String**s are used in the class, **struct Hjava_lang_String;** would appear here. If no objects exist, then this area is left blank.

The machine-generated header files also define a **struct** that holds the class's data. It's called something akin to **Classpackage_name_ClassName.** Java constants (**static   final**) become **#defined** quantities for the purposes of C++. Other data types behave normally, and as always, Java automatically changes **int**s and **boolean**s to **long**s, expecting you to follow along. Looking at listing 2, line 8, you can see the general pattern of the **typedef. DemonstrateNative** contains no data, so the **struct** is blank except for the required padding variable.

Immediately after this, Java invokes the **HandleTo()** macro on the class. This establishes the automatic parameter's data type, allowing it to be used in the function signatures that end the file. The **#endif** directive closes the header.

The Stubs File

All the stubs from a project can be placed in a single file, as can the C++ function implementations.

The information contained within them is largely useless to the programmer; it's entwined with the internal workings of the JVM. Only the commented line that precedes each stub concerns us. Here, the signature for each function is presented in a slightly different format, and it's necessary to learn it well to use many of the helper functions.

Refer back to listing 3, line 5.

```
/* SYMBOL: "DemonstrateNative/add(II)I", Java_DemonstrateNative_add_stub */
```

This is the signature for the **add()** method. Breaking it down part by part, we arrive at the following rules:

- ▲ The signature begins with the package name, followed by the class name, then the method name. Each term is separated by a forward slash (/).

- ▲ The parameters are contained within parentheses and encoded by type.

- ▲ After the closing parenthesis is the return type, encoded in the same manner as the parameters.

With these guidelines, it's easy to generate the signature for a method without Java's help, and this skill will become necessary in the next section. For instance, the signature for the method **setMinutes()**, contained in the class **java.util.Date**, becomes:

```
"java/util/Date/setMinutes(I)V"
```

The following table summarizes the symbols for parameters and return types. They are defined in the Java header file **signature.h**.

Symbol	Represents	Meaning
A	Any	Unused
B	Byte	Byte primitive
C	Char	Char primitive
D	Double	Double primitive
E	Enum	Unused
F	Float	Float primitive
I	Int	Int primitive
J	Long	Long primitive
L	Class	Package and class names, separated by / and terminated by ; Ex. L java/awt/Color;

Table Continued on Following Page

Symbol	Represents	Meaning
S	Short	Short primitive
V	Void	Void
Z	Boolean	Boolean primitive
[	Array	Precedes any other symbol, indicates an array of that type

The Helper Functions

Left to themselves, native methods can utilize all the capabilities of C++. However, to truly interface with Java, they must also be awarded additional functionality. A multithreaded program whose native methods are blind to this fact can easily fall into ruins. If an error occurs during the execution of a native method, it would be much more convenient (and make for much cleaner code) to take advantage of Java's elegant exception-handling system. For these two languages to truly be integrated, C++ must be able to call Java methods, just as Java can invoke C++ functions. Native methods should have the capability to create new objects, and to manipulate Java strings.

The mysterious Java header files provide programmers with all of these things, and more. Unfortunately, they are rarely documented, and their own syntax is confusing and misleading. Functions meant for public use are not differentiated from functions only Java should call. Here, then, is a thorough reference to the powerful helper functions.

Calling Java Methods from C++

Because function signatures have already been explained, the task here is a little simpler. Three different functions exist to call various methods from C++. Which one is used depends on the method type. Static and dynamic methods require separate procedures for invocation, as do constructors.

Most programmers call instance methods frequently. From C++, this is done using the function **execute_java_dynamic_method**. The complete signature is:

```
long execute_java_dynamic_method (ExecEnv *ee, HObject *obj, char *method,
                                  char *signature, ...);
```

The first parameter refers to a class named **ExecEnv**. Each concurrently running instance of the Java Virtual Machine is an execution environment. A value of **NULL** for this parameter indicates that the current execution environment should be used. In future releases of the JDK, this requirement will probably disappear; it's practically infeasible to use a value other than **NULL** here at the present time. In function calls, we will use **0** instead of **NULL**, so that **stdlib.h** doesn't need to be included. Just remember what **0** really means.

Next, **execute_java_dynamic_method** needs to know in which class the target method resides. A handle to this class must already exist, whether from a class passed as a parameter or from one created explicitly from a constructor. Because dynamic methods by definition require an instance to be called, if a reference to the desired class does not exist in C++, a new one must be made before this function can be used.

The third parameter is the name of the method as it appears in Java. This should be passed as a string.

Finally, this function wants to know the method's signature in the form of a string. This is where the signature-building rules from last section come into play. Only the later half, which specifies parameter and return types, should be applied here; the class and package names can be dropped as they have already been specified. This process probably seems tedious. Its only practical application is to distinguish between overloaded methods. In the event that more than one method uses the same name, the signature decides which version should be called.

All that need to be added now are the arguments meant for the method. C++ expects a variable length list and sorts it out itself.

Native methods that return values put them into a C++ **long** variable, which is then returned by **exeucute_java_dynamic_method**. A simple cast to the desired type in C++ allows them to be used just like any other piece of data. Methods which return objects in Java instead return handles to a native method; because handles are a 32-bit variable, they fit neatly into the grand scheme of this function. Returned handles should be cast to the appropriate handle type and stored in a local variable; this is enough to maintain a reference to the Java object.

Suppose a native method has a reference to a **java.lang.Integer** named **number**, and wants to call the instance method **number.intValue()**. The code would look like this:

```
execute_java_dynamic_method (0, number, "intValue", "(V)V");
```

Assuming the last three parameters match up correctly, C++ dispatches your method call, and Java never knows which language called it!

The good news is, dynamic methods are pretty simple to call from C++. Unfortunately, a qualification always follows a statement like that, and this is no exception. When an instance of a class exists in a specific location in the computer's memory, Java has no trouble finding it. When looking for data that belongs to the whole class, however, it needs a map. Every version of a class shares its constructor and static methods. Furthermore, without a handy reference to the class, Java could spend quite some time looking for what it wants.

Enter the function named **FindClass**. This helpful utility searches Java's class lookup table, matching names to numerical identities. It returns a value that other functions recognize much faster than they would a name. Although it's not necessary, utilizing **FindClass** can increase performance by shaving off the time Java normally spends translating between class names and memory locations.

Its signature looks like this:

```
ClassClass *FindClass (ExecEnv *ee, char *name, bool_t resolve);
```

The execution environment should always be **0**, and the class name a C string. For our purposes, the final parameter should generally be true.

C++ functions invoke static methods in much the same way as their dynamic counterparts. The only difference is, the second parameter is the class's identity according to Java's lookup table, rather than a concrete handle. **NULL**, or **0**, is a legal value for this parameter; it just means that Java will spend precious time trying to figure out where that class lives, rather than running your program.

The full declaration of **execute_java_static_method** is:

```
long execute_java_static_method (ExecEnv *ee, ClassClass *cb,
char *method_name, char *signature, ...);
```

If a C++ function wanted to obtain a random number using Java's math engine, it would need to call the static method **Math.random()**. Several lines of code would be necessary:

```
ClassClass *cc;
cc = FindClass (0, "java/lang/Math", true);
execute_java_static_method (0, cc, "random", "(V)D");
```

For efficiency's sake, these steps can be concatenated into a single line.

```
execute_java_static_method (0, FindClass (0, "Math", true), "(V)D");
```

However, this sacrifices readability for quicker typing. As before, the returned **long** represents the value returned by the Java method. Cast it to the appropriate type, then use it like any other returned value.

Native methods can produce new Java objects by triggering their constructors. The helper function **execute_java_constructor** takes the same arguments as **execute_java_static method**, but wants them in a different order. It returns a 32-bit value of type **HObject *.** Usually, this is immediately case to a handle type specifically named for the class in question. The full declaration is as follows:

```
HObject *execute_java_constructor (ExecEnv *ee, char *classname, ClassClass *cb,
                                   char *signature, ...);
```

After the returned handle has been safely stored in a pointer, it can be **unhand()**ed to work with its data and C++ can access its dynamic methods.

Let's use this knowledge to create a new **StringBuffer** in C++. For simplicity's sake, it will remain empty.

Before the object can be created, we need a place to put it. Remembering that C++ works with handles, the appropriate type is **Hjava_lang_StringBuffer *.** Simply declare the handle for now, and name it **sb**.

```
Hjava_lang_StringBuffer *sb;
```

Now invoke the constructor for **StringBuffer**, cast the resulting handle to the appropriate type, and store it in **sb**.

```
ClassClass *cc;
cc = FindClass (0, "java/lang/StringBuffer", true);
sb = (Hjava_lang_StringBuffer *) execute_java_constructor
     (0, "StringBuffer", cc, "java/lang/StringBuffer()");
```

When building method signatures, constructors are noted simply by the absence of a method name.

Learning how to call Java methods from C++ is an important step in smoothly integrating these two languages. Now it's time to learn how to work with a few items specific to Java.

Working with Java Strings and C Strings

Java's designers did an excellent job making the **String** class mimic a simple array of characters, while removing all the drawbacks inherent in using arrays. Words enclosed in quotes often serve as **String** objects, leading one to forget that one is actually working with an object.

This throws all sorts of snarls into C++ functions, because so many Java methods require **Strings** as parameters. C strings will not do; they are not recognized as objects. Rather than creating a new **String** by invoking its constructor each time one is needed, however, programmers can rely on the functions defined in **javaString.h** to help them.

Yet another of Java's header files, **javaString.h** anticipates every possibility. It will translate C strings to Java strings, and back. It allocates the memory itself, or it fills a specified array. It even creates and prints Java strings, without forcing the programmer to rely on the **String** class itself.

When strings are passed to a native method, they must first be converted to a format which C++ can understand. Two functions with this capability exist.

```
char *makeCString (Hjava_lang_String *s);
char *allocCString (Hjava_lang_String *s);
```

The first of these creates a **char** ***** and copies the string's contents into temporary storage. The second uses **malloc()** to set aside memory on the heap; it must be **free()**ed when the function no longer needs it.

```
char *javaString2CString (Hjava_lang_String *s, char *buffer, int size);
```

This copies the given string into a predefined buffer; although that buffer is then returned, it's not necessary to collect it.

```
unicode *javaString2unicode (H_java_lang_String *s, unicode *buffer, int size);
```

Rarely used, this gives C++ a way to access to the extended Unicode data contained by some strings. The Unicode data type is a 16-bit array of values that would otherwise be interpreted as C++ ints. All other string functions mentioned here truncate Unicode characters to 8 bits. Except when working with foreign alphabets, nothing beyond the standard functionality should be required.

```
Hjava_lang_String *makeJavaString (char *CString, int length);
```

To reverse the operations of the first two functions, use **makeJavaString**. It takes a null-terminated C string of the given length, and returns a handle to a Java **String** object.

```
void javaStringPrint (Hjava_lang_String *);
int javaStringLength (Hjava_lang_String *);
```

Provided as conveniences, these functions offer easy alternatives to doing common tasks in C++. The familiar **System.out.println (String)** method is mimicked by **javaStringPrint**. Rather than forcing a call to the instance method **length()** to find out how many characters a **String** contains, **javaStringLength** returns this value.

Multithreading in C++

Object defines three methods that greatly facilitate multithreading: **wait()**, **notify()** and **notifyAll()**. Available by default to all Java classes, native methods can't easily make use of them. The header file **monitor.h** instead implements functions with the same behavior that can be called from within C++.

```
void monitorWait();
```

Analogous to **wait()**, this suspends the thread running the native method until some other thread wakes it up.

```
void monitorNotify();
```

Equivalent to **notify()**, this wakes up the first waiting thread in this monitor.

```
void monitorNotifyAll();
```

Like **notifyAll()**, this awakens all threads waiting in the current monitor.

Observe the same multithreading practices within native methods as you do in normal Java methods. Throwing caution to the wind in C++ will completely wreck a well-planned thread design, and can lead to catastrophic deadlocks. Remember that native methods can be synchronized as well, and should be if they handle sensitive data!

Handling Exceptions in Native Methods

Although good programming practice dictates that errors should be resolved as they occur, sometimes Java needs to know about problems that arise during execution of a native method. In this event, **SignalError**, defined in **interpreter.h**, enables C++ functions to throw Java exceptions.

```
void SignalError (ExecEnv *ee, char *name, char *message);
```

The execution environment should be **NULL** or **0**. **Name** refers to the name of the exception, including its package, using forward slashes as the separator. The **java.io.IOException** would appear here as **java/io/IOException**. As the **Exception** and **Error** constructors both allow a message to be sent along, the third parameter takes a C string containing supplementary text. A properly formatted exception looks like:

```
SignalError (0, "java/io/IOException", "End of file");
```

Calling **SignalError** sets off a chain of events similar to what would happen if a Java method contained the following code:

```
throw new java.io.IOException ("End of File");
```

Execution of the native method ceases and control returns to its caller, who is expected to handle the exception.

Summary

By interfacing Java with C++, the inherent power of both languages comes to the surface. Applications benefit from speed increases, and from extension of their capabilities.

Although native methods are somewhat overused in the false belief that speed matters more than platform independence, in the arena of serious development they are still neglected. Since Java currently lacks the ability to print, play music, or handle a wide variety of images, using C or C++ code becomes the only means by which Java programs can perform these feats.

In this chapter, we've looked at the tools the JDK provides to ease the transition between the two languages. We've also seen the extensive library of helper functions that Java provides to extend exception handling, multithreading, and Java's string handling to C++ functions. These save the programmer from rewriting tedious processes for every native method.

Although currently buried deep in Sun's documentation, the interface between C++ and Java is poised to become the next big thing in the programming world. The combination of the flexibility of C++ and Java's powerful GUI, networking and multithreading capacities will give a great advantage to Java developers who know and understand C++.

GridBag Viewer
Applet

This is the code for the GridBag Viewer applet described in Chapter 11:

```java
import java.awt.*;
import java.applet.*;

public class gridBagger extends Applet
{
    Frame myFrame;
    Font fontItalics = new Font("Helvetica", Font.ITALIC + Font.BOLD, 16);
    Font fontPlain = new Font("Helvetica", Font.PLAIN, 14);
    Panel pnlGridBagLayout = new Panel();
    Panel pnlButtonRow = new Panel();
    Button btnAdd = new Button("Add Component");
    GridBagLayout gridBag = new GridBagLayout();
    GridBagConstraints gbc  = new  GridBagConstraints();
    int compCtr = 1;

    public void init()
    {
        Frame myFrame;
        Component comp;

        setLayout(new BorderLayout());

        pnlButtonRow.add(btnAdd);
        setFont(fontItalics);
        add("North", new Label("Click Button to change constraints..."));
        setFont(fontPlain);
        add("South",pnlButtonRow);

        add("Center", pnlGridBagLayout);
        pnlGridBagLayout.setLayout(gridBag);

        addButton(gridBag, gbc, pnlGridBagLayout,"Button " + compCtr++);

        // find frame
        comp = this;
        while (comp != null)
        {
            if (comp instanceof Frame)
            {
                myFrame = (Frame) comp;
                break;
            }
            comp = comp.getParent();
        }

    }
```

```
   protected  void  addButton(GridBagLayout gbl,GridBagConstraints gbc,
   Container parent, String caption)
   {
      Button  button  =  new  Button(caption);
      gbl.setConstraints(button,  gbc);
      parent.add(button);
      parent.layout();
   }

   public boolean action(Event e, Object arg)
   {
      GridBagConstraints gbc;
      GridBagLayout gbl;
      GridBagConstraintsDlg gbcd;

      gbc = gridBag.getConstraints((Component) e.target);

      if (e.target == btnAdd)
      {
         addButton(gridBag, gbc, pnlGridBagLayout,"Button " + compCtr++);
         return true;
      }
      else if (e.target instanceof Button)
      {

         gbcd = new GridBagConstraintsDlg(myFrame,gridBag,(Component)
         e.target);

         gbcd.show();

         return true;
      }

      return false;
   }
}

   class GridBagConstraintsDlg extends Dialog
   {
      String[] fillStrings = {"NONE","BOTH","HORIZONTAL","VERTICAL"};
      String[] anchorStrings = {  "CENTER","NORTH","NORTHEAST",
                                  "EAST","SOUTHEAST","SOUTH",
                                  "SOUTHWEST", "WEST", "NORTHWEST"};

      Font font = new Font("Helvetica", Font.BOLD, 16);
      GridBagLayout currGBL;
      GridBagConstraints currGBC;
      Component currComp, currParent;
      Panel pnlConstraints = new Panel();
      Panel pnlButtonRow = new Panel();
      Button btnOK = new Button("Modify");
      Button btnCancel = new Button("Cancel");
      Button btnChangeAll = new Button("Modify All");
      Button btnRemove = new Button("Remove");
      Choice fillChoice = new Choice();
      Choice anchorChoice = new Choice();
      gbcTextField txtGridHeight = new
```

```
        gbcTextField(gbcTextField.INT_REL_REM);
    gbcTextField txtGridWidth = new
    gbcTextField(gbcTextField.INT_REL_REM);
    gbcTextField txtGridx = new gbcTextField(gbcTextField.INT_RELATIVE);
    gbcTextField txtGridy = new gbcTextField(gbcTextField.INT_RELATIVE);
    gbcTextField txtInsetLeft = new gbcTextField(gbcTextField.INT_ONLY);
    gbcTextField txtInsetRight = new
    gbcTextField(gbcTextField.INT_ONLY);
    gbcTextField txtInsetTop = new gbcTextField(gbcTextField.INT_ONLY);
    gbcTextField txtInsetBottom = new
    gbcTextField(gbcTextField.INT_ONLY);
    gbcTextField txtIpadx = new gbcTextField(gbcTextField.INT_ONLY);
    gbcTextField txtIpady = new gbcTextField(gbcTextField.INT_ONLY);
    gbcTextField txtWeightx = new gbcTextField(gbcTextField.DOUBLE);
    gbcTextField txtWeighty = new gbcTextField(gbcTextField.DOUBLE);

    public GridBagConstraintsDlg(Frame parent, GridBagLayout GBL,
    Component Comp)
    {
        super(parent,"Modify Constraints",true);
        setFont(font);
        currGBL = GBL;
        currComp = Comp;
        currParent = currComp.getParent();
        currGBC = currGBL.getConstraints(currComp);

        // add valid strings to anchor choice control
        for (int i= 0; i < anchorStrings.length; i++)
           anchorChoice.addItem(anchorStrings[i]);
        // select current value
        anchorChoice.select(anchorStrings[currGBC.anchor
        - GridBagConstraints.CENTER]);

        // add valid strings to fill choice control
        for (int i= 0; i < fillStrings.length; i++)
            fillChoice.addItem(fillStrings[i]);
        // select current value
        fillChoice.select(fillStrings[currGBC.fill]);

        setLayout(new BorderLayout());
        add("South", pnlButtonRow);
        add("Center", pnlConstraints);

        pnlButtonRow.add(btnOK);
        pnlButtonRow.add(btnChangeAll);
        pnlButtonRow.add(btnCancel);
        pnlButtonRow.add(btnRemove);

        pnlConstraints.setLayout(new GridLayout(0,4));
        pnlConstraints.add(new Label("Anchor:",Label.RIGHT));
        pnlConstraints.add(anchorChoice);
        pnlConstraints.add(new Label("Fill:",Label.RIGHT));
        pnlConstraints.add(fillChoice);
        pnlConstraints.add(new Label("Grid Height:",Label.RIGHT));
        pnlConstraints.add(txtGridHeight);
        pnlConstraints.add(new Label("Grid Width:",Label.RIGHT));
        pnlConstraints.add(txtGridWidth);
```

```
          pnlConstraints.add(new Label("Gridx:",Label.RIGHT));
          pnlConstraints.add(txtGridx);
          pnlConstraints.add(new Label("Gridy:",Label.RIGHT));
          pnlConstraints.add(txtGridy);
          pnlConstraints.add(new Label("Left Inset:",Label.RIGHT));
          pnlConstraints.add(txtInsetLeft);
          pnlConstraints.add(new Label("Right Inset:",Label.RIGHT));
          pnlConstraints.add(txtInsetRight);
          pnlConstraints.add(new Label("Top Inset:",Label.RIGHT));
          pnlConstraints.add(txtInsetTop);
          pnlConstraints.add(new Label("Bottom Inset:",Label.RIGHT));
          pnlConstraints.add(txtInsetBottom);
          pnlConstraints.add(new Label("ipadx:",Label.RIGHT));
          pnlConstraints.add(txtIpadx);
          pnlConstraints.add(new Label("ipady:",Label.RIGHT));
          pnlConstraints.add(txtIpady);
          pnlConstraints.add(new Label("Weightx:",Label.RIGHT));
          pnlConstraints.add(txtWeightx);
          pnlConstraints.add(new Label("Weighty:",Label.RIGHT));
          pnlConstraints.add(txtWeighty);

          //txtGridHeight.setText(new
          Integer(currGBC.gridheight).toString());
          txtGridHeight.setText(currGBC.gridheight + "");
          txtGridWidth.setText(currGBC.gridwidth + "");
          txtGridx.setText(currGBC.gridx + "");
          txtGridy.setText(currGBC.gridy + "");
          txtInsetLeft.setText(currGBC.insets.left + "");
          txtInsetRight.setText(currGBC.insets.right + "");
          txtInsetTop.setText(currGBC.insets.top + "");
          txtInsetBottom.setText(currGBC.insets.bottom + "");
          txtIpadx.setText(currGBC.ipadx + "");
          txtIpady.setText(currGBC.ipady + "");
          txtWeightx.setText(currGBC.weightx + "");
          txtWeighty.setText(currGBC.weighty + "");

      this.pack();
   }

   public boolean action(Event e, Object arg)
   {
      if (e.target == fillChoice)
      {
         currGBC.fill = fillChoice.getSelectedIndex();
         return true;
      }

      if (e.target == anchorChoice)
      {
         currGBC.anchor = anchorChoice.getSelectedIndex() +
         GridBagConstraints.CENTER;
         return true;
      }

      if (e.target == btnOK)
      {
         updateValues();
```

```
        currGBL.setConstraints(currComp, currGBC);
        currParent.layout();

        this.hide();
        this.dispose();
        return true;
    }

    if (e.target == btnChangeAll)
    {
        updateValues();
        Component allComp[] = currComp.getParent().getComponents();

        for ( int i = 0; i < allComp.length; i++)
            currGBL.setConstraints(allComp[i], currGBC);

        currParent.layout();
        this.hide();
        this.dispose();
        return true;
    }

    if (e.target == btnCancel)
    {
        this.hide();
        this.dispose();
        return true;
    }

    if (e.target == btnRemove)
    {
        currComp.getParent().remove(currComp);

        currParent.layout();
        this.hide();
        this.dispose();
        return true;
    }

    return false;
}
void updateValues()
{
    currGBC.gridheight = txtGridHeight.intValue();
    currGBC.gridwidth = txtGridWidth.intValue();
    currGBC.gridx = txtGridx.intValue();
    currGBC.gridy = txtGridy.intValue();
    currGBC.insets.left = txtInsetLeft.intValue();
    currGBC.insets.right = txtInsetRight.intValue();
    currGBC.insets.top = txtInsetTop.intValue();
    currGBC.insets.bottom = txtInsetBottom.intValue();
    currGBC.ipadx = txtIpadx.intValue();
    currGBC.ipady = txtIpady.intValue();
    currGBC.weightx = txtWeightx.doubleValue();
    currGBC.weighty = txtWeighty.doubleValue();
}
```

```java
        int toInt(String s)
        {
            if ("RELATIVE".equals(s)) return -1;
            else if ("REMAINDER".equals(s)) return 0;
            else return Integer.valueOf(s).intValue();
        }
    }

class gbcTextField extends TextField
{
    public static final int INT_ONLY = 0;  // just allows digits
    public static final int INT_RELATIVE = 1;  // allows digits; shows
    RELATIVE for others
    public static final int INT_REL_REM = 2; // allows digits; else toggle
    RELATIVE-REMAINDER
    public static final int DOUBLE = 3; // allows digits and "." to enter
    precision
    boolean strSwitch = false;
    boolean is_String = false;
    int gbcType;

    public gbcTextField(int type)
    {
        super();
        gbcType = type;
    }

    public boolean handleEvent(Event e)
    {

        if ( e.id != Event.KEY_PRESS && e.key != '.') return
        super.handleEvent(e);

        // In case KEY_PRESS event period behavior gets "corrected"
        if ( e.id == Event.KEY_PRESS && e.key == '.')
        return   super.handleEvent(e);

        String s = this.getText();

        boolean is_int_char;

        if (e.key >= '0' && e.key <= '9') is_int_char = true;
        else is_int_char = false;

        if ("REMAINDER".equals(s) ||"RELATIVE".equals(s)) is_String = true;
        else is_String = false;

        switch (gbcType)
        {
            case INT_ONLY:
                if (is_int_char) return super.handleEvent(e);
                if (e.key == '.')
                {
                    int pos = s.indexOf('.');
                    if ( pos != -1)
                    {
                        s=s.substring(0,pos) + s.substring(pos + 1);
```

```
                    this.setText(s);
                    this.select(pos,pos);
                }
            }
            else return true;
        case DOUBLE:
            if (is_int_char) return super.handleEvent(e);
            else return true;

        case INT_RELATIVE:
            if (!is_int_char)
            {
                this.setText("RELATIVE");
                is_String = true;
            }
            else if (is_String)
            {
                this.setText((char)e.key + "");
                is_String = false;
            }
            else return super.handleEvent(e);

            return true;

        case INT_REL_REM:
            if (!is_int_char)
            {
                if (strSwitch) this.setText("RELATIVE");
                else this.setText("REMAINDER");
                is_String = true;
                strSwitch = !strSwitch;
            }
            else if (is_String)
            {
                this.setText((char)e.key + "");
                is_String = false;
            }
            else return super.handleEvent(e);

            return true;

    }
    return super.handleEvent(e);
}

public void setText(String s)
{
    if ("-1".equals(s))
    {
        super.setText("RELATIVE");
        is_String = true;
    }
    else if ("0".equals(s) && gbcType == INT_REL_REM)
    {
        super.setText("REMAINDER");
        is_String = true;
    }
```

```
      else
      {
          super.setText(s);
          if ("REMAINDER".equals(s) ||"RELATIVE".equals(s))
             is_String = true;
          else is_String = false;
      }
   }

   public int intValue()
   {
      String s = this.getText();

      if ("RELATIVE".equals(s)) return -1;
      else if ("REMAINDER".equals(s)) return 0;
      else
      {
         try
         {
             return Integer.valueOf(s).intValue();
         }
         catch (NumberFormatException e)
         {
             return 0;
         }
      }
   }

   public double doubleValue()
   {
      String s = this.getText();
      try
      {
          return Double.valueOf(s).doubleValue();
      }
      catch (NumberFormatException e)
      {
          return 0;
      }
   }
}
```

SendLifeSigns Application

This is the alternative code for the SendLifeSigns Application which will only work on platforms that don't have the flaw of preventing a packet being re-sent after one transmission or not allowing a datagram socket to be used more than once. You could run it on Windows NT for example. This example uses one socket and one packet. We've highlighted the important networking statements.

```java
import java.net.*;

class SendLifeSigns
{
    public static void main(String args[])
    {
        InetAddress      localAddress  = null;
        DatagramSocket   outSocket     = null;
        InetAddress      hostAddress   = null;
        boolean          verbose       = false;

        // Verify correct invocation
        if ( (args.length != 1) && (args.length != 2) )
        {
            System.err.println("Usage: java SendLifeSigns " +
                               "<monitoring computer name> [-v]");
            System.exit(0);
        }

        // Check if we are in verbose mode
        if ( (args.length==2) && (args[1].equals("-v")) ) verbose = true;

        // Get the address of the monitoring computer
        try {
            hostAddress = InetAddress.getByName(args[0]);
        } catch (UnknownHostException e) {
            System.err.println("The specified monitoring computer " +
                               "could not be found.");
            System.exit(0);
        }

        // Get the address of the local computer
        try {
            localAddress = InetAddress.getLocalHost();
        } catch (UnknownHostException e) {
            System.err.println("Could not determine the address " +
                               "of the local computer.");
            System.exit(0);
        }
```

```java
// Create a datagram packet with the sender's address in
// the message body
byte myAddressAsBytes[] = localAddress.getAddress();
DatagramPacket myAddress= new DatagramPacket(
        myAddressAsBytes,              // The data to send
        myAddressAsBytes.length,       // Length of data to send
        hostAddress,                   // The target
        2829);                         // Port number on the target

// Create a new outgoing datagram socket
try {
    outSocket = new DatagramSocket();
} catch (SocketException e) {
    System.err.println("Could not create socket.");
    System.exit(0);
}

// Continuously send data out
for (;;)
{
    try {
        // Send the packet
        outSocket.send(myAddress);
        if (verbose)
        {
            System.out.print(".");
            System.out.flush();        // force display update
        }

        // wait 5 sec. before sending the packet again
        Thread.currentThread().sleep(5000);
    } catch(Exception e) {
        System.err.println(e);
        System.exit(1);
    } finally {
        outSocket.close();
    }

    }
  }
}
```

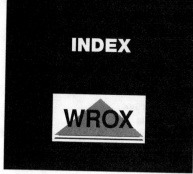

INDEX

M

Y

Register Professional Java Fundamentals and sign up for a free subscription to The Developer's Journal.

A bi-monthly magazine for software developers, The Wrox Press Developer's Journal features in-depth articles, news and help for everyone in the software development industry. Each issue includes extracts from our latest titles and is crammed full of practical insights into coding techniques, tricks and research.

Fill in and return the card below to receive a free subscription to the Wrox Press Developer's Journal.

Professional Java Fundamentals Registration Card

Name _____

Address _____

_____

_____

_____

City_____ State/Region _____

Country_____ Postcode/Zip _____

E-mail _____

Occupation _____

How did you hear about this book?_____

☐ Book review (name) _____

☐ Advertisement (name) _____

☐ Recommendation _____

☐ Catalogue _____

☐ Other _____

Where did you buy this book?_____

☐ Bookstore (name)_____ City _____

☐ Computer Store (name)_____

☐ Mail Order_____

☐ Other_____

What influenced you in the purchase of this book?

☐ Cover Design

☐ Contents

☐ Other (please specify) _____

How did you rate the overall contents of this book?

☐ Excellent   ☐ Good

☐ Average   ☐ Poor

What did you find most useful about this book? _____

_____

What did you find least useful about this book? _____

Please add any additional comments. _____

_____

What other subjects will you buy a computer book on soon? _____

What is the best computer book you have used this year?

_____

Note: This information will only be used to keep you updated about new Wrox Press titles and will not be used for any other purpose or passed to any other third party.

WROX

WROX PRESS INC.

Wrox writes books for you. Any suggestions, or
ideas about how you want information given in
your ideal book will be studied by our team.
Your comments are always valued at Wrox.

Free phone in USA 800-USE-WROX
Fax (312) 465 4063

Compuserve 100063,2152.
UK Tel. (44121) 706 6826   Fax   (44121) 706 2967

———— Computer Book Publishers ————

NB. If you post the bounce back card below in the UK, please send it to:
Wrox Press Ltd. 30 Lincoln Road, Birmingham, B27 6PA